From ACT UP to the WTO

From ACT UP
to the WTO

Urban protest and community building
in the era of globalization

EDITED BY BENJAMIN SHEPARD AND RONALD HAYDUK

VERSO

London • New York

First published by Verso 2002
© in the collection Benjamin Shepard and Ronald Hayduk 2002
© in individual contributions the contributors 2002
All rights reserved

The moral rights of the authors and the editors have been asserted.

10 9 8 7 6 5 4 3 2 1

Verso
UK: 6 Meard Street, London W1F 0EG
USA: 180 Varick Street, New York, NY 10014–4606

Verso is the imprint of New Left Books

ISBN 1–85984–653–X
ISBN 1–85984–356–5 (pbk)

British Library Cataloguing in Publication Data
A catalogue record for this book is available from the British Library

Library of Congress Cataloging-in-Publication Data
A catalog record for this book is available from the Library of Congress

Designed and typeset by Illuminati, Grosmont
Printed by R.R. Donnelly & Sons, USA

Contents

PART TWO
SEX, SOCIAL JUSTICE, AND THE NEW QUEER COMMUNITY ORGANIZING

Creating a new literature for a new era of community organizing

ERIC ROFES

I searched energetically for a book of inspiring stories about community organizing when I began preparing "Education for Action: Skills-building for Community Organizers and Social Change Activists," a new course at my university. I wanted my students – mostly undergraduates from rural and small-town California – to understand that when people motivated to overcome injustice came together and organized, they could successfully create change.

I found several texts that captured key moments in the civil rights movement, women's liberation, and labor organizing, and several book-length case studies of compelling organizing moments in anti-war activism, the Native American movement, and urban mobilizations. These historical accounts not only provided me with valuable insights into organizing strategies and tactics, but also inspired me with the simple heroism of ordinary people involved in mass social movements. Whether I was reading about the battle over the International Hotel in San Francisco, the fight to desegregate schools in Little Rock, Arkansas, or union struggles in Appalachian coal-mining communities, I was rocked by the narratives of movements which had ignited powerful social and political transformations.

My college students did not share my enthusiasm. Sure, they appreciated the organizing efforts of the 1940s, 1950s, and 1960s. They admired Ella Baker, Caesar Chavez, and Saul Alinsky and knew the difference between the Student Non-violent Coordinating Committee and the Southern Christian Leadership Conference. These young men and women are activists and don't take kindly to the media's depicting their generation as selfish slackers or corporate zombies. They realize that many people struggled to create a more open and participatory democracy. They neither take these gains lightly nor disrespect or diminish the efforts of earlier generations. But they are acutely aware that the movements highlighted in these texts are not their movements. They are the movements of their parents. In some cases, they are the movements of their grandparents.

This was driven home to me one day after we watched an episode of *Eyes on the Prize*. One of the undergraduates taking the class – a women with considerable organizing experience on environmental and globalization issues – followed me into my office and asked, "When are we going to start reading books and seeing videos about the activism of my generation?" It took me a few moments, but I soon realized what I had done. By creating a course almost entirely around social movement events meaningful to the Boomer generation, I had unintentionally affirmed the inaccurate, but often-stated belief that, since the 1960s and early 1970s, almost no organizing efforts of significance have occurred. The much-heralded, romanticized image of the 1960s as the golden age of organizing looms large over organizing efforts of the past two decades. If we as a nation constantly confront divides between age cohorts, we as progressive activists need to come face-to-face with our own generation gaps.

How could I have created a course which suggests that all of the great organizing moments took place before most of my students were born? After all, my own organizing efforts in the lesbian and gay liberation movement and AIDS activism took place primarily after 1980. What about more recent efforts to fight globalization, defend animal rights, combat welfare "reform," and counter the assault on the rights of immigrants, people of color, and women during the Reagan–Bush–Gingrich years? Why, in the year 2000, was I showing movies about Martin Luther King, Jr. and playing tapes by Joan Baez and Phil Ochs, and ignoring videos of Julia Butterfly, and music by Rage Against the Machine?

In your hands you are holding the book that will be the central text of my community-organizing course, alongside the Midwest Academy's *Organizing for Social Change* skills-building manual. Of course, I will link contemporary struggles with earlier efforts and show how earlier waves of feminism, the civil rights movement, and Third World liberation offer a foundation for contemporary efforts. My job as the instructor will be to illustrate ways in which specific values and organizing themes weave their way through decades of activism.

But I must remember that I created my course not as a nostalgic tribute to victories of the past, but as a course that would affirm and inspire the ongoing efforts of my students. To do this, it must prominently include more recent narratives of organizing around AIDS, sexual freedom, gender identity, corporate plunder, and globalization. It must illustrate how new technologies, together with new identities, have created new methods of organizing, and new populations demanding freedom. A course for activists of the twenty-first century requires a new literature capturing narratives of a new activism currently igniting our nation. This is the text for that course.

Urban protest and community building in the era of globalization

BENJAMIN SHEPARD AND RONALD HAYDUK

In November 1999, a radical coalition of students, youth, feminists, environmental, labor, anarchist, queer, and human rights activists converged in Seattle. Their target: the system of global capitalism. In blocking the meetings of the World Trade Organization, a movement was ignited.

In March 1987, a radical coalition of queer activists converged on Wall Street. Their target: "BUSINESS, BIG BUSINESS, BUSINESS AS USUAL!!!" It was ACT UP's first demo. Through innovative use of civil-rights-era nonviolent civil disobedience, guerrilla theatre, sophisticated media work, and direct action, ACT UP helped transform the world of activism. Countless groups would build on their methods over the next fifteen years.

Between 1987 and 1999, a new project in activism emerged unshackled by past ghosts. While ACT UP's work embodied the ethos of the new social movements, "the Battle of Seattle" marked the culmination of that decade's activism. *From ACT UP to the WTO* broadly considers the story of activism from ACT UP's birth to the WTO protests and the movements they inspired twelve years later. It further considers an ethos of vitality, a new brand of, dare we say, joy, perhaps rambunctiousness, involved in the new direct action – be it with age-old tactics such as picket lines or lockdowns, or newer approaches, such as hactivism or fax jams, which have entered the activist fray. There is something undeniably exciting about building new communities and identities on the foundation of social justice; perhaps it's just a new generation discovering the idea of solidarity. Nonetheless, the following essays trace the stories and overlapping themes of a new generation of social justice activists, their movements, and the ways they have revitalized a radical landscape.

While the new activism has brought about an optimism about the effectiveness of organizing not seen in recent years, much of the 1990s saw a retreat of progressive ideology and practice. Activism was portrayed by the dominant media as a relic of the past (Davis 1997). Capitalism and neo-conservatism appeared triumphant domestically and internationally during the post-Cold War age of "globalization." The influence of labor and environmentalism appeared in decline with the passage of the North American Free Trade Agreement (NAFTA) and the General Agreement on Tariffs and Trade (GATT). Both agreements, used to undermine local sovereignty, were passed by a Democratic congress and president. All the while, the role of the state was increasingly subordinated to the imperatives of "globalization" – a buzzword used to numb any opposition to the power of capital.

Yet, by the mid to late 1990s, labor made significant strides to revitalize itself – winning several struggles, and reaching out to workers in new industries. Simultaneously, a host of new forms of resistance began to emerge. The era of globalization has, ironically, helped create a new global activism. Despite the lack of major media coverage of many of the local battles within the new resistance movements, these protest practices have proven themselves to be effective. This emerging activism is the subject of these essays.

New economy, new action

The new activism grows from and responds to four key factors – globalization, shifting boundaries between public and private space, demographic change, and income inequality – all of which have transformed the landscape in which the new movements operate. Changes in communications technologies and economic restructuring have vastly increased the mobility of capital, creating unprecedented impacts on local communities and whole nations, opening the door for a radical transfer of information and wealth from public to private through the patenting of life, the privatization of government functions, and the concentration of wealth (Klein 2001b). It follows that these shifting boundaries between public and private space are radically changing the relationship between civil society and the state. At the same time

ACTUP/ACTNOW
SEIZE CONTROL
of the
FDA

Less than three months before the 1988 presidential election, Frank Young, the Commissioner of the Food and Drug Administration (FDA) and a Reagan appointee, has begun to make vague commitments to ensure swifter access to promising AIDS treatments. YET HE CHOSE TO IGNORE THESE TREATMENTS FOR OVER EIGHT YEARS, WHILE TENS OF THOUSANDS HAVE SUFFERED OR DIED.

NATIONAL RALLY: OCTOBER 10th, 1988
CIVIL DISOBEDIENCE: OCTOBER 11th, 1988

On October 10th, a mass rally of AIDS activists from around the country will be held at the Department of Health and Human Services (HHS) in Washington, DC to demand a compassionate comprehensive and informed response to the AIDS crisis and to demand universal health care. On October 11th a civil disobedience and demonstration will take place at the FDA in Rockville, Maryland to stop the "business as usual" policies that have contributed to the murder of so many people.

JOIN US:

Several civil disobedience training sessions will commence on September 3rd and continue every Saturday and Sunday of September at the Lesbian and Gay Community Services Center, 208 W. 13th Street, NYC.

YOU MAY PARTICIPATE WITHOUT PLANNING TO BE ARR

SHOW UP!

For more information come to an ACTUP/ACTNOW meeting. We m
day at 6:00 PM at the Center.

EIGHT IS ENOUGH.
ACT UP! FIGHT BACK! FIGHT AIDS!

ACT UP /ACTNOW

ACT UP-AIDS Coalition to Unleash Power is a diverse, non-partisan group of individuals united in anger and committed to end the AIDS crisis. ACT NOW (AIDS Coalition to Network, Organize and Win) is a coalition of AIDS activist groups working to end direct action at the local and national levels.

that 6,000 gay and bisexual men in New York City have already died of AIDS

that 300,000 gay and bisexual men, 25% of whom are men of color, have been diagnosed as HIV-positive

that, according to the city Health Commission, barring a cure, 80% of these can be expected to die within the next 15 years

that a city with nearly half a million HIV-positive citizens has provided 2 clinics to take care of them

that the mayor of the city with the most AIDS cases in the world, Ed Koch, has called for a complete defunding of the AIDS Anti-Discrimination Unit

that there has never been a municipal outreach on AIDS to gay men of color—and there won't be this year either. Koch just refused it again.

that the FDA continues to withhold over 40 drugs that have proven to be effective against AIDS

that people with AIDS have thereby been forced to obtain these drugs in other countries, and that the U.S. is requesting friendly nations not to sell them to American nationals

that the Helms Amendement has squashed any funding for educational materials aimed at the gay community

let the
record
show

that the nation's Surgeon General has said that the government's homicidal delay in recognizing and dealing with the AIDS crisis was a direct result of official homophobia

that women have effectively excluded from all drug testing treatments and, in fact, that women-specific studies on AIDS are practically non-existent

that despite growing numbers of lesbians with AIDS, the Center for Disease Control maintains no category for recording cases of lesbian infection and transmission

that anti-gay violence, particularly violence in which the attacker mentions AIDS, has increased threefold

that the federal AIDS Commission has said that the absence of any effective federal anti-discrimination laws has actually fueled the fires of AIDS infection nationally

ACT UP was formed in March 1987 to hold the government publ... WE SAY *FIGHT* BACK! devastated our community. We do so through direct action because we believe it is no longer enough to quietly take care of ourselves. We proudly participate in the Gay/Lesbian Pride Days because we recognize that every gay man and lesbian who dies of AIDS has died of homophobic violence. We march on behalf of the people living with this disease, and out of respect for those who have been lost to it. ACT UP! FIGHT BACK! FIGHT AIDS!

ACT UP IS A DIVERSE, NON-PARTISAN GROUP OF INDIVIDUALS UNITED IN ANGER AND COMMITTED TO DIRECT ACTION TO END THE AIDS CRISIS.

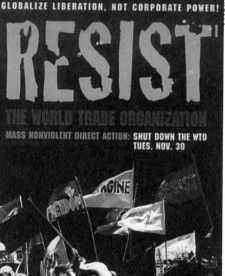

GLOBALIZE LIBERATION, NOT CORPORATE POWER!

RESIST
THE WORLD TRADE ORGANIZATION
MASS NONVIOLENT DIRECT ACTION: SHUT DOWN THE WTO
TUES. NOV. 30

COME TO SEATTLE! FESTIVAL OF RESISTANCE NOV 29-DEC 3, 1999

Early ACT UP flyers (*top*); flyer for the new global justice movements, organized to globalize democracy, not merely oppose globalization.

a demographic shift is radically altering the American cultural landscape. The US Bureau of the Census estimates that by 2030 no single ethnic or racial group will have a numerical majority in America. We are much closer to the multicultural US of 2030 than we are to Ozzie and Harriet's 1950s' white nuclear family (see Schmitt 2001). As such, the implications for shifting group relations and potential multiracial coalitions from these changes cannot be underemphasized (Sanjek 1998; Mollenkopf and Emerson 2001). Simultaneously, globalization has witnessed an exponential growth in inequality worldwide (Brecher et al. 2000; Danaher and Burbach 2000). Domestic social and economic inequalities only widened during the 1990s economic expansion, the longest in US history as the US maintained its position as the leader in inequality among advanced nations (Sanger 1997; Folbre et al. 2000). The vast majority of the wealth created by the recent expansion went to the upper 5 percent of US families, who increased their historic grip on over 43 percent of the aggregate income compared to the 5 percent held by the poorest fifth of the US population (Burtless 1990; R. Freeman 1999).

Economic inequality easily translates into the social inequality manifest in countless US social problems. The US prison population now represents 3 percent of the US male workforce, most being high-school dropouts for whom the job market has collapsed (R. Freeman 1999). Those without high-tech skills remain locked out of the new economy (Carlson and Theodore 1995; Wilson 1996). All the while, incarceration rates doubled, and then nearly doubled again, with disproportionate numbers of people of color locked up and subject to capital punishment (Beck and Harrison, 2001). For all intents and purposes, the US prison industrial complex became the primary housing provider for the poor, homeless, and mentally ill. In the meantime, political violence against people of color, queers, and the homeless continued (see Nichols 1999; and the Feinberg essay in part 2 of this volume).

Global capitalism, movement activists contend, is mauling the public: the "commons" are being turned into private malls; genes and seeds are being altered and patented; water is being dammed, bought, and sold as an increasingly scarce and valuable commodity; politicians and whole governments are routinely bribed and bent to capital's will; children are targeted and tracked at birth, fed advertisements and slogans in place of needed nourishment (Klein 2001b). At the same time, corporate globalization has steamrollered countless communities as neighborhoods lose ground to Gap, Starbucks, Wal-Mart and other chain stores. Mom-and-pop businesses are closed in large numbers; community gardens are bulldozed; and meeting places are replaced with fences and entrance fees, as public spaces are steadily privatized. The human cost of globalization is often social displacement. James Baldwin once said, "Urban renewal is Negro removal." Today, corporate globalization whitewashes the urban and cultural landscape, pushing the poor and dark-skinned out. In response to what it sees as the privatization and commodification of nearly every aspect of life, the global justice movement aims to reverse this process or at least to blunt capitalism's sharp edges.

Yet, changes brought about by globalization have also helped set the stage for new kinds of urban protest, community organizing, cooperation, and coalition-building (Hayduk 2002). We use the term "glocal" to describe the new intersections of local and global concerns. If globalization is an amorphous phenomenon, "glocalism" – political activism based on the insight that every local action has a global component – has been a coherent response. Throughout the last decade, periodic waves of glocal activism have percolated up from various pockets of the emerging global village, as activists offered solutions to the social and political problems posed by the global economy. Sweatshop activists challenged local Gap and Banana Republic stores for their Dickensian labor practices abroad and at home; city kids all over the world participated in the public/private debate by dancing in public streets intended only for commerce; garden activists fought powerful real-estate interests for green and open spaces; AIDS activists forced the hand of a sitting vice-president over his support for trade laws that prevented access to life-saving medications in South Africa; and labor rejuvenated itself, forming alliances with community-based groups to pass living-wage legislation in dozens of cities. As the twentieth century ended, the WTO protests in Seattle brought these innovative movements together in an explosive combination. Such are the narratives of *From ACT UP to the WTO*.

The essays in this volume detail the emergence of an extraordinary new brand of activism aimed at globalizing democracy, rather than corporate rule. They consider strategies of protest, ritual, and community building, reflecting a rejection of the monoculture for an alternative, more spontaneous, and authentic vision of the world. The new economy influences our experience of the world; its impacts upon various regions and communities affect how groups respond to its changes. Throughout the volume we highlight the continuities with earlier organizing efforts, as well as point out the unique nature of these new formations. In the end an ethos of joyful participation has allowed a new generation to act. If anything, the idea that activism can be both liberating and effective has shifted the way a generation looks at the project of social change.

Method and structure

From ACT UP to the WTO comprises five sections, addressing the new social movements, the use of street theater to reclaim public space, queer and sexual politics, new media/electronic civil disobedience, and race and community building. The intersecting link between AIDS/queer activism and the new activism is made in every section. The volume features essays on ACT UP's contributions to the global justice movements (part 1), queer and sexual politics (part 2), the new guerrilla street theater (part 3), the media and the new social movements (part 4), and contemporary approaches to harm reduction, housing, and anti-poverty work (part 5). Introductions before each section place the activism in a broader context and point to common threads between these diverse movements. For example, some groups maintain a trust or belief in traditional governmental institutions as a means for changing social conditions. Others have resoundingly rejected formal political processes and are building alternative or parallel institutions and spaces for community building.

This anthology considers a series of cultural practices and activist projects – from radical street protest to culture jamming – that for the most part have not previously been written about or seriously scrutinized. The authors span various disciplines, from academic research to grassroots organizing, and their essays reflect multiple ideological and methodological frameworks. What unites the essays in this volume is their focus on how various groups approach the goal of social change and community building in urban America: our emphasis is on practice.

The following essays employ both empirical and qualitative approaches (Reissman 1993) to the study of social phenomena. In most instances, interviews with activists, insider reports, and observing participant studies of the new social movements are emphasized (Kamanski 1992; Tedlock 1991). Mair (1988: 127) suggests that "We inhabit the great stories of our culture. We live through stories. We are lived by the stories of our race and our place." John McNight's (1987) point follows: "In communities, people know by stories. These community stories allow people to reach back into their common history and their individual experience for knowledge about truth and direction for the future." As such, stories, oral histories, can be used to assess changing conditions of communities. Stories help us define and identify with our communities.

The two build on each other. Ken Plummer (1995: 174) would argue that community plays a key role in storytelling. "Stories need communities to be heard, but communities themselves are also built through story tellings. Stories gather people around them: they have to attract audiences, and these audiences may then start to build a common perception, a common language, a commonality." As such, we have organized *From ACT UP to the WTO* in a way that emphasizes the link between storytelling and community building.

Just after actions these days, activists with computer access usually log on and contribute to a virtual radical community of independent media sites and listservs; this new generation of do-it-yourself organizers has created everything from news reports, video feeds, and photo documentation to online discussions and diaries (see essays in part 4). A number of the essays in this anthology were born from such interventions. Over the last decade and a half, as activism has moved from ACT UP to the WTO, what has emerged is a series of competing urban narratives, embodying different views of reality and strategy. At one recent action, the following announcement was made: "Reclaim the Streets actions pose an arrest risk. Our style of festival is their style of disorderly conduct." Consider *From ACT UP to the WTO* a place where discourses crash and intermingle.

Moving left? Go with LESC

That was our slogan. We, the editors, started organizing together through a New York City formation called the Lower East Collective (LESC) in the spring of 1999. LESC was born in 1997 "to make life miserable for bosses and bureaucrats." For years since the legendary Tompkins Square Park police riot in 1988, people had suggested that the battle against gentrification in Manhattan's Lower East Side was lost. LESC was a convergence of students, teachers, organizers, and newcomers who came to activism with a new, pragmatic approach, carefully picking and choosing our battles. While many of the issues we addressed had a long history of struggle on the Lower East Side – fair wages, critiques of consumerism, police accountability, and so on – the group embraced a new ethos of activism, rejecting the dourness and culture

of competing oppressions that characterized the declining old-style activism. Radical street performance, block parties, barbeques, and picnics were as much a part of the group's attitude toward community building as demonstrations. LESC projects included a community and labor coalition, a police and prisons project, a public space/gardens/housing group, an environmental justice group, and Reclaim the Streets.

A number of activists came to LESC after years of work with ACT UP – or groups, like WHAM! (Women's Health Action and Mobilization) and the Lesbian Avengers (see accounts of these movements in part 2), that were heavily influenced by ACT UP – and a desire to translate those skills into neighborhood organizing. LESC members consciously sought to emphasize activist work and praxis over long discussions about philosophy or ideology. Every three weeks the project groups would meet to present their work, in five minutes or less. As a result LESC, and by extension Lower East Side activism, was infused with an immediacy that focused attention on projects, not personalities. Ideas, tactics, strategies, and themes intermingled each meeting, forcing activists to grapple with how their issues overlapped and ways they could share resources. Along the road, the group was able to articulate what protest and community building were for, as much as what they were against: green space, affordable housing, a dynamic mix of cultures, living wages, and public space.

Ron comes to this writing from a Marxist/political science background, began his work as a social worker, worked in and around New York City government, and currently teaches political science. Ben comes from a sex/AIDS activist perspective; he provides AIDS housing in Brooklyn by day, while organizing at night. As such, we have a common interest in poverty-reduction work – Ron from a political perspective, Ben from a community economic development, religious background. The common thread, for all our differences in backgrounds and perspectives, was that we both recognized the importance of community building.

Our first action together was against the Disney Corporation in November 1999, one week before the WTO meeting in Seattle (see full account in part 3). It remains one of our favorite actions. LESC, the Reverend Billy and the Church of Stop Shopping, and SexPanic!, an ACT UP spin-off group, worked in coalition to disrupt business at the Times Square Disney Store. We shared anger over Disney's use of sweatshop labor, the eradication of public sexual cultures and local businesses from Times Square, and our fear that the company — and the homogenous corporate culture it epitomized — was colonizing all of Manhattan. It was one of those moments when queer social justice work overlapped with the new anti-corporate direct action. We were all learning. While neither LESC nor SexPanic! lasted, they were testaments to the new and revitalized, even fun, activist project born between ACT UP and Seattle. Shortly after getting out of jail we went out to one of the neighborhoods haunts, bought some sandwiches, told some lies, and laughed. For many of us, that was enough. If there is a theme to these essays, it's that liberation and laughter walk hand and hand. It's hard to have one without the other.

Bob Kohler, Vicki Larson, Ben Shepard, Ron Hayduk, Steve Duncombe (behind pole), and the Righteous Reverend Billy in LESC, SexPanic!, Church of Stop Shopping coalition action to disrupt the Disney store.

Introductory notes on the trail from ACT UP to the WTO

BENJAMIN SHEPARD

Something extraordinary has taken place over the last decade. Yet much of it stemmed from a single source. For all of my life as an activist, one group has remained a fixture on the cultural landscape: the AIDS Coalition to Unleash Power (ACT UP). I first heard about ACT UP when I was in college. "Silence = Death," the group's mantra, immediately spoke to me, informing me that I should let go of the shame I felt about needing to get tested for HIV (translated as: having had sex without condoms or with partners I didn't know). "Silence = Death" meant that the shame my godfather felt about having queer sex and testing positive was no longer necessary. In the years before he died, his veterinarian wrote that he had lots of pets as justification for prescribing so many medications he was taking for himself. They were drugs that AIDS treatment activists knew saved lives. Unfortunately, these life-saving medications had not yet been approved by the Food and Drug Administration (FDA) for human use. "Situation normal, all fucked up," ACT UP scribe David Feinberg (1994) concluded of the whole mess.

As the years went on, the notion that sexual freedom was OK would become an increasingly embattled idea. Many of my friends from the club days of the 1980s would encounter discrimination, positive test results, and social derision for their choices to live autonomous sexual identities. By the early 1990s, we went from ecstasy to ACT UP meetings together. One of the most important notions of ACT UP was that no one ever asked you what your identity was so long as you cared to

ACT UP/Golden Gate (415) 252-9200
Tuesdays, 7:30 pm, 592 Castro St.-Ste B

get involved. I protested, shared stories, watched friends die, and became queer with ACT UP. While there is not room to look at the group's history in its entirety, this collection serves as brief reconsideration of ACT UP's history and legacy on the activist landscape.

From rage to sartorial splendor

Fall 1993. We poured the ashes of friends we'd lost to the virus all over the steps in front of the California State House for my first action with ACT UP. I met everyone in the Safeway parking lot at 18th and Market Street for the bus ride from San Francisco to Sacramento. G'dali, one of the organizers from ACT UP/Golden Gate, gave a brief orientation. Wearing faded, beaten-up jeans with "Clean Needles Save Lives" and "Free AIDS Drugs" stickers, leather boots, and jacket, this fierce activist gently explained the best ways to hold our hands if we were arrested, among other tricks, including a brief primer on non-violent civil disobedience. Later, we recalled the names of all the friends we'd lost. I recalled my godfather, who'd died only three years earlier. Armed with a bundle of emotions ranging from rage to grief, placards, and whistles, we marched to the State House to protest Governor Pete Wilson's vetoes of health care spending. Drummers hit solemn measured beats. The Sisters of Perpetual Indulgence walked alongside a coffin carrying the ashes; a Gregorian chant droned through the air. The police beat a number of us with batons as we poured the ashes. One of my favorite memories of the day is the image of a man in a leopard-skin leotard, rhinestone drop earrings, and a lush moustache, carrying a sign proclaiming, "Looks Don't Kill, Wilson's Vetoes Do!"

ACT UP brought that sensibility – a certain sartorial splendor – to every action it did, and in so doing transformed the way activism was conducted. "Who do you have to fuck in this town to get arrested?" David Feinberg (1994) wondered during an office takeover when it seemed no one could get arrested at the FDA. I remember laughing out loud reading Feinberg's words. It was the same feeling as reading Woody Allen's *Without Feathers*, except that Feinberg was writing about maintaining a sex life, living, and ultimately dying with the virus.

That was the beauty of ACT UP. The group offered an outlet for an otherwise horrendous situation. Sometimes it was through humor, style, and camp; sometimes it was through direct action. The group recognized the subversive effectiveness of a joke, as well as the sentiment that many were tired of spending their days mourning lost friends, possibilities, and sexual communities. "Don't mourn, organize," IWW organizer Joe Hill pleaded on the eve of his execution after a frame-up for murder; ACT UP concurred. Long-time member Bill Dobbs explained the approach: "People have long wondered how we were able to cross the *au courant* downtown life with uptown politics. It combined sex, politics, and brains in an electric way. It drew the boys out of the bars and into the streets" (Bull 1999: 19–20). Over the past fourteen years, ACT UP members have died, high-risk groups have changed, three presidents have retired, and Monday night meetings have gone on as the group continued to set the tone for AIDS and cultural activism.

In 1988 Vito Russo said, "After we kick the shit out of this disease, I intend to be able to kick the shit out of this system, so that this never happens again." In other words, fighting the AIDS pandemic had come to mean fighting institutionalized racism, sexism, and the class system, in addition to homophobia. "Kicking the shit out of the system" meant fighting undemocratic international trade laws, an unjust immigration system, the prison industrial complex, poverty, unresponsive governments, budget cuts, a disaster in healthcare, and countless other manifestations of bureaucracies that put profits ahead of people. Oppressions overlap and influence each other, as do movements. This insight is the essential kernel of the story of activism from ACT UP to the WTO.

As the years wore on, ACT UP recognized that what had happened to queer communities would happen to people all over the world. Cleve Jones, the founder of the Names Project AIDS quilt reflected, "That's part of it. That terrible feeling of screaming as loud as you can scream and no one can hear you" (Shepard 1997: 261). Yet ACT UP built on these years. In the months before the Seattle protests, the group pushed for one of their greatest wins.

From ACT UP to the WTO

Long term ACT UP member Ann Northrop explained, "I got into the streets with ACT UP because I was taken with the tactics – direct action. We don't have the corporate power or the media. Our tool is our public humiliation." In the months before the Seattle WTO meeting, ACT UP used these tools to make Al Gore's life miserable. The problem was in South Africa, where an estimated 25 percent of the population has HIV. In accordance with WTO rules, the South African government under Nelson Mandela had passed a law stating that the country could bypass global intellectual property laws. In turn, the US vice-president threatened to sanction South Africa for manufacturing generic versions of expensive patented life-saving drugs. The US Trade Department bragged that Gore had held firm against poor countries standing up to world trade laws. In response, ACT UP members drove to Nashville for Gore's announcement of his plans to run for president, picketing his speech and placing signs in between Gore and the cameras proclaiming, "Gore's Greed Kills!" By the time the weekend was over, ACT UP had disrupted appearances in New Hampshire and New York, garnering significant news coverage and throwing Gore into a frenzy. Within the week, Gore's rhetoric on drugs had changed and he backed down. In a testament to the efficacy of a smart, well-targeted campaign, by the end of the year the group had forced a sitting vice-president to reverse the US trade policy.

Jimmy McNulty worked with ACT UP on that campaign. He recalled some of the direct action involved:

> The target was Charlene Barshefsky, the US Trade Representative (USTR), reporting directly to Al Gore, who was that day off to Seattle for the first of the WTO talks. So this was timed and targeted carefully and was the method that would, among other things, raise critical awareness and get some attention that led to the embarrassment, which led people to make public statements which bring the issue up out of their own mouth. Two weeks, three weeks later Al Gore acknowledged, "the activists were right."

A number of activists from ACT UP/New York, ACT UP/Philadelphia, and New York's Fed Up Queers used a decoy to clear the entrance to Barshefsky's office, where they locked themselves down and asked for a meeting with the trade rep. All this occurred within a federal building, on federal property close to the White House. McNulty explained, "As everybody knows, the whole fucking world is a con game.

You walk in with confidence, and we walked up the stairs. You can practically walk through armed guards. Then we walked right into the metal detector. I can't even remember because it was so intense, but I'm sure it went 'beep, beep, beep, beep, beep.'" The activists were on the second landing before anyone on the ground floor noticed them and pointed out they should not be there. Calmly they explained, 'This is an office takeover. No one is going to be hurt. This is non-violent. We have someone we want to talk to, Charlene Barshefsky.' Once inside the activists locked themselves inside Barshefsky's office, where they remained for an hour before being arrested and taken away. But that one hour was enough to force a change in federal trade policy. The November 27, 1999 issue of *Time* magazine on the upcoming "Battle in Seattle" specifically mentioned the USTR office takeover. The following spring the Clinton–Gore administration softened its stance on defending AIDS drug patents (see Shepard 2002, and the Sawyer essay in part 1 of this volume).

There is a famous poster in South Africa. With an image of Nelson Mandela's face, it reads "Survived Apartheid, Killed by Drug Company Greed." At the time of writing, Nelson Mandela and South Africa are being sued by thirty-nine drug companies for trying to produce their own AIDS drugs at cost (Cauvin 2001). Given how many people are affected by the virus, South Africa's democracy is threatened by lack of access to AIDS drugs. ACT UP's argument is that Africa needs the sovereignty to make its own decisions about what's best for its people. Community sovereignty versus corporate greed. In a sense, this is the theme of this entire volume. It's a civil war being fought on a thousand fronts across the world.

A note on 9/11

Our manuscript was already turned in when two planes crashed into the World Trade Center. This introduction is the only place it will be mentioned. Writing about history as it happens is never simple. For many, ourselves included, writing about 9/11 has proved incredibly painful. Bold pronouncements are premature. Now is the time for resilience and adaptation.

While the new activism had created an optimism about the effectiveness of organizing not seen in years, 9/11 reignited the apocalyptic ritual death dance between warring tribes we had hoped was a thing of the past after the Cold War (Moore 1990). If ever there were an example of a regime wrapping their militaristic agenda around a crisis, it is the treatment of 9/11. In turn, the message of the new movements became all the more urgent: the need to globalize democracy, not corporate rule. While the essays of *From ACT UP to the WTO* focus on the years between 1987 and the birth of the global justice movement in 1999, the subtext of the current panic runs throughout the volume.

Just as this new global movement emerged, the US administration was given (or generated) a crisis with which to justify labeling its opponents as deviants. Long before September 11, the powers that be sought to delegitimize activists as terrorists. On May 10, 2001, FBI director Louis Freeh testified at a Senate committee hearing: "Anarchists and extreme socialist groups – such as … Reclaim the Streets … represent a potential threat in the United States." The process became a great deal easier after 9/11, as the Attorney General claimed that those who opposed his approach to challenging terrorism "only aid terrorists." It was part of a classic script used to justify encroachments into the public sphere.

In light of the recent repression of activists, there are those who would suggest the global justice movement should wait out the crisis. The question of patience permeates Martin Luther King's "Letter from a Birmingham Jail," in which he states:

> My friends, I must say to you that we have not made a single gain in civil rights without determined legal and nonviolent pressure. Lamentably, it is a historical fact that privileged groups seldom give up their privileges voluntarily.… We know painfully through experience that freedom is never voluntarily given by the oppressor; it must be demanded by the oppressed. Frankly, I have yet to engage in a direct action campaign that was "well timed" in the view of those who have not suffered unduly from the disease of segregation. For years now I have heard "wait." It rings in the ear of every negro with piercing familiarity. This "Wait" has almost always meant "Never." We must come to see, with one of our distinguished jurists, that "justice too long delayed is justice denied."

As the global justice movements attempt to find their legs after 9/11, these are good words to remember. If we sit back too long, justice delayed may just become justice denied for yet another generation. The following essays are about people who had no time to wait.

PART ONE

Glocal proclivities and the new social movements

Social scientists, policymakers and community advocates have spent the last two decades scratching their heads about the wrenching social and economic changes understood as globalization. In 1993 and 1994, two key free-trade measures, the North American Free Trade Agreement (NAFTA) and the General Agreement on Tariffs and Trade (GATT), were enacted into law. These agreements expanded world trade and economic restructuring, while movements to establish national health care and enlarge the social safety net dwindled. For a while, the possibility of social change had begun to look bleak. Yet throughout the 1990s, rumblings of a new activism began to take shape, from the mountains of southern Mexico to the Lower East Side of Manhattan.

"Direct action is the driving force behind the new unrest," explains radical historian L.A. Kauffman (2000). "The key is action, not dull rallies where one speaker after another drones on, or meetings that just lead to more meetings, or studies that never end." Instead, most of the new organizing – from campaigns against police brutality to AIDS drug price wars – emphasize praxis over long debates. "Action Speaks Louder than Words" is the slogan of the Ruckus Society, a group that has been training activists in protest techniques since 1995. With an open mind and a willingness to consider the broad range of ways the new economic system affects countless communities and issues, contemporary activists revel in the quirky alliances developed within the fight for global justice.

One of the most important developments has been the emergence of a resurgent labor movement. In recent years, labor has evolved from a defensive position – epitomized by Reagan's firing of the air traffic controllers in 1981 – to one that emphasizes organizing the unorganized and projecting labor's power in the workplace. Wins in campaigns against United Parcel Service, the new telecommunications giant Verizon, and the Museum of Modern Art in New York, among others, have forced business to reassess the vitality of the new labor movement (Greenhouse 2000b; 2000c).

A major source of labor's new success is its re-embrace of its pro-immigrant and social justice roots. Not only is there a notable increase in participation by new immigrants, women, and people of color, but labor has also become increasingly aware of, and sympathetic to, international and environmental issues that impact workers. Coalitions of labor and community groups, including new immigrant rights groups, have won living wage campaigns across the country, with dozens of additional campaigns currently under way. The student anti-sweatshop movement, in partnership with labor and human rights organizations, has emerged as a rallying point across the country. "There's an understanding that these issues are tied up together," notes Laura McSpedon, a student anti-sweatshop organizer at Georgetown University, and "that to separate culture and identity and race and gender from class and the concerns of working people is artificial, and divides us in unproductive ways" (Kauffman 2000).

The massive mobilization of these and other groups in Seattle embodies just one of countless examples of activists finding innovative ways to work together and build community in fresh, often surprising, coalitions. An account by one Black Bloc anarchist, who found himself assisted by khaki-pants-wearing Gore supporters at the Bush inauguration protests in January 2001, embodied the new ethos: "This is a big thank you to whoever came to support the Revolutionary Anti-Authoritarian Bloc," he declared on an Indymedia website. "After being trapped at one point by cops and having to push our way out, only to have people trapped again, I'm glad there was some soli-fucking-darity. That's what it's all about. We will stand by you when you need us, and I'm glad to see it's vice versa" (Kauffman 2001).

Seattle was not one movement but the result of many. The first part of *From ACT UP to the WTO* looks at the vast cross-section of groups contributing to the new global justice movements. Lesley Julia Wood and Kelly Moore situate the new movements within social movement theory. The authors provide a conceptual framework for thinking about the new movements. They analyze changes during the past decade – both in social movement theory and in grassroots mobilizations – and the ways contemporary activists assess a broad range of possible targets for action.

L.A. Kauffman takes a macro-look at ACT UP's influence on radical politics from its formation through "the Battle of Seattle," while Esther Kaplan recalls A25, the 1995 New York City "Bridges and Tunnels" action, in which ACT UP worked in Seattle-like coalition to block every bridge and tunnel into and out of Manhattan.

Immanuel Ness presents a case history of the New York campaign to organize undocumented immigrants working for less than minimum wage in small greengrocers as a way of looking at where labor has been and how globalization has inspired a new labor activism. He outlines the ways labor has learned historic lessons and become a dynamic force within the new social movements. Ness's consideration of the local impact of a powerful global economic system exemplifies the new glocal thinking. Joel Lefkowitz further considers the unjust treatment of workers worldwide in his essay on the burgeoning global sweatshop movement and the new cross-border activism.

The essays in this section chronicle a year of glocal activism – from the protests against the World Trade Organization meetings in Seattle to protests against the World Bank and International Monetary Fund in Washington, DC, in April 2000, and against the Republican and Democratic Party conventions over the summer of 2000.

Starhawk recalls the personal agency that made the protests against the World Trade Organization meetings in Seattle so extraordinary. While only a few essays specifically address Seattle, this anthology focuses most of its attention on coalitions of movements that created the synergy behind Seattle and the series of dramatic radical protests that followed in its wake. Bronwyn Mauldin recalls the ways Jubilee 2000 helped position debt relief within the global justice movement during the Seattle WTO protests. Increasingly debt relief, AIDS, and global justice activists are working to ignite resistance to the new global health apartheid. Their unified theme is "Donate the Dollars, Drop the Debt, Treat the People, Save the Lives, NOW!"

For twelve years before Seattle, ACT UP was reinventing the activist landscape. ACT UP made battling drug companies a cornerstone of its work. Today, queer and AIDS activists are taking these lessons and applying them to the fight against inequalities of access to AIDS drugs across the world. After returning from South Africa and observing long lines of people waiting for treatments they were not going to get, Cleve Jones, the founder of the AIDS quilt, recalled a strange sense of déjà vu in seeing the long lines for medications that might never emerge: "It felt like 1981 at San Francisco General Hospital all over again." Years after the group's theoretical demise, ACT UP forced a sitting vice-president to stop sanctioning poor countries that manufacture or import generic versions of expensive life-saving drugs. As the World Trade Organization and the World Bank became clear obstacles to getting drugs into the bodies of people with AIDS all over the world, AIDS activists played key roles in protests against these institutions and within the battle for global justice. Eric Sawyer's essay discusses the campaign for global drug access.

Target practice: community activism in a global era

LESLEY J. WOOD AND KELLY MOORE

In 1965, environmental activism consisted of the provision of scientific information to the government, popular exposés of polluters, and the purchase of land to protect it from development. At the turn of the twenty-first century, it looked dramatically different. Community gardeners in New York City padlocked themselves to a giant papier-mâché frog to prevent gardens from being bulldozed (see Mikalbrown essay in part 3 of this volume). In cities like San Francisco, Adelaide, and Tokyo, cyclists in the pro-bicycling/anti-car movement Critical Mass regularly took over the streets on the last Friday of each month. Nationally and internationally based environmental activists converged on Seattle during the meeting of the World Trade Organization, forming human chains to prevent representatives from entering the meeting space, staging street theater, and confronting the police (see the remaining essays in part 1 below). Among the participants in the Seattle actions were community gardeners and cyclists from Critical Mass.

Why were the activists fighting to save community gardens in New York City at a meeting of an international trade organization? Did pro-bicycling/anti-car groups expect the WTO to build more public transportation and create bike-friendly streets? How did they know about Seattle, and what did they do when they got there? These same questions can be raised for all of the groups covered in this book: Why are community activists choosing new targets both locally and internationally? Why are they building decentralized coalitions using nonhierarchical models? Why are they using far more theater and direct action? And why has this led to more confrontation with police?

Our modest goal in this essay is to offer preliminary explanations for why and how community activists' targets and practices are changing at this historical moment. As professional sociologists who are also activists, we are well aware of the dangers of generalizations in a "movement" that is characterized by diversity. We hope to capture here the sources of new practices and targets, not the entire range. Of course these practices and targets are not new in themselves, but the ways in which community activists are linking them to national and international targets is new.

Community activism is activism in which the majority of members share a bounded geographic area in which at least one of their major targets is located. Although such activism has never been exclusively centered in cities, the degree to which its practices are also national and local has increased. We argue that the expanded targets and shift in practices are due to the changing locus of political power, access to resources, changes in policing and the convergence of earlier movements.

New targets, new structures

When anarchists smashed the windows of Fidelity Investment, McDonald's, Starbucks, and Planet Hollywood during the WTO protests in Seattle, they were not simply vandals making random attacks. Indeed, a subsequent communiqué was explicit in its explanation of the targets: those involved in gentrification, that had abusive labor practices, or with a record of human rights violations in the United States and overseas (Acme Collective 1999).

Unlike traditional responses to issues of gentrification or labor that targeted a company or a government, here activists attacked international corporations as sources of local, national, and international problems. This shift in community activists' targets can also be seen in other community-based movements. Three political and economic transformations help explain this change: the growth of international government and private/public governance structures that lack institutionalized methods of citizen influence; increased knowledge of targets and allies facilitated by increasing access to information; and a convergence of existing "political streams," long-standing bundles of ideologies, practices, values, and targets.

Activists' targets reflect the structure of systems of power: when the center of power shifts, activists' targets are likely to change also. When power is centered in a feudal system, petitioners target a lord or a king; as cities and nation-states arose, their governments became the target of individuals and group attention (Tilly 1978, 1995). The federated structure of the contemporary United States has made local, state, and federal governments the targets of activism. In a country in which power is more centralized, such as France, targets are more likely to be national.

In the last decade, the locus of power relevant to community activists has shifted between arenas in three ways. First, more power is centered in forums that include multiple states (e.g. the European Union, EU, and the Group of 8, G8). Second, national-level obligations are being returned to the local level through reductions in federal budgets and programs (Ekins 1992; Mander and Goldsmith 1996). Third, international hybrid public/private groups from the WTO to non-governmental organizations (NGOs), to which citizens have no institutionalized political access, have increased in importance. These changes have meant that activists have to strategize in new ways about the level of target that is appropriate. When taking on transnational actors, such as the WTO or McDonald's, do you direct attention toward the local outlet or the head office?

The internationalization of capital and the movement of labor across international boundaries has created a changed political arena. These macro-level forces have connected local governments with the actions of corporations regulated by national and international power structures, and pointed activists toward an exploration of how their own local problems are linked to the problems of people in other countries. Capital acquired elsewhere is often invested in urban economies and contributes to political campaigns.

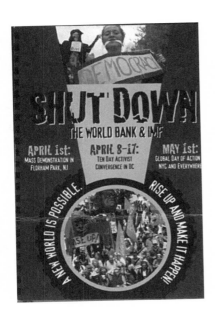

SHUT DOWN

THE WORLD BANK & IMF

APRIL 1st:
MASS DEMONSTRATION IN
FLORHAM PARK, NJ

APRIL 8–17:
TEN DAY ACTIVIST
CONVERGENCE IN DC

MAY 1st:
GLOBAL DAY OF ACTION
NYC AND EVERYWHERE

A NEW WORLD IS POSSIBLE.

RISE UP AND MAKE IT HAPPEN!

**S29
RTS
CAR
FREE
NYC**

COME IN COSTUME!!

Meet 8PM at
St. Mark's
Church, 10th & 2nd

NEW YORK CITY ROCKS!

RECLAIM THE STREETS

CLEAN AIR

TIMES UP!

CRITICAL MASS

Companies that do business in other parts of the world make decisions in the context of international considerations that affect the lives of local workers. And finally, emigration from chosen countries (made possible by legal changes that satisfy the labor needs of host countries) means that new skills, culture, and information are made available at a local level.

Yet because these international systems lack any mechanism for participation in decision-making, activists turn toward less conventional means. We thus see a local political theater group stage a short play and occupy a Disney store to protest the labor practices of the corporation's suppliers (see Shepard essay in part 3 of this volume); students demonstrate at the meeting of international corporations that use exploitative labor practices to manufacture college clothing (see Lefkowitz essay in this section); members of an anti-police brutality group go to Seattle to protest the suppression of political activism in the United States and all over the world; and an animal rights group from Chicago harasses and ridicules EU representatives as they try to enter a meeting space in protest against its failure to enforce strict environmental regulations that would protect valuable habitats. In all of these cases, local groups focus their attention on structures that appear to be geographically distant, but that actually exert a powerful influence on local issues.

Necessary resources

The mere existence of new targets in no way means that all groups will identify or have the capacity or desire to act against those bodies. Community activists are dependent on three types of resource in order to be able to act: information about targets, issues, and campaigns; human resources, such as organizing skills to facilitate movement building and engagement; and institutional resources that support movement stability and security.

Information about potential targets and allies has become easier and cheaper to access, particularly through the Internet. Twenty years ago, information about campaigns was disseminated through movement literature, sent by mail, personal contacts, or by the mainstream media. Today, arduous "phone trees" can be replaced by email. Desktop publishing can provide sophisticated imagery, and updates on campaigns can be easily shared. The importance of the Internet for organizing is often overrated, but few will argue that it has not altered the way movements disseminate

Time's UP! Critical Mass NYC

information about actions and campaigns, especially through the use of listservs and websites. Furthermore, the decline in price of video and digital technologies has helped to distribute imagery quickly and easily, facilitate ties between distant communities, make media relations faster and easier, and provide links between previously unconnected campaigns. The role of the media in building movements is not new, of course. Doug McAdam argued in the late 1960s that the media, particularly television, served as the principal vehicle of diffusion linking rioters in different cities. He also showed that activists staged events they thought were most likely to be covered by new media (McAdam 1982). What is distinctively different today is that in addition to staging newsworthy events, activists now produce and distribute their own images of action (for further discussion see the essays in part 3 below).

The acquisition of skills is made easier because identifying "fellow travelers" through electronic media is much quicker. Even if they meet in cyberspace, groups nearly always desire face-to-face meetings or gatherings. Such meetings appear necessary in order to broker the trust required of engaging in long-term organizing. Training and strategizing weekends, and their attendant social events, are popular ways to facilitate the development of shared identities, strategy, and process.

Along with skills, grassroots community movements have benefited from their ties to established institutions. Notwithstanding their potential role in professionalization and co-optation, institutions like the National Lawyers Guild and the War Resisters League, developed to protect and sustain earlier movements, have provided necessary resources and stability to the new community action coalitions.

The flourishing NGO sector has also been identified as a key actor in the new polity, influencing the targets and structures of direct action movements (Smith, Chatfield, and Pagnucco 1997; Tarrow 1999). As Western governments have shifted to the right, and NGOs have gained power, NGOs have become more willing and able to confront national governments. Despite their formal goals, NGOs may intentionally or inadvertently support grassroots movements. Decision-makers uncertain of the power of NGOs may provide openings for more radical action. Groups like Rainforest Action Network and Global Exchange provided significant funding for mass actions against the WTO and the International Monetary Fund/World Bank (Beck 2000).

Political streams

No group starts in a vacuum. The targets and actions of community activists in particular are highly influenced by the political traditions in their own city. For example, police brutality is a major issue in many American cities, and activists are typically focused on locally controlled police forces. But whom do they seek to influence and in what ways? Should they organize a Cop-Watch program? Petition city council? Demonstrate in front of the police headquarters? Organize those likely to be victims into a broad-based mass party? Hack police computers? Or fight with or heckle police at demonstrations?

One of the ways targets are chosen is according to the available political streams. All cities have different sorts of traditions from which members are drawn and ideas, tactics, and targets adapted. American streams include libearalism, pacifism and moral transformation, communist-style party organizing, and anarchism. In each of these streams, targets reflect organizational and movement histories. This is partially a matter of skill transfers, but also a matter of shared ways of understanding problems and solutions. Because community activists work in localized places, they may be more influenced by such streams than by groups initiated and organized nationally.

These streams have a genealogy, but are constantly adapted; occasionally, a bolder new stream is created. The best example of this in the contemporary United States is surely the creative direct action, affinity-group model. ACT UP pioneered a new political stream by drawing upon the affinity-group model used by American anti-nuclear activists, using the anarchist, pacifist, and civil rights tradition of localized decision-making; the direct action techniques of pacifists who physically confronted systems of power through "misuse" of spaces; and the feminist emphasis on process.

In the 1980s and 1990s, ACT UP targeted an amazing array of power sources at the local and national levels. Among them were religious groups and leaders, government agencies, government representatives, nonprofit organizations, for-profit organizations, individuals, and a form of domination in which power is maintained through a normalizing process, in which, to borrow from Foucault, "the whole indefinite domain of the nonconforming is punishable" (see Gamson 1991). Recognizing that these targets were intertwined, the group encouraged diversity in targets and local control over choices. Where to engage in direct action, then, was shaped by local understandings of the relationships between nominally independent systems of power.

This model of multiple targets is ascendant among community activists of many ideological stripes. Rather than rigidly viewing appropriate targets through a narrow lens, they are more likely to focus on multiple or shifting targets, and to engage in coalition work in new ways. Also, the choice of targets is not simply based on calculations of the likelihood of legal or bureaucratic changes. The availability of information and organizational strategies which favor coalition building means that some possible new targets – say, users of a product produced by an exploitative company – are placed in the background, while others – producers and multiple governments – are in the foreground.

We know that within this changed political context, these movements are choosing new targets in new ways. In order to understand these choices, we need to look more closely at the practices and tactics of the claimants themselves.

Practices

On May 1, 2000, over five hundred Mexican immigrant workers gathered at Union Square in New York City, ready to march to demand amnesty for immigrant workers. Behind them were clusters of other activists holding huge puppets of birds and workers. Young white anarchists wearing masks chatted quietly and handed out flyers on the history of May Day. Then the police surrounded the group, suddenly sweeping in and arresting eight people. After the scuffle, the march began, pausing to direct attention to stores that engaged in poor labor practices. It ended in a park, where some activists joined a bicycle parade to an abandoned lot under the Manhattan Bridge. On the bridge a banner read "Save the Land," and under it the activists cleared garbage and planted seeds. The police hovered menacingly nearby.[1]

In many ways, such a day in New York represents a new style of urban protest in North America. Like the changes in movement targets, these shifts are a result of the changing political and economic context. Increasingly, protests are organized through such diverse coalitions, using nonhierarchical models of democratic process, direct action and theatrics, and more confrontation with police.

Coalition building

One of the most interesting characteristics of the growing community direct action movement of the past five years has been an increasing emphasis on coalition building. The much lauded co-presence, if not coalition, between the "Teamsters and Turtles" in Seattle offered hope to activists who have been struggling to make the links between the labor and environmental movements. In US movements for civil rights and disarmament, such widespread coalition building has correlated with movement growth, creativity, and success (Meyer and Rochon 1997).

This facility at coalition building contrasts with the early days of identity politics when Joshua Gamson observed that identity-oriented groups like ACT UP had difficulty working in coalition with other movements (Gamson 1991). In the early and mid 1990s, the political context changed and ACT UP began to participate in coalitions against the Gulf War, homelessness, and the prison industrial complex, among others. Their theatrical direct action approach began to spread through a wide range of movements (see Kaplan essay in this section). Today, groups such as ACT UP/Philadelphia are playing key roles in anti-corporate coalitions, contributing their understanding of the links between political power and corporate power, and their experience with media-savvy confrontational tactics.[2]

Coalitions are built on three levels: ad hoc or project coalitions used to organize mass actions or events; longer-term local organizing coalitions, which link issues, organizations, and movements; and global coalitions between movements in different countries, which exchange information, human and material resources, and coordinate actions.

Each level of coalition building has a specific but related logic. The different levels overlap, contradict, and support each other. The strongest coalitions do not indicate an identity of interests, priorities, or tactics. Indeed, coalitions are strongest when they can emphasize their differences to potential supporters, while emphasizing commonality and cooperation to their targets (Hathaway and Meyer 1997). In projects, local organizing, and global movements, coalitions can provide needed leverage, resources, and information.

Coalition building has been facilitated by experiments with intentionally non-hierarchical organizing mechanisms inherited from the radical feminist, civil rights, antiracist, environmental, and anarchist movements. These approaches to organizing are attempts to overcome historical distrust between movements, and respond to histories of sectarianism and fears of infiltration. Often the only agreement between groups working on a particular action is on a limited tactical level, for example "Shut down the WTO." These coalitions are organized and maintained through the use of formal mechanisms like "spokescouncils" and "affinity groups" which aim to support differences of opinion.

Direct action

In 1998 in Philadelphia a diverse crowd of thousands, including a large "black bloc" of anarchists dressed in black, listened to speeches and marched along a permitted route through the city, demanding the release of imprisoned journalist Mumia Abu Jamal.

Less than two years later, on the same streets, many of the same people demonstrated again. This time, along with the rallies and marches, affinity groups of between five and twenty people moved into the streets to disrupt the movement of buses to the Republican National Convention. Traffic was snarled. Groups of people dressed as goats, clowns, and billionaires surrounded delegates. Police cars were attacked, and hundreds were arrested and many beaten. Giant puppets were built and confiscated, while an elaborate network of medics, legal observers, communications teams, and independent media supported the action.

There has been an explosion of tactical innovation. Street theater and fire breathing, inflatable suits, smashing of windows, electronic civil disobedience, and billboard alteration tactics abound. We can identify three features of these actions: theatrical but disruptive, reclaiming urban space, and confrontation with the police.

Theatrical but disruptive

The Radical Cheerleaders confused and alarmed loyal Republicans at the inauguration for President George W. Bush. With pompoms and sassy short skirts, Cheerleaders in many cities regularly bring their explicit radical feminism to actions, chanting for revolution and resistance. Such tactics, which take traditional images and subvert them, are wildly popular. Influenced by British rave culture and radical politics, and American movements which use costume and performance (albeit in different ways) to confound expectations, activists have dressed up like billionaires, petty dictators, and evangelists (see essays by Boyd and Grote in part 3, and by Talen in part 4, of this volume).

This is not to suggest that the theatrics are merely about visual display or media spin. The theatrics are central to a vision of a creative empowered society. The "carnivalesque" approach to protest is in part a backlash against routinized demonstrations and negotiated arrests, and is aimed at directing attention to issues of power and control. As the puppet-making network Art and Revolution explains: "We believe that our politics suffer without creative vision in the same way that our art suffers without political or social relevance" (Art and Revolution 2001).

Reclaiming the streets

This emphasis on reclaiming space has become central to many community actions (see essay by Duncombe in part 3 of this volume). In centers where urban space is increasingly controlled and privatized, actions that occupy space without a permit have become contentious in new ways. Reclaim the Streets events, whose non-permitted street parties had first gained wild popularity in Britain, started "liberating" streets from commercial and automobile activity in the United States and Canada in 1998. They explain: "It's about reclaiming the streets as public inclusive space from the private exclusive use of the car. But we believe in this as a broader principle, taking back those things which have been enclosed within capitalist circulation and returning them to collective use as a commons" (Reclaim the Streets 2001). This "reclaiming" of space, however, has been increasingly penalized.

Policing the people

With public space under increasing control, the widening gap between rich and poor, and the gentrification of inner cities as the wealthy return from the suburbs, policing strategies intervene more and more in public behavior. This has shrunk the stage on which social movements can operate without harassment. Where "quality of life" issues are heavily policed, police budgets and discretionary power have created a situation where even the tamest protest becomes the target of police attention. The right to assemble in front of public buildings has been challenged in New York City. Permits are needed to march on the street, use a bullhorn, put up a poster, or gather in the park. Increased repression, of course, has relatively predictable effects – generally stiffening resistance and tactical shifts. Historical studies have suggested that when repression is selective it can isolate groups, but when it is generalized it can radicalize moderate actors (McAdam, Tarrow, and Tilly, 2001).

Overwhelming evidence shows that the increase in repressive policing hits people of color hardest. In Los Angeles and New York City, communities have mobilized in response to police brutality. As white activists experience repressive policing in their own lives, they are becoming more interested in making the links between issues of globalization and issues of criminal justice. As a press release from the Black Radical Congress argues, "One of the most egregious manifestations of globalization in the US is the link between the rising funding disparities between prisons and public education" (Black Feminist Caucus 2000; see also Fletcher essay in part 5 below.)

The increase in police repression over urban space and protest has made policing a key concern for people of color and increasingly for white activists. As a result, distrust of the police is pushing white activist movements away from negotiated arrest scenarios and toward direct action tactics, which strategically avoid arrest while aiming to influence opponents. But people confront their targets too. In Washington DC at the inauguration ceremony of George W. Bush, a crowd of voter rights protesters and anarchists broke through a police checkpoint into the area that lined the president's parade route. Once there, they cheered, sang mocking versions of the national anthem, replaced the flags, and teased the undercover police.

Conclusions

In cities across the United States and Canada, community activists are working in loose coalitions and using creative tactics to confront multiple targets. The shifts in targets and practices in these movements take place within larger transformations in the political and economic context. And yet the relationship between such transformations and political practices is not direct. Political practices are adapted through processes and mechanisms like coalition building and brokerage, radicalization through police repression, and access to information which supports the building of political identities. These processes and mechanisms operate within politicized urban spaces, which have distinct political histories and affect communities in specific ways.

However, there are commonalities between the community movements across these cities. Increasingly, they are organized using nonhierarchical structures, engaged in theatrical tactics which disrupt the smooth functioning of power, and are heavily controlled and policed. Such evidence does not conform to existing distinctions within social movement theory between community groups and social movements, between identity-based and class-based struggles. They confound analysts who have argued that in a global era North American social movements will continue to become professionalized and less disruptive. Future work must focus on the mechanisms and processes which have allowed the flowering of this new movement.

Community gardeners in New York, cop watchers in Chicago, and housing activists in Toronto are making the links between the local and the global in new ways – by dressing up as daisies and disrupting city council meetings, taking on the police, and shutting down borders and global summits. These are community activists with a broad systemic analysis, who see multinational corporations, as well as the mayor, as responsible for local issues. From ACT UP to the WTO, they are struggling to use the tools of past movements in new ways and make challenges which are direct, creative, and accessible. There is no consensus on what constitutes "success." Nevertheless, these activists are defining a new moment in grassroots organizing.

Notes

1. The first part of the day was organized by a coalition of Immigrants Rights groups and Mexican organizations, and the second by Reclaim the Streets and Times Up! New York.
2. ACT UP/Philadelphia was a central organization in the protests against the Republican National Convention in August 2000; and played visible parts in the protests against the IMF/World Bank in April 2000.

A short history of radical renewal

L.A. KAUFFMAN

When tens of thousands of demonstrators shut down the World Trade Organization meetings in November 1999 with an exuberant and carnivalesque blockade, many observers were taken by surprise. To the political mainstream, the clashes in Seattle seemed to materialize from nowhere. According to the conventional wisdom of the last twenty-five years, after all, the left in the United States had virtually disappeared. It died when the US pulled out of Vietnam, or when Ronald Reagan was elected, or when the Berlin Wall fell. It fractured into the aggrieved and squabbling grouplets of identity politics or became the refuge of self-proclaimed victims and moralizing scolds. It was defeated, bloodless, and dull.

But all the while the left was ostensibly languishing (and parts of it certainly were), another history – another kind of radicalism – was unfolding. Seattle was the culmination of a thirty-year-long process of political reinvention: the creation, in the decades after the 1960s, of an effective, decentralized, multivocal radicalism based on direct action.

Most of this history of radical renewal is little known or poorly understood. It took place, for the most part, in movements that outsiders tended to view as "single-issue" and separate from one another, with little relevance beyond their own particular spheres: the gay and lesbian liberation movements, the feminist movement, the antinuclear movement, the radical environmental movement, and the AIDS activist movement, to name only the largest ones. In fact, these movements profoundly influenced both each other and the larger radical project and, across decades of political experimentation, created the new vernacular of resistance that has been demonstrated in the global justice movement of today. The single most influential group of people in this thirty-year process of innovation and reinvigoration were lesbian activists, both white and of color, who most often formed the bridge between one movement and the next, transmitting skills, insight, and expertise. The single most important organization, without question, was ACT UP, which introduced a vibrancy and flair to street politics that the left had lost, and created a new ethos of activism that was at once profoundly radical and pragmatic.

The roots of what has been called the "Seattle model" stretch back a good deal further than most realize, to the latter years of the anti-Vietnam War movement, in the early 1970s (see Starhawk's essay, "How We Really Shut Down the WTO," in this section, for a detailed account of how the Seattle protests were organized). Radicalized by the 1970 US invasion of Cambodia and disgusted with the machismo, infighting, and dogmatism of the late-sixties left, a new generation of activists began a tentative experiment with smaller and more decentralized organizational structures, and with a feminist-inspired politics that valued personal engagement over doctrinal purity.

Affinity groups – small, face-to-face groups that form the basic units for a protest – were first adopted as the building blocks for nonviolent direct action in 1971, during a stunningly ambitious and almost totally forgotten attempt by a group called the Mayday Tribe to blockade Washington DC in protest against the Vietnam War.[1] The group's slogan was, "If the government won't stop the war, we'll stop the government," and if that wasn't audacious enough, the Mayday Tribe's game plan also completely departed from the organizing style that had existed in the antiwar movement, and most radical activism, up until that point. There was no national leadership that called the shots; instead, planning for the action was decentralized, with affinity groups from around the country choosing their blockade targets and their tactical approach.

The Mayday Tribe's action did not succeed in the most literal sense, but the Nixon administration had to bring in squadrons of Marines and waves of assault helicopters to keep the government running, making more than 13,000 arrests in the process. What is more, a whole wave of activists was transformed by the experience of a new kind of direct action. As one participant wrote at the time, "Twenty thousand freaks carry the seeds now, and they've been blown to every corner of the land." These predominantly white radicals put down especially strong roots in the feminist, lesbian-feminist, gay, and radical ecology movements of the early 1970s.

In the late 1970s, activists from all these movements converged to fight the construction of nuclear power plants throughout the United States, and it was within this context that the direct action organizing model now used at the major anti-corporate globalization protests was developed and institutionalized. Quakers played a strong role in the antinuclear movement, especially at its inception, and they introduced their traditional consensus decision-making process – which some radicals were soon calling "feminist process" – to the world of direct action, melding it to the anarchist affinity group form. At this time, Quakers and other pacifists also made nonviolence codes a standard component of mass direct actions, although the antinuclear movement faced major disputes about whether property destruction constitutes violence, and how far activists can or should go in policing other activists – much as the global justice movement does today. Finally, it was in the 1970s antinuclear movement that the distinctive "spokescouncil" structure was adopted, through which representatives of affinity groups come together to make decisions for the action as a whole.

These elements – affinity groups, consensus process, nonviolence codes, spokescouncils – have formed the basis for large-scale direct action in a host of radical and progressive movements ever since, including major protests for nuclear disarmament in the early 1980s, Pledge of Resistance actions against US intervention in Central America in the mid 1980s, and Earth First! mobilizations from the late 1980s onward, to name only a few.

Very little about the structure or organizing methods of the anti-globalization movement is especially new, in other words. In many respects, the 1999 blockade of the Seattle

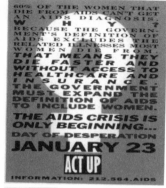

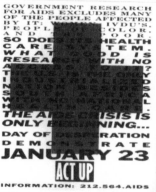

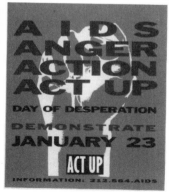

WTO meetings was planned no differently from the 1977 blockade of the Seabrook Nuclear Power Plant. Certainly, there were new technologies, from lockdown devices (first developed by radical environmentalists and animal rights activists in the 1980s) to cellular phones and the Internet. But the direct actions undertaken by the movement for global justice build on well-established practices of radical protest.

The novelty of the current movement lies in its vitality, ambition, and breadth. Two pivotal developments in recent activist history prepared the way: the style and sensibility that ACT UP brought to American radicalism, beginning in the late 1980s; and the growing interest, across the decade of the 1990s, in new kinds of collaboration between and among movements.

It is difficult to overstate the influence or importance of ACT UP. From its inception in 1987, the AIDS activist movement pioneered a punk-inflected style of outrageous and mediagenic direct action, employing protest in highly targeted ways that led to consistent concrete victories. The group's ferocious creativity had everything to do with the immediacy and immensity of the stakes: Illness and death were a constant presence in ACT UP, a powerful radicalizing force that made its experience unlike that of any previous social movement. "DESPERATE DYING HOPELESS PEOPLE WITH NOTHING TO LOSE ARE DANGEROUS AND UNPREDICTABLE," declared one ACT UP T-shirt. The fury — and fear — acted as potent inspirations, driving people to undertake daring actions and drawing them together in something like a wartime camaraderie.

ACT UP had one basic strategy: in the words of the late New York AIDS activist Aldyn McKean, "Make it more costly for those in power to resist than to give in." In the process, the group dispensed with a series of stultifying practices and assumptions that had become second nature on the left. ACT UP never entertained the notion that a group must hammer out its analysis before it takes action; it instinctively disdained rallies, where speakers drone on to the already converted. Where the antinuclear and other movements of the 1970s and early 1980s had opted for a homespun aesthetic of hand-lettered signs that were intended to connote sincerity and authenticity, ACT UP was shamelessly slick, using sophisticated computer graphics and stage-managing their actions for maximum visual impact. ACT UP wanted — *needed* — results, the sooner the better; it had no patience for the kind of radical purism that dismisses actual accomplishments as mere reformism.

The list of groups that took direct inspiration from ACT UP evokes some of the

fiercest and most effective activism from the late 1980s
onward: Earth First!, the Lesbian Avengers, WHAM! (Wom-
en's Health Action and Mobilization), BACAOR (Bay Area
Coalition Against Operation Rescue), ADAPT (American
Disabled for Attendant Programs Today), and many more.
"ACT UP just created – I don't know what the word is – a
restlessness or momentum," recalls René Francisco Poitevin,
one of the founders of Roots Against War, a San Francisco
Bay Area people-of-color group that played a central role in
the movement against the 1991 Persian Gulf War. "Direct
action was the thing. We were like: We know that shit works.
It can make a lot of trouble. So here we go."

The radical landscape of the early 1990s – ACT UP's heyday – was, however, a fractured one, where movements tended
to work in relative isolation from one another. It wasn't that
there was a high degree of tension or conflict between movements; it was more a particularism (some might say narrow-
ness) of political vision that had been part of the logic of
movement-building for decades.

The overarching trend in radicalism from the late 1960s
onward was proliferation – a profusion of causes, issues,
identities, and approaches. In the ensuing decades, even when
the strength and influence of radical movements were slight,
their sheer number and variety were breathtaking. Consider
feminism as just one example. In 1970, there were basically
two kinds of feminist: radical ones and liberal ones. By the
early 1980s, the political options included lesbian-feminists,
socialist-feminists, cultural feminists, eco-feminists, anarcha-
feminists, anti-porn feminists, pro-sex feminists, and a rapidly
multiplying array of feminisms of color. This tendency was
reinforced by the activist preference, throughout the 1970s
and 1980s, for small groups and local battles, captured in the
classic slogan of the time, "Think globally, act locally."

It is difficult to pinpoint exactly when this centrifugal force

became a centripetal one, though the emergence in the early 1990s of the environmental justice movement – a people-of-color-led movement that has fused ecological, economic, and racial concerns – was a clear turning point. Simultaneously, there
were major splits within both Earth First! and ACT UP over whether the movements
should focus on wilderness preservation or AIDS treatments as single issues or
reorient their activism to address class, economic, racial, and gender concerns; in
both cases, the broader-based radicalism prevailed. New movements in the mid to
late 1990s as diverse as the Bus Riders Union, Art and Revolution, United Students
Against Sweatshops, the Lower East Side Collective, and the Black Radical Congress
struggled in different ways to fuse multiple issues and perspectives in on-the-ground
campaigns. A new bumper sticker appeared in the late 1990s that captured the major
changes taking place in the world and the ways that radicals were beginning to
respond: "If you're being attacked globally, you'd better act globally."

The global justice movement that burst into view as the 1990s drew to a close,
however, has not subsumed the variety and specificity of local- and identity-based
concerns into some overarching theory, doctrine, or organization. The model for the
movement is the very model that radicals first adopted for direct-action blockades
two and a half decades ago: decentralized, based on coordination rather than unifi-
cation, deriving its strength and vitality from the autonomy and self-determination of
its component parts.

Note

1. The affinity group concept dates back to the Spanish Civil War of the 1930s, when it was
   used as the underground organizing structure by the Iberian Anarchist Federation, addressing both the security needs of a clandestine organization and anarchist ideals of decentralized power and free association. The idea was first adopted in the United States by
   the Motherfuckers, the Lower East Side chapter of Students for a Democratic Society, and
   by Weatherman for its 1969 Days of Rage, in both cases as a street-fighting formation
   rather like – in the Motherfuckers' words – "a gang with an analysis."

This city is ours

ESTHER KAPLAN

At 5 p.m. on Tuesday April 25, 1995, in New York City, a little over a year into Rudy Giuliani's tenure as mayor and just five months into the Gingrich Revolution, hundreds of homeless activists marched across the Brooklyn Bridge for a rally at City Hall. As they neared the Manhattan-side ramp, twenty-five activists peeled off to block the bridge just as rush-hour commuters headed their way. One of the activists, Lisa Daugaard, gleefully recalls that when police moved in to cuff them, a message came in over one officer's scanner. "Battery Tunnel?" she heard him say.

At that very moment, right across town, sixty City University of New York (CUNY) students had departed from another rally to block cars as they headed for that exit from Manhattan. A little farther uptown, twenty-five police-brutality activists dashed from a Chinatown movie house to seal off the Manhattan Bridge, the final artery to Brooklyn. And in Midtown, when a traffic light turned, seventy-five AIDS and disability activists, myself among them, briskly walked and wheeled our way deep into the entranceway of the Queens Midtown Tunnel for a traffic-stopping die-in. What the *Village Voice* dubbed the Rush Hour Revolt ultimately involved more than two thousand demonstrators, four rallies and 185 planned arrests.[1] In fourteen years of activism, I've never been part of anything quite like it.

The action may be a faded chapter of nineties' activist history by now, but what might today be referred to as "A25" is an early echo of the structure and style of the new direct action movement – interesting both for its strong parallels and for its distinct approach to some of the problems that plague the current movement. A25 was a large, multi-site, multi-issue action almost five years before the Battle in Seattle. It was a mass civil disobedience action at a time when no one but ACT UP had used that tactic in years. And it was a brash display of political unity – with majority participation by people of color – at a time when city progressives had never felt more divided.

A divided city

We all sensed that a storm was coming when Giuliani made a crackdown on the city's "squeegee men" a centerpiece of his campaign for mayor. But we didn't realize how soon. In his first week in office in January 1994, the former prosecutor, saying that windshield-wiping entrepreneurs "filled New Yorkers with dread," sent police officers out to round up and arrest them all. Two weeks later, the city posted signs in subway cars, urging riders not to give out pocket change to panhandlers, and arrests of the poor multiplied underground. Brutal sweeps of out-of-the-way homeless encampments followed, where the unhoused had their shelters and belongings bulldozed before being treated to three nights in jail. By March, the crackdown had extended to public urinators and marijuana tokers, and by April to the city's mostly immigrant squad of food vendors.

The deluge began in mid February, when the mayor announced that he would sell off several of the city's public hospitals to private bidders and that he planned to eliminate the city's Division of AIDS Services as well. And it simply didn't let up. In early May, he proposed a city budget splattered with massive cutbacks to the public schools, public universities, and youth services; in October he pushed a package of midterm cuts that threatened to eliminate soup kitchens across the city. By year's end, police brutality complaints had risen by 38 percent.

For activists, it was chaos. Looking back through my datebook from that year, I notice that in the space of a few months I appeared in court on disorderly conduct charges for an evening of staged squeegeeing; offered childcare for a day-long teach-in on the Division of AIDS Services; pulled a midnight shift as an observer at Penn Station, where reports of police beatings of the homeless were most severe; joined a demonstration protesting proposed tuition hikes at CUNY, and, like every other activist in the city, it seemed, went to meeting after meeting. Countless community coalitions sprang up – Youth Agenda to oppose the youth services cutbacks, the Harlem Coalition to Save Our Health Care to fight hospital privatization – each one a piecemeal attempt to limit the destruction.

During the course of that year, there were a few victories. Faced down by ACT UP and other AIDS activists, the mayor backed down on his threat to eliminate the city's AIDS division. The Board of Education and the United Federation of Teachers staved off a portion of the public school cuts. The health care union, 1199, along with local community activists, saved Harlem and Bronx public hospitals from the auction block. But it was a zero-sum game: if you won, someone else lost, and privately AIDS activists agonized that their victory came at the price of youth centers across the city shutting their doors.

Many advocates were struggling to find a way out of the bind, and some came together to form broad, citywide umbrella organizations, most notably the Same Boat Coalition, composed heavily of social service providers under the budget knife, and Breaking Bread, composed mostly of left-wing academics and community activists, including myself. But with unions and nonprofits locked in struggles that could mean the death of institutions, Same Boat could rarely turn out more than one hundred demonstrators for the rallies they planned – and ended up functioning best as a pre-email information exchange. And while Breaking Bread did pull out about eight hundred people for a forum on social change with bell hooks and Cornel West in June 1994, only one hundred showed up four weeks later for a follow-up strategy session, and that coalition soon closed shop.

The most significant things to come out of Breaking Bread were a few relationships among members of its racially and politically diverse steering committee, and a comment made by one of them, National Congress of Puerto Rican Rights chair Richard Perez, as he moderated that hooks–West dialogue. He said, "I can imagine a time when we'd have a level of unity where we could close down bridges and highways around the city and stop business as usual! And we could do this without having to form a single organization." It was an image of intense political coordination that went way past the dominant, but ineffective, coalition model of the time. A week, two weeks, three months later, and the image was still rattling around in our heads. Really, when you think about it, why not?

In early November, Lisa Daugaard and I (she a founder of the homeless advocacy group StreetWatch; me a longtime ACT UPer), nervously called up Perez and asked to meet about something we'd rather not discuss on the phone. The former Young Lord didn't ask any questions, but invited us over to his office the next afternoon. "Do you remember what you said back in July about all those bridges?" we asked. "What do you think about giving it a try?" Our first A25 planning meeting took place two weeks later in a noisy restaurant with about eight others. The meeting was contentious, even jittery, but almost everyone left ready to try what was then almost unthinkable.

Total coordination and total autonomy

William Broberg, a coordinator of the student arm of A25, now works as an attorney in Seattle – he was the one who finally got the WTO protesters there out of jail. Our post-Seattle conversations were my first exposure to the political structure behind these multifocal protests – the use of "spokescouncil" meetings to link independent acts of civil disobedience. Though our approach to organizing A25 was quite different from this Seattle model, the basic premiss – balancing unity and autonomy – felt extremely familiar.

Our goals for A25 were ambitious – to confront directly the disunity among New York City's activist communities and escalate the seriousness of the resistance – but our proposal was elegant in its simplicity: plan a militant, coordinated action that allowed maximum autonomy for each organization involved.

In the late 1980s and early 1990s, with labor in a deep slumber, most active organizations were community-based (Harlem, Bed-Stuy), identity-based (Haitians, African Americans, lesbians), or issue-based (abortion, AIDS), and it was common to hear complaints about the "Balkanization" of the left – in fact, by a few of the same people who are so taken by the current anti-globalization movement. Those of us who were building A25 were not among the bashers. We respected, and participated in, organizations like these – they'd been extremely effective at bringing our communities' issues into the public consciousness, whether AIDS discrimination or Puerto Rican independence – even as we wanted to push our own comrades to consider the potential for collective power on a grand scale. We also knew that part of what limited the effectiveness of coalitions like Breaking Bread was that none of us could really imagine a single organization that everyone could trust.

Our coordinating committee was not composed, as in the standard coalition model, of organizational representatives who changed from week to week. It was made up of specific individuals. To pull off our concept, we needed to bring in seasoned activists who had strong credibility within their community — enough credibility to bring in their organization without giving out all the information. "Key to our success was everyone in the room had a constituency," says Perez. "We weren't six people who could mobilize twelve people." And they each had to be people who could work comfortably in an egalitarian, collective body. "The careful and intentional pace at which we expanded was very important to me," says Thoai Nguyen, then an organizer with the Committee Against Anti-Asian Violence (CAAAV). "The importance placed on tactics and political principles over numbers was key."

Over time, we made a handful of agreements, each with a specific goal in mind. Each civil disobedience (CD) site would have an above-board rally to accompany it, to allow us to create buzz about the day of action without exposing our real plans. To minimize the risk of an injunction, no one but coordinating committee members would know any information about the other actions. We'd create a single common mission statement — subject to review by the planners of each action — that would be distributed on the flip side of each site's issue-based statement or fact sheet. We'd design a common press strategy, to guard against one "hot" action drawing all the attention — a strategy we implemented by offering the story to reporters on the condition that they cover every site. (That's why the *New York Times* had four photographers and four reporters on the story.) And that was it.

Beyond that, each team planning an action was on its own: Did they want to define the action by community, such as the South Bronx, or by issue, such as police brutality? Did they want the Brooklyn Bridge or Battery Tunnel? Did they want to keep logistics secret from their recruits, or trust each CDer to keep it on the down low? Their call. We were searching for a form of unity that could lay the groundwork for taking control of the city back from Giuliani and the forces of reaction he represented, but that would ask communities to sacrifice as little autonomy as possible.

On the coordinating committee, we asked much more of each other. No faxes, no emails, almost nothing in writing at all: every bit of outreach was one-on-one, face-to-face, and our meetings were long, intense, and frequent. At each successive meeting, if there was even one new person, we talked through and refined the strategy of the action, again and again. "I thought its simplicity was its best feature," says Nguyen. "We worked closely and held each other accountable for successes and failures, and we didn't rely on clumsy structures like the spokescouncil or affinity groups."

The color question

From the first thrilling news footage that came out of Seattle, it was evident that, as Elizabeth Martinez wrote in *ColorLines*, the great battle was "overwhelmingly white."[2] After Martinez opened up the debate within the movement, a handful of activists began to respond, in small and large ways: the Mobilization for Global Justice paid for buses for some mostly black ACT UPers from Philadelphia for April 16, 2000, in Washington; CAAAV joined with other activists to form Third Force, a people-of-color contingent for A16 and the Republican National Convention in Philadelphia; Nguyen and others organized trainings and teach-ins for people of color from Philly and New York City interested in participating in the protest at Republican National Convention (R2K). But many activists remain fairly cynical about the rate of change.

In contrast, race politics was fundamental to building April 25. It was, in part, our shared frustration with the creeping whiteness of coalitions like Same Boat that prompted us to explore this new model in the first place. In addition, "We came out of AIDS, CUNY, police brutality, homelessness, hospitals, all areas in which people of color were a tremendous component," recalls Perez, who spoke on a post-R2K panel about people of color and CD. "No one came out of an all-white milieu. Some of the anti-globalization activists are coming out of an all-white world."

From the outset, we talked openly about which communities were being hardest hit by the Gingrich/Giuliani one–two punch, and which communities were engaged in active resistance. We needed the Bronx, Harlem, and Brooklyn; we needed the unions, the food vendors, the cabbies, and the homeless; we needed African Americans, Haitians, Asians, and Latinos; we needed students, gay men, and lesbians. And we strategized carefully about who we could reach out to in each world.

Our vetting process consumed the first two and half months. Whenever the co-ordinating committee met, we'd each suggest a name or two and then have a lengthy debate about each person's ability to bring out a constituency, their political style, and who was best suited to make the approach. Sectarians were out; narrow nationalists, out; white activists without experience in multiracial organizing, out. If anyone felt that a candidate wasn't trustworthy, she was out. No one could come in unless everyone felt comfortable about them. I remember one meeting where the name of a certain respected sixties-generation lawyer came up (we were toying with the idea of having an attorney present at each meeting to thwart potential conspiracy charges) and I mentioned, almost as an aside, that I'd noticed he couldn't listen to women. And that was it – his name was tossed. I was a little stunned.

We had a few notable failures. Though we successfully recruited several black leaders – Shakoor Aljuwani of the Harlem Hospital Community Board, Brooklyn activist James Steele, Harlem priest Father Luis Barrios, Sabine Albert of the Haitian Women's Program – we never got full buy-in on the CD component from a black organization (Sharpton's operation was a near miss). Ultimately, says Perez, "we didn't find any militant organizations in the black community who bought into the multi-racial paradigm." We were equally conscious of trying to bring labor in, and we approached nearly every prominent labor progressive in the city. "When you look at where labor was then, it was extremely underdeveloped," says Perez. "It still is." Still, labor did join the legal rallies, and there was a strong African-American presence at the homeless and CUNY CDs.

In the end, at planning meetings, there was a level of ease in the room. No one spoke out of turn, in a sense: each of us was juggling a longstanding relationship with our own organization – in my case, ACT UP – with our personal and political commitment to making this unified action work. Losing credibility on either end was a little terrifying. I remember collapsing in tears one afternoon near the end, when I thought my ACT UP comrades, experiencing a crisis of faith about whether the other actions would come through, seemed on the verge of pulling out. Or the painful moment when Aljuwani said he didn't think he could deliver an action in Harlem – in great part because, late in the process, Harlem Hospital was saved from privatization. In this kind of intense environment, there was no room for posturing.

"I felt a real and visible sense of racial, class, and gender unity with the other members of the coordinating committee," Nguyen recalls, "whereas the current movements think of those issues – especially race and class – as secondary, if they think of them at all."

Discipline and trust

In early March I was in Philadelphia covering the trial of an old ACT UP comrade, Kate Sorensen, for *POZ*, the AIDS magazine where I now work. She'd been slapped with a $1 million bail after her arrest at R2K, plus ten felony conspiracy charges. (She ultimately stood trial for four.) Ten other felony trials came out of that week of action, and Sorensen is convinced that this is part of a national crackdown on activism. I suspect she's right, since the evidence of interagency coordination is so strong. But still, I kept wondering during the trial whether the loose structure of the direct action movement – undoubtedly a huge part of its size and appeal – had contributed to Sorensen standing trial for vandalism she'd had nothing to do with.

I asked Nguyen whether he'd had any fears with A25 that participants would do something to put others at risk, such as damaging property or physically confronting police. He said no, that he'd handpicked almost everyone in the police brutality CD, and "held each of them personally accountable to me, and vice versa. I also felt that the other coordinating committee members had the same m.o., and I trusted their confidence in the other participants."

The direct action style of April 25 came from two main sources: the tightly controlled, highly planned CDs of ACT UP/New York, whose members used to brag that the group, through hundreds of arrest scenarios, had never lost a single person in the system, and the security-conscious militancy of seventies-era radicals, like Perez, who'd experienced Cointelpro firsthand in the Young Lords. Our legal team was tight and effective; we already knew, from our experience with ACT UP, which precincts people would be taken to, how many lawyers we'd need for this number of arrests, and what kind of time commitment they'd have to make; how to run a 24/7 legal center until arrestees were all released; and how to use pressure from local elected officials – whom we'd already lined up – to expedite arraignment.

Many of our recruits – the CUNY students, young CAAAV members, homeless people – were fairly new to activism, and had never done CD before, so we committed to training them well and guaranteeing their safety. We created special segments of our CD trainings for minors, undocumented immigrants, and people with previous convictions, outlining clearly what the consequences might be and laying out important alternative roles they could play in the actions.

One of my favorite entries in our timeline for the action, adopted in early January, was "Week of action: Injunctions and restraining orders arrive." As tight as our security was, we had carefully built infiltration, and the possibility of conspiracy charges, into the plan. Nguyen had been a student organizer in Indonesia, where breaches in security could mean jail time or death; Perez's years in the Young Lords weren't so far off; and Broberg and I had ourselves received an injunction a few years before, while planning a CD to protest *Rust* v. *Sullivan*, a Supreme Court decision restricting abortion funds (discussed in the essay by Tracy Morgan in part 3 of this volume). These experiences set the tone.

We set very narrow restrictions on what any of us could reveal as we recruited for the coordinating committee. No unconfirmed CD participant knew where any action would take place; for two of the CDs, even the participants didn't know the locations until moments before. "If you handle secrecy right, people don't have to feel disempowered," says Broberg. "We had a very democratic process about which pieces of the tactical decision-making and information people were willing to relinquish knowing."

One of our final agreements was to use jail solidarity – we would work together inside to assure everyone's prompt release. But our approach was different from that, say, at R2K, where protesters all used noms de guerre and later fought every charge in court for nearly a year. We all gave the basic required information – legal name and permanent address only – and we agreed in court to accept ACDs (a kind of conditional dismissal that implies guilt), choosing as a group not to stand on ceremony so that we could be done with court and get back to our activist work. At a time when police response to activism was at least a bit more predictable, we made no major miscalculations of risk.

Speaking directly to activists

With our action on April 25, says Daugaard, "We targeted powerbrokers as a threat," but, even more importantly, "we targeted activists with a call to action." This emphasis is clear as I read back over our deeply moral joint statement, "This City is Ours":

"Every New Yorker is faced today with a historical choice, because our city is facing a degree of devastation that few of us have witnessed or expected in our lifetime," it read in part.

> Our political leaders want us to turn on each other: to blame teen mothers for the budget crisis, to blame Asian, Latino or Caribbean immigrants for unemployment, to blame homeless people and drug addicts for crime; to blame people with AIDS and other illnesses and disabilities for the collapse of our health care system; to blame youth of color for the failure of our educational system. We are committed to resisting this pressure.… This year, as we take to the streets together before Mayor Giuliani releases his proposed budget, we refuse to fight each other for the same scraps from the budget table. Today we refuse to give divisiveness and cruelty our blessing.… This city is ours, and we do not want it left in ruins.

As an effective challenge to the powers that be, our success was equivocal. Six years later, Newt Gingrich may be a distant memory, but Giuliani is still mayor of New York City. Still, his legacy has been damaged. His repeated efforts to introduce privatization into the public schools, whether through vouchers or for-profit school management, have failed. We now know that he only managed to implement his workfare program because of an election rigged by a now-disgraced municipal election leader. And his crown jewel, the drop in crime, has been permanently tarnished by horrendous incidents of police brutality on his watch, from Anthony Baez to Abner Louima to Amadou Diallo.

As a challenge to activists, it is possible to see the ripples of the action still. A25 cemented the relationship between CAAAV and the National Congress of Puerto Rican Rights, who had never before closely collaborated. The two groups not only went on to found the Coalition Against Police Brutality (CAPB), a people-of-color organization that now includes the black nationalist Malcolm X Grassroots Collective and the gay and lesbian Audre Lorde Project, but they formed the basis of Third Force, the people-of-color contingent that participated in A16 and R2K. The pressure exerted by the multiracial CAPB on Al Sharpton's narrow nationalism has slowly had its effect, too. When police shot Amadou Diallo in early 1999, the Reverend issued a call for two weeks of multiracial CD. A25 was a sort of coming out party for SLAM!, the Hunter College-based Student Liberation Action Movement, which filled out the ranks of the CUNY protest that day. According to Nguyen, SLAM! has become one of the few people-of-color-led organizations to do more than critique the race politics of the direct action movement; "it has taken on the responsibility to try to change it – despite a lot of resistance and denial."

During the thirty or forty hours we all spent together at Central Booking that spring in 1995, we experienced the kind of bonds that are by now familiar to veterans of the anti-globalization protests. "For a minute," Broberg recalls, "people gave themselves over to the vision of 'we' – a 'we' that was a whole lot bigger than we'd ever felt before." As Perez said to me recently, "It's important to create a tradition that speaks to these politics – that it's impossible to fight for your community without fighting homelessness and drug addiction; that it's impossible to fight for liberation and not fight homophobia. We were looking for a teaching experience, to show people what their power was." It wasn't a bad start.

Notes

This article was shaped by conversations and email exchanges with Richard Perez, chairman of the National Congress for Puerto Rican Rights; Thoai Nguyen, who is organizing Roma youth in the Balkans; Lisa Daugaard, who is now directing a project challenging racial bias by Seattle police; and William Broberg, a Seattle attorney. Thanks to Andrew Hsiao, who covered A25 for the *Village Voice*, for sharing his tapes from 1995 interviews.

1. For coverage of the protest, see for example Andrew Hsiao with Karen Houppert, "Birth of a Movement?" *Village Voice*, May 9, 1995; Jessie Mangaliman and Rob Polner, "Budget Protest Traps Thousands," *New York Newsday*, April 26, 1995; N R. Kleinfield, "Rush Hour Protest Causes Gridlock," *New York Times*, April 26, 1995; Elinor Tatum, "New York Police Break up Protest," *Amsterdam News*, April 27, 1995.
2. Elizabeth (Betita) Martinez, "Where Was the Color in Seattle," *ColorLines*, Spring 2000. For another influential article on race in the direct action movement, see Andrew Hsiao, "Color Blind," *Village Voice*, July 25, 2000.

How we really shut down the WTO

STARHAWK

It's been two weeks now since the morning when I awoke before dawn to join the blockade that shut down the opening meeting of the WTO. Since getting out of jail, I've been reading the media coverage and trying to make sense out of the divergence between what I know happened and what has been reported.

For once in a political protest, when we chanted "The whole world is watching!" we were telling the truth. I've never seen so much media attention on a political action. However, most of what has been written is so inaccurate that I can't decide if the reporters in question should be charged with conspiracy or simply incompetence. The reports have pontificated endlessly about a few broken windows, and mostly ignored the Direct Action Network (DAN), the group that successfully organized the nonviolent direct action that ultimately involved thousands of people. The true story of what made the action a success is not being told.

The police, in defending their brutal and stupid mishandling of the situation, have said they were "not prepared for the violence." In reality, they were unprepared for the nonviolence and the numbers and commitment of the nonviolent activists – even though the blockade was organized in open, public meetings and there was nothing secret about our strategy. My suspicion is that our model of organization and decision-making was so foreign to their picture of what constitutes leadership that they literally could not see what was going on in front of them. When authoritarians think about leadership, the picture in their minds is of one person, usually a guy, or a small group standing up and telling other people what to do. Power is centralized and requires obedience.

In contrast, our model of power was decentralized, and leadership was invested in the group as a whole. People were empowered to make their own decisions, and the centralized structures were for coordination, not control. As a result, we had great flexibility and resilience, and many people were inspired to acts of courage they could never have been ordered to do. Following are some of the key aspects of our model of organizing.

Training and preparation

In the weeks and days before the blockade, thousands of people were given non-violence training – a three-hour course that combined the history and philosophy of nonviolence with real life practice through role plays in staying calm in tense situations, using nonviolent tactics, responding to brutality, and making decisions together. Thousands also went through a second-level training in jail preparation, solidarity strategies, and tactics and legal aspects. There were also first-aid training, training in blockade tactics, street theater, meeting facilitation, and other skills. While many more thousands of people who had not attended any of these trainings took part in the blockade, there was a nucleus of groups prepared to face police brutality and provide a core of resistance and strength. And in jail I saw many situations that played out just like the role-play. Activists were able to protect members of their group from being singled out or removed by using tactics introduced in the training. The solidarity tactics we had prepared became a real block to the functioning of the system.

Common agreements

Each participant in the action was asked to agree to the nonviolence guidelines: to refrain from violence, physical or verbal; not to carry weapons; not to bring or use illegal drugs or alcohol; and not to destroy property. We were asked to agree only for the purpose of the 11/30 action, not to sign up to any of these as a life philosophy; the group acknowledged that there is much diversity of opinion around some of the guidelines.

Affinity groups, clusters and spokescouncils

The participants in the action were organized into small units called affinity groups. Each group was empowered to make its own decisions on how it would participate in the blockade. There were groups doing street theater, others preparing to lock themselves to structures, groups with banners and giant puppets, others simply prepared to link arms and nonviolently block delegates. Within each group, there were generally some people prepared to risk arrest and others who would be their support people in jail, as well as a first-aid person.

Affinity groups were organized into clusters. The area around the Convention Center was broken down into thirteen sections, and affinity groups and clusters committed to hold particular sections. In addition, some units were 'flying groups' — free to move to wherever they were most needed. All of this was coordinated at Spokescouncil meetings, to which each affinity group sent a representative who was empowered to speak on its behalf.

In practice, this form of organization meant that groups could move and react with great flexibility during the blockade. If a call went out for more people at a certain location, an affinity group could assess the numbers holding the line where they were and choose whether or not to move. When faced with tear gas, pepper spray, rubber bullets and horses, groups and individuals could assess their own ability to withstand the brutality. As a result, blockade lines held in the face of incredible police violence. When one group of people was finally swept away by gas and clubs, another would move in to take their place. Yet there was also room for those of us in the middle-aged, bad lungs/bad backs affinity group to hold lines in areas that were relatively peaceful, to interact and dialogue with the delegates we turned back, and to support the labor march that brought tens of thousands through the area at midday. No centralized leader could have coordinated the scene in the midst of the chaos, and none was needed — the

THE NEW YORK CITY CHIAPAS COALITION PRESENTS

SEATTLE IS JUST THE BEGINNING...

SATURDAY DEC. 11 THE FESTIVAL OF RESISTANCE CONTINUES
Noon to Midnight AT CHARAS /EL BOHIO COMMUNITY CENTER
605 East 9th Street between Avenues B & C
WITH POST- WTO / SEATTLE REPORT BACKS FROM
AMY GOODMAN, ABBY SCHER and DOUG HENWOOD AND MORE
LIVE MUSIC BY ANTIBALAS, PERFORMANCES BY FLY and
COATLICUE THEATER, MEXICA DANCERS, DANCE MIX WITH DJ CHROME,
VIDEO SCREENINGS OF "WOMEN FORWARD" AND "ZAPATISTAS," AND MORE!
Suggested Donation: $10.   More Info: 5×1-0302

organic, autonomous organization we had proved far more powerful and effective. No authoritarian figure could have compelled people to hold a blockade line while being tear-gassed – but empowered people free to make their own decisions did choose to do that.

Consensus decision-making

The affinity groups, clusters, spokescouncils, and working groups involved with DAN made decisions by consensus – a process that allows every voice to be heard and that stresses respect for minority opinions. Consensus was part of the nonviolence and jail trainings; we made a small attempt also to offer special training in meeting facilitation. We did not interpret consensus to mean unanimity. The only mandatory agreement was to act within the nonviolent guidelines. Beyond that, the DAN organizers set a tone that valued autonomy and freedom over conformity, and stressed coordination rather than pressure to conform. So, for example, our jail solidarity strategy involved staying in jail where we could use the pressure of our numbers to protect individuals from being singled out for heavier charges or more brutal treatment. But no one was pressured to stay in jail, or made to feel guilty for bailing out before the others. We recognized that each person has their own needs and life situation, and that what was important was to have taken action at whatever level we each could. Had we pressured people to stay in jail, many would have resisted and felt resentful and misused. Because we didn't, because people felt empowered not manipulated, the vast majority decided for themselves to remain in, and many people pushed themselves far beyond the boundaries they had set themselves.

Vision and spirit

The action included art, dance, celebration, song, ritual, and magic. It was more than a protest; it was the uprising of a vision of true abundance, a celebration of life and creativity and connectedness, which remained joyful in the face of brutality and brought alive the creative forces that can truly counter those of injustice and control. Many people brought the strength of their personal spiritual practice to the action. I saw Buddhists turn away angry delegates with loving kindness. We Witches led rituals before the action and in jail, and called on the elements of nature to sustain us. I was given Reiki when sick and we celebrated Hanukkah with no candles, but only the blessings and the story of the struggle for religious freedom. We found the spirit to sing in our cells, to dance a spiral dance in the holding cell, to laugh at the hundred petty humiliations the jail inflicts, to comfort each other and listen to each other in tense moments, to use our time together to continue teaching and organizing and envisioning the flourishing of this movement. It was one of the most profound spiritual experiences of my life.

I'm writing this for two reasons. First, I want to give credit to the DAN organizers who did a brilliant and difficult job, who learned and applied the lessons of the last twenty years of nonviolent direct action, and who created a powerful, successful and life-changing action in the face of enormous odds, an action that has changed the global political landscape and radicalized a new generation. And second, because the true story of how this action was organized provides a powerful model that activists can learn from. Seattle was only a beginning. We have before us the task of building a global movement to overthrow corporate control and create a new economy based on fairness and justice, on a sound ecology and a healthy environment, one that protects human rights and serves freedom. We have many campaigns ahead of us, and we deserve to learn the true lessons of our successes.

Note

Reclaiming can be found at www.reclaiming.org.

Community labor alliances: a new paradigm in the campaign to organize greengrocery workers in New York City

IMMANUEL NESS

On May Day 1999, a procession of hundreds of workers and community members wended its way through the streets of the Lower East Side of New York, chanting "no more green sweatshops" and "no justice no peas." The march was organized by a coalition of community and labor activists and recent Mexican migrants fighting for higher wages and improved conditions for workers in delis and groceries throughout the neighborhood. The events began a two-year organizing drive that unified Mexicans from El Barrio in East Harlem and activists throughout the city in the fight for improved working conditions for new immigrants. The new transnational immigrants are products of NAFTA, of regional and global integration that has forced peasant farmers off their land in Mexico into sweatshops and repressive workplaces in New York City and throughout the US.

Two years later, on May Day 2001, thousands of workers, immigrants-rights, and global-justice activists, including Reclaim the Streets and the Radical Cheerleaders, marched down Fifth Avenue, this time joined by hundreds of workers – a small fraction of the new immigrants demanding higher wages and dignity on the job. In the intervening years, union organizers, workers, and community residents waged a long campaign, including organizing new workers, community pickets, and street battles against employer oppression of workers. May Day 2001 was marked by political street theater in Union Square and on Fifth Avenue that encapsulated the struggle. Superbarrio man, defender of new Mexican workers, fought off employers, bankers,

May Day, 1999, Lower East Side Community Labor Coalition, New York City.

corrupt lawyers, fraudulent unionists, and the police to prevail in the struggle for dignity for new transnational workers. In the end, Superbarrio man, the masked crusader for the Mexican workers, prevailed, despite the fact that the real baton-wielding New York City police descended on the rally, assaulted the street actors, and arrested a random sample of participants.

Despite the police riot, the fact remains that Mexican workers in New York City are in motion, and working conditions for the vast majority have vastly improved as a result of this city-wide campaign that links the anti-globalization movement to the real struggles of everyday workers – victims of neoliberalism, which seems to work only for the ruling class. Through picket lines and direct action, unifying transnational workers with community members, the injustice is exposed every day and workers can gain the confidence to fight back. Though dismissed by many as an old intervention of the losers, the boycott line has emerged as the public symbol of resistance. When globalization and economic restructuring forced the labor movement to respond to the changing nature of the workforce, the police line held the promise for renewed power.

This chapter examines an effort to organize the low-wage immigrants employed in New York City's greengrocery industry, analyzing a new and highly successful organizing paradigm – collaboration among low-wage workers, unions, and community groups (the last an element long excluded from mainstream conceptions of union organizing).

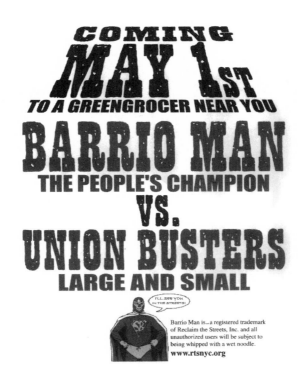

After nearly half a century of dormancy, American unions have taken up the banner of organizing new workers to build a larger and stronger labor movement. Achieving that goal, however, requires organizing efforts appropriate to a workforce that is very different from the workers in the heyday of the US workers' movement some sixty-five years ago. The workforce today is significantly more diverse than it was in the 1930s and 1940s, when white male workers in manufacturing dominated the employment landscape. There is a need, then, for strategies that conform to a changing corporate-led global economy. Like their predecessors, US workers today continue to struggle for fair treatment, decent wages, due process, representation, and greater political and economic power.

The new global economy

Industrial restructuring and the growth of subcontracting to small businesses un-organized by unions have occasioned a rapid expansion in low-wage jobs in the United States over the last two decades. Trade unions experienced in industrial organizing techniques increasingly require strategies for reaching workers in these new sectors. In this new environment, traditional campaigns that depend on older industrial models of organizing are not likely to succeed. Ironically, the growth of the global economy and capital mobility has increased the relevance of city-based community organizing strategies that target smaller, spatially dispersed firms employing relatively few workers.

Although workers are intimately connected to their communities of employment, there is a chasm between their workplaces and their neighborhoods. This disconnection was examined by Ira Katznelson in *City Trenches* (1994), a study of the failure of workers to unite around community concerns in the Washington Heights neighborhood of Manhattan. In the United States, the politics of the workplace is very different from the politics of the community. Though we can view workers as holding a large stake in their communities of work, they have almost no power in advancing their needs on neighborhood issues crucial to the survival of their jobs. What power do workers have when rising real estate values lead to exorbitantly high commercial rents, causing their employers to shut down and move? The relocation of industrial employment to low-wage areas in the United States and abroad has significantly changed the social and economic character of New York and other major cities. Industrial jobs in urban factories are frequently replaced by retail and domestic service jobs where workers work long hours in bad conditions for low wages and almost no benefits.

New immigrants and the degradation of work in New York

New York City, unlike other industrial centers in the United States, never developed a centralized and integrated system of production dominated by a few large monopolistic firms employing hundreds or even thousands of workers at a single site (e.g. auto plants in Detroit, steel mills in Pittsburgh). With the exception of a few department stores, even retail establishments have tended to be smaller in New York: only recently have the mega-stores so common elsewhere begun to appear. Vertically integrated businesses engender worker solidarity, unionization, labor militancy, and strike activity. By contrast, the horizontal structure of the New York City economy provides a favorable environment for deregulation and declining industrial standards, and weakens the ability of unions to organize workers.

Today, new immigrant workers in New York and other major US cities are an integral part of the global economy. There is growing evidence that the super-exploitation of these workers exercises a widespread pernicious effect, depressing wage levels generally, undermining workplace-safety provisions, and hindering union organizing efforts. Although new immigrants are critical to the economy and to the success of organized labor, most unions have tended to ignore them. Recently, however, there has been growing evidence that unions are beginning to take notice (Ness and Unger 2000). With new immigrants increasingly seen as vital to any upsurge in union membership, unions are now actively looking to organize them. At its October 1999 convention, the AFL–CIO called for an end to the employer-sanctions provisions of the 1986 Immigration and Reform Control Act (IRCA), which have penalized immigrant workers seeking to improve their wages and working conditions. In February 2000, the AFL–CIO announced its support for a general amnesty for undocumented immigrants (Bacon 2000).

Though the new rhetoric is indeed welcome, there are few examples of unions actually initiating broad, industry-wide campaigns to organize these new workers. This failure is due in part to the vulnerable status of undocumented workers and the cultural disconnection between union leaders and workers in new labor markets. Successful labor organizing today requires mobilizing and empowering immigrants

What's the REAL COST of DINNER on the LOWER EAST SIDE?

who do not reflect the demographics of current union membership. An example is the ongoing campaign to organize undocumented Mexican workers employed in small delis and greengroceries in New York City, a project that has brought together community activists, union leaders, and workers who had begun to organize themselves.

Stirrings on the Lower East Side

Recent immigrant workers have become part of the fabric of everyday life for most people in New York City. Over the last decade, nearly a million documented and undocumented new immigrants have entered the local labor market, mostly in low-wage industries. New Yorkers are quite familiar with these new immigrants, who perform many essential daily services for them. Immigrants are employed in construction and building rehabilitation; as cooks, dishwashers, and busboys in restaurants; and as taxi drivers, domestic workers, and delivery people (Sassen 2000). A majority are the victims of exploitative employers who force them to accept nineteenth-century working conditions and wages below the federally mandated minimum of $5.15 an hour. In the greengrocery industry, workers who clean, prepare, and package fruit and vegetables are required to work 12-hour days, six days a week, with no overtime pay or medical benefits. They receive wages well below the minimum, typically earning $250 for a 72-hour week (less than $3.50 per hour). When workers try to improve these conditions or join unions, they are fired and replaced with other recent immigrants. There are over two thousand greengroceries in New York City, employing fourteen thousand workers, mostly Mexicans, who work in conditions similar to workers in garment industry sweatshops. Most of the employers in the industry are Korean immigrants, whose establishments vary greatly in size from small shops employing two or three workers to larger markets employing twenty-five or more. Many own more than one shop.

The current effort to organize immigrant workers began in 1998 with the formation of the Lower East Side Community Labor Coalition (CLC), an alliance of progressive organizations dedicated to defending and improving the conditions of immigrant workers employed in the neighborhood. The coalition initially comprised two main groups: the Coalition for a District Alternative (CODA) and the Lower East Side Collective (LESC). CODA, a multiracial community organization, was formed in 1992 by veteran activists who sought to advance their agenda in the electoral realm while continuing to mobilize neighborhood residents around issues of concern (affordable housing, quality education, the environment, police brutality, etc.). LESC had come together in early 1997 as an organizing focus for younger activists looking to become involved locally. Although it did not take an explicitly electoral tack, many of its members (some of whom also joined CODA) worked that summer and fall to elect CODA co-founder Margarita López to the city council. That insurgent campaign, against an opponent backed solidly by mainstream politicians and labor unions, scored a stunning upset that even today is hailed citywide as a triumph of grassroots organizing. After victory in the September primary (tantamount to election in overwhelmingly Democratic New York City), Ernesto Jofre, the only labor leader to have supported the campaign, let CODA know that he would welcome a collaboration between the Lower East Side Community and his union, Local 169 of UNITE (Union of Needletrades, Industrial, and Textile Employees).

Later that fall, CODA and LESC members interested in workers' rights began meeting to discuss how immigrant workers in local businesses could be engaged and community support built for a campaign to improve wages and working

The next time you eat at a local restaurant or shop at a local green grocer, ask the owner or manager how much the employees are earning. Or strike up a conversation with an employee and ask what the working conditions are like.

All workers are legally entitled to a minimum wage of $5.15 an hour, no matter their immigration status. They are morally entitled to much more: a living wage that pays enough for basic necessities.

JOIN US!

To report underpayment or mistreatment of workers, or to join the organizing effort, call the **Lower East Side Community Labor Coalition (212) 473-3936**

LIVING WAGE ZONE

Because we can't stomach exploitation.

conditions. By January 1998 the CLC was formally in existence and actively involved in a campaign to make the Lower East Side a Living Wage Zone. Restaurants were chosen as the initial focus, as gentrification of the area had brought a proliferation of upscale eateries. They presented the stark contrast of well-heeled diners eating pricey food served up by immigrant kitchen help making substandard wages. A pamphlet – "What's the Real Cost of Dinner on the Lower East Side?" – was produced to educate consumers, while ESL classes were set up at CHARAS/El Bohio, a local community center, and promoted among the workers in an effort to have contact with them away from their employers. Inquiries were made to the Hotel Employees and Restaurant Employees Local 100, to honor their jurisdiction, but they were concentrating on cafeterias and larger restaurants uptown.

Meanwhile, engaging workers on the Lower East Side was proving extremely difficult. Impediments included the implanted wariness of immigrants, the fact that few CLCers were fluent in Spanish, the difficulty of contacting workers for the most part confined to kitchens, and the problem of scheduling ESL classes that the workers could attend, given their long and grueling hours. The campaign seemed stalled.

The Mexican American Workers' Association

Then, in April 1998, the character of the campaign changed dramatically. CLC members happened one afternoon upon a small but lively demonstration in front of Leshko's, an old-style Ukrainian coffee shop on Avenue A. There a group called the Asociación Mexicano–Americano de Trabajadores (AMAT; Mexican American Workers' Association)[1] was protesting the unfair firing of two workers and demanding that they be paid the back wages owed them. Jerry Dominguez, the group's founder and lead organizer, said actions of this sort were used wherever AMAT learned of abuses and was asked to help. Based in El Barrio (East Harlem), the group had built up an extensive network of contacts with Mexican immigrant workers throughout the city, particularly in delis and greengroceries, where workers have more contact with the public and so are more accessible to organizers.

A week later, the demonstrators were back, now greatly augmented by CLC activists. Patrons were asked to boycott the restaurant, and most complied; within an hour or two the owner had relented and agreed to a settlement. CLC had found the partner it needed. In short order AMAT agreed to join the coalition, and plans were laid to redirect the campaign toward workers in the neighborhood's twenty or so greengroceries.

The idea was to move beyond the reactive struggles AMAT had been waging in particularly egregious instances of abuse. However successful in righting individual wrongs, these actions did little to change the general pattern of day in, day out abuse endemic to the industry. An employer could be forced to cough up wages that were owed, but the industry-wide practice of paying well below the legal minimum went untouched. It was thought that by harnessing worker militancy to a community's power to boycott, a more permanent and general improvement in wages and working conditions could be achieved. A community presence would protect these very vulnerable workers from summary firings or exposure to the Immigration and Naturalization Service (INS). This strategy, if successful, could serve as a model for communities throughout the city.

One last detail remained to be decided. Some in CLC thought that the community could itself strike and then enforce a bargain with the employers. Some of these were wary of unions generally and were oriented more to the independent workers center paradigm. Others were simply concerned that the community organizing aspect of the campaign might be diminished were a union to be brought in. The prevailing view, however, was that workers needed the power and resources of a union if they were to engage their employers and achieve a legally enforceable collective bargaining agreement. It was time to pitch the campaign to Ernesto Jofre and Local 169.

UNITE Local 169

This was a union CLC activists could feel comfortable with. Long a champion of low-wage immigrant workers, it was led by Jofre, a labor activist from Chile who had been imprisoned for three years by the Pinochet regime before being exiled to the United States, in 1978. It helped also that the union's offices were convenient to the area targeted by CLC. Through the early months of 1998, CLC members had met regularly with Jofre to discuss possible organizing efforts. In the meetings, he had stressed that workers would be welcomed into the union, regardless of their immigration status or the size of their employer (many unions, for bottom-line reasons, spurn the very idea of organizing small shops). He was waiting only for CLC to find an entrée to the workers. Now AMAT was aboard and he was listening.

In conversations AMAT and CLC held with workers employed at greengrocers around the city, many workers expressed a strong desire to join a union that could raise their wages and provide protection from employer abuse and unfair treatment. In the Brighton Beach section of Brooklyn, AMAT had already organized to the extent that workers there seemed ready to move. Although eager to try out the community-labor strategy on their home turf, CLCers made the trek out to Brooklyn to lend a hand. Soon Local 169 joined the effort, and in August Dominguez was hired as a full-time organizer. In time, as the campaign expanded into other areas of the city, additional Mexican activists, including Manuel Guerrero, were hired and trained as labor organizers.

For now the target was a ten-block stretch along Brighton Beach Avenue, where the population was made up largely of recent Russian émigrés who frequented about twenty large and small Korean-owned greengroceries.

From August to November 1998, Local 169 ran a campaign to sign up workers. Hundreds of workers met with union organizers, CLC members, and other supporters to discuss the campaign. Workers had to be convinced that it would improve their conditions and that they would not face the threat of deportation. On any given night, dozens of workers met with organizers on street corners, at local diners, and in the homes of Mexican workers in the neighborhood. More than 75 percent of some five hundred workers, and a majority in every store along the corridor, signed union recognition cards indicating that they wanted their employers to recognize the union and bargain collectively for a contract. With a majority of workers signed up, the union presented the cards to the employers and called for elections, which were held in the winter of 1998. Once employers discovered this support for unionization, they hired union-busting law firms to oppose the organizing effort. Employers fired workers who led the drive and intimidated others to end their support for unionization. In addition, employers immediately raised wages to comply with federal and state wage and hour laws. Wages rose dramatically, from about $2.50 an hour to more than $5.00, and employers promised to comply with government minimums in the future. This employer carrot-and-stick approach effectively ended the campaign in Brighton Beach.

Some workers considered the effort a success once wages increased and working conditions were improved. With National Labor Relations Board (NLRB) protections so ineffective in defending the rights of workers – particularly immigrant workers – to organize into unions of their choice, the campaign was unable to convince workers that they could successfully defend their interests against the employers. Even the strongest supporters of the union could not convince their co-workers to vote the union in. The Brighton Beach drive, though successful in increasing wages – at least temporarily – demonstrated the futility of holding NLRB elections when employers are able to intimidate workers. Though many local residents supported the campaign and CLC members held protests twice weekly, there was no grassroots community organizing or sustained boycott that could pressure the owners to recognize the union. Once the drive ended, wages dropped to their previous level.

Back on the Lower East Side

Even during the Brighton Beach drive, efforts had continued on the Lower East Side. Union organizers continued their work among greengrocery workers, while CLC activists built support among church groups and community-based organizations. In the fall of 1998 a parade of over two hundred people, led by a mariachi band, marched from CHARAS/El Bohio to every greengrocer in the neighborhood. The idea was to put employers on notice and show workers that they had the community's support and that of the several elected officials who marched that day.

On the Lower East Side it was decided to forgo NLRB elections and to demand instead employer recognition and bargaining upon demonstrating that a majority of workers had signed union cards. It was felt that community boycott lines could pressure employers to accede to that demand, while at the same time protecting workers from reprisals.

By late spring, a majority of the 125 workers employed at seventeen greengroceries had signed union recognition cards with Local 169. On May 1, CLC held a rally and march to protest working conditions in the stores and demand union recognition. Over three hundred workers, community residents, and elected officials joined the march, again led by a mariachi band, and again stopping at each of the stores. CLC and the union invited the owners to a meeting at the local Boys Club, but only one owner and a representative of the Soho–Greenwich Village Korean Merchants

Association attended. A second invitation was totally ignored. The letter of invitation had explained that the campaign wished to deal with the stores as a unit and to negotiate a neighborhood-wide agreement (ensuring the stores' economic viability and including union recognition to protect workers' gains), so that no store unilaterally complying with the labor laws would be put at a competitive disadvantage. CLC indicated that if serious negotiations toward a union contract were not begun, boycotts against the stores would be initiated.

The first boycott was begun in late June 1999 at two stores on lower Avenue A – Graceland, a greengrocery, and Gracefully, a gourmet food shop. The same family owned both stores, as well as a third, Adinah's Farms, on Avenue C at Second Street. The hope was that the owners could soon be brought to the table, and that an agreement responsive to the needs of workers, owners, and community could be arrived at. Instead, the owners dug in their heels and resorted to union-busting tactics. They blasted loud music at protesters; printed slanderous leaflets identifying CLC and the union with the Mafia and with the drug dealers who had once occupied the corner; and on one occasion sent four goons in a limousine to threaten protesters physically. On several occasions customers assaulted protesters or tried, unsuccessfully, to provoke violence from the boycott line. In mid August, workers at Adinah's went on strike when they were illegally fired for supporting the union drive. A majority of workers there had signed union cards with Local 169, which after the firings filed an unfair labor practice charge with the NLRB. The campaign was expanded on 25 October, when a consumer boycott line was initiated at 7th Street Fruit and Vegetable, a store on First Avenue owned by a Lebanese immigrant family. By late summer 1999, the campaign had received substantial media coverage (*New York Times*, *New York Newsday*, *El Diario*, *The Villager*, and other papers, as well as several television stations).

An essential element of the campaign's success was the effort to lobby government agencies to enforce wage and hour laws. CLC and Local 169 appealed to the US Department of Labor and to New York State attorney general Elliot Spitzer. By December 1999, the Department of Labor had issued judgments for back wages against Adinah's, and the attorney general's office had launched a citywide investigation of the industry. The coalition organized daily leafleting at the stores, particularly between 4 and 7 p.m., cutting deeply into sales. The pressure from consumers in the neighborhood shielded the workers from reprisals from their employers.

In December 1999, after six months of community boycotts and the perseverance of the workers on strike at Adinah's Farms, the owners finally agreed to recognize Local 169 and agreed to a contract at Adinah's. At Graceland and Gracefully an agreement was signed that guaranteed the owners' neutrality in union elections. Daniel Lucas (1999), a worker at Adinah's Farms, said of the victory:

> We have shown other workers in this industry that this can be done. I know that all store managers treat workers the way they treat us. The strike was the only way to show our power and to put pressure on the company. Now that we have won I feel proud. There are so many workers who are afraid. They can see that we are not afraid and that we won our strike.

By the winter of 2000, two other stores in the neighborhood – Fuji Apple and Hee II Market, both on First Avenue – had quickly agreed to sign contracts. Two months later, a total of six stores in the Lower East Side had signed agreements with the union. These improvements in wages and working conditions have raised wages for workers in other stores throughout the neighborhood, and indeed throughout the city, as owners try to avoid being targeted. The campaign has also received ongoing support from Manhattan members of the New York City Council, led by Margarita López, which held hearings on wages and working conditions in the industry.

Korean Employers Association

Throughout the greengrocery organizing campaign, CLC and Local 169 have encouraged Korean store owners to form an employers' association that would recognize the union and bargain collectively on behalf of employers in the produce industry. This effort was made at the inception of the campaign and continued as it expanded throughout New York City. The idea is that, rather than organizing and bargaining store by store, it is better to solve the problem of illegally low wages and substandard working conditions by reaching an industry-wide master agreement. This, of course, requires having most of the workers sign union cards. By the spring of 2000, efforts in that direction had begun. Mexican workers throughout the city have become aware that they are owed back wages for years of being underpaid, and are flowing into the Local 169 union hall to join the union and seek back pay.

By the summer of 2000, Attorney General Spitzer had concluded that not one store of the dozens he had investigated was in compliance with minimum wage laws.

Even the owners admitted that the laws have been ignored for many years, stating only that most stores are now paying the minimum hourly wage. Because they voluntarily raised wages, the owners claim they do not require oversight from the union. Workers' testimony in many instances contradicts the contention that wages have been raised to legal levels; even where they have, the experience in Brighton Beach suggests that such raises will not be permanent in the absence of a union contract. Unfortunately, although the union and CLC have expressed the hope that employers will recognize the workers' right to organize, the Korean owners remained divided.

The Fifth Avenue campaign

An effort to expand the campaign beyond its promising beginning on the Lower East Side began with the organization of workers at three stores in central Greenwich Village in the immediate vicinity of Local 169 headquarters. The three stores, all on Fifth Avenue, cater heavily to office workers in the area and employ two to three times as many workers as even the largest of the Lower East Side stores. The initial target was Valentino Market, a gourmet deli at 13th Street, where a three-day community boycott led to union recognition and shortly thereafter a collective bargaining agreement. Meanwhile, despite early signs of cooperation, the effort to gain recognition from the Han Family, owners of three large markets – East Natural and Abbigail's on the Fifth Avenue corridor, and Soho Natural further downtown – became a major struggle as the owners hired a union-busting law firm to resist the organizing drive. Though nearly all the workers had signed union recognition cards, the owners refused to accept them as evidence of support for the union. Instead, they immediately raised wages and threatened workers with firing if they supported Local 169. Since the overwhelming majority of the twenty or so workers employed at East Natural supported the union, the local called for an election. However, that request was withdrawn, when better-paid, quasi-managerial employees were transferred to East Natural from the other stores, effectively packing the bargaining unit in favor of management.

Thus, CLC and Local 169 became embroiled in a dispute that has continued to the present day. Though some community members were committed to maintaining the boycott lines, the situation required building alliances with workers' rights groups beyond the Lower East Side. The boycott lines were expanded and staffed primarily by Mexican immigrants, most of them members of AMAT. New-found support came also from students at two area universities – New York University and New School University.

With worker support, the boycott lines were expanded to include all three stores owned by the Han family. Their union-busting tactics included two separate attempts to bring in unions that would sign sweetheart deals or no contract at all. In July 2000, CLC members went to Abbigail's to inform the owners that boycott lines were being set up that day. While there, they witnessed a manager giving workers union cards from a Brooklyn-based non-AFL–CIO union. Then, in October, the Han family formed an association of employers meant to block serious unionization efforts. The employers brought in International Longshoremen's Association Local 1964 from Jersey City, and signed recognition agreements at East Natural and several other stores. Local 1964 has publicly admitted that a primary goal was to stop the consumer boycotts. The contracts signed by the local were negotiated without the support or knowledge of the workers. This effort to create a company-dominated union was challenged by Local 169, CLC, and the workers. At a hearing held in Washington in January 2001, the AFL–CIO ruled that ILA Local 1964 is not the legitimate representative of workers at East Natural Market, and that Local 169 retains the right to organize workers there.

The evidence established that UNITE's strategic campaign to organize greengrocers and the combination of tactics used under the plan, have proven successful in a number of locations. With this proceeding resolved and only one union in the picture, UNITE stands a reasonable chance of consolidating its support and winning representation of East Natural employees (AFL–CIO 2001). Workers at another store nominally represented by Local 1964 – Jin Market, a Tribeca greengrocer that employs about twenty-five workers – have signed cards with Local 169 and wear baseball caps at work indicating their support. In mid January, CLC threw up a boycott line at the store, which continues to be honored by a majority of residents and workers in the neighborhood. On 20 February, the AFL–CIO concluded that UNITE Local 169 has the right to organize workers at Jin Market for the purpose of reaching a collective bargaining agreement, despite the existence of a contract between the ILA local and the owners.

Citywide mobilization and organizing

By March 2001, the greengrocery organizing campaign had gone citywide. Thousands of workers were streaming into Local 169 headquarters to sign union recognition cards and, with the help of union lawyers and a team of law students, to file back wage claims against their employers. What started in June 1999 as a campaign to organize immigrant greengrocery workers on the Lower East Side has captured the attention of Mexican workers throughout the city. The dramatic success of these organizing efforts has emboldened these workers to sign recognition cards calling for unionization, testify for back wages at the attorney general's office, and build on the early success of the campaign.

The Korean owners continue to debate whether they should recognize workers' demands for union recognition and negotiate as a group with worker representatives and Local 169. CLC and the union continue to explore ways of educating owners on workplace standards and the rights of workers, but maintain that the first step is the recognition of the rights of workers to assemble, organize, and join the union of their choice – rights that are guaranteed by the Thirteenth Amendment and statutory law, but flouted regularly by employers.

Conclusion

This campaign has demonstrated the power of community–labor collaborations. With increasing numbers of undocumented immigrant workers now convinced they can defeat their employers and demand their rights in the workplace, prospects for building a broader movement for worker rights become suddenly brighter. At the beginning, the greengrocery campaign was disparaged by many labor leaders as a waste of resources. They believed it could not succeed in mobilizing workers in large numbers, since the stores were small and were dispersed throughout the city. They believed also that immigrant Mexican workers were too vulnerable and intimidated to join the effort.

At the time of writing, the local labor movement is taking credit for the campaign as a far-sighted effort to build union power by mobilizing and organizing dis-empowered workers. The potential of this effort is enormous. Greengrocery workers throughout New York City have already improved their conditions, and the organizing drive is poised to bring thousands of new members into the union movement. The campaign has demonstrated to new immigrant workers from Mexico that the union movement cares about them and that they can advance their interests through organizing. The campaign is also testimony to the capacity of community members to effect change for people who work among them. In the new economy, work is conducted in public, not inside closed factory gates, making it easier for community residents concerned with workers' rights to pressure employers to treat their workers fairly. The consumer boycott has proven an effective mechanism to defend workers against employer abuse. In a seemingly cynical world, the greengrocery organizing effort has shown that most people indeed have a social conscience and, when given the opportunity, will take a stand with those willing to fight for basic human rights and justice in the workplace.

Students, sweatshops, and local power

JOEL LEFKOWITZ

With a well-focused strategy, "Students at a growing number of schools across the country have decided to take action about the fact that their school logos are sewn onto clothing by poorly-paid, often-mistreated workers in sweatshops around the world" (Fishkin 1999). The movement against sweatshops focuses on decisions that students have the power and the right to influence: the licensing of university logos, a business worth nearly $6 million a year to the leading campus (the University of Michigan), and $2.5 billion overall (Miller 1999; Van der Werf 1999). But the movement's significance is far greater than its contribution to changes in that industry; it offers new possibilities for "expanding the scope of conflict" (Schattschneider 1975), part of the new "power repertoires" (Piven and Cloward 2000) of "globalization from below" (Brecher, Costello, and Smith 2000).

In their classic book *Poor People's Movements: Why They Succeed, How They Fail* (1979), Frances Fox Piven and Richard A. Cloward describe how protest movements emerge, the forms they take, and the consequences of their actions. They argue that movements arise when conditions "come to seem both unjust and mutable"; the social location of protesters shape the "strategic opportunities for defiance"; and the impact of defiant disruptions depends not only on the customary contributions withdrawn by the defiant but also on what those affected by the disruption can concede, and on the "political reverberations of those disruptions" in other arenas (Piven and Cloward 1979).

This chapter applies Piven and Cloward's analytic framework to the student movement against sweatshops, drawing attention to the similarities between it and the student anti-apartheid movement of the 1970s and 1980s that focused on pressuring universities to divest their portfolios of stocks in corporations operating in South Africa, and placing the student strategy in the context of global commodity production.

Students educated themselves and each other about the injustice of apartheid and sweatshops. These student movements worked to redefine university investment and production decisions as public matters for democratic decision rather than private enterprise. As students took action, and succeeded, they inspired other students with the idea that they could bring about change. Both movements focused on campuses, where students have leverage, and sought decisions within the control of their university targets. Both movements reverberated beyond the campus, not only increasing the visibility of the issues they raised but sparking decisions in other institutions, parallel to the student demands.

Injustice

To develop and maintain awareness of the injustice of racism in South Africa, students confronted their campuses by building shanties on college grounds that dramatized conditions under apartheid (Soule 1997); in the current campaign students have constructed mock sweatshops.

> Students toiled at sewing machines amid barbed wire ... at the University of Wisconsin–Stevens Point, calling attention to working conditions at sweatshops they say produce shirts, caps and other merchandise bearing the campus's name.... "Nike pays Michael Jordan more money a year than Nike pays 30,000 Indonesian workers," was scrawled on a cloth banner tacked to the fenced-area where 15 protesters operated a mock sweatshop. (Maller 1999)

Similarly, at universities across the country, sweatshop opponents have staged mock fashion shows, in which students model "college apparel" while announcers describe "the harsh labor conditions under which the clothing was made" (McFarland 1999; Silverman 1999). Several tours of colleges in the United States by sweatshop workers provided students with direct testimony about those harsh conditions, and introduced students to the workers who produce college-logo apparel (Palms 1999;

Lin 1999). Some students have also traveled to see workers and working conditions in factories in other countries (Nicklin 1998). In addition, the issues involved have been clearly expressed in talks by the indefatigable Charles Kernaghan, executive director of the National Labor Committee.

These educational efforts have refuted the claim that there is no alternative to market-disciplined low wages, drawing attention to both the tiny share of the retail price that goes to workers' wages and the high salaries of corporate executives (Silverman 1999). Students have emphasized the particular plight of women workers in sweatshops, drawing attention to forced birth control and sexual harassment.

Mutability

By showing that wage demands could be met without much impact on prices or profits (as Kernaghan points out, wages account for less than 1 percent of the retail price of a university-logo T-shirt), students have shown theoretically that sweatshop conditions are mutable. And by taking actions that have yielded concessions, they have shown practically that change can be brought about by student power.

Jo Freeman points to the importance of "protesters whose success is then emulated by others" with information "spread largely through the media and informal communications networks" (1999). Referring to the success of a sit-in at Duke University early in 1999, Richard Applebaum and Peter Dreier describe precisely this phenomenon: "The Duke victory quickly inspired students on other campuses" (1999). In addition, although administrators insisted that "university officials' hands are tied … because the U.S. companies would never agree to full public disclosure" of factory sites (Nicklin 1998), student pressure yielded just such disclosures, reported under headlines like "Apparel companies put factory locations within mouse click" (Kaplan and Krauss 2000).

Student leverage

In a brief mention of student movements, Piven and Cloward note that "a favorite criticism of the student peace movement, often made by erstwhile sympathizers, was that it was foolish of the students to protest the Vietnam War by demonstrating at the universities." They contend that

Stop sweatshops march, December 1999, New York City.

The students were not so foolish, however. The exigencies of mass action are such that they were constrained to act out their defiance within the universities where they were physically located and could thus act collectively, and where they played a role on which an institution depended, so that their defiance mattered. (Piven and Cloward 1979)

As with the divestment strategy of the anti-apartheid movement, students against sweatshops have concentrated their collective defiance on campuses, focusing on the relationship between their universities and the use of sweatshop labor. Students have relied on a classic tactic in the repertoire of protest: the sit-in. The combination of a well-focused strategy and confrontational tactics has brought students success.

Referring to the events of the spring of 1999, Applebaum and Dreier reported that "at every university where students organized a sit-in (Duke, Georgetown, Arizona, Michigan, and Wisconsin) they have wrested agreements to require licensees to disclose the specific location of their factory sites, which is necessary for independent monitoring" (1999).

Concessions

Students against sweatshops have pressed universities to adopt codes of conduct for factories licensed to make products bearing their logos and to develop effective means of monitoring compliance with those codes. They have emphasized a very specific procedural demand, that universities "withdraw from the Fair Labor Association [FLA], an industry group the students say does a poor job of monitoring work conditions ... [and] join the Worker Rights Consortium [WRC]" (Healy 2000). Students have been critical of the FLA, "which we pronounce 'flaw' [because it] was designed by corporations to protect themselves" (Silverman 2000). "Under the [FLA's] bylaws the garment firms control the board's decisionmaking" (Applebaum and Dreier 1999). Unlike the FLA, the WRC "would rely entirely on surprise inspections" (Van der Werf 2000).

At Tulane University, a spring 2000 sit-in ended with an agreement to hold a student referendum to decide on affiliation with the FLA, WRC, both, or neither, in the fall (Cowen 2000). About 60 percent of the students in the low-turnout referendum voted for affiliation with the WRC (Bacon-Blood 2000).

Sometimes responding to sit-ins, dozens of other universities have agreed to student demands by affiliating with the WRC. Piven and Cloward observe that elites often choose concessions "with which they had experience" (1979); principles of conduct and oversight of conformity with those principles are familiar to university decision-makers from the anti-apartheid era.

Reverberations

Although not every student sit-in has yielded concessions, Alberto Melucci argues that since movements "challenge the dominant cultural codes, their mere existence is a reversal of symbolic systems embodied in power relationships" (1985). In effect,

Stop sweatshops demonstration at Gap, December 1995, New York City.

this was the point made by students against sweatshops at the University of Toronto, who "achieved their goal of getting world-wide coverage of their sit-in" (*Toronto Star* 2000). Even where administrators did not yield to student demands, student protests have had an important agenda-setting impact. As California congressman George Miller declared, "The student involvement got this on the agenda" (quoted in Krupa 1999).

Just as the divestment movement spilled off-campus, with cities and states, as well as universities, selling stocks in, or restricting purchases from, companies operating in South Africa (Sandalow 1990), opposition to sweatshops has spread off-campus. For example, citing influences including the anti-sweatshop activity at Duke University, a city council member in Oberlin, Ohio, sought legislation regulating city purchases (Melendez 1998). Similar legislation has reportedly been "adopted by more than two dozen municipalities" (Greenhouse 2000a). Controversy has grown over whether states can adopt purchasing policies sensitive to the conditions under which goods are produced, such as Massachusetts legislation restricting purchases from companies operating in Burma (Amar 2000).

Rather than a boycott, the traditional point of consumption strategy, the movement against sweatshops utilizes new opportunities for leverage in the contemporary economy. College logo merchandise, like many similar commodities, is designed, produced, and marketed in global commodity chains (Gereffi 1994). The corporations controlling these commodity chains scatter production to factories in various countries, owned by companies even more far-flung, in order to cut costs. And they have the workers add college logos to bring higher prices. But adding the college logo also brings licensing agreements that may be, and have been, influenced by the colleges, especially by defiant students. In short, students have expanded the repertoire of protest in the contemporary economy by adding to traditional strategies institutional pressure through the global commodity chain.

Students have focused attention on the injustice of sweatshops in a variety of creative ways and taken action to improve working conditions and wages. They have succeeded, and in doing so have created new methods of influence in the global economy.

Jubilee 2000 Northwest: breaking the chains of global debt

BRONWYN MAULDIN

Standing on a cement barricade, pressed up against the Rent-a-Fence by the crowds behind me, I strained to see past rows of police in riot gear, past limousines and buses, through the rain, to see who was entering the Exhibition Center. Around me a spontaneous chant rose up, "We're here! We're wet! Cancel the debt!"

It was the evening of November 29, 1999 in Seattle, the opening reception of the World Trade Organization. Twenty thousand of us surrounded the Kingdome football stadium and parking lot: Sunday school teachers, steelworkers and anarchists, Indian fisherfolk, Korean farmers, and South African trade unionists. Tomorrow we would stop the WTO in its tracks. That night, we demanded cancellation of the debts of the world's poorest countries.

A group of "debt cancellation dignitaries" had been given special dispensation to pass through police lines and complete the human chain around the Exhibition Center with several hundred feet of gold Mylar. They included Ann Pettifor of Jubilee 2000 UK, Rep. Maxine Waters of California, Bishop Vincent Warner of the Episcopal Diocese of Olympia, Njoki Njehu of 50 Years is Enough, John Sweeney of the AFL–CIO, and Hanna Petros of Ustawi.

Some WTO delegates left their vehicles and scurried into the building without acknowledging the shouting crowds a block away. Others gave indignant interviews to the swarming press about how demonstrations would have no impact on the ministerial meeting. A handful of European NGO representatives came outside, asking

Petros to join them at the reception. "Your message needs to be heard on the inside too," they said. A policeman intervened to keep Petros out of the building.

Why did a small group of debt cancellation activists in the Pacific Northwest of the US add its voice to the demonstrations against the WTO? How did we turn out so many supporters? What did we learn about our community and leadership as a result?

A short history of Jubilee 2000

The global Jubilee movement began in the mid 1990s in Britain as a campaign calling on the International Monetary Fund (IMF), World Bank and wealthy G7 countries to cancel the unsustainable external debts of the world's poorest countries by the end of the year 2000, under a fair, transparent process. After nearly twenty years of structural adjustment lending, many developing countries[1] now spend more in debt service payments to the IMF, World Bank and wealthy countries each year than they spend on health care and primary education for their own citizens. UNICEF estimates

that nineteen thousand children die every day due to the debt – they die of preventable diseases because their governments must cut spending on sanitation and health care to pay off foreign and multilateral debts.

The call for debt cancellation was based on the jubilee year outlined in the book of Leviticus in the Bible. Every fifty years all debts should be forgiven, slaves set free, and land returned to its original owners. In the beginning, the Jubilee campaign was seen as an act of charity. It quickly spread through Europe, North America and eventually to more than sixty countries around the world.

In the countries of the global South there has long been activism against the IMF and World Bank, particularly against structural adjustment policies. It tended to be part of larger, long-term movements, pro-democracy, human rights, the women's movement and labor organizing. While activists in the South had support from individuals and organizations in the North, there was no mass movement within the wealthy lending countries against the IMF and World Bank until the creation of Jubilee.

Jubilee South argues that since the actual amount loaned has been repaid several times over, continued interest payments are illegitimate wealth extraction. Structural adjustment requires borrowing governments to answer to lending agencies rather than to their own citizens, thus undermining democracy. Jubilee South sees the movement to cancel the debt as returning to the people of the South wealth that has been stolen by the North, through centuries of colonialism, slavery, and neoliberalism. Having allies in the North pressure their elected officials put Third World debt on the global agenda; within five years debt cancellation went from radical impossibility to mainstream certainty.

Jubilee Northwest

The Jubilee 2000 Northwest Coalition was born when Seattle activist Hanna Petros returned from the human chain for debt cancellation at the G7 summit in Cologne, Germany, in the summer of 1999. Petros, a native of Ethiopia, is a tireless fighter for justice for Africa. She is the founder and executive director of Ustawi, a Seattle nonprofit organization whose mission is to promote sustainable economic and environmental alternatives for Africa. Ustawi often brings leaders and intellectuals from Africa to educate the American public and policymakers. Returning to the US, she met with representatives from various organizations and churches, including St Mark's Episcopal Cathedral, labor union locals, the Washington Association of Churches, leaders of the African community in Seattle, the Global Economy Working Group of the Church Council of Greater Seattle, and People for Fair Trade, a local group created to organize against the upcoming WTO ministerial. From this group grew the Jubilee 2000 Northwest Coalition.

Petros arranged for Dennis Brutus, South African poet and anti-apartheid leader who is now an activist against the IMF and World Bank and honorary commissioner of the Jubilee 2000 Africa campaign, to speak. His message was that debt cancellation and global trade policies are inextricably intertwined for people of the South. If debt is cancelled without changing global trade policies to put people before profits, then the economic crisis that developing countries face today will only continue. At the same time, there can be no truly fair trade among nations until the debt is canceled and lending policies that keep poor countries economically and politically subservient to wealthy governments and transnational corporations are ended.

It was a timely message. Organizing against the WTO had been going on in Seattle since February 1999. Many members of Jubilee Northwest were actively involved. Michael Ramos of the Washington Association of Churches participated in weekly meetings with key anti-WTO organizers. Sally Soriano of People for Fair Trade, one of the great unsung heroes of the Battle in Seattle, recognized that our work on debt was integral to the challenge to the WTO and helped bring our group into the coalition. Others, such as Rosalinda Aguirre of Washington State Jobs With Justice, acknowledged the links between local labor and Third World debt. I was part of an ad hoc group doing research and public education on the WTO. When Ramos suggested in late August 1999 that Jubilee Northwest organize a human chain to highlight the Third World debt crisis during the WTO meeting, we were ready.

Why and how we took our message to the WTO

Jubilee Northwest organized a human chain for debt cancellation as part of anti-WTO activities for several reasons. First, we wanted to call the world's attention to the ordinary people of the global South, who have been hurt the most by corporate globalization and the free-trade model promoted by the WTO. Second, we wanted to activate the existing base of grassroots support for debt cancellation. We had a long list of supporters, whom we contacted by mail, phone and email, to encourage participation in the human chain. We also spread the word through national and international Jubilee networks. Third, we saw this as a way to bring debt cancellation supporters into the larger movement for global economic justice. Therefore we encouraged Jubilee supporters to join activities against the WTO, including the events of November 30. We did this by sending out information about those events to our lists, and sharing our lists with other organizations, where appropriate. We spoke to churches, labor union locals, and community groups about the debt crisis and global trade policies, and what their members could do about them.

Our fourth goal was to expand support for debt cancellation by reaching out to people who were becoming part of the anti-corporate globalization movement. As they learned how the WTO shapes global trade policies, they heard about the role of the IMF and World Bank in creating and maintaining the chains of debt. We wanted to integrate debt cancellation and global trade policies, by giving them an opportunity to take action against the debt creators. We participated in the monthly anti-WTO planning meetings and subcommittee meetings. We went to meetings of other groups organizing against the WTO. We sent our press releases not only to the media, but directly to organizations and email lists.

Fifth, we wanted to ratchet up the pressure for debt cancellation on the major global economic decision-makers who were in Seattle that week. We wanted a lot of people standing in the streets demanding debt cancellation.

Many organizations and individuals provided immeasurable support for our human chain. The AFL–CIO made civil rights and labor organizer Rev. William Orange available to coordinate the mechanics of our human chain and lead our peacekeeper training. The Independent Media Center made their facilities available for Jubilee Northwest and Jubilee South representatives to get our messages out. Two thousand steelworkers joined our march because they understood that as the debt crisis undermines workers' rights and wages in other countries, it ultimately puts downward pressure on their own rights and wages in wealthy countries.

In the month preceding the WTO action, I received calls and emails from all sorts of people around the world: a Denver Sunday school teacher saying he was bringing his class, Malawians looking for funds to come join the chain, a *Time* magazine writer asking how we were organizing the chain, and a group of San Francisco wiccans wanting to hold a ceremony as part of the chain. People from Pakistan, Australia, and Boston said they could not come, but wished us well.

What did we learn about our community and the role of the global South?

The rules of the global economy are often unfair and unequal. They are designed to benefit wealthy people within a country, and wealthy countries vis-à-vis poorer ones.

For debt cancellation to have a positive impact on people in the global South, Jubilee cannot work in isolation. We will not succeed without our allies in the larger global economic justice movement. Twenty thousand people turned out on November 29 because they understood that putting people before profits requires both canceling debt and changing global trade rules at the same time. Since then, debt relief activists have joined ACT UP and a broad coalition of groups to call for debt cancellation and health care for all. In June 2001 Jubilee USA, AIDS activists, and labor leaders marched on New York demanding "STOP GLOBAL AIDS NOW!"

As our steering committee internalized these lessons, we saw our community as part of a global movement striving to change fundamentally the economic and power relations between nations. Do we only look to other people in wealthy countries for leadership? No, we must put the people we claim to want to help at the center of our work. After all, they are the ones who live with the effects of debt and disastrous trade policies on a daily basis. Our human chain made debt cancellation part of the fair trade lexicon and of the ongoing movement for global economic justice. When we all caught our breath after an amazing week of citizen action, we knew we had not reached an endpoint, but a beginning.

Notes

1. This essay uses terms like "developing world," "Third World," and "global South" interchangeably, as none of them is completely accurate.

An ACT UP founder "acts up" for Africa's access to AIDS

ERIC SAWYER

One AIDS activist's story

I have been living with HIV for a very long time. Twenty years have passed since February 1981 when I developed shingles, my first HIV-related symptom.

I am alive today because I have had access to the latest treatments as soon as they become available. I am alive today because I fought governmental and societal inaction to force the US government and US-based drug companies to respond to the HIV epidemic in a responsible way. I am alive today because I put my life and body on the front lines: on the streets protesting as an activist, in the laboratories of drug companies as a guinea pig testing new drugs and treatments, and into the public arena as an openly gay man living with AIDS.

I am an international treatment activist today because I am angry that my friends in the developing world are dying due to lack of access to the treatments and health care I rely on to thrive with a fatal disease. I am an international treatment activist because I was born with a sense of humanity that tells me that every life matters and deserves to be fought for.

I am proud to be a founding member of ACT UP/New York. I am also a co-founder of Housing Works, a non-governmental organization that provides housing, medical services, and drug treatment for homeless people with HIV. In ACT UP/NY I helped to establish three committees: on housing and treatment access programs for homeless people with AIDS, on HIV and tuberculosis co-infection, and on global AIDS issues. The Global AIDS Issues Committee dealt with AIDS in developing countries – including treatment access – and helped fight for the release of the HIV-positive Haitian refugees detained at Guantánamo Bay, Cuba.

One of the most important lessons that we learned in ACT UP is that people with HIV and AIDS must take a leadership role in the fight against AIDS. Few people but us care enough to fight to change public opinion about AIDS. Few but us care enough to fight for a cure to AIDS. And few but us are willing go to jail to fight for access to treatments for all people living with AIDS.

The beginning: ACT UP/New York

ACT UP began in March 1987 following a speech given by Larry Kramer at the Lesbian and Gay Community Services Center in New York City. Larry called many of his friends that he knew were concerned and trying to do something about AIDS, and asked us to be in the audience to help him organize "civil rights style" demonstrations to draw attention to the lack of government activity on AIDS.

During the late 1980s and early 1990s ACT UP successfully drew the world's attention to AIDS. We developed our tactics by studying the Vietnam anti-war effort, the civil rights movements in the US and South Africa, and the gay rights movement.

ACT UP lessons

We knew from the anti-war and civil rights movements that demonstrations including peaceful civil disobedience actions that involve risking arrest receive far more media attention than simple street marches or political rallies. Television

ACT UP because AIDS is **genocide!** ACT UP because people with AIDS must have a say in choosing treatments to be tested, and in designing trials! ACT UP because **over 300,000 people worldwide have died of AIDS!** ACT UP because the INS deports people with AIDS and HIV infection! **ACT UP because AZT isn't free!** ACT UP because there is no national health care! **ACT UP because women are the fastest growing group affected by AIDS!** ACT UP because fags & dykes are under attack! **ACT UP because nearly 50% of the people living with AIDS are people of color!** ACT UP because there is no legal needle exchange! ACT UP because we die & they do nothing! ACT UP because tens of thous...

...ling group...because fags & dykes a... because nearly 50% of t... ople living with AIDS are people of color! ACT UP because there is no legal needle exchange! ACT UP because we die & they do nothing! ACT UP because tens of thousands of homeless people have AIDS! ACT UP because HIV discrimination must end! ACT UP because there is 1 AIDS death every 11 minutes! ACT UP because out of 15 drugs targeted by health officials in 1985 as "high priority", 7 still have not been tested! ACT UP because people of color are excluded from drug trials! ACT UP because the FDA has approved only 3 drugs for use against AIDS! ACT UP because women are routinely excluded from drug trials!

Years before protease inhibitors, Eric Sawyer (*second to left*) at the 1992 International Conference on AIDS, Amsterdam.

producers seem to think that pictures of police arresting demonstrators make interesting television news. Thus, ACT UP tried always to include some action in our demonstrations that would get us arrested.

We realized early in our ACT UP experience the importance of street theater, witty chants, slick graphics, and sound bites. Often the coverage we received was limited to fifteen seconds on the television news. Reporters seldom covered our issues accurately. We learned that witty chants and slick graphics were a better way to make sure that the media reported the facts correctly.

An example of this occurred when we were pushing for the development of housing for homeless people living with AIDS. We collected old furniture, loaded it into my pickup truck, and placed the furniture in the middle of the street in front of the New York City housing commissioner's office. We hung a big banner between two streetlights that read "Squatters Camp for Homeless People with AIDS." Then we sat on the furniture while rush-hour traffic tried to drive around us, until we were arrested. The police had to cart our old furniture away in garbage trucks and tow my old pickup truck to the police vehicle pound; the demonstration kept city employees busy for more than an hour. This gave reporters time to ask sufficient questions to understand the dangers of homelessness for people with AIDS and to communicate these dangers to the public. The next month the housing commissioner announced that the city was budgeting $25 million dollars for new AIDS housing programs. It seems the demonstration was a success.

ACT UP also quickly learned that doing our homework was crucial to the success of an action. We taught ourselves to become experts, both to enable us to answer reporters' questions and to debate successfully with government and scientific officials. We learned that it helped to advance our cause when we were able to suggest workable solutions to the problems we were protesting about. Some problems were not the result of ill will, but rather occurred because no one had yet found workable solutions. We found that when we suggested solutions, they were often adopted. This was especially true if an elected official or prominent public figure was sufficiently embarrassed in the media. Thus, ACT UP always prepares fact sheets that include a list of demands that summarize workable solutions. We also learned to have lawyers present at all demonstrations to guard against police abuse and to help those arrested get out of jail sooner. Videotaping of demonstrations also helped prevent police abuse and win court cases.

It helped that many ACT UP members were employed by corporate America, because this taught us the importance of using modern technology to carry out our activism. We quickly learned that telephone, fax, and email zaps are an effective means of advocacy. By overwhelming the communications systems of government officials and others we were trying to influence, we often got what we wanted.

All these tactics – part civil disobedience, part street theater – succeeded in getting ACT UP's message into the public eye and played an important role in the group's many accomplishments, including forcing the government to shorten the drug testing and approval process; securing a seat at the table for people living with HIV/AIDS; increasing funding for AIDS research, housing, care, and education; and creating legislation to protect the rights of people with HIV.

The global AIDS story

Some of ACT UP's most powerful actions – our political funerals – were copied from the South African anti-apartheid movement. During the 1990s, we carried the ashes of people who had died of AIDS, or the actual bodies of the dead, to the feet of those who contributed to their deaths through inaction or inappropriate action.

The tactics of the global justice movement influenced ACT UP, and as the 1990s progressed ACT UP in turn began to devote itself more strongly to global issues surrounding AIDS. When treatments began to emerge that helped rich people with HIV live longer and healthier lives, activism became more important than ever, because the majority of people with AIDS in the developing world had almost no access to these treatments.

It is estimated that 25–40 percent of people aged between 15 and 45 in some areas of Africa are infected with HIV. Life expectancy in some African nations has been reduced 25–33 percent, from 60 years of age or more to 40 years or less. An estimated 4 million people in Africa will die of AIDS this year, and there are already millions of AIDS orphans.

An estimated 90 percent of people with HIV live in developing countries and have no access to any proven treatments for HIV. Patients with drug-resistant tuberculosis and other deadly diseases also need medications they cannot possibly obtain due to their price. Patents on pharmaceuticals now last twenty years from the date of the patent application, and patented drugs are often priced ten times higher than is necessary to make a profit.

Until a few years ago, the General Agreement on Tariffs and Trade (GATT) did not cover pharmaceutical patents, and few cared if developing countries quietly made copies of needed patented drugs; large pharmaceutical corporations had no viable market in those countries anyway. But under today's GATT, which set up the World Trade Organization (WTO), drug companies have become extraordinarily aggressive in enforcing patent rights around the world, no matter the cost to public health and welfare.

Global trade law allows exceptions to patent protection in some cases. The WTO's Trade-related Aspects of Intellectual Property (TRIPs) agreement includes provisions for "compulsory licensing" and "parallel importing." Governments can respond to a medical emergency by manufacturing generic equivalents of patented drugs locally or

GREED
═
DEATH

by importing such drugs at the lowest available world price. The United States commonly uses the compulsory licensing provision itself — for cable television, music, and computer technology, for example — but has furiously opposed efforts by Thailand, South Africa, and other developing countries to use the same provisions for lifesaving medications.

The US government (including the US Trade Representative, the State Department, the executive branch and Congress) has in recent years supported the multinational pharmaceutical companies seeking to protect their patent rights, without balancing concern for human lives. US government policy is more restrictive that the WTO agreement, and the US government has used its clout to stop other countries providing critical drugs to their own citizens by threatening economic sanctions.

Drug companies say they need to protect their profits in order to recoup the money they spent to develop existing drugs and to reinvest in the research and development (R&D) of new drugs. But this is a major exaggeration. Many drugs — including the AIDS drugs AZT, ddI, ddC, d4T, 3TC, and ritonavir (Norvir), and cancer drugs like paclitaxel (Taxol) — were largely developed by the National Institutes of Health (NIH) or by university researchers with funding from NIH grants. US taxpayers paid for much of the research on these drugs, and then the government and universities licensed them to drug companies (sometimes in the final phase of clinical trials) for very small royalty payments, sometime as little as 1.5 percent of sales. The R&D costs for many drugs that have generated billions of dollars in sales were mostly paid with tax dollars, with the drug companies' investment limited to the final stages of the clinical trial process. Such costs have long since been recouped.

In addition, drug companies invest surprising little in R&D. For example, Abbott's 1998 annual report listed R&D costs as 9.8 percent of sales. The Pharmaceutical Research and Manufacturers of America (PhRMA), an industry trade association, states in its press releases that industry R&D costs average 20 percent of sales; in contrast, marketing costs average 30 percent of sales. In addition, drug companies' return to investors is the highest of any industry, averaging 25 percent, but in some cases topping 33 percent. Pharmaceutical companies are among the richest corporations on the planet.

Generic versions of antiretroviral drugs such as AZT, ddI, and ritonavir are being produced and in some cases are already being sold for less than 10 percent of the cost of the patented equivalent. Brazil produces generic versions of eight antiretroviral drugs, which it provides free to its citizens with HIV/AIDS. Many of the expensive brand-name AIDS drugs are cheap and easy to make. Yet they are being sold almost exclusively by multinational drug companies for excessively high prices that put them out of reach of over 90 percent of the people worldwide who need them to save their lives.

The pharmaceutical industry cares little for markets in the developing world – which account for only a tiny percentage of its profits – but cares very much that precedents are not set and that knowledge is not obtained that might threaten high drug prices in the US and other major global markets.

Planting the seeds for a global campaign

Because health care is a human right, and because of the ever-widening gap in access to health care that exists in the world, members of ACT UP/New York and several other groups came together to form the Health Global Access Project (HealthGAP) Coalition. We started HealthGAP because most of the world's people are denied access to life-saving medications due to abuse of drug patent protections, excessively high drug prices, and unfair government policies.

The coalition focused the media's attention on US trade policies and related government threats to withhold foreign development aid and restrict the ability of countries to trade with the US due to the patent infringement concerns of US-based drug companies. We exposed the lawsuits of drug companies attempting to block access to affordable generic drugs. The public outrage we created in the US and elsewhere led to widespread demands that the US government stop putting drug company profits before human lives.

The basic idea for a campaign for access to affordable medicines began during the planning process for the XI International Conference on AIDS held in Vancouver in July 1996.

I was the North American representative to the conference's Community Liaison Committee. The Community Liaison Committee met during the eighteen months prior to the conference to advise organizers on everything from theme, to program content, to speakers, to related cultural activities.

The time frame for the planning process of the Vancouver conference corresponded to the eighteen months of clinical trials testing triple-combination antiretroviral therapy using protease inhibitor drugs. It was a period of false hope, marked by speculation by the media and ill-informed zealots that the new therapies might be a "cure" for AIDS. Those of us who dealt with AIDS on a daily basis knew that the new drugs were not a cure, that they worked for only about half the people taking them, and that only a small minority of the world's people with HIV could afford them.

The wake-up call

I was asked to give a speech at the opening ceremony of the conference to share my outrage over the lack of global access to HIV treatments and to issue a wake-up call to tell the world that the new drugs did not represent an end to the AIDS crisis. I stated that nothing had changed for the majority of the world's poor, who were continuing to die at genocidal rates around the globe. I challenged the drug companies to consider tiered pricing, and said that if they did not do so, activists would fight to have their patents revoked – just as patents on antibiotics had been invalidated to make drugs available during World War II. My speech ended with an ACT UP demonstration and a chant of "Greed Kills, Access for All!"

After the speech, I was inundated with requests for media interviews and speaking engagements. The theme for the next international AIDS conference, held in Geneva in 1998, was "Bridging the GAP," but many activists found ourselves asking "what bridge?" However, the theme did serve a purpose, for shortly after the Geneva conference activists launched HealthGAP in response to frustration over the lack of access to treatments for poor people in the developing world.

HealthGAP was started by Alan Berkman, MD, a New York physician who treats low-income persons with AIDS, along with members of ACT UP/New York, ACT UP/Philadelphia, ACT UP/Paris, Search for a Cure, Ralph Nader's Consumer Project on Technology, *AIDS Treatment News*, the AIDS Treatment Data Network, and many

ACT UP/NY occupied Senator Joseph Bruno's office
to demand access to AIDS drugs, spring 1998.

others. HealthGAP also works with Médecins Sans Frontières/Doctors Without Borders (MSF), Health Action International, South Africa's Treatment Access Campaign (TAC), Partners In Health, and groups of people with AIDS from around the world.

Alliances formed

Shortly after starting HealthGAP, we met with Jamie Love of the Consumer Project on Technology. Love educated us about global trade policies, the WTO, GATT, and such technical issues as compulsory licensing and parallel importing of drugs. I knew we had found the missing link in terms of information to challenge drug company pricing and patents. Love also introduced us to a variety of other consumer, fair trade, environmental, and international public health organizations.

At around the same time, a legislative battle was brewing over two opposing US trade bills: the African Growth and Opportunities Act (AGOA) and the Hope for Africa Act. Activists including members of ACT UP/New York, ACT UP/Philadelphia, Citizens' Action Campaign, Essential Action, and a number of trade union organizations, along with friendly congressional officials such as Jesse Jackson Jr., Barbara Lee, and Maxine Waters, organized demonstrations opposing AGOA and suggested language for the competing Hope for Africa bill.

During the planning of a demonstration in opposition to AGOA, we obtained a copy of what we called the "smoking gun memo." The February 5, 1999 memo, from a State Department staff member, intended to convince a New Jersey representative that the Clinton/Gore administration was doing everything in its power to support the interests of several large international pharmaceutical companies in the representative's state in their battle to prevent the South African government producing its own generic versions of AIDS and cancer medications. The memo listed courses of action, including 301 Trade Watch List inclusions and threats to withhold trading rights and foreign aid from South Africa if the country did not stop pursuing the production of inexpensive drugs.

ACT UP attacks Gore's greed

Love and I were outraged at this information and at the fact that Vice-President Al Gore had taken an active role in issuing some of the threats at various meetings. I wanted to chain myself to the fence in front the vice-president's residence in protest, as I knew such an action would garner considerable attention in view of his impending presidential candidacy. But my suggestion that we include a stop at Gore's residence as part of our upcoming AGOA protest march in Washington, DC, met with dissent. ACT UP/Philadelphia was especially opposed, fearing that such an action would confuse the media and draw attention away from what they saw as the more important fight over the AGOA bill. I agreed to delay my protest against Gore until the next opportunity, but we began to spread the word about the VP's actions.

The tide started to turn on the global drug access issue in February 1999, when several members of ACT UP/New York rented a van and headed down to Tennessee to disrupt Al Gore's presidential campaign kick-off. We went armed with information about the vice-president's role in denying AIDS drugs to poor South Africans and signs reading "Gore's Greed Kills – AIDS Drugs for Africa." Leaving ACT UP/NY's media machine behind to spin the story, a handful of activists hit the road, driving all night to change history.

The action had a major impact, due as much to the lack of one story, as to the presence of another. The media were already bored by a lackluster campaign by two candidates perceived to be equally dull. They were ripe for something interesting to write about, and we gave them the hook they were looking for. By disrupting several of Gore's early campaign appearances with protests about a single issue, we succeeded in turning coverage about the campaign into coverage of our cause.

Confronting power with truth: face to face with Al

One of my favorite actions during the campaign was the one which put me face to face with the vice-president. A group of activists had gotten up very early one Sunday morning in March to drive from New York to New Hampshire to a church barbecue fundraiser for Gore. We arrived at the church during a gentle rain that moved the event indoors to the church basement. We appeared in "party loyalist drag" – posing as heterosexual couples even though all of us were queer – to pay Al a visit of consequence. I hoped to get a face-to-face meeting with Gore, having met with his wife Tipper the preceding week following a disruption in New York City. The plan was to have me and my "wife" refrain from disrupting the event, but instead to stick around to meet and greet the VP after the disruptions by others, and to attempt to get his response to our questions on camera.

Our cover was blown due to the luck of our placement within the crowd. My "wife" had registered us both while I parked my car, filling out our name tags with assumed names. The ten activists spread out throughout the room to blend in, and my "wife" and I took up a post near the speaker's platform. As luck would have it, a photo-op "plant" family with two kids in strollers was positioned right next to me. Soon the dad handed me his camera and asked if I could snap a few shots of him and his family with the VP. When Gore approached, we ended up first in the handshake line. When Al reached for my hand and said, "I'm Al Gore and I want to be your next president," I replied, "Nice to meet you Mr Vice-President, I'm Eric."

"Eric," asked Al, "Eric who?" A cellphone in my shirt pocket blocked my view of the assumed last name my "wife" had put on my name tag, so I said "Eric... er, umh... Sawyer... Mr Vice President." At this point Al pushed my phone out of the way and read "Eric Sandman" on my name tag. He said "Eric Sawyer or Sandman? Sawyer, right... Oh yes." Since I had spent twenty minutes with his wife three days before, discussing our concerns, the name recognition hit him. Gore continued, "And you're not from New Hampshire, are you Eric Sawyer?" To which I replied, "Well, no sir, I'm from New York." Al then said, "Well you certainly have traveled a long way to see me today, haven't you Eric Sawyer?" I replied "Yes sir, Mr Vice-President, and contrary to what you may think, I really do want you to be the next president of the United States." He ended with, "I don't doubt that you do."

Gore then proceeded to the kiddie photo-op. The secret service detail attempted to push me out of the way, to the objections of the dad, who called out, "No, wait, let him back over here, he has my camera and he's going to take pictures of the kids with Al and me." Through a forced grin, Gore said, "OK, let Eric back over here to take the pictures!"

When the vice-president began speaking, one by one we disrupted his speech and were ejected by the secret service agents. When I jumped up onto a picnic table and yelled "Al, what are you going to do about the millions of Africans dying from lack of access to AIDS drugs?", the secret service escorts that had been keeping me company near the stage grabbed handfuls of the flesh of my love handles and pulled me off the table to the floor, back onto my feet, and out the door.

The next week, we received an invitation to meet with folks at the White House about our concerns.

Victories achieved

Since the spring of 1999, the movement for more a balanced government policy on pharmaceutical patents and trade rules has seen fantastic progress. Few issues have emerged from obscurity to widespread public awareness so quickly. The issue of drug pricing and access has become a world-class moral cause, and large numbers of people have come to agree that sentencing poor people to death to protect drug patents is not acceptable.

Activists continued to hound Gore on the campaign trail, but we backed off after he convinced the administration to stop pressuring South Africa and Thailand on the issue of generic drugs, and to increase requests for global spending on AIDS for the first time in ten years. In November 1999, activists staged a sit-in at the US Trade Representative's office in Washington, DC, to bring further attention to the drug access issue (see Introduction to this volume). On December 1, World AIDS Day, as the streets of Seattle erupted in protests outside the WTO meeting, Clinton gave a speech to global trade delegates promising that "the US will henceforth implement its healthcare and trade policies in a manner that ensures people in the poorest countries won't go without medicine they so desperately need." Clinton followed up with an executive order in May 2000 that turned his promise into policy. In February 2001, newly inaugurated President George W. Bush agreed to uphold Clinton's order.

In March 2001, hearings began in a lawsuit brought by thirty-nine international pharmaceutical companies against the government of South Africa over a law that would allow the country to manufacture or import generic versions of life-saving drugs. The trial – and associated protests around the world – focused global attention on the issue of drug access, and generated reams of mostly unfavorable press coverage for the drug companies. Faced with this shift in public opinion, several companies agreed to lower their prices and to show some flexibility in the area of patents, even as activists prepared to hammer home further the need for affordable drug access at the Summit of the Americas/Free Trade Association of the Americas meeting in Quebec City in April.

AIDS activists began working with student groups on campaigns to ensure that drugs developed through government-funded university-based research remain in the public domain. A petition drive at Yale University concerning the drug d4T (Zerit) led Bristol–Meyers Squibb, which holds a license for the drug, to agree to allow other companies to produce inexpensive generic versions for sale to South Africa.

A time for action

Today, activists continue to organize against global financial institutions such as the IMF and the World Bank, which mandate structural adjustment policies that deny countries the right to spend their money on health care and education. We continue to work with international groups such as MSF and TAC to pressure drug companies to reduce their prices on life-saving medicines for AIDS-related opportunistic infections as well as antiretroviral drugs. Although some success has been made in improving access to drugs for people with AIDS in South Africa, activists are now calling on drug companies to increase access to medications for all life-threatening diseases, not just AIDS, and for all poor people, not just those in Africa.

History will recall how we responded in the face of the AIDS pandemic, and will judge us if we fail to act. It is time to stand up as human beings concerned about our brothers and sisters in the developing world to demand that the human right to health care be provided to everyone in the world, no matter how much money they have, what country they live in, what religion they practice, what color they are, who they love, what drugs they take, or how they make the money they need to feed themselves and their children. Just as a virus recognizes no national borders, our solidarity must encompass all who are affected by the AIDS epidemic. It is time to demand that pharmaceutical companies drop the prices they charge poor people for drugs to a level that is affordable in the countries where most poor people live. It is time to demand that our governments, churches, foundations, and rich people pay for the purchase of essential medicines and the provision of health care to poor people everywhere. We must never forget that access to health care is a human right. And we must not rest until every man, woman, and child has access to safe shelter, sufficient food, clean water, and good health care.

PART TWO

Sex, social justice, and the new queer community organizing

It is difficult to overestimate the impact AIDS has had on a new generation of activists. Throughout the 1990s AIDS activists had to acknowledge that AIDS was spread as much by racism, sexism, and the class system as by homophobia. Lesbians took a leadership role in AIDS activism that proved transformative. As the AIDS crisis progressed unchecked, the so-called "sex wars" raged and a new wave of anti-censorship feminists sought a distinct path from 1970s feminism. From their work with ACT UP, lesbian activists went on to lead groups such as the Lesbian Avengers and Fed Up Queers. Judith Butler (1990) envisioned a world in which gender could be viewed as performative rather than biological. Social constructionism combined with feminist theory to acknowledge the distinct nature of heterosexism and sexism, sexuality and gender. AIDS prevention activism, with its emphasis on practices rather than identities, contributed to a dynamic new world-view. This philosophy, queer theory, sought to problematize questions of sexuality and gender. Queer theory envisioned a world positioned against heteronormativity ("regimes of normal") not against heterosexuality. The rubric of "queer" offered a political space, for kinky heterosexuals, sex workers, bisexuals, and gender deviants, as well as lesbians and gay men. The result was a queer politics that emphasized broad universalistic discourses as opposed to interest group representation (See Warner 1993; Sedgwick 1990).

As the decade progressed, a chasm emerged within gay, lesbian, bisexual, and transgender (GLBT) politics. On one side were queers who sought to link the GLBT movement with broader social justice issues; on the other were single-issue gay assimilationist organizations aspiring for a place at the national policy table. Queers, who envisioned their movement as a critique of social, sexual, and economic regimes of the normal, rejected the commercialization of the gay movement, while mainstream gay groups sought to portray the gay community as "just like everyone else." The subjects of public sex and reproductive rights became flashpoints for a debate about public and private spaces and cultures. While mainstream gay and lesbian groups argued that the only thing wrong with the society was that it discriminates against gays, queer activists linked their work with larger social justice movements. The result was a significant schism between gay assimilationists and queer grassroots activists. Early in 2000, the Millennium March on Washington would come to symbolize a queer/gay assimilationist split nationwide. The essays in this section consider these developments.

In 1997 Eric Rofes wrote: "Among the most effective ways of oppressing a people is the colonization of their bodies, the stigmatizing of their desires, and the repression of their erotic energies." The essays in part 2 place the battle for sexual self-determination within larger struggles against economic and cultural colonialism. Liz Highleyman begins the section by situating AIDS/queer/sexual civil liberties activism within a larger battle for social justice. Leslie Feinberg and Bob Kohler place these struggles within the broad context of gay liberation's historic struggles against police brutality, while considering the evolution of queer activism toward a broader universalizing discourse. Sarah Schulman discusses the birth of the Lesbian Avengers, while Tracy Morgan builds on Schulman's themes to consider mobilizations for women's reproductive rights and sexual freedom. Eric Rofes and Benjamin Shepard consider strategies to battle persistent institutionalized homophobia and genderphobia.

For many, queer community is formed on the basis of freedom of the body. Queer and AIDS political activism ranges around battles from sexual freedom, to AIDS education and advocacy, abortion rights, anti-racism, as well as a critique of homophobia. Freedom of the body means freedom to choose in the broadest sense. Lauren Berlant and Michael Warner (1999) note: "By making sex seem merely frivolous, merely personal, heteronormative conventions of intimacy block the formation of non-normative public sexual communities.... Making a queer world has required the development of the kinds of intimacy that bear no resemblance to domestic space, to kinship, to the couple form, to property, to the nation." Essays by Susan

Wright (a policy director for a national advocacy and lobbying organization promoting tolerance of sexual minorities), Liddell Jackson (the founder of one of New York's longest-running sex parties), and Jim Eigo (an AIDS prevention activist), assess the history, function, and unfinished business of a building a more sustainable, egalitarian public sexual sphere. Overall, the essays within part 2 fit together to address the successes and dilemmas of building community through sex and gender liberation. They are all part of a project aimed at creating a queer world beyond the inequalities of heternormativity.

Radical queers or queer radicals? Queer activism and the global justice movement

LIZ HIGHLEYMAN

The year 2000 was hailed as "The Year of the Protest." From N30 to A16 to S26, the turn of the millennium saw a series of multi-issue protests that brought together a range of progressive activists into what some are calling the "convergence" movement. Bursting onto the public radar with the Battle of Seattle in November 1999, the emerging movement set its sights on the World Trade Organization and its sister financial institutions that determine the ground rules for global trade. A broad range of progressive constituencies came together, including the much heralded "Teamsters and Turtles" labor/environmentalist alliance, death penalty opponents, pro-democracy activists, anti-capitalists, and black bloc anarchists, leading Green presidential candidate Ralph Nader to claim, "There's never been an event in American history that has brought together so many disparate groups."

Yet an explicitly queer presence was surprisingly absent at the year's mass actions. While many gay, lesbian, bisexual, and transgender (hereafter referred to as "GLBT") people were involved, it was generally as individuals who happened to be queer, rather than as a visible, organized presence waving the rainbow flag. This lack of visibility warrants examination, since queer activists gave birth just a decade ago to a major resurgence of urban activism.

A brief history of radical queer activism

The AIDS Coalition to Unleash Power (ACT UP) came together in New York City in March 1987 to address the mounting death toll within the gay community; chapters soon sprang up in cities across the United States and Europe. The group resurrected a kind of radical activism that had not been widely seen since the 1970s, imbuing it with their own brand of queer style and sensibility. "United in anger and committed to direct action to end the AIDS crisis," ACT UP engaged in office occupations, road blockades, and demonstrations at international AIDS conferences and the head-quarters of government bureaucracies.

In its early years ACT UP served a dual purpose as an AIDS activist and a queer liberation group. But tension between these roles was always present, and soon led to the formation of Queer Nation (QN), a new group specifically grounded in queer identity politics. The unabashedly pro-queer group organized kiss-ins, anti-bashing actions, and protests against homophobic officials and institutions. As had happened before in male-dominated progressive groups, some women within ACT UP and QN wanted to focus on their own issues, and in 1992 the struggles against sexism and homophobia came together under the banner of the Lesbian Avengers (see Schulman interview, below).

From its early days there was debate within ACT UP about whether its proper focus was solely HIV/AIDS or the social and economic context surrounding the epidemic. ACT UP brought together both long-term queer activists who saw AIDS activism as a way to link queer liberation with a broader social justice agenda, and assimilated gay white men who had been shaken out of their complacency by the deadly virus and were now literally fighting for their lives. As the 1990s progressed, several ACT UP chapters began to fall apart. In New York, ACT UP's Treatment and Data Group spun off to form the Treatment Action Group (TAG). In 1990, ACT UP/San Francisco split into two groups, one of which (ACT UP/Golden Gate, later renamed Survive AIDS) focused on treatment advocacy, while the other was deter-mined to work on a wider range of issues. The treatment advocacy groups lost much of their radical edge as their members gained seats at the table with the very univer-sity researchers, government officials, and pharmaceutical company representatives they had once screamed at from the streets.

By the late 1990s most ACT UP chapters were moribund. A major exception is ACT UP/Philadelphia, which successfully made the transition from a single-issue, gay-identity-based group to an inclusive social justice organization that has taken an active role in the convergence movement. Although much smaller than during its heyday, ACT UP/New York remains active in a variety of causes, and veterans of the group have spearheaded several subsequent activist efforts. The tiny ACT UP/East Bay has consistently maintained a broad, social justice focus. By the mid 1990s most of the original members of ACT UP/SF had left the group, and the name was assumed by so-called AIDS dissidents, who believe that HIV does not cause AIDS and that antiretroviral drugs are poisons that cause the symptoms associated with the syndrome. Although strongly grounded in queer identity politics, ACT UP/San Francisco and other dissident chapters have been involved in actions supporting animal rights, opposing the execution of Mumia Abu-Jamal, and other progressive issues shared with the convergence movement.

The mainstreaming of a movement

The emergence and decline of ACT UP and QN took place in the context of a changing gay movement (the "L" would not be widely added until the 1980s; the "B" and "T" not until the 1990s). As GLBT people gained mainstream acceptance, the movement lost its radical edge and became increasingly assimilationist (for a history of the early gay liberation movement and its shift toward assimilationism, see Bronksi 1998; Duberman 1999; Teal 1971).

The post-Stonewall gay liberation movement was about "releasing the homosexuality in heterosexuals, and the heterosexuality in homosexuals" – that is, developing a novel approach to the very way sexual identity is conceptualized. Both gay liberation and the feminist movement of the same era offered a critique of traditional gender roles, the nuclear family, marriage, and compulsory monogamy, and both made common cause with progressive movements of the day, including anti-war activists, free-speech proponents, and advocates for "Third World" liberation.

By the mid 1970s, however, the gay movement had increasingly come to adopt a civil rights, identity politics model. In a diary entry from the early 1970s, gay activist and historian Martin Duberman (1999) wrote "I feared that the net effect might be to win recognition of gay people as a legitimate minority, but a minority wedded to dominant mainstream values. A new world would not be ushered in, but the old world reaffirmed – with the addition of a few prosperous, well-educated, middle-class white queers." It is a critique echoed by queer radicals today (see Shepard 2001).

With the election of Bill Clinton in 1992, large national GLBT groups such as the

National Gay and Lesbian Task Force (NGLTF) and the Human Rights Campaign (HRC) intensified their quest for a place at the mainstream table, focusing on same-sex marriage, gay inclusion in the military, "hate crime" laws, and increasing the economic and political clout of the GLBT community. With a Democratic administration in the White House that gave lip service to GLBT concerns, many gay men and lesbians traded in their sticker-covered leather jackets and combat boots for neckties and sensible pumps.

Paralleling the mainstreaming of the GLBT political agenda was an increased commodification of the gay identity. This increasing consumerism encouraged the movement to play down its radical edges to position itself as a more attractive market. As Tom Thomson (2001) notes, "It's not surprising that the thorough interconnection of corporate power and queer activism has discouraged the development of even mild critiques of capitalism and state power within queer political discourse."

At this point in the GLBT movement's evolution, it's worth asking whether gay, lesbian, bisexual, and transgender people are in fact a progressive constituency. Identity-based movements bring people together on the basis of shared characteristics and oppressions, and often expect that their members will share certain moral values, political beliefs, and cultural tastes. But as societal oppression declines, there is less to hold an otherwise disparate identity group together.

As GLBT people gain mainstream acceptance, many feel a decreased need or desire to align themselves with marginalized groups or radical causes. By now, many GLBT people have well-paid professional jobs, and have no interest in abolishing capitalism. Others want to join the legislature or the military, and have no interest in overthrowing the government. Still others desire a monogamous marriage and children, and see little reason to challenge traditional ideas about relationships and families. While progressive queers often argue, for example, that the GLBT movement should support adequate welfare, tenants' rights, and labor issues because many GLBT people are poor or working class, it makes as much sense to suggest that the GLBT movement should support a capital gains tax cut because many GLBT people are wealthy. One often hears gay conservatives described as a contradiction in terms. Yet based on exit poll data from the November 2000 election, an estimated 25 percent of GLBT people voted for Republican candidate George W. Bush; clearly, conservative gays are no longer a fringe element, if indeed they ever were.

Whither the "queer left"?

Queer radicals today face a dilemma. Should we try to steer the mainstream GLBT movement in a more progressive direction, or work with other progressive activists in groups that are not queer-focused? Can – and should – a movement focused on gay and lesbian identity expand to encompass a full range of progressive causes? And how can a movement organized around sexual identity embrace the intersecting identities of gay men and lesbians (and bisexuals? and transgendered people?) who are also women, people of color, disabled, youth, or working class?

Progressive queer activists have had some degree of success in pushing the mainstream GLBT movement to adopt progressive causes. The NGLTF has responded favorably to critiques that it has not been sufficiently inclusive of bisexuals, transgendered people, people of color, and queer youth. The organization has been persuaded to take stands against the Gulf War, the death penalty, and the International Monetary Fund (IMF). The Ad Hoc Committee for an Open Process, which included many long-term radical gay and lesbian activists, encouraged greater grassroots participation in the planning of the April 2000 Millennium March on Washington, an event Ben Shepard (2001) characterizes as "a profound chasm within the movement itself."

ACT UP with "Anti-Racist Skinheads & Punx against Homophobia" at LGTB march on Washington, 1993.

Even as gay left institutions such as *Gay Community News* have dissolved in recent years, queer activists have continued to address progressive issues from a queer-identity-based perspective. Queer Watch, a small group formed in 2000, was able to persuade several national GLBT groups to sign an anti-death penalty statement. GLBT working people continue to organize, forming queer labor groups such as Pride at Work. Progressive queer groups exist in several US cities, including Boston's Queer Revolt, San Francisco's Lesbian and Gay Insurrection (LAGAI), Chicago's Queer to the Left, Queers for Racial and Economic Justice, and a new network calling itself the Queer Liberation Front, after the post-Stonewall group of the same name. Yet on the whole, the queer progressive/left tendency remains small, and has failed to capture the imagination of the broader GLBT community.

One of the most visible factions of the contemporary radical queer milieu is the transgender (TG) movement, which has taken many people by surprise with the sheer speed and magnitude of its growth in the 1990s. Although it is in many respects an identity-based movement for transgendered, transsexual, and intersex people, some activists (such as GenderPAC) advocate an expanded scope that includes all people affected by gender-based oppression. While the gender movement has its assimilationist elements, activist groups like Transexual Menace and TransAction have

ACT UP Women, with Black Block at 1992 Pro-Choice March in Washington.

followed in the footsteps of ACT UP, engaging in direct action and street protest to call attention to issues such as violence and police brutality against gender-variant people.

The post-Stonewall gay liberation movement advocated a broad sexual and gender liberation agenda, which shared similarities with the "sexual revolution" of the same era and with the "free love" movement dating back to the late nineteenth century. But today there is little emphasis on sex within most of the GLBT civil rights movement. Repeal of sodomy laws has been accorded a low priority by the GLBT establishment. A group called SexPanic! formed in 1997 to counter the demonization of queer sex – attacks that were often coming from assimilationist gay men and lesbians as well as from the religious right and the straight establishment (see essay by Eigo below, and by Shepard in part 3). But the group never succeeded in mobilizing large segments of the GLBT population.

Sex workers have become increasingly organized and active in the 1990s, demanding reform of laws that punish consensual commercial sex. Aided greatly by the Internet, sadomasochist/BDSM social, support, and activist groups have sprung up in large cities and small towns across the country. Polyamory groups, proponents of responsible non-monogamy, and advocates for nontraditional relationships, are increasingly visible. But there is really no all-encompassing sexual and gender liberation movement that has succeeded in bringing together elements such as the leather community, fetishists, polyamorists, sex workers, producers and consumers of pornography, and advocates for the sexual self-determination of youth. Today the "sex activist" label is most often applied to those who write and teach about sexual technique or who do art and performance related to their own sexual experience, and there is little emphasis on connecting sexual and gender issues to a broader social justice agenda. Many pro-sex advocates seem to feel that if they have attended the latest orgy, they have done their part for social change.

What do we want? Everything!

In the absence of a strong queer progressive or sexual and gender liberation movement, some queer radicals have opted to devote their energies to the new convergence activism. Activists from many different struggles – some previously unaware of each others' existence – emerged from the fog of tear gas in Seattle as a real movement, albeit one that has so far resisted adopting a particular name or a specific agenda. The global financial institutions are perhaps the ideal impetus to bring so many different activists together. In promoting free trade at all costs, they run roughshod over national and local laws regarding consumer safety and environmental protection. In advocating the free movement of capital and goods – but not of workers or consumers – they encourage corporations to shift production to the poorest countries, creating a race to the bottom that impoverishes workers in the developing world while undermining labor in developed countries. With their structural adjustment policies, they impose cutbacks in health care, education, and other social services. In their very workings, they are undemocratic, with decisions made by a small elite rather than those who are most directly affected. Under the banner of "neoliberalism," the gap between the haves and the have-nots has widened as power and wealth are concentrated in ever fewer hands.

The recent upsurge in activism has occasioned a flood of ink (see the essay by Klein in part 4, and other essays in this volume), but a few notable features of the new movement should be mentioned here. The convergence movement prides itself on its grassroots, leaderless structure and its flexible tactics. Like the radical queer activism of the 1990s, the convergence movement has borrowed heavily from anarchist and feminist principles, which reject hierarchy and value broad participation and consensus decision-making. It insists on a consistency of means and ends. As described by Cindy Milstein of the Institute for Social Ecology, "We're not putting off the good society until some distant future, but attempting to carve out room for it in the here and now." The convergence movement derives its strength from the concerted efforts of multiple autonomous individuals and affinity groups working without a centralized platform or leadership – potentially a great advantage, since authorities cannot decapitate a movement that has no head.

Like the radical queer activists – and like the Zapatistas, whom many credit with kicking off the struggle against neoliberalism five years before Seattle – the convergence movement has mastered the means of communication, using eye-catching visuals and sophisticated technologies to disseminate their message outside the control of the mainstream, corporate media (see the essay by Nogueira in part 4). "For once in a political protest," says veteran activist Starhawk (see essay in part 1), "when we chanted 'the whole world is watching!' we were telling the truth." In addition to using email and the Web to plan and coordinate every aspect of their work, convergence activists also use the Internet to conduct "cyber actions" such as email "zaps" of global corporations and government officials – the latest version of the phone and fax "zaps" pioneered by ACT UP (see interview with Dominguez in part 4).

It is too early to forecast the fate of the convergence movement. As Alexander Cockburn notes, "Once in a generation you can catch the ruling class off guard. Then you spend twenty years paying for it" (Cockburn et al. 2000). The movement has already met a level of repression that is unusual at such an early stage, facing increased police mobilization, stepped-up surveillance and infiltration, and stiffer jail sentences. For a truly anti-authoritarian movement to be successful, it cannot rely on brute force to overthrow "the system" or make people fall into line. Rather, it must persuade people that its goals are in their own best interest. The convergence movement has tapped into a popular sentiment against growing corporate domination. Now it must find ways to bring the global struggles home and show how they are relevant to people's everyday lives and, perhaps most important, must better define what it's for as well as what it's against.

Where was the rainbow in Seattle?

While the queer presence at last year's convergence actions may have seemed minimal, the influence of queer and AIDS activists has nevertheless been considerable. With their queer sensibility and mastery of the media, queer activists attracted a greater share of attention than their small numbers would otherwise warrant, and the influence of radical queer groups can be seen in many non-queer activist organizations. At the WTO protest in Seattle the sight of a small group of Lesbian Avengers topless in the cold rain was among the most memorable images.

Many of the most active queer participants within the convergence movement are veterans of ACT UP, QN, and their sister groups. In general, these activists came to the queer and AIDS movements from a background of social justice activism; the queer presence within the convergence movement does not include a large proportion of HIV-positive activists. In a testament to their high degree of influence, queer and AIDS activists have been among the most visible and active coordinators of actions (though no one dares call them "leaders"). In fact, at the Republican National Convention protest in Philadelphia last summer, three ACT UP/Philadelphia members were arrested as "ringleaders" and held on unprecedented bails as high as $1 million.

Nowhere is the synergy between AIDS activism and the struggle against global corporate domination more evident than in the fight for affordable AIDS drugs for poor countries. Multinational pharmaceutical companies have used the patent and intellectual property laws of the WTO and individual countries to block the local manufacture or importation of cheap generic anti-HIV drugs in developing countries such as South Africa and Brazil. There could hardly be a better example of corporations putting profits before people. Activists from ACT UP/Philadelphia, ACT UP/New York, and South Africa's Treatment Action Coalition – along with non-AIDS-focused groups such Médecins sans Frontières/Doctors Without Borders and Nader's Consumer Project on Technology – came together to form the Health Global Access Project (Health GAP) Coalition, which has spearheaded activism in support of drug access (see essay by Sawyer in part 1 and the Introduction). Such efforts have already resulted in reduced drug prices, reams of negative publicity for the pharmaceutical companies, and an agreement by one company to allow off-patent production of its AIDS drugs.

Barriers to queer inclusion

Given the resistance of the mainstream GLBT movement to addressing progressive issues outside the realm of gay identity politics, one might ask why more queer radicals are not active in the convergence movement. Does it make more sense to join forces with the progressive multi-issue movement rather than trying to influence the GLBT movement? Might we have more success persuading the convergence movement to embrace sexual and gender liberation than in convincing the GLBT movement to embrace non-queer progressive causes? Who are our best allies, mainstream and conservative GLBT people, or progressive and radical heterosexuals?

The lack of a visible and organized queer presence in the convergence movement is a "Catch 22" similar to that described by Elizabeth Martinez in her analysis of the absence of people of color. Queers are not eager to participate in the movement because it doesn't include enough queers; the movement does not include enough queers because queers are not eager to participate. The fact that some of its most visible members are queer or AIDS activists has received little notice. Is it a positive development that the presence of out queers is seen as unremarkable, or is it a sign of a reluctance to acknowledge the role of queers in the movement?

The convergence movement is, on the whole, quite queer-friendly. Most non-queer progressives include homophobia in their laundry lists of issues. However, queer issues – and sexual and gender issues more broadly – are not a high priority for a majority of non-queer activists. In part this is due to a hostility – especially among older white male leftists – towards identity-based organizing in general, what Duberman (1999) describes as a "horde of disgruntled, righteous, straight leftists" who "deplore the derailing of class struggle (and their own leadership) for the trivial self-therapies of 'imagined' identity politics." Some leftists argue that a focus on identity takes attention away from the class and economic issues they feel are paramount. Some still harbor the belief that racism, sexism, and heterosexism are outgrowths of capitalism, and that we must first abolish capitalism in order to liberate people of color, women, and queers. In reality, these "isms" preceded capitalism and exist under a variety of economic and political systems, and other societal forces (such as religion) have played as great a role in propping up racism, sexism, and homophobia. There is little reason to assume that these "isms" would not persist in a post-capitalist, post-statist society unless they are actively confronted and eradicated from the outset.

But queers face additional difficulties that go beyond those of other identity groups. Progressive thinking has evolved with regard to racism and sexism, and most now agree that the issues of people of color and women are integral to the larger project of achieving social justice. The convergence movement is roughly half women, has adopted feminist principles, and recognizes that global corporate domination disproportionately affects women worldwide. Although people of color are still not present in the movement in proportion to their numbers in the population (see Martinez 1999; Crass 2000), issues of racism are widely acknowledged, as is the fact that people of color bear the brunt of corporate exploitation and environmental devastation. But when it comes to queers, the issues of sexuality and gender are still downplayed. There remains a sense among some on the left that issues of sex, sexuality, desire, and gender are frivolous, a luxury of the privileged or a waste of time. They are seen as private rather than public, and are associated with leisure rather than work. Usually whites can work against racism and men against sexism without their own identity being called into question; however, heterosexuals (especially men) who work for queer liberation must confront the risk of being seen as queer themselves, a prospect that remains highly threatening for many radical men. Add to this the pervasive American erotophobia that regards sexual issues as distasteful and those who draw attention to them as somewhat suspect.

Despite this, parts of the traditional socialist left have made considerable progress in including queers and queer issues. In the late 1980s and early 1990s, sectarian socialist and communist groups were more or less forced to seek alliance with radical queers, who were at the time the most visible face of militant urban activism. What may have started out as opportunism has in some cases evolved into real alliances, as socialist activists worked together with queers and began to rethink their outmoded ideas about homosexuality and other forms of sexual and gender non-conformity as symptoms of "bourgeois decadence." Various groups, such as the Democratic Socialists of America, now have queer caucuses; the Workers World Party has become an outspoken supporter of GLB and especially transgender causes, and the sponsor of Rainbow Flags for Mumia through its International Action Center. However, while some traditional leftist groups have accepted GLBT as a marginalized identity, others remain squeamish about queer liberation struggles, especially those that explicitly involve sex. And a few continue to oppose queer identity and (especially male) same-sex relations; these include the Revolutionary Communist Party, which states in its program, "education will be conducted throughout society on the ideology behind homosexuality and its material roots in exploiting society, and struggle will be waged to eliminate it and reform homosexuals."

Some so-called Third World revolutionary groups have also developed a new attitude in regard to queers, a marked departure from earlier movements in China, Cuba, and elsewhere. For example, the Zapatistas consistently link their cause with the struggles of all marginalized people. Subcomandante Marcos (1994), responding to speculation that he was homosexual, proclaimed:

> Marcos is gay in San Francisco, black in South Africa, Asian in Europe, a Chicano in San Ysidro, an anarchist in Spain, a Palestinian in Israel, a Mayan Indian in the streets of San Cristobal … a woman alone in the Metro at 10 [p.m.] … an underground editor, an unemployed worker … a non-conformist student, a dissident against neoliberalism … and of course a Zapatista in the mountains of southeastern Mexico.

Likewise, the once anti-gay African National Congress in South Africa marked the end of the apartheid era in 1994 when it adopted the first national constitution that explicitly included sexual orientation.

A queer convergence

The age and gender diversity of the convergence movement, as well as its large anarchist/anti-authoritarian element, help promote a queer-positive atmosphere. Anarchism – along with feminism – has long been concerned with breaking down the artificial barriers between the public and the private spheres. The anarchist tradition embraces play as eagerly as it does work: remember "If I can't dance, I don't want to be part of your revolution." It values personal freedom as well as social justice. In addition, younger activists – whether homosexual, bisexual, heterosexual, or refusing labels altogether – have grown up in a more queer-accepting culture and widely embrace more fluid conceptualizations of sexuality and gender; few are as concerned as their elders with reifying identity-based categories.

The lack of queer participation in the convergence movement cannot be laid entirely at the feet of clueless heterosexual activists. Many queers – especially those who have had experience working with homophobic straight leftists – distrust (or even dislike) heterosexuals and are more comfortable organizing within the queer ghetto. Radical queers must combat heterosexism within the convergence movement by being visible and by overcoming the urge to put off addressing our issues as sexual and gender minorities. In addition, we must encourage the developing movement to resist alliances with unrepentant homophobes, and insist that we not be hidden in the closet in a misguided attempt to make the movement more comfortable for union members, communities of color, and others presumed to be less tolerant of queers.

Heterosexual progressives can be the best allies of radical queers in areas where the mainstream GLBT establishment fears to tread. Heterosexual anarchists and some socialists have a long tradition of critiquing marriage, monogamy, the nuclear family, and accepted notions of child-rearing. Non-queer groups such as the ACLU have taken the most principled stands on freedom of sexual expression, while the mainstream GLBT movement has increasingly adopted censorship tactics. Leadership in struggles against the death penalty, police brutality, and the unjust prison system has come from non-gay groups such as Amnesty International and the Quakers, while the GLBT establishment pushes for "hate crime" laws. As mainstream GLBT "leaders" have become more visible, some heterosexual progressives have come to believe that these "leaders" speak for all queers. They fear that opposing positions espoused by the GLBT establishment will be viewed as homophobic; queer radicals must make it clear that this is not the case.

Although identity-based politics has accomplished a great deal in making the progressive movement – and society as a whole – aware of the issues and concerns of marginalized groups, we may have to move beyond identity politics to advance on a broad-based progressive social justice agenda. In an ideal world, the need for activism based on race, sex, or sexual orientation may become a thing of the past, but the movement is clearly not there yet.

Radical queers and heterosexuals alike should understand that GLBT people do not – and should not – have a monopoly on issues of sexuality, desire, and gender. As Duberman (1999) notes, the queer movement has developed a body of thought concerning

> the historicity and fluidity of sexual desire, the performative nature of gender, and the complex multiplicity of attractions, fantasies, impulses and narratives that lie within us all....To understand how and why sexual and gender identities get socially constructed is to open up a new way of talking about politics, about how relations of power get established, [and] about the role of the state in reinforcing and policing that set of relations in the name of maintaining the stakes of the already privileged.

Just as issues of race must be addressed by white people and issues of sex and gender must be addressed by men, issues of sexuality and desire must be addressed by heterosexuals – not as a way for the dominant group to "help" the marginalized, but because social inequalities and stereotypes negatively affect all of us.

Radical queers have succeeded in harnessing erotic/sexual energy to enliven their activism in a unique way; indeed, this is part of what is meant by "queer sensibility." Such energy makes radical queer activism exciting and compelling, and keeps activists motivated and involved. As it stands, the introduction of an erotic component into non-queer activism tends to feel oppressive to many women and to bring out the worst competitive macho tendencies in some men, but perhaps in the future people of all genders and sexual orientations will be able to marshal this life-affirming force against the forces of death we confront in our struggles for justice.

Finally, we must never lose sight of the fact that on a worldwide basis, a majority of people are unable to live openly queer lives or to explore alternative gender roles or different relationship and family structures due to harsh material conditions. The struggle against global corporate domination directly contributes to the queer struggle, because sexual, economic, and social liberation must go hand in hand.

Note

Thanks to Leslie Cagan, Bill Dobbs, Benjamin Doherty, Phillip Fucella, Mitchell Halberstadt, Jesse Heiwa, Imani Henry, Chuck Munson, Mary Patten, Susan Raffo, Kate Raphael, Ben Shepard, and jeff subhumyn for helpful information and comments related to this essay.

Jail house rocks, "Matthew Shepard lives!"

LESLIE FEINBERG

One Police Plaza, Central Booking, New York

"Matthew Shepard lives! Matthew Shepard lives!" we thundered, as cops dragged another activist into our cellblock. Each new prisoner received a hero's welcome from his peers: cheers, applause, hugs, a shower of kisses. We were packed into a makeshift men's "bull" pen: sixty-eight gay and bisexual men, one drag queen who had fought the cops at the 1969 Stonewall rebellion that ignited the gay liberation movement, and – unknown to some of the police – one transgendered female. In addition, a nearby cellblock held thirty-three lesbian and bisexual activists. We were held in an old central booking station, long unused.

We were all arrested on October 19 for taking our anger about the horrific murder of a young gay Wyoming student onto the streets of New York. That demonstration, built by a grassroots and word-of-mouth mobilization, swelled at times to more than ten thousand. Earlier in the evening, thousands of us gathered in front of the swank Plaza Hotel in midtown at the height of rush hour to hold a political funeral for Matthew Shepard. The rally bristled with placards linking the anti-gay lynching of Shepard to the racist lynching in June of James Byrd, Jr. in Jasper, Texas.

Some eighty of us were the first to get busted when we stepped off the curb to take our march onto Fifth Avenue. Cops cinched our hands behind our backs with plastic handcuffs and dragged us into four police vans that blocked the avenue. Police rounded up all the legal observers, march negotiators, and marshals they could get their hands on. Three precincts were used to house the volume of prisoners. I was in a group that was brought to the old Central Booking Station. All were locked up without water or food. Some had their desperately needed medications confiscated. We were not allowed to make phone calls or see our attorneys, and were not told what we were charged with.

Each new wave of arrivals was urged to turn the benches into makeshift stages for an impromptu rally. Activists rose up above our noisy throng to regale us with the details of the battles we'd missed. "After you all got arrested, we started marching on the sidewalk," one young man said. "But the cops pushed and shoved us. They even drove up on the sidewalk on motorbikes headed right for us. So we took the street." We roared at that news.

Others filled in what happened next. At 55th Street, the police barricaded the avenue to divert everyone onto the side street. Then cops targeted the march leadership for a further round of mass arrests. Another activist picked up the narrative. The crowd headed west to Sixth Avenue, only to run into another cop barricade, "which we overturned," he said. "We made our way through traffic to get back to Fifth Avenue so we could march past St. Patrick's Cathedral – which we did. "Anti-gay bigot Cardinal O'Connor has got to go," he concluded. An older gay activist told us how marchers had been trapped between lines of riot-police in Times Square. Cops on horseback charged into the crowds. Our anger was tangible as he told us how police wildly flailed at people with night sticks, bloodying those they could reach.

Thousands of people – broken up by police into smaller groups – all converged eventually on Madison Square Park at 23rd Street. Richard told us, "Two police helicopters were hovering over the park. That's how a lot of us knew where to go. There were thousands of us covering every inch of the streets, the park, every bench. All of us were united. This is the best thing I've ever been part of in the gay community!"

"Now there's anger coming through"

Behind bars, the deep emotion shared by people all across the United States about the torture and murder of a gentle, young Wyoming student was thick as resin. I saw a man sitting on a bench, staring straight ahead, hands tightly clasped. "Are you OK?" I asked. He looked at me with tears in his eyes and nodded slowly. "I've been

Gay activists demonstrate anger over the killing of Matthew Shepard, New York City, October 1998.

quiet," John Boyle said. "Now there's anger coming through." Keith Cyler took in all those packed into the cell with an expansive gesture. "Look: here's a lawyer, a school-teacher, a clerk. There's young people just getting fired up for the first time, old-time act-uppers – a large cross section of the population. People are angry."

Many told me maddening accounts of police brutality and bigotry. Fred described how cops held him for hours in tight handcuffs that cut off all feeling in his hands. By the time the police found a knife to cut them off, he had passed out unconscious.

His lover, David – who is HIV-positive – saw it all happen. "I'd rather lose a finger than have my lover be so stressed out from worry," Fred said. After Fred had passed out, David asked the cops to see if his lover was still breathing. "Relax!" a cop barked at him. "If that was your wife face-down on the floor unconscious, would you relax?" David retorted.

For those who might forget how righteous anger against oppression can nurture tender, compassionate consciousness, I had my own personal reminder that night.

I was the only female-bodied person in the men's cellblock – that I knew. As a gender "outlaw," just producing identification papers left me vulnerable to grave legal and physical dangers. I had already endured one brutal "pat-down" by male cops, but we were still awaiting transfer to the custody of Department of "Corrections" officers. I wondered how I would survive the perils of the night. However, from the moment I was arrested, many of the men detained with me recognized me as a trans activist and author. Once inside the cell block, a small group of gay and bisexual men approached me. One brother wrapped his arm around my shoulder. "We know who you are," he said. "We are honored to count you among us tonight. We'll do every-thing we can to help you." And they did.

'It's just the beginning, folks!'

At 1 a.m., the police announced they were going to "chain-gang" us. We were trans-ferred in manacles, chained together, to the lower Manhattan Tombs jail. As I looked around at the prisoners there – predominantly African American and Latino – I was struck with the irony of the situation. This capitalist jail was built on one of the northern end-stations of the great underground railroad that transported African peoples from chattel slavery more than a century ago. I also recalled that in the early eighteenth century, the Carolinas passed a law that no more than twelve African people could attend the funeral of a slave – because the gatherings became a catalyst for political resistance. And now the administration of Mayor Rudolph Giuliani had tried to bust up a funeral march. It couldn't stand the fact that thousands would be calling for mass solidarity against the racist and anti-gay lynchings that are a hallmark of counter-revolutionary terror under capitalism.

One of the people I was chained to in the police van, Jason Chappell, was a former organizer of the Borders Bookstore union drive. He saw a connection between three recent New York events: a demonstration by forty thousand construction workers, the Million Youth March, and this Shepard protest. "Each time," Chappell noted, "there has been an overreaction by Giuliani and his police force." I was also handcuffed to Sylvia Rivera, a Puerto Rican drag queen who had fought the cops at the Stonewall Rebellion in 1969. Then, too, the police and courts and jails were used as weapons to repress an already downtrodden community of African-American, Latina, and white gay drag queens and butches – many of them young, hungry, and homeless. Decades of anger exploded that night in the streets of Greenwich Village. And a new social movement emerged from that blast of rage.

It was a contingent of that mass movement that took the streets of Manhattan more than thirty years later to organize even wider sectors of the population into the struggle against the rising cesspool of anti-gay and racist violence. Inside a Tombs cell, in the early hours of the morning, Sylvia Rivera concluded, "Tonight is just the beginning, folks. This is the rebirth of Stonewall. Another piece of history in the making." And she ought to know.

From Stonewall to Diallo

BENJAMIN SHEPARD INTERVIEWS BOB KOHLER

March 1999, Bob Kohler was arrested for engaging in an act of civil disobedience, protesting the forty-one shots fired against unarmed Amadou Diallo, an immigrant from Guinea. Kohler's arrest was just one of over a thousand made in the month since eight activists – five women and two men from a group called Fed Up Queers – chained themselves together to block traffic on lower Broadway, separating themselves from the broader rally over Diallo's death (Flynn 1999). The gesture struck a chord (although the seven activists continued to face stiff charges after charges against 1,200 other arrestees were dropped). As a veteran of the Stonewall Riots and member of Gay Liberation Front, Kohler was familiar with police brutality.

> I do not equate my oppression with the oppression of Blacks and Latinos. You can't. It is not the same struggle, but it is one struggle. And, if my being here as a longtime gay activist can influence other people in the gay community, it's worth getting arrested. I'm an old man now. I don't look forward to spending twenty-four hours in a cell. But these arrests are giving some kind of a message. (Trebay 1999)

In the months following the Matthew Shepard Political Funeral (see Feinberg essay above), queer activists had sought to outline the links between police brutality and violence against queers and people of color. While the broader lesbian, gay, bisexual, and transgender communities mobilized against the violence to Shepard, Kohler was part of a group of radical queer activists agitating to force GLBT communities to translate their struggles into broader questions of social justice – never a simple

Bob Kohler (*center*) and Sylvia Rivera (*right*) during the Gay Liberation Front years. Little did either of them know, they would spend the next thirty years on the struggles they began with Gay Liberation Front.

process. To an extent, the task describes Bob Kohler's entire career as an activist – from work with the Congress on Racial Equality (CORE) to Gay Liberation Front, through ACT UP and Fed Up Queers. Kohler recalled his start with CORE and Harlem Riots of 1966:

BK   I don't know that there was one catalyst, Ben. In those days anything, a bottle breaking could be a catalyst for a mini-explosion of people and anger.... In the late 1960s, there were riots everywhere. I don't think that the gay riots would have occurred had we not been influenced by all of the other riots in the straight radical community. So that was there.

I had to crawl out on my belly of the Harlem CORE office to my car, which was okay. Of course, when I went in Francis Foster said to me, "You know, things are bad and push is going to come to shove and I'm not going to have the time to say, 'Hey, he was one of the good guys.' So, before you really commit yourself, know that you are going down if there is time to go down." I mean, I was not happy crawling out with fires all over the place and the anger, but I felt okay.

And then I went down South to the first pool that had just been desegregated. And I went down with two black people, a man and a woman. And when we jumped in the pool, every white person jumped out of the pool. And it was really funny. We were the only three in the pool. And we said, "What do we do now?" Joan couldn't swim and so she held my hand. She said, "Don't let go of my hand." Okay. And they were running around the pool. And you know how – this is awful, but – Southerners, their voices get high when they get upset. And they were screaming, "The niggers are in the pool! The niggers are in the pool!" And that's all they kept saying, over and over and over…. And I remember Pete and Joan saying, "Yeah, the niggers are in the pool. We know."

And finally, I was looking at Joan and we were talking and suddenly it appeared like she was floating up and I thought what the hell? They were emptying the pool [*laughs*]. The water kept going down and [t]here we stood. And I said, "We're not going to sing because that was going to be too silly to sing, 'We Shall Overcome'" as they are draining the pool. And so finally we got down on our knees and we said, "We gotta get out of the pool. This is too silly." And so we got out and we left that night to get back East. That was CORE.

And finally, the reason that I left was that it was at the point where whites should get out. The blacks needed to handle this by themselves. And we needed to leave. And we were pledged to nonviolence and I thought I don't know if I can deal with somebody spitting on me again. And Francis also told me that in the South the only thing worse than a "nigger" was a "nigger lover." And it was true, because you were a traitor to them.

We had to have training where we would sit at a milk counter and they'd spit on you, the instructors, that was bad enough – spit on your face, you know. But when people really spit on me, it was nasty. Getting really called nasty stuff, it gets to ya after a while.

So it was good. Our time was up. "Ours" meaning white people was up, and CORE, the movement, could no longer be nonviolent.

Gay liberation

BK   By the end of the 1960s I said I was going to take two years off. After a career change I didn't know what to do and I was doing nothing. And I used to go in the park all the time and that's where the street kids were. I got very friendly

Gay Liberation Front march from the House of Detention to a Black Panther rally at Union Square.
Lois Hart is front center, Kohler, obscured, third from left.

with them and, even though I was older and represented a father figure to them, I wasn't old enough to be the dirty old man, so they trusted me. And they'd confide in me. Their wigs, their stolen credit cards, anything – all their contraband I'd keep for them. They lived in the park. And those were the kids who rioted. And I'd gotten to know them and I kind of thought I had seen what happens to black people in Harlem; I had seen what happens to poor white people – I had seen all of that, but I had never seen this with gay teenagers. It was something I just didn't know about. Fourteen-, fifteen-year-old kids with cigarette burns all over their bodies from a father who found out they were gay – or were permanently scarred, and certainly mentally scarred forever. And thrown out and living out of bags in Sheridan Square and washing in the little fountain. I did not know that. I had never understood that there were groups like that.

So I got to know them very well. I got to know all of their problems, what they were doing, about their operations. You know they were all going to be huge stars when they got the operation. It got me very angry and the only thing I could do then was give them money and when I say money, I say quarters, not bills. And I would collect clothes for them. I was doing that for months and then Stonewall happened.

The kids, we were doing the same thing of listening to their bullshit. A couple of them were primping to go down to cruise at the piers where the Jersey cars came. And whenever they'd go down there or knew they were going out hustling, that's when I'd get the credit cards and anything valuable and I was gathering all that. During Stonewall, if I'd been arrested, I'd still be in jail now. I had so many credit cards, so much stolen merchandise. It was unbelievable.

But I was there and suddenly all of the things that had been welling up inside me about these kids came to fruition. Not in any way a revolution. I still will defy anybody who tells you otherwise – my best friend Sylvia, I don't care who it is – I do not believe that anybody saw anything. These kids started a riot because that was the only thing that they knew to do. They used to cut each other's faces open when they'd grab a bottle. And I used to drag these kids to St. Vincent's hospital with blood pouring down their faces. I was like a gay Florence Nightingale. But I was the only person they had. It took a lot of that. It was heavy. And I didn't see the explosion coming. I'd see only minor explosions. I should have seen it coming because there'd been raids over time. But suddenly this raid was [*slaps hands*] – a riot.

And nobody knows who started it and nobody can know because you don't know a riot is going to start, so therefore you're not looking to see anybody start anything. You hear something. Maybe it's a bottle break. Maybe it's a fire in the trashcan and then it's a riot. So all these bullshit people who say "I saw this. I saw that": you didn't see nothing. Well, one thing you didn't see was drag queens in high heels. I can tell you that. They weren't there. It was the kids who started it and then the whole street erupted. But it was just – the kids had the best time of their lives. That was fun. And that broke up the week and they were glad when it happened on Wednesday night. And glad when it happened again. And by Saturday night… they still… none of those kids knew because they didn't have that kind of a mind.

But we knew by the second riot that something was happening. So that's when the organizing started. The first Panther flyer out on the street read: "Are homosexuals revolting? You bet your ass we are!" I'll never forget that.

The spirit of gay liberation front…

"Oppression is like a large tree with many branches, each branch being a part of the whole. They cannot be separated; they draw from each other," Lois Hart, one of the Gay Liberation Front (GLF) founders, explained. Of course, GLF and the vision of gay liberation linked with universal struggles for social and cultural transformation would not last (see Teal 1971). But that did not prevent Bob from agitating for the GLF alliance with the Black Panthers. At the same, the Gay Activist Alliance (GAA) split with GLF to focus exclusively on gay issues, exposing a split that would follow the movement. The assimilationists, such as GAA, thought the only thing wrong with our society was that it oppresses gays, while queers, such as Kohler, envisioned gay liberation as a critique of social, sexual, and economic "regimes of the normal" (Warner 1993; Teal 1971; Shepard 2001).

For the next three decades, Kohler would build on Hart's advice, staying involved with the movement, with ACT UP, SexPanic!, and eventually Fed Up Queers (FUQ). By the time of the Diallo protests, Kohler's career had moved full circle – back to the struggles against police brutality and racism, and their tenuous link with homophobia. GLF's view was always, to borrow a Deni Cavello phrase, "Any oppression is too much oppression."

BK   Of all the groups I've worked with, I think Fed Up Queers, the group that helped ignite the civil disobedience after the Diallo shootings and later the AIDS drugs for Africa campaign [see Sawyer essay in part 1], come closest to working in the spirit of Gay Liberation Front. The FUQs think the stencil on the street is as important as the blockade. It's just as revolutionary. Like all the "No More Prisons" signs on all the sidewalks, it takes a while to push an idea into the consciousness. I see so many contributions by today's radicals, including a fierce group of young lesbians.

BS   "You remember the old Margaret Mead statement, "Never doubt that a small group of thoughtful, committed citizens can change the world. Indeed, it's the only thing that ever has." I think that's the ethos of what's happening now.

BK   The last year allowed us to believe Margaret Mead. We've allowed ourselves to act on Margaret Mead's statement. We've allowed ourselves to act, to make mistakes…

…and even succeed.

The reproductive rights movement, ACT UP, and the Lesbian Avengers

BENJAMIN SHEPARD INTERVIEWS SARAH SCHULMAN

I met Sara Schulman on a hot summer day in her East Village Apartment, not far from Veselka, a deli featured in her novels. Meeting her, one is reminded of a trajectory of radical women's organizing from the suffragettes, through her own contributions with the reproductive rights movement in the 1970s, ACT UP in the 1980s, and the Lesbian Avengers and the Irish Lesbian and Gay Organization in the 1990s. "Access to Resources (Xerox machine)," she playfully listed as the most important quality for Lesbian Avengers in their *Dyke Manifesto* (see Schulman 1993: 296). An ethos of activism emerges within the do-it-yourself story of Schulman's work with these groups. I began by asking Schulman about the relationship between being a writer and being an activist.

SS   I think, because of the kinds of writing that I've done, because of the content, there's been no place for it in the culture. So I've had to be involved in politics to change the world enough to make a place for what I want to write.

The gay and lesbian writers of my group – many of them are dead now. But my generational group, it was very intertwined because there was no audience for your work except for other gay people. There was no venue for it except gay underground venues. So you were describing the people who were actually reading your work. So if they didn't feel that it was authentic and it didn't resonate with them, they wouldn't read it. There was no voyeurism going on, there was an immediacy there and that's why so many of my peers, like David Feinberg,[1] and all those people, did both....

BS What got you to become an activist? What was the crux?

SS I had a fairly left-leaning mother. She was a social worker. My father had been a deserter from World War I and he had been in jail. And we were taken to anti-war demonstrations. My grandmother, who I lived with, was a socialist. And the Cold War occurred when I was a child. Abortion wasn't even legal when I was in high school in the seventies. So, it was a time of tremendous social transformation. You had to be kind of dead to not notice. And the feminist movement happened. My family had been through the Holocaust. Being Jewish, you know that kind of thing…

What happened was I got down to college. My family was very homophobic.

I was basically exorcized from it as a teenager. I dropped out of college, the University of Chicago, actually. I left school and I went to Europe. And I met people who were involved in helping women from Spain – which was still fascist at the time – go to France to get abortions. So I had hands-on, front-row experience of illegal abortion and how it operated. So when I came back here in 1979, the Hyde Amendment eliminated Medicaid abortion. And my friend and I just immediately went to CARASA (Committee for Abortion Rights and Against Sterilization Abuse) – it was the day of the Hyde Amendment – and got involved in the abortion rights movement. So, you are a teenage girl and abortion becomes legal in 1971 and then in 1979 – I'm seeing it taken away. Then of course, the next year, Reagan is elected. That just felt like a very immediate place for me.

BS Tell me about the work of CARASA.

SS CARASA was the radical wing of the reproductive rights movement. In those days, there was NARAL (National Abortion Rights Action League), which was single-issue abortion rights. They were looking at birth control, childcare, the whole thing that would allow a person to have some sort of autonomy. And these were a mixture of socialist feminists, the left wing of the feminist movement. Unfortunately the whole thing self-destructed in 1982 around homophobia. The lesbians in the group were increasingly out. Suddenly, we wanted to say "lesbian liberation" and talk about lesbian stuff in the context of reproductive rights and they just wouldn't do it. And it was very much old left arguments: 'It will alienate the working class; it will alienate Latinos. You are trying to turn this into a lesbian organization.' And we all got kicked out. And that was very upsetting and horrible. And I didn't do anything for four years until I came into ACT UP.

So, I went from the feminist movement to the mixed-gay movement, which didn't exist at that time. And what was interesting at the beginning of ACT UP was there was a certain group of these guys – Mark Rubin, Marty Robinson. They were people who had been in gay liberation politics. But that was not the mainstay. The main people in ACT UP had been apolitical, totally apolitical. So when this thing happened they really didn't understand a lot about how to run a meeting, how to do things; and a lot of women had been trained in the feminist movement this whole time and had an incredible skill. So a lot of the women rose to a position of leadership because they had organizing skills.

BS   One of the things that I think is kind of interesting is the link between reproductive rights and AIDS activism that unfolded there.

SS   Okay, this is the whole issue around the Hyde Amendment. You can't say somebody has a right if you don't give them access to that right. If you have a right to abortion but [the government] won't pay for it, then you really don't have it. So with AIDS, people started saying, I'm a citizen and I have a right to health care. That was the initial argument because the first argument was "drugs into bodies."

BS   But I think sexual self-determination was a big issue.

SS   Well, that was later. That's with the evolution of AIDS politics. Before ACT UP, the whole issue of the bathhouses that got covered in my book there. You know, very few people fought to keep the bathhouses open. But I think we know that closing bathhouses does not end unsafe sex. We know that as a fact. And, of course, people said that back then…

A personal theory of activism

SS   In a way, I'm an old-time lefty more than anything else and I've always been interested in political movements that have concrete political goals, that have issues for campaigns, that mobilize people, that create countercultures – that stuff has attracted me.

BS   All the essays in this book emphasize praxis.

SS   The theory is not complex. You have to have an idea that is winnable. You have to have a campaign that is viable. And you have to follow every step of it. It's quite easy. If your goal is not winnable then you are in trouble. And if you don't have an idea of how to reach your goal, you'll never reach it. It sounds simple, but it's very hard to get people to follow it.

BS   Defining a goal is a hard thing to do.

SS   What I liked about ACT UP is that the goals were very concrete and easy to win.

BS   They get harder and harder to win as the years go on.

SS   Well, they get more complicated. The cooptation of ACT UP made everything really complex, and the relationship with the drug companies… We'll see what happens. It feels like the protease time bomb is ticking and people are getting sick again.

A proliferation of groups

SS   In the new kind of organizing after ACT UP, gay people said they were gay. Certainly there were plenty of straight women in ACT UP. But straight women dropped out of the fight for women's rights. And I do understand what happened there. I think its because straight men never got onboard, especially with abortion rights. And people had to choose between having a happy personal life or being politically active. So many of the women I knew who were involved with the women's movement, they just had to stop. It was inorganic for them.

ACT UP and then all those groups – Church Ladies for Choice came out of ACT UP; Queer Nation came out of ACT UP; Lesbian Avengers came out of ACT UP – everything came out of it. You know, Housing Works, they all came out of ACT UP.

BS   And that is why this book is called *From ACT UP to the WTO* because a lot of the theatrics that people are using now started in ACT UP.

Lesbian Avengers at the annual Dyke
March, New York City, June 1996.

SS Yeah, except that those strategies didn't start in ACT UP. You read in that
book (see Schulman 1993) about the Women's Action Brigade disrupting Congress
in 1983. That's when we got together with CARASA. So that was the direct action,
and before that the Lavender Hill Mob. You know, there was stuff in the sixties by
gay groups that used direct action. These were old tactics that had been used by
gay people before. And some of the same people – us and the guys, like Marty
Robinson etc. – they're all dead now. But in the sixties and early seventies they did
direct action around gay liberation stuff. For example, there was a meeting of
psychiatrists. In those days, homosexuality was considered a psychiatric disorder.

They interrupted it and got arrested. So when ACT UP started, they brought those tactics. And those of us who were in the women's movement had those tactics. We were all the old lefty/fringe/bohemian types. We weren't the stockbroker types.

BS   ACT UP certainly contributed to an activist use of media.

SS   Well, ACT UP people were very connected. It's interesting when you look at the media coverage, because ACT UP was never a middle-class, white male organization, never… But if you look at media coverage, it looks like it was because that's who they saw, because that's who the media is. So they would take the microphone and put it in front of Larry Kramer when there'd be some incredible organizer there that they would just ignore. So the representation of it is very stilted…

The Lesbian Avengers

SS   Well, what happened was, like I said, we were in ACT UP, and we realized that younger women were not getting it together and learning the skills that we had. And we thought we'd just start this small group in New York to teach them basic skills. And the people who started the Avengers were just hard-core political people – you know, people who had been in the Cuban Revolution, Irish Republicans, a woman who had been in CORE (Congress on Racial Equality) and me and people who really knew what they were doing. And we came up with this idea and it just went "boom!" It just became so large so fast, and then it just fell apart.

BS   Why?

SS   It fell apart because organizations just fall apart, and there was an anarchist thing, and some things can't be sustained. But probably twenty to thirty thousand people went through it.

BS   What was the peak? What was the thing you were most happy about?

SS   The best thing was the march on Washington that we did without a permit. Forty thousand dykes. We started the Dyke March. That was the best thing that we ever did. No permit. That was so great because the official march on Washington that year was so lame – 1993, it must have been. That was great. We ran a few ballot measure campaigns in other states that were really wonderful. You know, we did a lot of really great stuff. But, organizing lesbians is a very specific thing because it is a very disempowered constituency. It's people with no experience of power, with lots of acting out and destructive behavior, and you have to kind of handle that. So these things can be great and they go bad very fast. That's the way it is.

BS 1993, that was sort of a sad time, when the split started happening.

SS When the right-wingers started to come out… Well, Clinton got elected and then after two weeks he had done "Don't ask, Don't tell…" It happened too fast. We were like, "and that was it? Already?" [*Laughs*]

And then we had the strategic split inside ACT UP. I can't remember what year that was. But it was basically about working inside pharmaceutical companies and government agencies. And what happened was that the more professional people – the people who had gone to Harvard, the people who could talk the talk – who had corporate backgrounds, were getting into these committees and working inside these companies and getting access to better treatment. And the people who were more marginal and forgettable were left on the outside. And so it's like – those guys are all still alive, all of them. Well, not Steve [Gendin], but most of them. And the people who died were more marginal. You know, Vitto Russo didn't have health insurance…

So we had our own two-track system going on. I mean, those guys saved their own lives. You can't blame 'em for that…. Its amazing they went so long. The leadership died. That's part of the cooptation was the desperation. No one is to blame. It was a very difficult situation emotionally. People did an amazing job.

Also, coming from the East Village arts community, which was so totally devastated by AIDS, I feel like the creature from the Black Lagoon – I'm one of the few people alive from that time. People who had risky personalities were more likely to die than people who didn't. And those people who had risky personalities were the ones who invented new ideas that moved the whole world forward.

The Irish Lesbian and Gay Organization

BS What about ILGO?

SS   Well, you know, when Anne and Marie started, they innocently applied to march in the [Irish] parade and ended up in the middle of this whole thing and did the best they could for a few years and got overwhelmed by really strategizing and organizing it. And honestly, my feeling is, my way of doing politics, which I laid out to you before – you have a goal that is winnable, you plan a campaign that is specific, and you carry through each step – did not fit in with the culture of ILGO. ILGO has a very repetitive culture. They're very comfortable doing the same tactic over and over again, and I can't do that because I want to win.

It's a difficult thing because it's not just true in ILGO – it's true in much of the left. It's like, for years, we used to hand out leaflets and it really took ACT UP for people to stop doing that because it didn't work. It didn't work from the thirties, but they did it anyway. And some personalities can't try new things. They can't think of new things. They feel insecure doing new things. They only feel secure doing what they know. But they did a great job for five years.

Note

1. Author of several books including *Queer and Loathing* and long-time member of ACT UP/NY.

From WHAM! to ACT UP

TRACY MORGAN

Whereas once legal abortion was undeniably understood to be a partial guarantor of women's freedom and women's physical safety, by the late 1980s it was fast being depicted as an act of senseless violence. The religious right had worked long and hard, in a grassroots and populist fashion, to alter profoundly the terms of the debate about abortion in America, and its efforts were beginning to meet with success. With abortion depicted as the casual snuffing out of innocent *life*, the pro-choice movement began to assert that women who choose abortion are neither amoral nor unethical decision-makers; they are people in psychic pain. Abortion was no longer seen as protecting women from septicemia, death, and forced motherhood. Rather, choosing abortion now caused women agony and distress. To be found defensible, abortion had to be traumatic. Adding insult to injury, "Pro-Child – Pro-Choice" usurped "Pro-Woman – Pro-Choice" as the slogan du jour. While the former worked implicitly to support the notion that women who chose abortion were callous child haters or legalized assassins, sadly the latter had become a too-radical and un-domesticated statement about women qua women, outside the family context. As it became more commonplace for women to be valued as fetal containers, it also began to seem more likely that the terrifying world of Margaret Atwood's *The Handmaid's Tale* would soon be brought to life.

Looking for a movement

I remember sitting in 1988 with friends from college, many of us Women's Studies graduates, talking about yet another impending, and in all likelihood dismal, Supreme Court decision regarding reproductive rights, wondering what we might do to galvanize some kind of response. Not drawn to lobbying, and hence not drawn to NOW (National Organization for Women) or NARAL (then the National Abortion Rights Action League), we were an energetic but rudderless bunch of twenty-something white women, living in New York City, spinning our wheels. If there had been a movement in the streets, we would have been there. But there wasn't.

As a proto-activist, I began to explore whether NARAL and NOW were the only games in town and if so, why? I read the *Village Voice*, searching for hints of something vibrant to join. There was No More Nice Girls, CARASA (Committee for Abortion Rights and Against Sterilization Abuse), and the Guerilla Girls but these groups struck me as rather insular. I remember thinking you probably had to be asked to join them. While things were looking pretty bleak on the reproductive freedom front, I clung to the belief that there had to be thousands of women floundering nearby wondering what to do with their feminist energy. I met a woman who told me about a group called the Reproductive Rights Coalition (RRC) and she gave me the date and time of their next meeting.

At the RRC meeting I found a group of about twenty racially diverse women in their mid to late thirties and older handing out flyers, seated around a huge table. Among them were union leaders, lawyers, physicians, public health policymakers, and women of the not-so-New Left, better known as socialist and communist party members. I was familiar with some of their names, having followed the movement in feminist newspapers like *Off Our Backs* and *Sojourners*: Dr Helen Rodriguez-Trias, Suki Ports, Dr Vicki Alexander, and the convener of the meeting, Verniece Miller of the Center for Constitutional Rights. I, on the other hand, had no recognizable affiliation or recognized authority to speak of, apprenticing as a film editor by day and hitting the phones at NARAL by night to pay the rent. I symbolized what this group pretty glaringly lacked: the youthful novitiate.

The pressing issue was the *Webster* decision, expected to be delivered in July, and the talk at the table focused on how the RRC might best respond. Among other things, including the view that life begins at conception, the 1989 *Webster* decision

ACT UP Women's Action, International Conference on AIDS, San Francisco 1990.

would bar both public employees from performing or assisting in an abortion, unless it was to save a woman's life, and the use of public buildings for performing abortions even if no public funds are involved. Under consideration were a march and a rally. There seemed to be unanimous agreement that meeting attendees should go back to their organizations, rally the troops, getting co-workers, union members, and clients to protest what was expected to be a punitive Supreme Court decision. I wondered what that meant for me? Should I call my friends? The meeting crackled with tension, so I listened. When I finally did share my thoughts, I suggested that we create a really catchy poster advertising the march and wallpaper the city with it, mirroring the group ACT UP. I recall that the mention of ACT UP changed the energy of the group and a subtle resistance was palpable.

Generationally speaking, young feminists in the late 1980s were reared on the words and ideas of pro-sex feminists, many of them lesbians: Dorothy Allison, Pat Califia, Amber Hollibaugh, Audre Lorde, Cherrie Moraga, Joan Nestle, Carol Vance,

Ellen Willis and others. They described a feminist politics where the quest for pleasure, rather than the removal of danger, would be primary. The words of Gayle Rubin (1984), probably the most theoretically sophisticated of feminist sex theorists writing at the time, nicely capture the sensibility that animated my activism and that of many of my peers:

> The time has come to think about sex. To some, sexuality may seem to be an unimportant topic, a frivolous diversion from the more critical problems of poverty, war, disease, racism, famine, or nuclear annihilation. But it is precisely at times such as these, when we live with the possibility of unthinkable destruction, that people are likely to become dangerously crazy about sexuality.

Witness the 1986 *Hardwick* anti-sodomy decision, the murder of abortion providers, the bombing of women's clinics. With the advent of AIDS and the rise of Republican conservatism, the body – to borrow Barbara Kruger's phrase – became a battleground.

Direct action and the birth of WHAM!

My desire to take part in direct action was ever increasing. I wanted people to take us and our message seriously. On July 3, the day the *Webster* decision was announced, a small group of us planned to do civil disobedience, blocking traffic on the Brooklyn Bridge, burning flags, and carrying posters that told Supreme Court justices to "Get Off Our Backs". I remember dressing up as a pregnant woman with the cover of that week's *Village Voice* pinned to my belly. It read, in bright red and yellow, "Abortion Without Apology". As planned, we were handcuffed and taken away to a police precinct and a holding cell. The next day, my picture was in section A of the *New York Times* and in *Newsday*.

On Wednesday, July 5, 1989, ten thousand people hit the streets of New York City marching from downtown Foley Square to a rally in Union Square. The event accommodated a general outpouring of rage and opposition, signaling that the time for a more street-oriented movement in defense of reproductive freedom had arrived. Thanks to this momentum, WHAM! (Women's Health, Action and Mobilization!) was formed.

WHAM! had wobbly legs at first. We struggled to find meeting space. We had no money to make flyers and were unable to finance even the most basic of activist necessities. We lacked a lawyer. We had few if any media contacts. We had no one

lesbian bashing • hysterectomy •
AIDS • cervical cancer • rape •
bulimia • forced child-bearing
• Operation "Rescue" • pap smears •
incest • anorexia • endometriosis •
RU-486 • pre-menstrual syndrome
• forced sterilization • mastectomy
• domestic violence • chlamydia
• sexual harassment • IUDs • pelvic
inflammatory disease • Caesarian
section • liposuction • urinary
infection • forced abortion • breast
cancer • gynecology • clitorectomy
• yeast infection • breast implants
• cystitis • ovarian cancer •
fibroids • Dalkon Shield • ab...

WHAM! Women's Health Action a...

WOMEN'S HEALTH CARE IS POLITICAL

BREAST CANCER
AN EPIDEMIC

WHAM!
WOMEN'S HEALTH ACTION AND MOBILIZATION
212/713-5966

ONE WOMAN DIES
EVERY 3 MINUTES
WORLDWIDE
FROM A BOTCHED
ILLEGAL ABORTION

Take direct action for
free, safe, legal abortion
WHAM! Women's Health Action and Mobilization (212) 713-5966

SUPPORT
VAGINAL
PRIDE

BECAUSE WOMEN'S HEALTH CARE IS POLITICAL.

WOMEN'S HEALTH ACTION AND MOBILIZATION
WHAM! 212-713-5966

WOMEN DON'T

...ted thousands of Americans are suffering and dying from AIDS—without ever receiving an AIDS diagnosis.

...cause there are at least 15 documented symptoms of AIDS that the Centers for Disease Control (CDC) refuses to include in
...l case definition. Acute pelvic inflammatory disease, pulmonary tuberculosis, and rapidly progressing cervical cancer are
...m. These symptoms are occurring routinely in patients with seriously compromised immune systems—mostly women and
...drug users.

...he seriousness of CDC's omissions, the American Medical Association (AMA) recently stated in a public letter to CDC
...William Roper, "…*you must exercise your leadership by acting as quickly as possible to revise the case definition.*"

...C EXCLUDING WOMEN'S SYMPTOMS? The CDC claims many of them aren't life-threatening. Yet pelvic inflammatory
...women with HIV.

GET AIDS.

...ymptoms occur in people not infected with HIV. But so does common herpes, which *is* included in the current
...cluded because it can become severe and difficult to treat in the presence of HIV. But so can vaginal
...erion must be applied to all symptoms of AIDS.

...have enough research yet. Meanwhile, numerous published studies and hundreds of frontline health care
...ow HIV affects women. And, today women are the fastest growing population with HIV disease. According to
...e current [CDC] definition does not incorporate recent information on the manifestations of HIV disease in women
...e to integrate all currently available information into the case definition may be compromising women's health."

...NDERCOUNTING AIDS CASES KILLS. The CDC's failure to include these symptoms in their AIDS definition suppresses the true scope of
the AIDS pandemic. It distorts epidemiology vital to providing health care, investigating treatments and determining funding levels.
It leaves many individuals and physicians uninformed—tragically affecting education, prevention, diagnosis, and treatment, as well
as access to public benefits and insurance disbursements.

THEY JUST

WHEN WILL THE CDC DO ITS JOB? The CDC is the federal agency set up to chart the course of epidemics in this country, and to make
policy to stop the spread of illness. The CDC is failing. Instead of gathering accurate information and developing effective education
policies, the CDC continues to promote obstructive procedures such as mandatory testing—a plan that only serves to drive people
away from treatment.

The CDC's persistent refusal to expand the AIDS case definition is nothing short of willful and deadly negligence. This is why AIDS is
a crisis. *Every* American should be outraged.

Join the undersigned individuals and organizations and *demand* the immediate revision of the case definition of AIDS to include *all*
the symptoms identified by researchers and clinicians working with HIV-infected people. *Demand* that the CDC adjust its method of
collecting statistics to reflect "modes of transmission" instead of listing "risk groups." *Demand* that the CDC publicly support
voluntary and anonymous HIV testing.

DIE FROM IT.

place to work from. In fact, we were transient. Judson Church allowed us to use their meeting space but that was limited and could never become permanent. We would have meetings there and seemingly emotionally disturbed members of the anti-abortion group Operation Rescue would come in to disrupt them. With no home, no money, and few men (who tend to have money and power) in its membership, the organization was frail.

Nevertheless, in late August, we planned a series of demonstrations called October Outrage! The idea was to target Operation Rescue churches, fake abortion clinics, and the New York City-based National Right to Life Committee headquarters in an effort to keep the energy flowing that the July 5 demonstration had culled, and to increase our membership. While the demonstrations themselves were far from hard-hitting, I think they served to make us real to ourselves – always an important first step. We saw what we could do on a shoestring and without much experience, stealing xeroxing from our temp jobs, writing our first press releases, and dealing with police on the streets.

While October Outrage! was kicking off, Cardinal O'Connor announced his desire and intention to go on a "rescue," meaning an abortion clinic blockade. His pro-nouncement made the front page of *Newsday* on October 2, 1989. The next day, Victor Mendolia, a member of ACT UP, called wanting to know if, in response to the Cardinal's statement, WHAM! would want to work together with them to plan a demonstration against the Catholic Church's anti-gay, anti-abortion, anti-safe-sex, and anti-woman stance. I was thrilled and took his offer to the general WHAM! meeting for approval. A few of us were appointed to represent WHAM's interests in the demonstration planning and were asked to report back to the group from time to time.

"Stop the Church," as the demonstration was called, brought WHAM! into the spotlight. Held on December 5, 1989, at St Patrick's Cathedral, it drew over five thousand people to the streets on a cold Sunday morning. Inside, over one hundred people were arrested laying down in the aisles of the church, chanting "Your dogma is killing us!" With the Sunday morning mass completely disrupted, ACT UP and WHAM! had created bedlam within and without. The next day, every newspaper in New York City ran articles, editorials and columns responding, largely negatively, to the action.

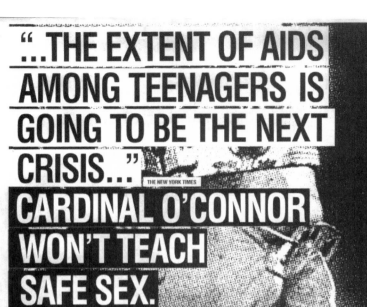

"...THE EXTENT OF AIDS AMONG TEENAGERS IS GOING TO BE THE NEXT CRISIS..." THE NEW YORK TIMES

CARDINAL O'CONNOR WON'T TEACH SAFE SEX.

STOP THE CHURCH

ACT UP
AIDS Coalition To Unleash Power

WHAM!
Women's Health Action and Mobilization

FIGHT ITS OPPOSITION TO ABORTION.
FIGHT ITS MURDEROUS AIDS POLICY.

TAKE DIRECT ACTION. TAKE CONTROL OF YOUR BODY.
For information call: 212-989-1114

MASSIVE PROTEST
SUNDAY • DECEMBER 10
9:30 AM
ST. PATRICK'S CATHEDRAL
5TH AVE. & 50TH STREET

At that point, although I was still devoted to WHAM!, I found myself becoming more involved with ACT UP. Shortly after Stop the Church, I was invited to go with ACT UP (on a financial scholarship) to Atlanta to demonstrate against anti-sodomy laws and to protest the shoddy AIDS-related epidemiological work being done by the Centers for Disease Control. I went to Atlanta, joined an affinity group, was arrested again, and, upon returning, became a regular attendee at ACT UP's famous Monday night meetings. I only dropped in on WHAM! from time to time and soon faded from the scene altogether, as I devoted my time to AIDS issues, especially as they concerned women and the Centers for Disease Control (CDC).

The CDC Working Group was campaign focused. We were single-minded in our pursuit and developed a complex strategic plan designed to change the definition of AIDS. We did a major postcard mailing responding to the CDC's proposed change to the definition. We held teach-ins nationwide. We had national days of local CDC office takeovers. During the International AIDS Conference in San Francisco, we took out a full-page newspaper ad in the *New York Times*, signed by over five hundred politicians and service providers, which read: "Women Don't Get AIDS. They Just Die From It."

Despite the successes, there were conflicts – such as how closely involved with outside institutions, politicians, and the state ACT UP should be – which resulted in the CDC working group becoming ad hoc.

The Holland Tunnel action

The biggest event the ad hoc group coordinated was in response to the 1992 Casey Supreme Court decision, which imposed a 24-hour waiting period on a woman requesting an abortion. We decided to choose a key exit route out of the city on what would be July 4 weekend and block it as a response to the ruling. Because we had no organizational backing, it was not clear how we would get people to participate. So, we made a poster that we wheat-pasted liberally which said, "Women Power, Time's UP! Shut Down the Holland Tunnel in Response to the Casey Decision." It gave no date for the action and no time either. Instead we listed three pre-action, civil disobedience trainings that a potential participant would have to attend. What was key was that no one knew the day or hour of the planned action. We wanted to train them in civil disobedience and create group solidarity. We trained about three hundred people in civil disobedience techniques and principles. We spoke of Gandhi and King.

We arranged for a pre-action meeting to be held at the Lesbian and Gay Community Services Center, but at the last minute they were served with an injunction, which would be brought against them if they allowed us to meet. Suddenly, we were homeless and forced to take our group down the street to a park. Someone in the group offered the roof of their building as a meeting space. At that meeting, which was dark and unnerving, we checked people's IDs at the door. Anyone who had not been through the CD training was not allowed up. Then, at the meeting, we collected support sheets from arrestees and gave them each a small piece of paper with an address on it, telling them to go to one of four locations.

The next morning some new people showed up at these appointed spots, which signaled to us that while our security was good, it was not foolproof. We sent them away. In these meeting spaces, no one was allowed to use a phone or to leave the premises. The police were at some of the locations but we later lost them through our creative tactical maneuvering. It was the mid-afternoon, on July 3, when over two hundred people blocked traffic. Some people chained themselves to each other to slow down the arrest process. Police did not arrive on the scene for at least ten minutes, enabling us to shut the Tunnel down successfully.

Conclusion

While the above is a kind of timeline, chronicling events over a number of years, there are a few things worth noting about the change in tactics. Our work became much less democratic and much more hierarchical. We expanded the affinity group model, so popular in WTO protests now, to accommodate the movement of hundreds of people. It is of crucial importance to note that our move toward a less democratic process reflected an increasing awareness of forms of surveillance being used to scare people away from direct action.

Beyond patient and polite: a call for direct action and civil disobedience on behalf of same-sex marriage

ERIC ROFES

The passage of the Knight Initiative by 62 percent of California voters in March 2000 may come to be seen as a turning point, igniting more intense activism in support of full participation in the institution of marriage. Even if progressive forces had defeated Proposition 22, marriage in California would still have been restricted to a man and a woman. Some of us have grown impatient and are no longer satisfied with strategies which fail to confront mainstream resistance to same-sex marriage directly.

We've had enough of people thinking this is too radical an issue to win mainstream support, except in rare parts of the nation which still value participatory democracy. We are tired of liberal politicians and patronizing journalists denouncing the Knight Initiative while simultaneously arguing that marriage should be reserved for mixed-sex couples. We're not content with heterosexuals enjoying the advantages of state-sanctioned marriage while same-sex couples grovel for a watered-down imitation – domestic partnership. And we're dissatisfied with this struggle remaining in the hands of gay organizations that conceptualize activist strategy only through the lens of the traditional legal and electoral machinery.

Some activists have had enough of the patient and polite organizing methods of the past decade. We've learned the ACT UP lessons that were so critical to AIDS organizing in the late 1980s. Some of us may quit the courts, retreat from legislatures, and exit professional press briefings. Instead, we may take up the tactics most necessary for social change but largely absent from a contemporary queer movement composed almost entirely of suit-and-skirt lobbyists, splashy television advertisements, and upscale black-tie dinner banquets: direct action and mass civil disobedience.

We're tired of lefter-than-thou people thinking this issue is not "radical enough" to merit the attention of progressive queers and their allies. We see no contradiction between working to democratize the institution of marriage, even as we make efforts to undercut the cultural dominance of this problematic institution. We can work, in the long haul, with groups such as the Boston-based Alternatives of Marriage Project, to demand opportunities which nurture and support forms of organizing our relationships outside the confines of state-sanctioned marriage, but will also recognize that, for the foreseeable future, marriage will remain a hegemonic institution to which access should be guaranteed regardless of sexual orientation or gender. Smug middle-class gay activists have the economic and social capital that allow them to hold marriage at a distance, but many poor and working-class LGBT couples understand the legal, economic, and social benefits which would accrue to them once same-sex marriage is won. Likewise, for queers in relationships with recent immigrants to the United States, marriage affords the opportunity to avoid lengthy and expensive legal procedures to try to avoid being separated by the authorities and instead win official citizenship.

In this next, more militant phase of efforts to win same-sex marriage, justice-minded individuals, liberal politicians, and civil rights leaders may no longer be granted the luxury of talking out of both sides of their mouths. One will either be for full and democratic participation in the institutions of our culture, or be an advocate for discrimination. There will no longer be a viable position of neutrality.

Queers should refuse to attend mixed-sex weddings

These days, when I receive an invitation to the marriage of heterosexual friends, family members, or students, I am filled with outrage. What nerve! Sending an invitation to me (and, often, my lover) with no reference to the fact that I am being asked to participate as an observer in an event in which I am not legally permitted to be a central participant! There is no note acknowledging the disparity and injustice, no sheepish apology for participating in an institution of segregation, no phone call checking-in about the politics of it all.

It may be time for queers to stop letting heterosexuals off the hook. They embrace marriage uncritically only because we let them. And they will continue to be blind to the politics of engagements, marriage, and weddings until they are forced to see them as segregated rituals and institutions that must be challenged, undermined, and transformed. Lesbian, gay, bisexual, and transgender (LGBT) people and our allies may be ready to take direct action by refusing wedding invitations and articulating our reasons loudly, holding demonstrations at daily newspapers which continue to run marriage columns that are not accessible to all, and disrupting television shows, such as *Who Wants to Marry a Millionaire?* or *The Newlywed Game*, which are conceptualized around an institution currently founded on exclusivity and bigotry.

Social change on cutting-edge issues rarely occurs in the absence of a direct action strategy. Building on rich traditions of militant organizing, inspired most recently by ACT UP but rooted in the tactics of the Civil Rights Movement, women's liberation, and antinuclear activism, these efforts may be what is needed to transform current campaigns for equal access to marriage into an authentic movement for social justice and participatory democracy. Activists may take their struggle directly to the people, using powerful organizing methods strategically designed to create a critical consciousness about the politics of marriage, inspire a movement of street activists passionately committed to bringing about change, and force the issue into an arena of intense public scrutiny.

Same-sex couples must undermine the marriage bureaucracy

Holding a mass queer wedding every time there is a march on Washington or the mayor of San Francisco organizes such an event in City Hall may no longer be enough. These polite and patient rituals are in the same relationship to the direct action strategies proposed here that the AIDS quilt was to ACT UP. A marriage simulation does not in and of itself function as civil disobedience. And many people have come to believe that candlelight vigils are an inadequate response to anti-gay votes. Such vigils are not the same as political protest. We may need more than candles, more than photo ops, more than sloganeering. The time may be right for the kind of carefully crafted actions that demonstrate a new level of serious intent about this issue, and place same-sex marriage in the public eye in a compelling and confrontational manner. We may soon see national networks of activists plotting massive civil disobedience actions focused on undercutting key points of access to the institution of marriage.

There has been a small but very important stream of civil disobedience actions in the marriage fight. They have involved members of the clergy who violate orders from denominational authorities and perform same-sex marriages at tremendous risk to their careers. These clergy members have been put on trial, censored, and even defrocked for their actions. In the post-Knight Initiative era, let's hope we see more clergy with integrity take similar actions.

At the same time, LGBT activists themselves might be ready to follow the lead of these clergy members. We might see coordinated days of action when same-sex couples attempt to register at the local county clerk's office. Imagine the impact if same-sex couples in rural areas, small-town America, urban centers, and suburban neighborhoods throughout the nation on the same day and at the same time showed up couple-by-couple and stood in line to fill out the forms to register for marriage. Imagine if they requested the proper forms and replied to refusals with a pre-determined response grounded in passive resistance. Imagine if they were all trained to alert local media outlets, organize teams of vocal supporters, and articulate a calm, impactful message in response to this closed institution. Imagine if they returned every day for a week or a month voicing the same powerful statement.

Or imagine same-sex couples chaining themselves peaceably to the front doors of the offices of their neighborhood justice of the peace and singing songs of liberation as they were carted off to jail. Or choosing to appear in large numbers outside the churches where prominent politicians or celebrities were getting married, silently holding up signs stating "Participation in Marriage is Participation in Injustice," or "Saying I Do when We Can't = Bigotry" Or crashing local wedding ceremonies at the moment where the officiator asks for any objections, standing up and reciting a speech about the shameful inequity of access to marriage.

Justice-minded heterosexual couples must boycott marriage until it is democratized

It has been wonderful to witness large numbers of supportive heterosexuals – especially heterosexuals under the age of thirty – decrying barriers to same-sex marriage. As the debates intensify and the stakes increase, LGBT activists will begin to urge these folks to back up their rhetoric with principled action. Justice-minded heterosexuals could make a major contribution to undermining the status quo by refusing to participate in the institution of marriage until it is open to all. The Boston-based Alternatives to Marriage Project is leading organizing efforts to popularize alternatives to patriarchal marriage for all people.

Some heterosexual allies already understand that marriage is a form of heterosexual privilege that comes at the expense of queer rights, gender equality, and social justice. They understand that marriage grants them a whole set of advantages, benefits, and legal privileges that are subsidized by queer folks and others who do not marry. We actively pay for what many others see as normal, universal, and sacred. This leads many activists to argue that we should be fighting for the strong domestic partnership laws currently in place in many northern European nations – for both same-sex and mixed-sex couples. In these nations, marriage simply becomes a religious "add-on" outside the realm of state sanction.

During a period when same-sex couples cannot marry, the taking of such vows by mixed-sex couples will increasingly be named for what it is: an act of willful participation in an institution that is neither democratic nor open to all. Heterosexuals getting married is analogous to Christians joining a club that excludes Jews, men working as partners in a law firm that has no female partners, or whites supporting the flying of the Confederate flag over public buildings intended to serve people of all races. No matter how one wishes to frame them, such choices are inherently ethical choices: participation in rituals and institutions that exclude sectors of society puts you on the side of discrimination and oppression.

It may be time not only for true heterosexual allies to say no to marriage until all people have equal access, but also for all principled people to engage in public education around their refusal to accept privilege. Will we begin to see groups marching outside religious institutions and county clerk offices under banners such as "Hetero-Couples Refusing to Marry Until All Can Marry," or "Until All Are Welcome, None Must Participate: Free Marriage Now!"? Will we begin to hear from the children raised by mixed-sex couples who take a justice-minded stand and refuse to get married until same-sex couples can get married? Is now the time to put an economic dent in the wedding industry, as a result of large numbers of heterosexuals refusing to open their wallets for marriage licenses, wedding receptions, bridal dresses, photographers, and honeymoon excursions? Imagine if heterosexual allies publicly burned their marriage certificates?

There is an important historical precedent for this kind of privilege-refusing action. During the Civil Rights Movement, a number of white people repulsed by the injustices of racism declined to participate in key institutions of segregation. They refused to utilize white-only public facilities, ride on buses which forced Blacks to the back seats, and sit at segregated lunch counters. Likewise, there have been men who resigned from clubs that excluded Jews, women, and people of color, and people with inherited wealth who have given away their legacies to organizations in poor communities working for economic redistribution. It is time for such visionary pioneers to emerge in this battle against heterosexism.

Some argue that the queers predisposed to militant activism do not see marriage as a priority and view the institution as problematic; those who value marriage may be less inclined towards tactics of direct action. As in all social justice movements, radical activism won't be everyone's cup of tea. Yet we have learned from voter initiatives such as those ending affirmative action and jettisoning bilingual programs in public schools that California is the right's testing ground for regressive initiatives. The passage of the Knight Initiative by voters of the largest and most trend-setting state in the nation should compel us immediately to break through earlier barriers to militancy and rethink our cautious strategy and limited tactics.

Social change movements that lack a direct action component and don't take seriously the power of civil disobedience risk becoming nothing more than symbolic demands and rhetorical hype. Same-sex marriage will become a reality throughout the United States sometime this century. It will come about more expeditiously, and with a greater public understanding of the links between gay marriage and participatory democracy, if we replace strategies of pleading and bargaining with the tactics of a true social change movement.

Note

The author is grateful for the feedback of Wayne Hoffman, Joan E. Biren, Diane Sabin, Dave Orphal, Liz Highleyman, Kate Clinton, Margo Okazawa-Rey, Jim Mitulski, Eileen Hansen, Will Seng, Marshall Miller, and Michael Scarce as he worked on this essay.

Amanda Milan and the rebirth of the Street Trans Action Revolutionaries

BENJAMIN SHEPARD

We met in the park across from Stonewall Inn. A group of club kids with Afros, guys with loop earrings, high heels, and Mae West sunglasses, led the crowd as we stepped off:

> One: we are the people!!!!!!!!
> Two: a little bit louder!!!!!!!!!
> Three: we want justice for Amanda!!!!!!!!!

we chanted over and over again. The infectious chant carried us most of the way from the Sheridan Square downtown to 100 Center Street, where the Amanda Milan trial was being held the following day. Milan, a transgender woman, had been murdered in Times Square on June 20, 2000, days before Manhattan Pride march. Shortly after Milan's death, Stonewall legend Sylvia Rivera had successfully reformed her Street Trans Action Revolutionaries (STAR) to make sure Milan was not forgotten. In the time since Milan's death, her memory has come to symbolize the unfinished business of a GLBT movement, which has all too often left transgender people at the back of the bus. Once at Center Street, we began reading names of transgendered folks who, like Amanda, had been lost – some to bigots' violence, the whereabouts of some unknown, others to drug overdoses, and others casualties of a subterranean black-market economy, where so many transgendered people find themselves, at the margins of our cities and history.

"It was believed for centuries that it was necessary to hide sexual matters because they were shameful," Michel Foucault (1980: x–xi) observed on the question of gender insubordination and its implications for a repressive culture. "We now know that it is sex itself which hides the most secret parts of the individual: the structure of his fantasies, the roots of his ego, the forms of his relationship to reality. At the bottom of sex there is truth." Certainly, sex structured the form of Amanda's relationship to reality. Rumors abounded about Milan's death. In the weeks following, the papers ambiguously dropped hints about a "transpanic." Melissa Schlarz, a long-time trans advocate, had seen it before:

> My time hanging around the Times Square transsexual scene goes back to the mid 1970s. Amanda Milan was just the latest. People from all over the world, transgenders, come to Times Square. Everyone knows that's where something is happening. In the past it was always the West Village or Times Square. What exactly was she doing? The trial is coming, we'll have to wait and see.

According to the Audre Lorde Project, 25-year-old Amanda Milan was brutally murdered in front of Show World, a former porn house, where many trannies worked in the Times Square neighborhood of Manhattan. Milan was an African-American woman of transgender experience. According to accounts, two men began to verbally assault Amanda Milan in front of the Port Authority terminal, with one man exclaiming, "I know you're really a man." While Amanda tried to get into a cab, eyewitnesses say that one man handed the other a knife, which was used to slash her throat. She bled to death on the way to St Vincent's Hospital. Some reports indicated that several onlookers laughed and applauded as the assault took place.

Transsexuals have been dying in New York for years. What makes the Milan case significant is that until Amanda Milan no one responded. Transgender folks, loosely defined as moving from one gender to another, have always been misunderstood and quite often marginalized. "They have always been people of the shadows, people of the night," Schlarz explained.

> I knew a lot of friends when I was younger, they never went out during the daytime. It was a life filled around the night. Transsexual people are still illegal in New York State. There is no protection. You can be thrown out of your home, thrown out of your job; you can be denied healthcare. So we're fighting for basic civil rights now. I've known lots of people who died of drug overdoses, people who died of violence, people who drank themselves to death, and some of them I remember very vividly. So I would like this to be about her and about us. I did not know her but I've known hundreds of girls like her.

When Rivera heard about Milan, she told herself that this time it was going to be different. This was not going to be an unsolved murder. So she made sure "the girls came out." In the days before the demo, Bob Kohler, Sylvia Rivera's long-time friend, put out the call for the pre-trial demo:

> I know you all realize how important this action is and if you multiply that by 100 you come close to what it means to the trannie community. For what it's worth, it is also extremely important to me – I have been involved in trannie issues for a very long time and, of course, Sylvia has been a part of my life for over thirty years.... It is an extremely important event for a community whose time, as Sylvia says, "has come." In my mind, it is equally as important to the LGBTQ community as a whole. Sylvia has been there for us at every turn and she is counting on us to help support her now.

Bob was referring to Sylvia's lifelong willingness to put herself on the line for the cause of gay liberation. As Sylvia will tell you, in the year after Stonewall, drag queens petitioned and were arrested fighting for the gay rights bill. "Drag queens could be out there," Sylvia, who was one of the arrestees, explained.

Back then, Rivera was a young street kid, who'd risen to fame through a willingness to engage in direct action. When she was arrested during the Matthew Shepard political funeral, an unresolved 25-year-old charge from that era popped up. It was one of countless charges faced by an activist who'd first been arrested as a teenager back in 1963. She explained:

> Yeah, it was a 25-year-old warrant. It was for breaking the window at Silver Dollar Restaurant in the Village, from a fight with the owners. Most of my arrests have been in a lot of political things. And part of my arrest record was loitering with the intent of prostitution. And out of all them arrests all the times that I have been in and out of jail, I have only served time once. I did ninety days for possession of heroin. That's the only time and I promised that I would never visit Rikers Island again and I haven't.

Rivera co-founded the original Street Transvestite Action Revolutionaries (STAR) in 1971 with the late Marsha P. Johnston as a caucus from the Gay Liberation Front. The feeling was that the nascent Gay Liberation Movement needed to bring a little bit more focus to the transgender community. In addition, there were a lot of transgender youth who needed both services and a public voice. When STAR was formed, it was the nation's first trans political organization. The Street Transvestite Action Revolutionaries would serve as a radical street action group to promote the rights of transgender people. They did this by forming a space for transgender people to live and by maintaining a visible trans presence in the streets.

I asked Rivera why Street was in the title. "Because we were street kids. And we needed to emphasize that." Sex work remained a subtext for much of our conversation, which I asked Sylvia about,

> Well, it happens historically because the mainstream gay community who have obtained their rights have left us off of all of their bills. People do not have to hire the transgender women or men because there are no laws protecting us. And this is part of one of my arguments with the community right now. And that's one of the reasons why at the beginning of this year I decided to resurrect STAR. If we continue to be invisible, people are not going to listen to us. And if we ourselves don't stand up for ourselves, nobody else will do that for us. And we have allowed them to speak for us. There was nobody out there who was willing to step on their toes. And this is why STAR has had to come back to existence and we have to push people like the Human Rights Campaign, the Empire State Agenda, the Community Center. Every big corporate group that is gay and lesbian has to be put in their place.
>
> I'm just tired of seeing our children, our future, out there prostituting their lives away, taking drugs, being turned away from proper housing or medical care. I will turn fifty on July 2. I have been out there on the streets for forty years and nothing has changed for my community. It makes me very angry to know that there are women out there that have college degrees that are standing on drugs, selling their bodies on the street corners. It does not make any sense. And the same thing with the youth. Everybody praises the Hetric Martin Institute. Hetric Martin is the worst institution there could be for a transgender child. The staff there are not trans friendly and the gay and lesbian children are less friendly than the staff. And they are more abusive than the heterosexuals. And so these children go to the street. We have no other choice. It's the only way to survive. The law says it's a crime. It's a victimless crime.

Beyond Matthew Shepard

Shortly after Milan's death, STAR organized a call for an end to anti-trans violence, and also to recognize the intersections of transphobia, racism, sexism, classism and homophobia. The message was that the lives of trans people of color are not expendable. On July 24, 2000, the memorial service for Amanda united the trans community as never before. There were powerful testimonials from her friends and family, and a particular call for trans self-reliance from Octavia St Laurent. Then there was a march to the murder site. Activist after activist spoke, the refrain the same: "We were on the streets in Matthew Shepard's memory – Now is the time to be on the streets for Amanda!"

Yet the mainstream gay communities have not been in the streets for transgender people. In the years after STAR's demise as the movement assimilated, the guys in the Brooks Brothers' suits distanced themselves from, in Larry Kramer's words, "those guys, girls, whatever you call them…" (see Crimp 1988: 251; Shepard 2001). And the transgender legacy of Stonewall was left behind. However, there is progress on certain fronts. The Sex and Gender Liberation Institute of the 1999 National Lesbian and Gay Task Force Meetings in Oakland was a highlight of the weekend. Nevertheless, the problems on the streets persist.

Under attack in the West Village

Much of the current anti-trans violence begins with a tolerance for anti-trans rhetoric, even in gay communities. Melissa Sklarz suggests that "The initial problem started in the far West Village, which strangely enough is still going on today where the community, the people that own homes there, feel that they are being victimized by the transgender prostitutes." The result has become a class war between home owners at the center of New York's affluent gay West Village and transgender sex workers, many homeless, who have traditionally worked the meatpacking district on the periphery of the city. Yet with the move toward privatization, once accessible public areas, such as Times Square, have become hot commodities for real estate. "The doors have already been closed, sex clubs shut down, youth centers closed. The places for trans youth to go, places where this stuff used to go on, such as the Chelsea piers, were fenced off," one advocate argued at one of the increasingly vocal West Village community forums on prostitution. "Most of these hookers are not white. They are black and Hispanic," one observer screamed. The subtext at many of these meetings is a cultural sexism and racism, with a transphobia at its center. "These are not our regular Greenwich Village queens that we've enjoyed and appreciated," a member of a local street association noted. "These are low-class, vulgar transvestites that come from other areas of the city" (Horowitz 1998).

I attended one of these forums, where I mentioned that New York state was approaching its five-year time limit on welfare reform and these were just workers, making a living like anyone else. I was booed. "Tell 'em to go work at McDonald's!"

one man screamed. When I replied that the job market for applicants without general equivalency degrees has absorbed more workers than it can absorb (see Wilson 1996) and that there are ten applicants for every one job opening for workers without GEDs (see Carlson and Theodore 1995), the screaming just got louder.

And the attacks continued. While the mainstream gays on the "left" demonized transgender sex workers, the city's real-estate-driven Quality of Life Campaign successfully pushed for the closure of several clubs, including Edleweiss, the Greenwich Pub, and Butterfield, where trans folk worked and hung out, shut down because of obscure city ordinances. As Stonewall teaches us, attacks on queer spaces are also attacks on queer identity.

The attacks on transgender identity function on many levels. While the APA did away with diagnosing homosexuality as a psychiatric disorder in the early 1970s, the term "gender identity disorder," used to refer to trans folk, remains a psychiatric classification within the current APA Diagnostic and Statistical Manual of Mental Disorders, volume 4 (see APA 2000). The overinclusive category pathologizes gender nonconformity in its broadest terms, classifying anything from "cross dressing" to "involvement in a transvestic subculture" among symptomatic criteria for mental illness. Psychiatric diagnosis on the basis of social, cultural, or political affiliation evokes the darkest memories of medical abuse in American history (Wilson 2001). Recall that women suffragettes who demanded the right to vote in the early 1900s were diagnosed and institutionalized with a label of "hysteria" (Mayor 1974). Bolsheviks, immigrants, and labor organizers of the same period were labeled as socially deviant and mentally defective (Dowbiggin 1997). In truth, transgender support organizations, such as STAR, are the primary source of support, education, and civil rights advocacy for gender-variant people, families, friends, and allies (Wilson 2001; Wilson and Hammond 1996).

Building a community

For a number of years in the 1970s and 1980s, Sylvia, who suffered from chemical dependence, was homeless herself. (She's been sober for over two years now.) Nonetheless, she continued organizing, organizing a community of trans squatters who lived on the piers on the West Side of Manhattan. Like many of the street kids, they have since been pushed out of that space. But the process was just a part of Sylvia's lifetime of building spaces, such as the original STAR House, where transgender people can be part of a community.

As activists will contend, the idea of a unified community is still very new. Until ten years ago, there were transvestites and cross-dressers and transsexuals and pre-op and post-op and there was no single unifying identity. The concept of a social and political identity for transgender people is still fresh. Yet activists have worked to turn it from an idea into something that is real. Once you can define it, you can start defending it.

The new mobilization among trans folks is already bearing results. In spring 2001, when a transgender dancer was dismissed from a local dance club, STAR organized a midnight picket line outside the club. Building on a nascent queer/labor alliance (see Krupat and McCreery 2001), members of STAR, the Housing Works Transgender Working Group, and the New York Direct Action Network Labor Group packed a rambunctious line, successfully turning almost all patrons away while offering suggestions for some better spots to go to. The club closed within a few weeks.

Sklarz ponders,

> Would the police have worked on a murder like this in the past, we don't know. I knew transsexuals, who were sex workers, who would get in fights with straight men, who would go to prison. I knew girls who would go to men's prison even though they had been living as women for years. I think it's only with this heightened political environment that police, specifically, and our culture, in general, are beginning to look at all these people differently and the right of these people; however odious sex work may be, it's something. You pointed out when you sat down: what do you do with people that have been thrown out of their schools – they are incapable of working, yet you've got to survive.

A call for social justice

Martin Luther King (1986) once said that "Human salvation lies in the hands of the creatively maladjusted." Perhaps. However, labeling any person's gender expression as mental illness is oppressive, with a widening segment of gender-nonconforming youth and adults subject to diagnosis of psychosexual disorder, stigma, loss of civil liberty, and political violence (Wilson 2001; Wilson and Hammond 1996).

"For many, Amanda Milan has become not a martyr, but a rallying cry. The activism around her death showed the world transgender people belong in the queer community and that what happens to one transgender girl at four in the morning outside the Port Authority is about everyone," Sklarz concluded. The message from activists is that there is no difference between Matthew Shepard and Amanda Milan. The response to her death tells the non-queer community: enough, today the violence stops. "It is not OK anymore. It is not OK for people to die because they are sex workers or die because they have AIDS or die because of drugs and alcohol."

STAR was born from Gay Liberation Front and its vision of global solidarity. Throughout the years, Sylvia Rivera has maintained that spirit. While she considers the Matthew Shepard political funeral – where she spent the night in jail – one of the best demonstrations she ever attended, she considers sleeping in the street to protest cutbacks on homeless services, as she did last January, just as important. "We're not free till everyone is free," Rivera maintains. "Part of our mission statement is to be out there for all oppressed people."

The challenge of sex and gender liberation requires building spaces for countless identities and genders on a foundation of social justice. To the extent that we challenge today's culture of sexual privilege, we are all offered the possibility of social transformation. These are things we can all benefit from. Gender fluidity is truly a revolutionary idea. "It's between the ears," Schlarz repeated. When that is free, STAR's work will be done.

When private clubs serve the public

SUSAN WRIGHT

Whatever your sexual fantasy, most likely you keep it buried deep inside yourself. That's because we're taught to hide our sexual desires, even from ourselves, by making sick jokes about sex or feeling shocked repugnance at the possibility these fantasies could be exposed. It feels dangerous, and for some of us that makes it even more exciting.

But the only way to know yourself sexually is to acknowledge your desires and to face the things that drive you wild. For millions of people, their fantasies include things like sadomasochism – the consensual exchange of power and/or the intense stimulation of the body and mind. Some have fetishes for things like rubber and leather, or for certain parts of the body like feet or breasts. Most people get off on watching real glistening bodies grinding in animal pleasure, while many others enjoy being watched as they lose themselves in ecstasy.

This is a good and healthy thing. Unfortunately there is a small minority of Americans who think the only way you should have sex is the way *they* want do it – missionary intercourse between married couples for procreational purposes. Well if that's what they want, then fine; but it's not what I or millions of other people want. The problem is, this anti-sex minority is controlling what kind of sexual experience the rest of us can have.

One of the places this happened was in Baltimore City, where three SM clubs were closed down by the zoning board. Starting in December 1999, the SM–leather–

fetish community in Baltimore City lost their right to do SM in any setting other than their own home. The consequences of losing these educational venues were so serious that local and national SM activists were able to enlist some behind-the-scenes support from a few civil rights and GLBT organizations to help fight for the right to have SM clubs.

Most GLBT organizations don't respond when the police crack down on "public sex." Instead, privacy rights have long been touted by gay activists as a surefire way to gain our sexual freedom. Yet state legislators have long regulated what happens in private. One example is the old sodomy laws that continue to be selectively enforced against queers. The Supreme Court has used the "right to privacy" to give people the right to have an abortion, buy contraception, and to acquire certain kinds of pornography. But the Supreme Court has also refused to invoke the right to privacy to strike down state laws that prohibit sodomy, as well as hundreds of laws that restrict the sale of sex toys, pornography, and sexually related activities. That's why the sexual freedom movement is fighting for the right to have consensual public sex, as well as consensual sex in private.

Defining public sex

Too often public sex is narrowly defined as the places where gay men meet other men – in T-rooms, parks, backrooms, or bathhouses. But there are millions of people of every sexual orientation who regularly engage in consensual public sex. Most of this sex happens in so-called "private clubs" that are open to the public.

Aside from the SM–leather–fetish communities, swingers are the largest community of sex-loving people practicing public sex. People in the "lifestyle" are generally heterosexual and bisexual couples who quietly gather together in hundreds of private clubs across the country to socialize and sometimes have really hot sex. The sheer number of these clubs indicates that they fulfill a need that our society doesn't otherwise satisfy. Swing clubs or sex clubs offer a safe haven for public sex, complete with consent from one's spouse and condoms available on every shelf.

For legal purposes, sex clubs are usually licensed as private clubs and you must be a member to enter. But these clubs are open to the public, allowing people to sign up on the spot and pay extra for their "membership." Defining the space as "private" has allowed these clubs to get around those pesky state and local statutes that restrict our sexual expression. The question is – how long will sex clubs be able to function under the privacy label?

In particular, zoning laws have become the vanguard of anti-sex legislation. Zoning laws passed by city councils have restricted adult bookstores, peep shows, and strip joints in a growing number of cities across America. Many municipalities also have zoning laws that restrict the formation of private sex clubs. In some cities, for-profit private clubs must go through a public hearing held by the city council. When alcohol is brought into the picture, the situation gets even more complicated.

Baltimore City crackdown

In Baltimore City the zoning laws were so vague that zoning officials could basically interpret them as they wished. In late 1999 a zoning official decided that the regulations regarding adult entertainment (which were originally written for strip clubs) were deemed applicable to the three local venues that catered to SM practitioners.

First the zoning officials targeted the Phoenix Society, a five-year-old nonprofit, social and educational group. The Phoenix Society caught the attention of zoning when it moved its clubhouse to a residential area in Brooklyn, Maryland. The residents complained about the unusual number of cars parked on the streets during evening hours, so a zoning-enforcement officer visited the club. Phoenix was cited for having an improper occupancy permit and for providing adult entertainment without a license. The Phoenix Society left the building and the group disbanded.

Only a few days later a zoning official attended a party hosted by a private group at the PlayHouse Studio and Gallery. Zoning Superintendent Donald Small said his officer "observed about thirty people in various stages of dress engaging in behaviors we certainly believe were adult entertainment." The proprietors of the PlayHouse Studio were fined $500 and told by authorities to cease holding SM events. PlayHouse did not have a license for adult entertainment but they were in a building in the proper zone to have such a license.

Then Club Orpheus was cited and fined for providing unlicensed adult entertainment, specifically a weekly fetish dance party hosted by the SM organization called Baltimore Bound. Orpheus remained open as a nightclub and dance hall but SM activity could no longer take place in the "dungeon" that Bound promoters had recently installed in the club's basement.

Housing Department spokesperson Zach Germroth denied that they were singling out and closing SM establishments, citing a larger eighteen-month-old citywide crackdown on zoning violations. But Superintendent Small acknowledged that the closing of the Phoenix Society was "what really fired this whole thing."

Building a campaign

Quite likely the zoning officials thought that no one would protest their actions. But they didn't realize they were dealing with a large and well-informed SM–leather–fetish community in Baltimore City. The number of concerned people is not surprising when you consider the statistics provided by the 1990 *Kinsey New Report on Sex*, which states that 5 to 10 percent of US adults practice some form of sadomasochism. The Internet has helped an increasing number of people acknowledge their SM interests and fantasies. These millions of adults are joining and creating new educational and social groups in exploding numbers.

In Baltimore City, the activists protested that SM clubs couldn't be licensed as adult entertainment venues because the regulations had been amended in October 1999 to prohibit "flagellation." Therefore it was impossible for an SM club to operate as an adult entertainment establishment. Yet the zoning officials were citing these clubs for not being licensed as adult entertainment. Rather than let this contradiction sit unopposed, the local SM–leather–fetish practitioners formed an advocacy group called Baltimore Advocating Tolerance & Education for Alternative Sexual Expression (Baltimore AT EASE). They also called in help from the National Coalition for Sexual Freedom (NCSF), a national advocacy and lobbying coalition that has a special commitment to the SM–leather–fetish communities because its members suffer significant discrimination and persecution due to their sexuality.

The local activists realized that the first step to getting back their SM clubs was to win over the mayor and city council. A letter-writing campaign was started that sent 150 pro-SM letters to Mayor Martin O'Malley's office. When it became known that Mayor O'Malley would attend the GLBT Triangle Ball at the Hippo early in 2000, Baltimore AT EASE seized the moment. During the Triangle Ball, the director of Baltimore AT EASE, Leigha Fleming, went on stage and pinned a distinctive Leather Pride pin on Mayor O'Malley's lapel. The activists also publicly pinned the mayor's chief of staff and the head of the city council just to be sure the pin would be recognized. Numerous members of the SM–leather–fetish communities proudly wore their own Leather Pride pins, and they each went through the receiving line to shake the mayor's hand and thank him for his support in amending the zoning laws. It was a memorable event and certainly prompted city officials to listen to the pleas of this vocal subculture in their city.

Representatives from Baltimore AT EASE and NCSF met with the Baltimore City Council President Sheila Dixon to discuss a resolution to the crisis. "Obviously, it's of great concern to us if a group is being unfairly targeted," said Dixon's chief of staff, Anthony McCarthy. "We want to make sure there's no discrimination going on here." As Judy Guerin, NCSF's executive director, explained, "We let it be known that we were ready to launch a national media frenzy detailing how Baltimore was persecuting a sexual minority. We were really prepared to do that, as well as take some legal actions that we think would have worked."

Building a community

Once the doors were open, SM activists spent months educating the mayor and city council that SM practitioners must be allowed to get together to teach each other the techniques involved in things like safe bondage and SM. Of the five hundred educational and social SM–leather–fetish organizations in America, most sponsor hands-on workshops and educational demonstrations. Some, like TES in New York City, have workshops several times a week to meet the high demand. These social organizations are run by volunteers who offer to spend their time showing others how safely to have a good experience exploring their sexuality.

Is this public sex? Most people would say so. But as well as being sexually satisfying, it serves a necessary educational need. Mainstream society is rife with harmful stereotypes about SM that confuse consensual activities with violence and abuse. In reality, SM is a loving form of sexual expression. The community is governed by the creed known as "Safe, Sane and Consensual." This means that all participants must understand and agree to what they're doing. Key to consent is that at any time the activity can be stopped if it doesn't feel good.

Safety education isn't the only thing that's needed. SM practitioners come together to talk about limits, how to set them, and how to ensure that activities are consensual. They discuss things like: In what ways can people be coerced into having sex? When can limits be pushed? What about scenes that involve humiliation – when do they cross the line and become verbal abuse? These questions and many more are discussed constantly by educational and social groups.

But it's not enough to talk. We have to show each other how to safely and pleasurably stimulate the human body. So SM practitioners play together at parties. Parties have rules that must be followed, which include "Safe, Sane and Consensual." There are also basic etiquette rules that prohibit touching anyone without permission, or interrupting a scene, for example. Parties also offer a way for our community to self-police our members. Most parties have volunteers who act as Dungeon Monitors – an oxymoronic name for people who watch to make sure scenes are done safely and consensually. These volunteers are empowered to step in and stop a scene if they see something going amiss. Parties offer a communal environment, and a safe place to get together with someone new.

Some SM practitioners want to gather simply to offer support to each other. People who do SM often feel isolated and rejected because of their sexuality. According to a survey by the National Coalition For Sexual Freedom, 80 percent of SM practitioners are closeted about their SM activities because of fear of persecution or discrimination. Many people never tell their family or friends, while some feel they can't even tell their partner about their desires because of the misrepresentation and stereotypes about SM.

Despite these inequalities, there are some members of the SM–leather–fetish communities who resist the "mainstreaming" of SM. These practitioners believe it takes away some of the mystery and power of SM to expose its workings for everyone to see. Some say this sort of sexuality inherently cannot be explained. Others have claimed that SM isn't a team sport, and that it's subject only to the desires of those involved. Still others like their sexual expression to be considered "edgy" or "dangerous" because it adds to their own experiences in some way.

Yet it seems everyone knows someone who has been persecuted or arrested because they do consensual SM, or because they cross-dress, or because they have a body modification. These people don't deserve to lose their jobs or custody of their kids, and they don't deserve to be stigmatized by sex-phobic people. That's why activists and advocacy organizations are being actively supported by the SM–leather–fetish communities in their outreach efforts. Allowing bigotry and intolerance to continue in the name of some sort of "mystique" is clearly a self-defeating attitude.

Working for our rights

Another case in point is the San Diego Six. Just before the Baltimore closings, in the fall of 1999, six people were arrested in San Diego for engaging in SM activities at a party in a rented space. The six adults were charged with "lewd and indecent behavior." The SM–leather–fetish communities rallied to raise tens of thousands of dollars for their defense. When the first defendant, who pleaded not guilty, was brought to trial in late 1999, the jury threw out the case. Charges against the other five were dropped, and the Police Department's Vice Unit finally began discussions with local educational and social groups so SM events could take place in San Diego.

In Baltimore City, after successful outreach to Mayor O'Malley and the city council, Baltimore AT EASE continued to pursue options with the zoning board. It took six months of dialogue before a compromise was reached. The Zoning Administrator David Tanner wrote a letter to NCSF on May 30, 2000, stating:

> After consideration of our discussion and review of your written description of the types of SM activities, I agree that SM activities will not be considered adult entertainment or adult entertainment businesses as defined in the Zoning Ordinance of Baltimore City. The establishment of SM activities in a private club setting would comply with the Zoning Ordinance of Baltimore City. At our last meeting, we reviewed the definition of private clubs, both non-profit and for-profit and what zoning district would allow them. We also agreed to continue an open dialog concerning this issue.

Now that Baltimore AT EASE and NCSF had gotten the city officials to agree, thousands of dollars were needed to pay the lawyers who would write the new zoning code. Baltimore AT EASE sponsored a series of creative efforts that raised money over the following year, including a formal Christmas cocktail party, a Valentine's dance and dinner, a crab feast in Kent Narrows, a picnic in Patapsco State Park, and even a Fetish Casino night complete with "kinky bucks" for people to play with. They also sponsored a variety of educational workshops from "How to talk to the cops" to sensual massage and basic bondage.

Finally, on May 1, 2001, the new zoning code was accepted and went into effect in Baltimore City. SM educational and social clubs were legal in Baltimore. This success was seen as a major victory by the sexual freedom movement. "It shows how effective this movement can be when mobilized and focused on its goals," stated Judy Guerin, executive director of NCSF. "This issue reached a high level of visibility within the Mayor's office as a direct result of the efforts of Baltimore AT EASE and the strong support of the local and national communities. This demonstrates how a united community effort can bring greater understanding and directly effect change."

However, this success in Baltimore City doesn't mean that clubs in other cities are safe. In June 2000 in Attleboro, Massachusetts, a private party was raided and the owner was charged with running a "house of ill-repute." The participants paid a nominal door fee for a party in a private apartment, yet they were accused by the media of engaging in sex for pay. Even worse, one woman was arrested for engaging in consensual SM (paddling another woman's buttocks with a wooden spoon) under the archaic statute "Consent is not a defense to assault."

Our sexual freedom continues to be chipped away through municipal legislation and random enforcement of blue laws. There is a lot of work ahead for the sexual freedom movement. The main goal is to improve the attitudes toward sex in our society and gain tolerance for everyone who engages in alternative sexual expression.

The joy of public sex

Joining a group of people who are in naked or near-naked states in an erotically charged atmosphere is a liberating experience. It's considered shocking simply because we aren't taught how to talk about sex, much less learn different ways to enjoy sex. Public sex and nudity are only frightening when you haven't experienced them. Somehow that can make it all the more powerful when you do it. Revealing your body and allowing yourself to enjoy the positive erotic response can be more healing than any other life experience. It's the sort of total acceptance that many of us haven't experienced since our toddler days. I will never understand why this release of inhibitions is censured and condemned when it should be celebrated. Though the sexual freedom movement is still in its infancy, we can only hope that more organizations stand on the side of freedom for consensual sex, whether it's done in public or in private.

Jacks of Color: an oral history

BENJAMIN SHEPARD INTERVIEWS LIDDELL JACKSON

I first met Liddell Jackson after one of the SexPanic! "emergency" town hall meetings. Unlike most of the folks in the room, Jackson did not seem particularly worried about the future of public sexual culture in Manhattan. "Gay men are incredibly resourceful," Jackson explained. "We've been through this before in 1985 when we lost all the clubs and they came back. They will again this time." Jackson, a black man from Memphis who came to New York via Brown University in 1976, approaches today's attacks with the same confidence he has maintained for over two decades as an organizer in New York. Sitting in his Upper West Side apartment, Jackson and I discussed his efforts to help build queer organizations which deal honestly with questions of race, culture, and difference. Jackson, the founder of Jacks of Color – New York's longest running sex party, run by and for men of color and their friends – explained his approach to building community through public sexual culture. He began with a recollection.

Black and White Men Together

LJ My lover Mitchell and I joined Black and White Men Together in 1980. Back then, it was really just a glorified pickup place for black and white men to meet each other outside of the bars and the baths … until people like myself got in there because our weekly gatherings quickly evolved into consciousness-raising sessions. It wasn't just about let's just get together and see whom we can pick up. It was like, we are all here and this is a cohesive group of us coming here every week. Let's sit down and talk. We have a valuable opportunity here. It's about learning about each other's communities. And so Mitchell and I, and some of the other really steady attendees, rapidly turned that organization from a glorified fuck club to a very important entity addressing issues of racism in the gay male community.

The Discrimination Documentation Project

Then Black and White Men Together in 1982 and 1983 created something called the Discrimination Documentation Project. It was created to address what was beginning to be seen as a rising measure of carding black gay men as they went to bars. The guy who was the founder, the late Henry Weimhoff, a sweet guy and a therapist at the Institute for Human Identity, really fashioned the test. He based it on the NAACP Housing Tests of the fifties.

And so the first place we went was a bar called Circles in the East Fifties, which was one of the major bars that had been accused of having racial quotas. We sent in about five or six different groupings of black and white men – a black and white couple, two black men and a white man, three white men and a black man, and the last one was always an all-black group. And yes, it was true: every time it was a group, with the exception of a black and white couple, the black men would be carded. And the black men who came as a group on their own – well, they were carded and denied admission. They would say, "You don't have enough ID. You need three pieces of ID. You've only got two." A New York Driver's License – they would say, "You need more ID." And if you produced three, they would say, "That one doesn't even look like an ID." We set up a base at a nearby bar, a restaurant/coffeehouse thing. After the last group tested, then we sat there and said, now it looks like we've got discrimination here. And so, armed with this information, we went to the bar as an entire organization and asked to see the manager. Now, you've got thirty black and white gay men saying, "We want to see the manager." And when the manager came out and we reported this to him, he sheepishly admitted that that had been the case. And we asked him to promise not to do that again and he agreed that he would not, and then he graciously welcomed us in for a free drink on the house. Now you know, as far we were concerned, this was our first time out of the gate and we saw it as a victory.

The second case was the Ice Palace – a much more difficult campaign. I remember sending the press release to Arthur Bell, a *Village Voice* columnist who used to write the column which Michael Musto writes now, the gay "about town" column. He was an old Gay Activist Alliance/Stonewall veteran. He called me and said, "This is a frontier that we have not even begun to address in our community – racism. I'm going to write about this in my column." And the Ice Palace became a long-time campaign. The Ice Palace never capitulated, but after a year of the picket they went out of business. That case put us on the map as an entity in the lesbian and gay community. By 1984, we changed our name to Men of All Colors Together to speak to the other people of color coming to our meetings.

Public sexual culture

When I first got here, baths were the thing – Man's Country was the most popular interracial club. I met two ex-lovers there. There was outdoor sex still going on; there was T-room sex still going on; there was truck stop stuff…. This was the late 1970s so the concept of sexual freedom was something that was not unfamiliar to us. That continued until 1982 or 1983. And then GRID turned to AIDS.

It was 1982 when guys started dying. And people whom you knew started getting sick…. Yet, in the midst of all this we were still having sex. We hadn't stopped having sex. We just had to have it safer. And also in the early eighties there was a gradual springing up of safer sex parties. There were clubs like the Anvil and the Mineshaft.

My favorite thing was the sex clubs. At that point a safer sex club was a place where you walked in and checked your clothes. You brought your own beer, and you went into the play areas to have sex. And they were safe sex clubs because they had condoms and lube everywhere. It was given. There was a body politic that said, "this is the collective contract." And if we're going to stay alive, this is what we have to do for the contract.

We also felt responsible for each other. The one thing that I have always believed, coming out of the gay male communities dealing with an epidemic, was that it taught us how to show each other a level of respect…. The advent of safer sex gradually developed a custom, a tradition of talking, negotiating: what are we going to do, are we going to do any fucking? Who's going to fuck whom? Do we have condoms? We actually had to talk to each other, and in talking to each other we developed different levels of caring for each other. You were talking about keeping yourself safe and him safe too. And you developed this alliance and you could feel really good about having kept each other alive. That's a level of humanity you hadn't had before. And if you had had sex and enjoyed it, you'd exchange numbers and say, "Let's do this again…" The sex clubs created some sort of close circles, because a lot of the same guys kept coming, and a lot of the same guys started to know each other and started to trust each other and hang out and play with each other. There was a level of camaraderie that developed and then – not to sound schmaltzy – a brotherhood.

ACT UP and sexual freedom

Society was not listening to us. Luckily we had an ACT UP that was getting something done. And at that point, when ACT UP first came around, people were like, "ACT UP, you go! I may not be able to go out there and scream but I'm behind you all the way." Because nobody else was listening to us any other way. If you can get people to listen and get drug trials done and get drugs out there that are going to be affordable, thank you. So there was a lot of support for them, especially among the sex community.

BS I've always thought that their pro-sex message was part of their movement vitality.

LJ That wasn't lost on people. Many of the sex guys were in ACT UP, especially the ones who were like artists and freelancers, not corporate people. And they would be in ACT UP meetings and then be in sex clubs later. In the first years of ACT UP, the joke was that it was the best cruising you could do on a Monday night. You could go to ACT UP and have a date before that meeting was over.

I was a political organizer all along. And I stayed that way all through the 1990s. But I was also somebody who went to as many sex clubs as possible because I liked them. I liked what they did, what they were trying to do. I was one of those few political activists who would speak out about sex parties and the importance of supporting them.

People would look at me like I was crazy because they were not putting together the need to have the gay male community be a political entity that also embraces sexual freedom. I was at the opposite end of that spectrum. We need to celebrate the sexual part of ourselves expressed at these places by being open about saying that we were going to these places; these places are keeping us alive. They need our support and not in the dark of night, in the cloak of secrecy. They need us to be proud, to stand up and say "yes, I do go there. It needs more funding. It needs more condoms and lube. It needs to be supported by the Department of Health. These places are good."

Jacks of Color

This all came to a head for me in 1990. It was a conversation at Wally's with me, my friend Kobi, who's black, and another guy named Jay. I turned to them and I said, "Why are we the only three black men in this place. This makes no sense to me." They were like, "I guess they didn't want to come because it's nothing but white guys." "Yeah, but it's a safe sex club." "Now is the assumption that black men and other men of color don't want to do safe sex? That's ridiculous, I'm sure they do, but they don't have any place to go." And so, as is my history, rather than complain about something, what I tend to do is create it.

And out of that I created Jacks of Color. Everyone I talked to tried to talk me out of it, tried to tell me black men or other men of color would not support it.... When we first opened it, we created it just for men of color and after the third or fourth party we opened it up to men of color and their friends, because during those first parties I talked to so many white men whom I knew, whom I played with, who said to me, "Well thanks a lot. One of the reasons I seek you out is I like being with men of color and there are very few at these places and usually the ones who are hesitant to interface with the white men. At least I have a really great time with you every time we go out. I wanna be in a multiracial place. And now you create a club for men of color and I can't go to that either." And I thought, "You know, that's absolutely right." There are so many white guys out there who got it. They figured out how they need to interface with the larger society and they don't need to be shunned or cast aside. They need a space for them to practice that. They are going to be the keys for our society.

So, anyway, Jacks of Color, once it really started to thrive, which was in 1995, I started to get major numbers and then I started to get imitators, which I thought was good 'cause it increases the number of spaces we can go. Afrodesiac, In the Hood, Blatino, Ariba, The Basement all started from Jacks of Color. So there was a movement. Yet Jacks of Color is still the only inclusive one.

BS   I went to a black gay bar in Chicago called The Generator. When you get inside you know why it's called The Generator. I just think that bottom-up, building a community through public sexual space is still so important. Do you feel like you built a community there?

LJ   Yes, there's a Jacks of Color family that is quite large. And it expands out into all sorts of different arenas and it even includes women now. That sense of embracing sexual expression has really become pervasive among certain sectors of the political activist community and I'm very happy about that. I like seeing people embrace that sense of sexual experience within themselves. For one thing it opens up a level of trust among people.

The city as body politic / the body as city unto itself

JIM EIGO

For more than three decades I've worked as an activist for a number of progressive causes. All that work has taken place in cities – for more than two decades, in New York City; for the past fifteen years, for AIDS and gay activist groups. I was raised in the Bronx and in Philadelphia, and my idea of what society is and could be has been shaped from my experiences of people working together (or failing to) in the dense and diverse neighborhood of Manhattan's Alphabet City, my home for the last twenty-three years. In my early formal protest work, against the war in Vietnam in the late 1960s and early 1970s, the city figured more as setting than as cause or content of my protest.

After my college years in California I returned to New York City in 1978 to embark on a writing career. From my work with the Pledge of Resistance, a group that in the 1980s worked against the Reagan administration's Central American wars, I learned how the New York cityscape might be effectively used as a player in a protest movement. In 1984 the Pledge held a Wall Street rally that used the ravines of Lower Manhattan as echo chamber. A week-long protest outside the midtown offices of Senator Al D'Amato used the city street as classroom. And every Thursday morning for over a year, Pledge members demonstrated outside the tiny Marine recruiting station that quite dramatically sits on an isolated island in the middle of Times Square.

New York City: AIDS disaster area

Although a gay man who supported gay causes, I didn't purposely work with gay activist groups while I was involved with other causes. I thought the "wider" campaign for international justice more important than narrowly gay issues. AIDS changed that. I didn't have AIDS myself, but as a writer, resident of the East Village, and gay man, I'd seen my profession, neighborhood, and kind decimated by a disease and by federal neglect. By 1987 I'd volunteered for the Gay Men's Health Crisis, taken the HIV test, and knew I was HIV-negative. But when the political dimension of AIDS became clear, I joined the newly formed activist group AIDS Coalition to Unleash Power (ACT UP).

Late in November 1987 I went to the Gay & Lesbian Community Services Center in the West Village to attend a forum asking whether the gay movement, in the wake of the Supreme Court's decision *Bowers* v. *Hardwick*, should uphold local sodomy laws, provided those laws were aimed at homosexuals. But I never got to the second-floor forum. On the ground floor I was waylaid by a meeting of ACT UP. About a hundred other people attended. For passion, intelligence, and range, no meeting I'd ever attended was its rival. It would be a few years before I missed another weekly ACT UP meeting (and only because I was out of town on ACT UP business).

At that first meeting, a pharmaceutical chemist, Iris Long, a housewife from Queens with a background in drug research, gave a report. She was gathering information on government-sponsored AIDS clinical research. She announced a weekly study group; I decided I'd attend. I was a writer and a pretty quick study and hoped that, working with Iris, I could make an immediate impact on AIDS activist work. As it turned out, between 1988 and 1992 I put my writing "on hold" to engage in full-time AIDS activist work, all of it as a member of ACT UP, most of it in the area of experimental drugs.

Soon our AIDS-treatments study group was turning out treatment-related fact sheets and analyses for the general organization. Under the Freedom of Information Act, we gathered huge amounts of data on the federal AIDS effort. Our study group, Treatment and Data (soon known as T&D), became an ACT UP subcommittee (and, a year later, a full-fledged committee). The T&D subcommittee's parent committee, the Issues Committee, was ACT UP's self-styled think-tank. By 1988, ACT UP was shifting from a local to an international organization.

But before it became a major player in federal AIDS policy, ACT UP was a local organization, one that could only have flourished in New York City. The city has been a gay mecca for over a hundred years. ACT UP required large numbers of smart, dedicated, skilled queers. In its first years it drew upon the street savvy and organizational expertise of a score of veterans from the early Gay Liberation movement. ACT UP could only have made its immediate impact in a media capital. The city grid, Manhattan's canyons, gave ACT UP an unequaled battlefield for a few years of highly videogenic skirmishes with police and local officials. From 1987 through 1991, the organization's legion of wheat-pasters kept the city plastered with one artistically and politically provocative poster after another – informative, newsworthy, and doing extra duty as recruitment tools and constant advertisements for the group and its causes.

ACT UP's street demonstrations gained the group its initial notoriety. Its first, in early 1987, protested the high cost of the first anti-AIDS drug, AZT (azidothymidine), and targeted Wall Street. The ACT UP float at the Gay Pride Parade in June wheeled a moving jail with AIDS prisoners down the city's central thoroughfare, Fifth Avenue – a graphic protest against the very real threat of an AIDS quarantine. It put the group on the media map. On a chilly, thrilling evening in November, when a city council member invited ACT UP to come through the barricades, ACT UP became the first group to hold a protest on City Hall steps. Mayor Ed Koch was mortified.

The media feasted. By the time of the group's first anniversary in early 1988, ACT UP could mobilize more than a thousand people, whose presence at Wall Street at morning rush hour kept all downtown snarled for the rest of the day. Small "affinity groups" within the larger group would secretly plan mini-actions, frequently involving colorful, inventive, media-ready acts of civil disobedience that would take place at the same time as a major ACT UP street action. (In my first year in ACT UP I was arrested four times in AIDS-related civil disobedience in New York City and convicted once for a sit-in at the Department of Health, the first conviction for AIDS-related civil disobedience in the United States.)

ACT UP's second anniversary action – three thousand converging on City Hall, the biggest demo ACT UP ever mustered in the city – coincided with a dozen affinity group actions. Gran Fury, a group of artists, smuggled its parody of the *New York Times* (entitled "New York Crimes") into hundreds of vending machines in downtown New York. The affinity group I belonged to, Wave 3, wore a special

T-shirt for the occasion. It said: "NYC – AIDS Disaster Area."

At first ACT UP's T&D Committee applied the data it collected to local activist work, forming affinity groups to target the five local hospitals that were conducting federally funded AIDS research. In February 1988, on behalf of my affinity group, I wrote a critique of AIDS research at New York University (NYU). We delivered copies to NYU's AIDS researchers. One suggestion of our (fairly primitive) critique was that the federal AIDS research effort initiate "parallel trials." A drug's major "clinical trials" gather data on a drug's effectiveness in human subjects. They're very strictly limited to people who meet rigid criteria. We advocated parallel trials which would enroll anyone with HIV who had no available treatment options. In 1988, an overwhelming number of people with AIDS were routinely excluded from trials due to gender, illness, or conflicting medications. Data collected from parallel trials, while not clean enough to secure a drug its final approval, would yield a wealth of data on how a drug worked in the target population. Our group sent our critique to Dr Anthony Fauci, head of the federal AIDS effort. In a few weeks, in a speech in New York, Dr Fauci was using several phrases that seemed lifted from ACT UP's critique. But one he rephrased: "parallel trials" had become "parallel track." (Detailed analysis of how ACT UP's concept of parallel trials became government policy can be found in several books: see Nussbaum 1990; Arno and Feiden 1992; Epstein 1996.)

ACT UP's influence on the federal AIDS effort most likely occurred because ACT UP was now a worldwide grassroots organization. The United States government respected and feared the organization's strength, and several people in high places agreed substantially with our analyses. We'd become expert in several fields, from insurance to immigration. We

A few months into its existence ACT UP designed and produced its "palm card." As you'll see it's our business card. For the first year and a half of our existence it was our most important educational/outreach/recruiting tool. We'd order them by the thousands. We left them everywhere. If the AIDS commission testified in NYC, there would be a card on every seat, and so on. The description of the group on the card was recited verbatim before every Monday night meeting for years. Our two most notable logos, ACT UP and SILENCE = DEATH, are on the front and back of the card respectively; our most famous slogan, "ACT UP, Fight Back, Fight AIDS," is on the back. Even when the group had no money we somehow would always find enough money to print up a new batch of palm cards.

represented communities directly affected by the disease, and we could bring thousands out onto the streets to dramatize our demands.

By 1991, when expanded access to AIDS drugs became codified in a policy statement I helped draft, I decided to extricate myself gradually from AIDS committee work and return to the private writing that had sustained me before my public career. For the past few years I'd ventured more and more beyond activist circles into the halls of power. It was not a place I felt at home and, duty done, I decided it was time to recharge my batteries.

ACT UP, meanwhile, was rapidly becoming a victim of its own successes. How could a radical grassroots activist group maintain its identity even as it was meeting daily with federal, state, and city officials about projects sponsored by several of its committees? How do street activists negotiate with power when power corrupts? How "pure" can you afford to remain when thousands of your members are dying and your goal is to bring them relief? How much should the full group have control over what its subcommittees do, over what its individuals proclaim, in the group's name?

Monday-night meetings had always been barely controlled chaos, with hundreds of members vying for time and attention for their worthy projects. Now, dozens of ACT UP's committees, subcommittees, and ad hoc groups – many with notable accomplishments – were coming into ideological conflict. Turf wars between rival factions would rage across the floor at weekly meetings. A large portion of T&D had formed a new group, the Treatment Activist Group (TAG), and would shortly decide it was easier to leave ACT UP than endure increased sniping from members opposed to any discussion with federal officials.

I chose to leave AIDS work rather than make the jump from ACT UP. So long as ACT UP was a vital, viable group united in purpose, I could challenge people in power and believe that I was speaking as the representative of a large (and growing), nationwide grassroots movement. Because I'm HIV-negative, I felt I could not simply speak as an individual when I challenged AIDS policy – I had no right. In 1989, when 99 percent of ACT UP was voting in support of what T&D was doing, I felt I had that support. But by 1992 only 65 percent consistently voted to support that effort, and it was clear the numbers were slipping even as ACT UP's tangible successes on the treatment front were mounting. So ACT UP divided and large numbers of members left. When I was no longer sure for whom I was speaking I shut up.

COME FUCK WITH US

"The next time you see unprotected anal sex in a sex club, remember: Tapping a top on the shoulder and offering him a condom and some lube is a very powerful way to express your affection for a brother."
— Michael Callen

AIDS Prevention Action League (APAL) is an open organization for AIDS prevention through direct action, advocacy and education. Our goal is to support gay men in reducing HIV transmission and sustaining a sexual culture in which we can survive.

APAL is creating livable models of HIV prevention for the second decade of AIDS.

NEW YORK AIDS DISASTER AREA

GOVERNOR CUOMO IS DOING NOTHING. DO SOMETHING—ALBANY MARCH 28

FOR INFORMATION: ACT UP 212-989-1114

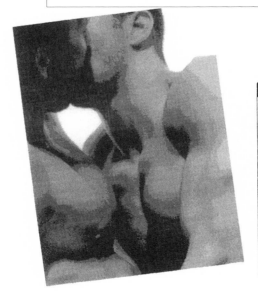

AIDS	PREVENTION	ACTION	LEAGUE

Save Our *Sex* Party!

"The next time you see unprotected anal sex in a sex club, remember: tapping a top on the shoulder and offering him a condom and some lube is a very powerful way to express your affection for a brother."
- Michael Callen

The Hottest Safer Sex Party of the Year!

**540 West 21st Street
Thursday-September 7, 9pm Until**

$5 *Suggested Donation!*

In spring 1992 I attended my last ACT UP meeting (although I'd continue to attend ACT UP demonstrations). By summer 1992, I resigned my last AIDS appointment, wondering if our federal success on treatment issues had helped undermine ACT UP locally. But I knew we were facing a global disease and any hope for a cure (and a vaccine for those who were not infected) depended on the health of the national research effort.

The Giuliani administration's war on sex

The city was a prerequisite for the modern gay movement. The concentration of people that the city affords makes sex contacts between people of minority sexual tastes more common than elsewhere. Areas that become known as homosexual hangouts draw like-minded people. In twentieth-century Manhattan, whole commercial districts arose to service gays in neighborhoods that would never have coalesced had the areas not been notorious for gay sexual contacts.

In early 1995 it became clear that New York City government under the new Republican mayor, Rudy Giuliani, had undertaken a multi-pronged campaign that, if successful, would shut down every gay male sex space in town. The Department of Health (DOH), after years of tolerating gay male sexual hangouts, began padlocking commercial sex venues, one by one, for violations of an outdated state health code. In addition, a Democratic city council was poised to pass a rezoning plan that had originated in a Giuliani-dominated planning commission. Rezoning would exile adult establishments to narrow strips on the city's outskirts, a move most businesses wouldn't survive.

The danger to queers seemed acute. The US Supreme Court doesn't recognize gay people's right to sexual expression, so when local government actions infringe on the sexual activity of some gay men, all gay people are endangered. When ACT UP began in 1987 its message was unwaveringly sex positive. One reason the group took off so quickly was because its weekly meeting was the sexiest space in the city for a gay guy to be on a Monday night. Urban gay men had seen their community sex spaces erode in the age of AIDS. ACT UP would be a first stand in reclaiming that space, in asserting our right to it. Yet by 1995, a handful of men who'd recently mounted the barricades for ACT UP were now spearheading efforts to close gay spaces, loudly flouting that long-held principal of gay liberation: securing protection of gay people's sexual freedoms was the basis for securing other gay rights. Most gay men in New York City seemed utterly ignorant of the threat, or indifferent to it.

Sometimes city officials acted against gay spaces in the name of AIDS prevention. Was this to divert attention from the utter paucity of city-sponsored AIDS prevention programs for gay men? DOH officials privately acknowledged that most unsafe sex occurs at home and that AIDS prevention programs could use commercial sex spaces to promote safer sex. Still, city officials were poised to crush what slender public sexual culture has sprouted in the age of AIDS.

A history of modern male homosexuality is the history of our spaces, especially in densely populated New York City, where so much "private" life, sexual and other, takes place in semi-public settings. Against great odds, gay people in the past have fought, covertly and overtly, to keep their social spaces. The contemporary gay movement dates from the Stonewall Riots of 1969, an early victory over a city administration that would have shut us down. Yet in 1995, sex was under attack in community after community across the country.

In early 1995, toward the end of the twenty-fifth-anniversary year of Stonewall, NYC found its most prominent gay journalists – Duncan Osborne, Gabriel Rotello, and Mike Signorile, all ACT UP veterans – calling for city action against gay spaces. Each fresh screed outdid the last – lurid depictions of sex clubs as "killing fields" where everyone not driven to "suicide" was driven to "murder." A gay PR man (and former ACT UP member) acted as literal tour guide for a straight reporter through a gay sex den. Tabloid papers and local television news fed for weeks on the story. How had this come to pass in the home of Stonewall, birthplace of ACT UP, and Queer Nation?

These stories had the ring of classic scapegoating, raising the specter of HIV-positive predators willfully infecting the unwary in the backrooms of NYC, when in fact research showed that HIV-positive men were the most conscientious practitioners of safer sex. But these facts don't conform to the persistent, pernicious stereotype that said gay and HIV-positive men were sexual vampires. Blaming HIV-positive men for fresh HIV transmission, treating them only as vectors for disease, supported a kind of sexual quarantine that comfortably fitted with the prevailing bureaucratic view: we deal with AIDS by containment rather than care or cure. The stories also erected insuperable barriers between positive and negative gay men, dirty gays, and respectable ones, predicating a yardstick by which a "tolerant" straight society might grade gay men. Those who fell furthest from monogamy's norm would be forced to stop unhealthy, antisocial sexual conduct.

Five years earlier ACT UP would have slapped the source of these stories with a zap. But in April 1995 the only organization in NYC speaking out against the city's abrogation of gay men's sexual freedoms was small and only a month old. A core of ACT UP veterans formed the AIDS Prevention Action League (APAL) to oppose the juggernaut of real estate interests and ambitious politicians at work behind the camouflage provided by tabloid fags whose call for the closure of gay spaces was putting fellow gay men at the mercy of vice cops – and betraying the central tenet of AIDS activism. For nearly a decade, in matters ranging from testing to treatment, activists had worked to increase the power of community members over their lives in an epidemic and under a social order that gravely eroded it. Now gay journalists were arguing that gay men couldn't be trusted with autonomy. Fags were the predatory sexual animals that straight society had always imagined; someone please step in and save us from ourselves.

In reality, gay men themselves developed the models for AIDS prevention programs, reducing a yearly infection rate from 10 percent to 1.4 percent by the early 1990s. By early 1995, recent estimates that infection rates might be rising prompted a re-examination of AIDS prevention efforts around the country – and should have.

So APAL would promote safer sex in all the places that gay men have sex, working to provide community members with knowledge, materials, and space for sexual expression that supported community health. I came out of retirement as an activist to join. Our plan was to advocate for a sex-positive AIDS prevention policy with city officials, to work with operators of sex venues to facilitate safer sex, to work with our peers to implement fresh prevention strategies, and to promote our message in the media.

AIDS and the closure of gay sex spaces

In the age of AIDS, New York City began closing commercial sex spaces in earnest in 1985, mostly bathhouses and hard-core sex clubs, for violations of a state sanitary code that prohibited establishments from allowing anal intercourse or fellatio on the premises. (It was later amended to forbid vaginal intercourse as well.) For inspection convenience, the code never distinguished between protected and unprotected sex, or oral and other intercourse. In 1988-89 a second spate of padlocking focused on X-rated movie houses. During the administration of Mayor David Dinkins in the early 1990s, "safer sex" sex venues opened and flourished. But in 1995 the city shut down nine X-rated cinemas for sanitary code violations. With increased enforcement, DOH inspectors were supplemented by vice cops – unqualified personnel and gay men's historic tormentors. After witnessing code violations at a particular venue and sending its owner a warning letter, the city would obtain a court order to close a sex space for all purposes for a year.

In meetings with city officials, APAL argued that the sanitary code mocked current HIV research. More than 90 percent of the department's inspection reports cited fellatio, an activity that AIDS prevention organizations had recategorized as low risk. Code enforcement aimed at stopping blow jobs wouldn't put a dent in transmission rates. Because the code failed to differentiate between protected and unprotected, oral and anal, enforcing it was tantamount to promulgating dangerous misinformation. And in fact the city inspection team was transforming a sanitary code into morality code, requiring X-rated theaters to even suppress masturbation, eliminating indisputably safe sexual activities.

MEMBERS OF APAL ARE HERE TONIGHT TO TALK WITH YOU ABOUT KEEPING SEX CLUBS OPEN, MAKING THEM SAFER AND MAKING THEM OURS.

APAL argued that you can't prosecute safer sex; you have to engage individuals to practice it. Studies suggest some gay men are likelier to have safer sex in public settings than in private. APAL argued for keeping sex spaces open so safer sex materials would be readily available. Because of city actions, some owners, afraid to acknowledge sex was occurring on the premises, stopped providing condoms to patrons. Yet the city chose to intensify enforcement.

Giuliani's first fame had come as federal prosecutor. A residual prosecutorial rage informed his every initiative as mayor, featuring a quality-of-life campaign bent on arresting everyone from streetwalker to jaywalker. His administration began to initiate sting operations on sex workers. Sex businesses that couldn't be closed for health code violations were harassed for supposed violations of the building code or the liquor code. Moreover, his campaign to zone adult-use businesses out of residential neighborhoods accommodated city real estate moguls' plans to mall Manhattan even as it suited the mayor's puritan strain of (fallen) Catholicism. In an atmosphere like this, the call for the closing of gay sex venues (and the lurid stories that accompanied these actions) was red meat. And the yahoos fed.

This island is my land

The mayor's major anti-sex initiative, the city's complete rezoning, would, if approved by city council, give businesses with substantial sexual content a year to relocate to narrow bands, most of them far from the neighborhoods they served, much of the land unusable. When APAL members spoke out at public hearings against rezoning the city, our most persuasive arguments were personal. I'd identify myself as a writer, gay man, and AIDS activist. I'd explain that pornography was integral to many people's safer sex programs and that restricting its physical access would endanger them. Tampering with the safer sex culture that had arisen in this epidemic could be murderous.

Some of my writing was homoerotic fiction. Under rezoning some of my published work would be unavailable in my own neighborhood. Because "gay" is a sexual affiliation, literature, theater, and film can't be gay without being sexual. Restricting businesses based on sexual content would impinge disproportionately on gay people, discrimination New Yorkers should reject.

I'd say I opposed rezoning most of all because I'd used commercial sex venues all my sexual life. I had my first sexual encounter with another man in a porn theater. I was grateful to live in a city that afforded me a place where, in my confusion and inability to face down a homophobic society, I felt I could finally deal with my sexuality and no one would judge me. Many gay men still came out at commercial sex places. All the gay men I knew used them at some time. They'd done my community inestimable service and I hoped they'd continue to do so.

In September of 1995, New York City's Planning Commission voted to support rezoning, 7:6 – shockingly close considering that the year before, without opposition, it passed a year's moratorium on sex-related businesses. The swing vote on the Commission, a last-minute mayoral appointee, absent for the entire rezoning debate, should in decency have abstained. APAL and its allies, a few handfuls of dedicated, savvy people, had managed to sway several commission votes. In speeches delivered on the day of the vote, many commissioners credited gay opposition with changing their opinions. Although APAL had been adept at shaping perceptions inside commission chambers, we'd been unable to rally a grassroots constituency. With the support of the Planning Commission, the bill to rezone New York easily passed city council in October.

Out of the jaws of defeat

In the ten months of its existence, the AIDS Prevention Action League spent much of its time and energy fighting the city's shutdown of gay sex spaces. But it also undertook some initiatives to make the city's sexual landscape safer and hotter. Our float for Gay Pride Day burlesqued sex acts on a bed and in a booth. The crowd roared approval. Our X-rated Pride Day posters touted oral sex as safer sex. Our Pride Day leaflet invited our peers to "Come Fuck with US." Forgoing the reductive slogans of most AIDS prevention material, APAL's Postcard Project circulated short, complex sex stories drawn from the lives of APAL members, which focused on sexual decisions made or deferred in the age of AIDS. Though cautionary tales, they were as absorbing to read as pornography.

APAL decided that the generation of pleasure in the name of community would be a worthy end in itself. APAL's Save Our Sex Party, September 7 at Zone DK, was AIDS prevention work as well. The fucking onstage, in defiance of a health code, was an education, and it spread its energy to the party at large: 450 men of different races, shapes, ages, and classes coming together in a model of supportive, safer public sex in the face of city harassment.

A commercial sex establishment is only as safe as its clientele make it. APAL drafted Sexclub Guidelines that rejected intrusive monitors and inspection, yet committed cooperating sex venues to maintaining standards of safety. Yet, the real prevention work in sex clubs would have to be done with patrons. APAL's Sexclub Project proposed a friendly takeover of sex spaces in which project members – not experts but peers – would converge on a particular sex space on a designated evening and provide information to other customers, swap stories with them, and ask their opinions. What would a supportive sex space look and feel like? What concrete steps could achieve it? How many people does it take to infuse a space with a new attitude? APAL worked with a gay movie house in the East Village to try to create a model.

Can a space serve erotic and social functions? Can each reinforce the other? Group sex as an expression of community might be a rather utopian ideal. Short of that, the project aimed to transform existing venues into supportive sexual networks, hotter for me if it's hotter for you. While some young gay men couldn't envision a future for such places, APAL aimed to help create sex spaces in which we all could imagine a future together.

ACT UP in its first several years had been notably effective on three fronts: articulating issues, generating corresponding public actions, and using the media. APAL had been good at the first but spotty on the others. In the wake of APAL's enormously successful Save Our Sex Party, I'd hoped that AIDS activism had ripened into its sensual phase, where every action was a carnival, a gumbo of sex and play and politics, in defiance of a disease and a regime that would throttle all pleasure. It was not to be. Just before Christmas the group held one last (successful) community forum (plus a pornswap that doubled as civil disobedience since the sale of sexual material took place in defiance of rezoning), and then packed it in.

The web and fabric of gay New York City

For a few months APAL brought together my sex life, my politics, and my writing. The city I lived in and loved had been the site and the content of APAL's efforts. Although APAL discontinued operations, the threat to gay spaces continued, so I began to write articles and address local groups, disseminating arguments I and my APAL colleagues had formulated in our defense of gay sex spaces. By 1997, gay journalist Gabriel Rotello was arguing that, since significant new HIV infection was occurring among gay men, we should abandon current safer sex strategies and supplant our diverse sexual landscape with a new, unified communal norm – serial monogamy. He'd turned his guns on monogamy's greatest enemy: a core group of gay "multipartnerists" said to pose a danger to all gay men. In their indiscriminate coupling, they had the potential to carry HIV infection beyond their core group.

I argued that, at a time when many men consistently practiced safer sex, it was not the rate of partner change that determined infection rates and that effective AIDS prevention had to target individuals and their situations. It had been my experience that multipartner sex could be compatible with, even foster, safety. For more than a dozen years I'd been a more or less promiscuous practitioner of my version of safer sex, a personal expansion of that hoary AIDS prevention slogan "Come on me not in me." My personal sex life had come to stress nonpenetrative sex acts, the wearing of condoms for occasional anal sex, and unprotected oral sex without taking ejaculate into my mouth. I told the groups I spoke to that this would seem unacceptably risky to some gay men and unaccountably stodgy to others. I supported them all in their right to make their sexual decisions and asked that they refrain from interfering with mine. Fear of infection had ceased to be the primary reason I kept safe. Applying lessons community activism had taught me, I had sex to promote personal, partner, and group well-being, believing that long-range prevention (supporting habits to be maintained over a lifetime) would be fueled by desire rather than fear.

Safer promiscuity would not be the right prevention strategy for every gay man. But many men had been practicing it successfully throughout the epidemic. For these men multipartnerism had not been a threat to safety but a source of it. Community norms can promote safer sex; communal sex is one way. And when safer sex becomes the norm at a commercial establishment, it can promote safer sex in other contexts. Closing sex spaces interfered with my own practice of safer sex and diminished the pleasure I shared with dozens of other gay men in any given year, interactions that I and they cherished, and that strengthened the web and fabric of gay New York City.

I pointed out that during this epidemic every sexually active gay man had attained a body of knowledge. Hundreds of thousands of gay men had altered their sexual expression to devise safer models that more nearly met their needs than monogamy could. Pooling these bodies of knowledge would be a more effective prevention project than eliminating spaces for the promiscuous.

In a quest to subvert the current order, some queers had found a polygamy of potential – that anyone might be anyone else's lover – a useful tool for opening up the airless, asocial, closed circuit of the state-sanctioned couple. The time was past due for a prevention activism to augment our treatment activism and transform all our sexual spaces. Gay male sexual culture would be healthier when infused with a sense of community, every gay man sharing in the well-being of every man he had sex with. Sexual health was a lot more than freedom from a pathogen. Safer sex would be unsustainable unless it engaged individuals to make personal decisions that promoted sexual pleasure.

The last stand

In spring 1997 a coalition of gay academics, activists, writers, and artists formed Sex Panic! in an attempt to articulate an alternative vision of gay life to the vision of "faith and family" put forth by mainstream gay groups in the late 1990s. SexPanic! flared brightly for a few months, issued a few brilliant papers, held a few exciting, well-attended forums, and flared out.

"Rezoning New York City Will Not Improve My Quality of Life" read a sign a little girl held as she sat in a stroller on a cold, brilliantly sunny morning in early March 1998. The girl's mother, a dancer at a stripclub, wheeled her around and around outside a federal courthouse in Lower Manhattan. Mother and daughter were among two hundred New Yorkers – workers in the city's "adult" establishments, their dependants, their patrons, their defenders – marching to protest the mayor's planned city rezoning.

On that March morning a federal court would decide whether rezoning could proceed and turn 98 percent of the city into a censorship zone. Except for the New York Civil Liberties Union, traditional anticensorship forces had been muted by the thrust of the rezoning campaign. For three years the mayor had lied. He'd said he wanted to exile adult businesses from residential neighborhoods because they bring drunkenness, noise, and gaudy signs. But there were laws against such disruptions that most stores abided by; the city's own study of adult businesses failed to link them to crime. Only one thing united the range of businesses that rezoning targeted: they dealt with sex. The First Amendment should be protecting these businesses, but so far in the long battle through several courts justice had been fooled. On the eve of what the mayor hoped would be his final court victory, he publicly admitted his goal was a city free of commercial sexual materials.

All the city's power structure – Republican mayor, Democratic city council, the *Times*, the tabloids, the relevant money men – had consolidated behind the proposed rezoning, a classic late 1990s' alignment of prudery and greed. Although the bluenose mayor had been rezoning's mouthpiece, its motor was economic. Real estate interests, which had seen the money to be made when they drove adult businesses off 42nd Street to make Times Square safe for Mickey Mouse, drooled over the prospect of cleaning up by cleaning out the whole city.

Although tens of thousands of gay New Yorkers and visitors to the city regularly used its commercial sex spaces, few gay men were speaking out against their shut-down. Most of them were carrying placards among the strippers and civil libertarians at this March demonstration, a chilly last stand. This was the first time imperiled workers in New York City's adult industry rallied to keep their jobs in the face of the city's attempts to zone them out of business. Over the next few months they'd march again in front of courthouses, in City Hall Park, and through midtown. But their fate had been written before they'd begun, and no judge would undo the decision a state court had already handed down: the city was free to shut down or exile adult busi-nesses. In 1999, a last dim hope for justice, the US Supreme Court, refused to hear the case.

Rezoning had changed how rank-and-file gay men had sex. I live in the East Village, an arty, mixed-race neighborhood with a large gay population. At the start of the campaign to sanitize the city, in 1995, the East Village boasted six commercial, explicitly sexual, gay male meeting places. By early 1999 none of these six sex spaces remained.

Most gay New Yorkers did nothing to resist rezoning because public talk about sex embarrasses them and they figured they had sexual options. Well-connected gay men could (with some inconvenience) plug into an increasingly private, underground sex scene. But nothing is beyond the arm of the law: one long-standing private gay male sex club in Chelsea was closed when a disgruntled member reported its exist-ence to authorities. And with the shuttering of every sex space is the irreversible eradication of a very particular social scene.

The asshole is a revolution!

In the early 1990s, even as I was enmeshed in AIDS work, I began to take notes for short pieces of fiction I wanted to write, sex fiction. I'd begun to feel that the preservation of the homosexual urge through the plague years was an important pursuit. Several of those short stories have now been published. In spring 2000, on the strength of that writing, I was hired to be the staff writer for a group of soft-core pornographic gay magazines. A month later I was asked to become the managing editor for *Playguy* magazine, responsible for writing most of the magazine's text. The closing piece in the December 2000 issue, the first one I edited, is a mock "inter-view" of a model who appears in various stages of undress and arousal in a graffiti-decorated public restroom. It runs like this:

PLAYGUY   The last time we spoke to you, Ivan, you explained your philosophy of sexual anarchy. How do you put it into practice in your daily life?

IVAN   Mostly I wait in out-of-the-way men's rooms. Then I lure unsuspecting straight dudes into sex acts that are dirtier than anything they ever imagined. Every guy who fucks me over a filthy toilet leaves the john a little more twisted than when he came in. Score another blow for a free society!

PLAYGUY   You live by such a high standard yourself. Don't all the guys you have sex with disappoint you?

IVAN   I have my fun. I'm just out to queer mankind, one guy at a time. The way I figure it, every asshole is a revolution waiting to happen.

PLAYGUY   It sounds like yours happened already.

IVAN   Every day, dude. It's happenin' every day.

Would I literally reduce the revolution to an asshole? In times as repressed as ours, maybe the most appropriate site for revolution is fantasy where I can help keep alive the spark of those sexual potentialities that in reality are under political and viral siege. For the time, I've moved my political work from the streets and the meetings to the mags. Those of us who work in the highly censorable field of gay soft-core porn today work with one hand tied behind our backs. Nor can we be overtly political since we are engaged in a commercial venture.

And yet I know from the letters and emails and phone calls I receive that the magazine I edit is a prime instrument for hundreds of young guys who are just coming to terms with the desires they feel for other guys. And many of our middle-aged readers live utterly closeted lives in communities where they're afraid to be gay except in the private sessions they have with our magazines. Our pictures and stories tell these guys there are others out there who, like them, desire other guys. We open them up to worlds of possibilities. Even if circumstances of their lives are such that they cannot live out of the closet right now, they can anticipate it.

And meanwhile, out in the streets? The Giuliani administration in its dying days (as of this writing, the guy has less than a year left in office) hasn't been as rabid in its prosecution of "sin" as it has been in the past. There's a glimmer. But there are also disturbing rumblings beyond city hall, suggesting that New York City's war against sex will outlast the mayor who spearheaded it.

Within the past few weeks the metropolitan area's three mainstream liberal newspapers, the *Times* (notorious for protecting its real estate interests even at the expense of personal and civic freedoms), the *Daily News*, and *Newsday* have, almost out of the blue and in mysterious concert, written inflammatory, misleading articles or editorials condemning the amount of sex materials still available for sale in the city. This, even though the amount has been drastically reduced and the few dozen remaining "adult businesses" (serving a metropolitan area of 14 million) are but shadows of their former selves and so not "adult businesses" at all. Real sex only takes place in establishments as underground as the catacombs!

When the ground of sexual activity has shrunk to the brink of disappearance, where to? At a time of impossibility, it's the job of fantasy to open things up. Of course I don't believe that the worlds I write every month in the magazines I work for will ever be literally realized. In fact that's a major reason I feel compelled to write them. The beauty, the benefit, the consolations of all-male pornography have always been in the effort to sketch a landscape of erotic (im)possibility. At the edge of the imagination of every young guy who is coming to terms with his desire for other guys there is an exciting, frightening new world of limbs and cock and butt – a world of all but infinite potential. Every month I plow this turf. If such a world were do-able, we smutmeisters wouldn't have to delineate it. But we try to keep alive an idea of a utopia, which in these dark times for freedoms, (homo)sexual and other, exists more and more as (im)pure idea. Besides, I want to bring you and your buddies more and better orgasms.

Note

This essay draws from the following earlier essays: "New York City's War on Sex: Some Notes from the Fore (& the Aft)," *Steam*, vol. 3, no. 4, Winter 1995/96; "Bodies of Knowledge," *b-2K* 1997, GMHC, New York; and "The Day Fun City Died," a column for the website www.cruising forsex.com, posted in two parts in January 1999 (part two was published with a few revisions in the *New York Blade*).

Sunflower with cellphone: garden activist working to save the gardens.

PART THREE

Public versus private spaces, battlegrounds, and movements

Naomi Klein argues that the spirit of the new social movements is a radical re-capturing of public space through a burlesque of "do it yourself" activism.[1] No theme better embodies the dilemma of globalization than the question of where and how the lines are drawn between public and private spheres. For many, there is the feeling that public space is gradually being eroded. Citizens' rights to participate within the various geographies of the public sphere are limited by encroaching corporate domination. As city governments cement relationships with large transnational companies – whether by design or by default – the imperative to privatize public space becomes more and more compelling. During the 1990s, battlegrounds emerged as contending interests clashed, between real estate and neighborhood public space advocates. The following essays explore the battle for public space in the era of globalization.

Dwindling park benches

A recent joint study by Harvard University, the New York City Department of Planning, and the Municipal Arts Society reported that many publicly designed spaces in New York City have failed to provide respite from encroaching privatization and urban claustrophobia. Gates that should be open are padlocked, ledges designed to be welcoming are lined with spikes, plazas are cluttered with dumpsters, water

New York's community meeting space for countless insurgent groups and community builders was facing eviction at the time this book went to press.

A new generation of public space activists are taking the DIY ethos to build communities with what they have, even if that means shaking up the now sterile Times Square, with or without a permit.

The Dance Liberation Front activist group's "Twist-a-thon" 2000 dance protest against New York City's cabaret laws. Times Square was awash with dancing defenders of free speech. The Hunger March Band is a constant at such events.

fountains do not work, and chairs and tables meant for public use are appropriated by restaurants (Dunlap 2000).

As more public space is usurped, activists have moved to reappropriate the private. Beginning with the awareness that strategies must change and adapt to be successful, a new generation of activists has forged a novel style of street protest that departs from the tired old-style street pickets and rallies of days past. The result is innovative guerrilla theater and radical street performance. Experimental groups like Queer Nation, Reclaim the Streets (RTS), the Theater of the Oppressed Laboratory, Art and Revolution, the Reverend Billy and the Church of Stop Shopping, and the Surveillance Camera Players have pushed the limits of where reality ends and theater begins, blurring the boundaries between public and private spaces. Long-established theater groups (such as the Living Theater and Bread and Puppet) and new formations (such as the Ransom Corp and the Dance Liberation Front) have turned homogenized public spaces into landscapes for public performance and community building. The Church Ladies for Choice, an ACT UP spin-off group, have used the public arena, public spectacle, to highlight the needs of women to gain safe access to abortion clinics. Jan Cohen-Cruz reports in this section on the ways their work utilized the public sphere to highlight the need for sexual freedoms in the broadest terms. Such is the cultural spirit that runs throughout the new public space movements.

Countless groups – from garden activists, to strippers, to sex shop owners, to guerrilla theater actors – have participated in the debate over public and private spaces. Even rave-goers moved from private clubs to semipublic warehouses to create new movements in public spaces. Throughout the late 1990s, RTS pumped new life into environmental/social justice movements by successfully organizing street dance parties/actions, mobilizing gyrating bodies into the streets of cities around the world. Steve Duncombe considers the ways their use of dancing as liberation demonstrates the ethos of the new activism.

Public panic!

Nothing divides the private from the public more than the notion that the personal sphere is where intimacy appropriately takes place. For many, sex is the most intimate, and therefore the most private, act of all. Over the past decade, a conservative politics of "family values" has brought a new hyper-vigilance around public order, policing the divide between the public and the personal. While activists work along the lines of the IWW mantra – an injury to one is an injury to all – the public/private divide dislocates these interconnections. Notions of what is private allow us to turn our backs to injustice. For many, the private sphere is seen as an ideology of capital, heteronormativity, reproduction, family values, and privilege (Berlant and Warner 1999). The public is a place for conversations, for cross-class contact, and for community building. Public sexuality is an integral component of queer world-making (Crimp 1988; Dangerous Bedfellows 1996; Delaney 1999). As more and more public spaces have been shut down and community spaces have been put at risk, SexPanic!, "a pro-queer, pro-feminist, anti-racist direct action group," called for queers to respond.

Part 3 outlines a series of battles within the current public/private debate. "This is a free-market economy. Welcome to the era after communism," New York Mayor Rudy Giuliani declared as he red-baited garden activists, explaining his reasoning for selling off New York's community gardens. Yet, after numerous protests and mass arrests, the mayor backed down, reversing his policy of privatizing community gardens. With enough pressure and creative coalition building, public space activists often do succeed, but not without losses. Positioning the garden movement within the public/private debate, Kerstin Mikalbrown reports on the struggle of garden activists to save a beloved community garden from developers and contributors to the campaign of a popular mayor.

Using the example of the group Billionaires for Bush (or Gore) at the 2000 Republican and Democratic conventions, Andrew Boyd outlines the ways guerrilla theater techniques are being successfully employed by the new movements. Jason Grote builds on Boyd's themes as he recalls the delightfully absurdist defiance of the Students for an Undemocratic Society's parody "celebrations" during the first widespread inauguration protests in a generation in January 2001. These two campaigns underline the subversive and liberatory use of humor and satire as tools of resistance in the face of entrenched problems.

Do it yourself

In the era of globalization, few public or private spaces remain immune to the pressure of global capital, big real estate, telecommunications, and the Internet. All types of public spaces – from community gardens to cruising spots – experience the same pressure. Those attacking the environment are quite often the same people calling for closure of public sexual spaces. Follow the money: public spaces where people gather are privatized for profit. The result is a "blandification" of countless urban geographies. As parks are replaced with chain stores, unique neighborhoods become, in the words of Reverend Billy, "seas of identical details." Essays by Stephen Duncombe and Carmelina Cartei consider the use of public space for public ritual, performance, and transformation.

Groups like the Church of Stop Shopping have led efforts to revitalize private spaces, targeting Disney and Starbucks outlets and turning them back into public arenas for democratic conversation. Shepard's essay recalls one such "shopping intervention." Guerrilla theater, as used by the Church of Stop Shopping, offers countless tools to confront privatization. The technique engages and educates a crowd, shows new members another vision of reality and, most of all, gives passersby an entrée into the new social movements. The Disney invasion was part of the new ethos of "do it yourself" (DIY) culture (see McKay 1998). DIY activists echo Margaret Mead's view that only small groups have ever changed the world. This new activism suggests that movements don't need charismatic leaders; any small group of people can create change themselves. The essays within this section outline a vast resistance to the malling of our cities, analyzing the link between globalization and the nature of public/private spaces and interests.

Notes

1. Remarks made during the panel "Can Movement and Party Challengers Work Together?" at "Independent Politics in a Global World" Conference at the CUNY Graduate Center, New York, October 7, 2000.

Culture jamming a SexPanic!

BENJAMIN SHEPARD

In June 1997, a flyer was passed out during Manhattan's Gay Pride Parade. It warned,

> WE'RE IN DANGER... WE'RE UNDER ASSAULT   Giuliani has closed down bars and dance clubs, including Cake, Crowbar, Edelweiss, Rounds, Sound Factory, Limelight and many others. He's fenced off the piers, zoned adult businesses out of the city, and padlocked sex clubs and theaters. Cops have entrapped more and more men in gay cruising grounds, parks, bathrooms and the streets of Chelsea and the Village. Queer New York is being shut down. Not since Stonewall have we faced so much harassment. What is our response?

New York, the East Coast's queer mecca, was in the midst of a sex panic and a group borrowing that name had come to the Gay Pride parade to raise the alarm. Transgender, dyke, bisexual, butch, SM, gender deviant, fetish, sex work, and queer people of color – communities were being squeezed out and their meeting places shut down. Public spaces citywide – from community gardens to cruising grounds – had become battlegrounds. SexPanic! formed in spring 1997 to protect "public sexual culture and safer sex in New York from police crackdowns, public stigma, and morality crusades" (SexPanic! Mission Statement 1997).

New York's neighborhoods had become lost in a sea of identical details, with the distinct aspects of communities, such as queer sex spaces in the West Village and knish shops in the East Village, lost to chain stores. Times Square, where the "mallification" of New York was most severe, became an epicenter of the panic. The

Square's public spaces – long a convergence point for cultural outsiders – had been sold and fenced off. Its homeless, cruisers, and pilgrims of all kinds, who had made this geography unique, were told to move along or face arrest. Combinations of globalization, powerful real estate interests, and a conservative regime contributed to the privatization of much of the city's other public spaces and cultures, but not without resistance. The following is a dispatch from a series of citywide battles against the expanding "blandification" of one urban geography.

For SexPanic! public sexual culture offered a place to find a notion of self within the city. Queers, like every other community in New York City, needed meeting spaces where people could converge for contact, to build community and to organize. Club closings, police raids, and privatization of public spaces challenged such possibilities. The Chelsea piers, a cruising space on the west side of Manhattan where gays had converged as long as anyone could remember, represented just one of many queer spaces under assault from the moralists on the one hand and real estate on the other. To the extent that queer spaces transgressed social, spiritual, and aesthetic limitations, as Jean-Ulrich Desert (1997) points out, they were unique and in danger of being lost. A flyer for a SexPanic! rally, "Queer Pier Facts," announced:

> In the past we fought to claim this space –
> In the present it is under attack –
> Will we let them take it from us in the future?

SexPanic! and many other activist groups emerged to protect these liberated zones. SexPanic! was a call to arms, a challenge to the queer communities to respond.

The backlash against public sexual culture unfolded as New York's mayor Rudolph Giuliani began his "Quality of Life" campaign to clean up New York (See Burr 1998). To stabilize the city, the mayor argued that civil liberties would have to be sacrificed. On May 17, 1994, he told the *New York Times*: "Freedom is about the willingness of every single human to cede lawful authority a great deal of discretion about what you do and how you do it." Soon after his election, a number of gay writers – such as Michelangelo Signorile, Andrew Sullivan, Gabriel Rotello, and Larry Kramer – and other "progressives" followed the new mayor's lead and strategy. Welfare moms, promiscuous queers, street people, strippers, and artists became targets of this cleansing. To the extent that undesirable communities embodied the city's decline, they were driven from public view as chain stores took their place. The result

QueerCarnival
TAKE BACK CENTRAL PARK

OCTOBER 10, 10:10 PM
MEET: CENTRAL PARK WEST & 79TH
DRESS UP & SHOW OFF
BRING NOISE & FLASHLIGHTS
CRUISE THE PARK
MAKE THE RAMBLE
A SAFE SPACE FOR
ALL QUEERS

QUEERS ARE BEING ENTRAPPED, ARRESTED, BEATEN, AND JAILED BY COPS.
SIMPLY FOR BEING QUEER. THIS IS PART OF AN ATTACK ON QUEER VISIBILITY.
THE CRACKDOWN ON PUBLIC SEX IS ONE ELEMENT, AS ARE THE CLOSINGS OF
QUEER SPACES ACROSS THE CITY AND THE ZONING LAWS THAT ELIMINATE SEX-
ORIENTED BUSINESSES, MANY OF THEM QUEER. WE WILL NOT TOLERATE THIS
CRACKDOWN. THESE ARE OUR SPACE. THIS IS OUR PARK.

QUEER NEW YORK IS BEING
SHUT DOWN!!!

PADLOCKED!
Mayor Giuliani has harassed
and padlocked
• Gay and lesbian bars,
including Cake, Crowbar
Edelweiss, Rounds, Rawhide
• Dance clubs, including Limelight,
Sound Factory, Tunnel, Vinyl
• Sex clubs, including He's Gotta
Have It, the Vault, Zone DK
• Theaters, including the Adonis, the
Capri, David, the Hollywood Twin,
King, Naked City, the New David,
Prince

FENCED OFF!
The piers where we have played
for years are being torn down,
fenced off, and patrolled to keep
us from meeting each other.

ZONED OUT!
Giuliani has zoned 85 percent of adult
businesses into oblivion, taking Times
Square away from us and giving it to
Mickey Mouse. Adult bookstores, video
stores, strip clubs and even bars with go-
go dancers will have to close all
over the city.

SHUT UP!
Public discussion is curtailed. Tune in
the media and all you hear are conservative white gay male voices calling for assimilation. They say gay liberation was a mistake, activism is un-
dignified, and marriage is all we
need. Other opinions, including all lesbian opinions, are shut out.

ARRESTED!
In the past six months entrapments and
arrests of gay men on charges of public
lewdness have increased
by 40 percent.
• Men have been pressed by the NYPD,
Authority police, parks police, Metro
North and LIRR cops
• Over 65 men have been arrested in the
World Trade Center men's room this year
alone
• Men of color are routinely reviled
more harshly than white men.

THIS IS A SEX PANIC!

It is policing in the name of quality of life. But whose quality of life? It is repression in the name of
AIDS prevention. But it goes against everything we know about safer sex practices. Effective AIDS
prevention respects pleasure and the complexities of our sexual lives.

FIGHT BACK! Contact SEXPANIC! at 212-252-4925
Come to a meeting at the Lesbian and Gay Community Center, Thursdays at 8 pm.

Join SexPanic! In a March to
KEEP NEW YORK SEXY!
Come Topless and Turgid to
Times Square!

The Supreme Court turned down a request to
prevent Rudy Giuliani from enforcing New York
City's XXX-Zoning law. Now 96% of New York is
a censorship zone. Bookstores have changed
their titles, video booths are gone and dancers are
wearing tee shirts - if they are working at all.
Current adult businesses are now in a store-by-
store battle with zoning inspectors to stay open or
move to unusable land on the city's outskirts.

New York's City's XXX-Zoning ordinance says that
women working in commercial establishments
may not show their nipples and that men may not
be discernibly turgid. So who's working? Mayor
Giuliani has shut down a unique industry in New
York and put thousands out of work! His vision for
a sanitized city safe for Disney, tourists and rich
real estate moguls does not include working class people.

WANTED

Tell Rudy he can't zone free expression or ban sex out of our
city! Take off your top or throw on a thong and join us for a
legal rally!

42nd street and 8th Avenue
Whatsday, August XXth, X-oclock.

*note: xxxxxx ruling says that women may go topless in public as long as it is not for commercial
gain. Men parade on beaches all over New York in thongs, both with and without socks stuffed in it.
So come topless, come turgid or just come sexy!

DANGER!

WE'RE IN DANGER   The media
tell us AIDS is over, and we want too badly to
believe it, HIV continues to spread. A new generation is at risk. Meanwhile, we feel burnout
and despair. Sexual liberation is mocked, our
community's past achievements are forgotten,
and lesbian voices are drowned out.
What's happening to us?

ASSAULT!

WE'RE UNDER ASSAULT Giuliani has closed bars and dance
clubs, including Cake, Crowbar, Edelweiss, Rounds, Sound Factory, Limelight, and
many others. He's fenced off the piers, zoned adult business out of the city, and
padlocked sex clubs and theaters. Cops have entrapped and arrested more and
more men in gay cruising grounds, parks, bathrooms and the streets of Chelsea and
the Village. Queer New York is being shut down. Not since Stonewall have we
faced so much harassment. What is our response?

TURDZ!

OUR "SPOKESMEN" ARE TURDS They have bad answers for
real questions. They say we caused AIDS; they blame us for spreading it;
they tell us to get married. Andrew Sullivan, Michelangelo Signorile, Larry
Kramer and Gabriel Rotella talk all the time. But look what they're saying:
they don't like gay culture, they don't believe in safer sex, they don't
trust you. They reduce lesbians to sexless homebodies and want gay
men to be the same. Are shame, enforced monogamy, and
small-town values what you want?

GET INFORMED
SPEAK UP

JUNE 25
7-9pm

SEX PANIC! TEACH-IN
Lesbian and Gay Community Services Center, 208 W 13St., in the Assembly Hall

For further information call 212-229-9102

JOIN US

was an expanding blandification of a place considered to be one of the most colorful geographies in the world.

SexPanic!'s goal was to challenge the steamroller of big real estate and corporate interest homogenizing the cultural landscape. The Disney Company had successfully lobbied New York's mayor to shut Times Square's red-light district in exchange for Disney's business there. In Mayor Rudy Giuliani's New York, small-town family values were set firmly against burlesque. Either you were for the redevelopment program or you were for decay. This dichotomy, in turn, reinforced norms of white, procreative heterosexuality (Pendleton 1997). Times Square's queerness was seen as a threat to a cultural heterosexuality, the normative power of which sought absolute hegemony (Watney 1987). There would be very little room for those who lived less than "straight" lives in the new Times Square. Giuliani's goal was to make the city welcoming for tourist dollars. And it was working.

"During a sex panic, a wide array of free-floating cultural fears are mapped onto specific populations who are then ostracized, victimized, and punished," notes Eric Rofes. Historian Allan Bérubé defines a sex panic as "a moral crusade that leads to crackdowns on sexual outsiders" (*Gaywave* 1997). Stereotyping, when used as a political tool, turns prostitutes into "fallen women." Inconsequential threats such as public sex are translated into calls for absolutist positions, moral barricades, quick fixes, and imaginary solutions. Fear of difference lies at the core of a generated panic (Weeks 1985).

Moral panic has always been used to erode opposition to hitherto unacceptable impositions on civil liberties. During Reconstruction, rape panic over interracial sex was used to ignite rage before lynchings. Similar processes of using panic as a political means continue today. In August 1999, the New York City Parks Department altered the city's Parks Rules, stating that groups of twenty or more would be required to obtain permits or face arrest (*City Record* 1999). Activists cried foul, pointing out that the rule stifled freedom of assembly and could be selectively enforced against activists. In response, New York Police Commissioner Howard Safir justified his position by describing how "perverts" expose themselves in parks and how the new rules would address this problem. The statement was directed to stir up fury about public sex, long a wedge issue dividing progressives. Safir's deliberate use of child seduction hysteria (see Jenkens 1998) was one of many circumstances in which moral panic was deployed to silence opposition to the city's repressive policies. Given the public's acquiescence to panic hysteria, all of the city's public spaces were in danger if the motivations behind it went unquestioned. And SexPanic! knew it.

"SexPanic! came on like a lightning bolt," said one observer recalling the summer of 1997. The group's response to the mallification of Manhattan involved combinations of guerrilla flyers, teach-ins, cyber- and street-based direct actions, community organizing, slide shows, poster campaigns, and the use and abuse of media. Every action was designed with the purpose of forcing people to rethink their assumptions about the public panic. The group's rejection of sexual shame and advocacy for the notion of queer as a rejection of the bland normal, as opposed to just heterosexual (Warner 1993) established a theoretical basis for defending public sexual culture. SexPanic!'s vision of queer even offered room for kinky hets such as myself to get involved. SexPanic!, and a number of other direct action groups in New York City, such as the Church of Stop Shopping and Reclaim the Streets, drew attention to the relationship between assaults on public culture and the urban politics of gentrification, crime prevention, safety, real estate development, HIV prevention, and cultural erotophobia.

The aim of the activism was to "culture jam" the panic – mixing an industrial narrative of sameness with a personal story. The practice of culture jamming involves making use of what you have, what is around you, and recouping it with creativity and vitality. Some culture jammers take old movie footage and turn it into their own stories. *The Encyclopedia of Culture Jamming* posits: "There's a great cosmic battle between organic chaos and mechanical order. On one side: life, libido, novelty; on the other: machinery, standardization, law" (Gross 2001). In New York City, what would emerge were competing narratives of a panic. On one hand were marketing pollutants in our mental environment, on the other was a series of battles to reappropriate privatized spaces. The culture jammers' job was to subvert the blandification script with a community-creating story. The following were pressure points.

Skirmish #1: from cruising to community

In the summer of 1997, Lisa Duggan wrote "There are many panics going on" (quoted in *LGNY* 1997). "Sex panic and homophobia and police brutality. Make the Connection," a SexPanic! flyer proclaimed, listing issues ranging from gender phobia, to XXX zoning, public space, racism, sex work, and war on the poor. "DUMP RUDY

NOW OR WATCH THIS LIST GROW LONGER," the 1997 flyer concluded. Sex-Panic!'s goal was to connect the dots between the panics. Those fanning the flames ranged from city administrators, to developers, police, and even gay journalists – all lined up in opposition to public sexual culture. Some panics involved safer sex, others the rights of adult entertainers. Still others demonized men who have sex with men. Their offense was engaging in sexual acts in semi-public places such as public toilets, parks, YMCAs, movie theater balconies, alleys, backstreets, ships, trucks, piers, docks, booths in porno arcades, bathhouses, back rooms, sex clubs, SM dungeons, and even cyberspace (*Gaywave* 1997). All the while, *Bowers* v. *Hardwick*, the legal case prohibiting queer sex, remained the law of the land.

Visible signs of public sexual culture were targeted. In the summer of 1997, the New York Police Department carried out undercover sting operations resulting in the arrests of 119 men charged with indecent exposure, soliciting sex, and other "lewd" acts (Neff 1997). Entrapment and wrongful arrests increased 40 percent from the year before (*Badpuppy* 1997). During one three-day sting by the Port Authority Police, ninety men were arrested in the men's room in the PATH station concourse of the World Trade Center (Goldstein 1997; Shindler 1997).

The issue at hand was, who filled these public spaces? Cruising spots which benefited low-income gays of color were fenced off. Sociologist Susan Christopherson (1994) notes, "The practice of citizenship, originating in the urban experience, is being transformed to emulate consumer behavior." Cruising is a place for people who do not have the money, or wish to use it for a hotel room. As such, the practice was extremely dangerous within the current climate. The question was, is public space accessible for nonconsumers, nonshoppers, in today's New York?

Answering the question, SexPanic! held a number of "queer-ins" in Central Park's Ramble, where police had been harassing men for "loitering" in the park, in some cases entrapping and beating gay men. The goal was to retake the Ramble's history and utility as a cruising space. Queers converged with flashlights looking for the "cops in the bushes," chanting "Push, push, in the bush!" and "We're here, we're here, we're fucking in the park."

SexPanic! was not the only direct action group in town battling the hyperregulation of public space in Manhattan. Following up on a large, pulsing, illegal street party, Reclaim the Streets pranked the police and called for a "massive protest" in Tompkins Square Park. The idea was to test the new park rules calling for groups of twenty or more to get permits before converging. Some one hundred police cars arrived only to find croquet players and ladies' clubs, both illegally converging in groups of twenty. When the police saw what was going on, they quickly left, exposing the selective enforcement of the law. The unconstitutional law was intended as a tool to control protests and "perverts in the bushes."

Park spaces had become contested grounds after the city's legal public sexual spaces were closed down, fenced off, and privatized. All public spaces felt the squeeze. Even community gardens, where neighbors converged to build community, were being bulldozed and sold off to developers (See Mikalbrown essay in this volume). Much of the pressure over public space began with a zoning law.

Skirmish #2: XXX zoning

In the fall of 1995 the city zoning law was passed. "We changed the rules," the mayor stated in September 1997:

> by adopting the same laws that apply to drug dealers and zoning regulations, we have cut the number of sex shops drastically. We made sure that no sex shop could operate within a set number of feet from schools, churches and community centers. Basically, with the tight new regulations, it will be nearly impossible for a sex shop to open in this city. In my opinion, one is too many. (Burr 1998)

Mayor Giuliani hoped to shut down nearly every adult business which dealt with sexual materials – strip clubs, bookstores, video stores, movie houses, and others. If implemented, the zoning law would turn 98 percent of Manhattan into a censorship zone. If the city's zoning law was fully enforced, New York City's sexual cultures: its arcades, clubs, Christopher Street's T-rooms, and so on, would all be relegated to the outskirts of Queens, Staten Island.

What was at stake were notions of community, or *Gemeinschaft* and *Gesellschaft* (Tönnies 1887/1957). *Gemeinschaft* refers to the idea of urban life as a village in which people live and work; they know one another, care for, and are committed to their community. *Gesellschaft*, on the other hand, refers to the loss of involvement with their community that people experience because of industrialization. Forced to work and play far from home, people lose any connection with the people of their neighborhoods. Cruising grounds, clubs, gardens, and other public spaces represent a small bit of *Gemeinschaft* in a rapidly transforming urban world.

Rally to "Keep New York Sexy!"

A SexPanic! flyer Jim Eigo wrote for a rally protesting the zoning law noted: "New Yorkers have learned to work, play, shop and party in close proximity. Sex is part of daily life. Don't let Rudy zone it out like toxic space." Intermediate associations were being lost as meeting spaces were padlocked, bulldozed, or shut down. Sociologist Philip Selznic (1992) outlines the problems which occur when these connections dissipate: "People lose the benefits of community when they are stripped of their group attachments and left naked before an impersonal or central authority." Those charming elements of city life, which make people feel part of something, were being lost. As public spaces disappeared, New York was being transformed into a place where people were left trembling.

SexPanic! formed, in part, to fight the zoning law. Immediately after its passage in 1995, Larry Flynt's former lawyer, Harold Price Ferringer, filed suit over the constitutionality of the law. By 1998, as the law made its way through the final chapters of the court battle, SexPanic! organized a series of rallies. After two successful demonstrations against the zoning law, SexPanic! sought to reappropriate what had been lost: Times Square. You would be hard pressed to find a drag queen, a cruiser, or even a massage parlor in today's Times Square. For a brief moment Sex Panic! wanted to kick up some of the cobwebs within a now sleepy neighborhood. The plan was for a jazz funeral, bringing joy and unabashed sex-positive bodies back to Times Square, if only for a day. The theme of the rally would be "March from Show World to Disney World to Stop Censorship, Save Jobs, and Squash Rudy's XXX Zoning Law."

On May 13, 1998, we were to meet at the corner of Show World, a porno theatre at the heart of the lost district, which the *New York Times* described as New York's supermarket of sex. We hadn't done much outreach for this rally. When I got to the corner, only two strippers had arrived ahead of me. It looked a little bleak. Slowly but surely, the whole corner filled with strippers, club owners, and more members of SexPanic! Along with a drum corps led by some former Lesbian Avengers, the chant "More Booty, Less Rudy, Keep New York Sexy!" pulsed through the sleepy streets. The chant took a rhythm of its own. The rest of the core activists arrived and we began to move. We marched west down 42nd Street to the Disney store, where the matinee lines waited to get into *The Lion King*. People smiled, laughed, and enjoyed the point we were making. Hecklers scorned the scene. The entire matinee crowd chanted with us: "No strippers, no peace!" And for a brief moment, delight refilled a territory thought of as lost for good.

Prank #3: taking a bust at the Disney store

In August 1998, Supreme Court Justice Ruth Bader Ginsberg rejected Ferringer's appeal. The following August, SexPanic! looked to organize a legal topless march through Times Square to mark the anniversary as a day of infamy. As outreach, I took the idea to the Lower East Side Collective (LESC), a convergence of activists who had done excellent work around public space issues in the city. It was suggested I contact Reverend Billy and the Church of Stop Shopping.

The next day I received a phone call from the Bill Talen, a local actor and instructor at the New School for Social Research, who had created the alter ego Reverend Billy and the Church of Stop Shopping. Its aim was to protest the consumerism overwhelming Manhattan, specifically to torment Disney and their flagship Times Square store. The reverend's gospel preached that when you enter the Disney store, "consumer narcosis" overtakes you and you forget who you are. In response, Reverend Billy, dressed in a minister's garb, had taken to delivering extemporaneous non-shopping sermons in and outside the store. Gradually, he encouraged others to come with him for "shopping interventions" at Disney. Although nothing ever came

Cops enjoying the performance at the
Disney Store.

of the proposed topless rally (I was one of only three potential marchers), in Talen
I found a wonderful fellow prankster.

The underpinning for Talen's character emerged from Jimmy Breslin's 1998 adage
that Times Square used to be a place where stories happened. Our job was to start
more stories. I began to participate in a number of non-shopping interventions. As
with the vision of the "strip-in" and other nonviolent, civil disobedience actions
around the city, Talen and I hoped to up the ante on the contested space within the
Disney store. The corner of 42nd Street and 7th Avenue was historically a place
where people from all over the world came to commune within the city's holy, neon
glimmer. One foot in the gutter and the other in the clouds, some preached; others
merely sought contact (Benderson 1997; Delany 1999). Currently, unless you are in
the neighborhood to shop, police ask you to move along.

An affinity group from LESC, SexPanic!, Reclaim the Streets, and the Church of
Stop Shopping staged a sit-in at the Disney store on November 15, 1999. Our goal
was to bring attention to a series of Disney offenses in the new Times Square. We
listed reasons for the sit-in on a flyer. Among others, we posited: "We're here to

protest the inauthentic … the use of entertainment as ideology … the celebration of the bland … Disney eradicates difference." We called for an end to Disney's support for the mayor's polices and requested that the company admit that their homoerotic cartoon star "Hercules" was gay, concluding: "Whose world do we want it to be – Disney's or ours?" (see Barber 1995).

After weeks of planning, two or three activists at a time trickled into the store. Once inside we performed a small play about the neighborhood, after which we locked down, blocking traffic to the cash register. We distributed lyric sheets to everyone in the store before leading the crowd in a resounding rendition of Disney's classic, "Whistle While You Work … for 15 cents an hour," in homage to Disney's Haitian and Indonesian sweatshops. The song was the cue for the Reverend to begin a non-shopping sermon, which further disrupted the somewhat excited shoppers and befuddled staff. Chants of "Put down the mouse!" and "Hercules is Gay!" filled the store before police were able to move in, arresting six of us. "It is my civil right not to live in a shopping mall," I screamed before being locked in the paddy wagon. For a moment, the sterilized private space had been transformed into a public theater, once again a place where stories begin.

Prank #4: reclaiming public space with stories

Two weeks after the Disney action, Reclaim the Streets held a roving street party in Times Square on the busiest shopping day of the year, November 26. The action began in Union Square, where marshals led over a thousand people on an im-promptu subway run, away from cops at 14th Street, up to 44th and Broadway. Once crowds flowed out of the 42nd Street subway, we kicked on our sound system and placed a tripod on the corner of 44th and Broadway, stopping traffic with dancing bodies for over an hour. The action, commemorating national "Buy Nothing Day," protested the role of globalization in homogenizing local geographies. The intention of the action was to involve the thousands of unsuspecting shoppers already clutter-ing the streets. Once confronted with the street party, in one grand culture-jamming moment, many joined in, thinking they had stumbled onto the production of a music video at nearby MTV. Sometimes magic realist narratives, like all stories, become reality-creating machines. By the end of the day, forty-five activists had been brutally arrested for dancing, rather than shopping, in the New York City streets. A group of some fifty of us followed the arrestees to the police station, playing drums, danc-ing, and telling stories as we waited for them to be released. The action would anticipate the following week's World Trade Organization uprising in Seattle; many Reclaim the Streets activists left jail for flights to the West Coast the following day. What had started as a movement about the quality of life in one small town had become part of an international resistance effort.

In the end, the stories of SexPanic!, the Church of Stop Shopping, and Reclaim the Streets outline different battlefronts in a public/private debate. In the era of global-ization, there remains a need for civic society in between the market and govern-ment. These groups are part of a burgeoning movement in do-it-yourself activism aimed at preserving public space and civic culture. Through radical street perform-ance, culture jamming, protest street parties, and other pranks, spaces left for dead regain life; public sexual cultures are remembered/re-enacted; and new stories emerge. Not a bad outcome; after all, even communities need stories to exist within.

Stepping off the sidewalk: Reclaim the Streets/NYC

STEPHEN DUNCOMBE

[W]hen you come to challenge the powers that be, inevitably you find yourself on the curbstone of indifference, wondering "should I play it safe and stay on the sidewalks, or should I go into the street?" (RTS/London)

Through direct action we demand that a different philosophy govern our lives and, at least for a moment, we free ourselves to what life could be like. (RTS/NYC)

New York City, October 4, 1998

It's a damp afternoon in early October. The clouds are low and periodically a light mist rolls down. For the past twenty minutes groups of young people have been strolling up to "The Cube," a large steel sculpture on a traffic island marking the entrance to Manhattan's East Village. Carrying portable radios and dressed in the young hipster uniform of oversized clothes, they look like they're either coming home from or launching out on an all-night rave. Some look more anxious than others, and the most anxious of the bunch scurry around yelling into cellphones and advising newcomers of their legal rights. People tune their radios to the frequency of a local pirate radio station and Goa trance music flows from fifty boomboxes. The crowd is visibly excited.

Meanwhile, a block south, an old bread truck is parked by the curb. Jammed inside is a portable transmitter, a couple of DJs, a sound engineer, and enough marijuana smoke to levitate the vehicle. A block west a small crew of people, desperately trying

to look nonchalant, wait next to a supine bundle of 30-foot steel poles, linked at the top. Further down and around the corner sit another small group, huddled around what looks like a garden wagon covered in a tarpaulin.

A little after 3 p.m., as the crowd had grown to more than a hundred, a signal is given. Led by a man holding aloft a large orange traffic sign with outlines of a man and woman dancing, the crowd moves tentatively off the curb of the traffic island and onto the street. "Move, move" the anxious ones yell and the crowd breaks into a run down Astor Place. One short block and they turn onto Broadway – the major thoroughfare that runs the length of Manhattan. In the middle of the street the metal pipes are being pushed into the air forming a tripod. Once the tripod is up and stable a young man scrambles up and seats himself on top. The garden cart is wheeled out, its tarp ripped off, and – after many frustrating tries – a small generator fires up, powering a compact receiver and amplifier. Heavy beats pump from the sound system, echoed by the boomboxes now turned to full volume. Curious crowds come off the sidewalk, people start to dance and soon three hundred hipsters have turned Broadway on a Sunday afternoon into a street party.

The New York Police Department shows up, at first slowly and then in force. They stand by bewildered, unsure what to do about the young man perched precariously 30 feet above the pavement, and not knowing how to confront a street full of ravers, some with painted faces, a few decked out in Marie Antoinette garb, and one energetic fellow in a bright blue bunny suit. It's Reclaim the Streets and New York City has never seen anything like it.

But the world already has. Reclaim the Streets/New York City is only the latest incarnation of a philosophy and style of protest that has erupted throughout the world, from London and cities throughout the UK, to Helsinki, Prague, Sydney, Tel

Aviv, and Berkeley, California. There are no official chapters of RTS, only a shared concern with public space and a common practice of carnivalesque protest. What follows is an unofficial history and personal analysis of one such outbreak, in New York City.

From London to New York

Reclaim the Streets began in London in the autumn of 1991, during the burgeoning anti-roads movement in England, when a small band of individuals got together to take direct action against automobiles. This group disbanded, but reformed four years later in response to two dramatic occurrences. One was the 1994 battle for Claremont Road, a residential street in East London that was to be demolished to make way for a busy traffic thoroughfare. In place of the usual petitions and marches to save the street, protesters in this campaign simply moved in – occupying every house on the block (save one house owned and occupied by a feisty 92-year-old woman, who refused the Department of Transport's order to move.) Claremont Road was then turned into a festival: houses were painted, barricades built, a large tower erected, and parties held, turning the area into a 24-hour community of protest up until Claremont Road's last hour.

In 1994 the British government also passed the Criminal Justice and Public Order Act (CJA). Not only did the CJA effectively outlaw political protests, but the act singled out as unlawful unpermitted parties with sound systems playing repetitive beats – in other words: raves. Thus the state linked protesters and ravers, making both their demands for public space illegal. This coalition, armed with the action model pioneered on Claremont Road, fueled the rebirth of Reclaim the Streets. In 1995 the reformed RTS threw its first street party on Camden High Street in London, shutting down the street to cars and opening it up to partyers for the entire day. This was soon followed by another party/protest and then another and another. These grew steadily in size and scope. In July of 1996, some eight thousand people took over the M41 motorway in an anti-road demonstration, and on April 12 in 1997, an estimated twenty thousnd people descended on and danced in Trafalgar Square in London to protest the general election. Meanwhile, the idea of Reclaim the Streets had spread and soon cities across the UK and Europe were hosting their own protest parties (*Do or Die* 1997; Jordan 1998).

Reclaim the Streets crossed the Atlantic in 1998, touching down, not too surprisingly, in the Bay Area. On May 16, armed with couches, chairs, carpets and a sound system, RTS/Bay Area took over Berkeley's Telegraph Avenue, a common site for protests over public space ever since the infamous People's Park protests in 1969, when police shot and killed a demonstrator. Back in New York City a young philosophy student named Louis read about this protest and other RTS actions in an anti-car magazine called Car Busters (Stagg 1998). Excited by what he had read, he organized a meeting at Blackout Books, the anarchist book store where Louis and a number of us volunteered. That first meeting brought together the usual suspects of the direct action protest scene in the East Village, albeit with a slightly younger face. But as word spread, so did the circle. Soon meetings included sound engineers from Steal this Radio, a local pirate radio, party promoters and DJs, performance artists and the manager of a club, and, importantly, a number of protest newbies brought in by the simple promise of a politicized rave.

The meetings were messy: chaotic and long, reflecting the inexperience of a number of newcomers to political organizing. But the chaos reflected something else: a certain studied non-professionalism, an unspoken commitment to keep things messy in order to allow for maximum participation of those who were new to organizing. But newcomers didn't come to RTS because of messy meetings (and more experienced politicos didn't leave despite them); instead they came because those meetings, and the action that was being planned, symbolized a philosophy that had been percolating in the cultural underground for the past two decades: Do-It-Yourself.

DIY was an ethic born in reaction against a dominant society that considers culture primarily in terms of a profit-generating, commercial enterprise. If you were a punk musician in the early 1980s and wanted to play your unpopular, and therefore unprofitable, music, then you had to rent out the local VFW hall and organize the venue yourself. If you wanted to write about the music you loved that mainstream magazines like *Rolling Stone* didn't acknowledge, then you did it yourself, publishing a zine. And fast-forwarding to the present day: if you want to party, and most of your friends are under twenty-one and broke, then you find a warehouse, cobble together a sound system, and you throw your own rave. The key in all of this culture is participation. If you don't participate, it doesn't happen.

Reclaim the Streets is a protest that only works if everyone participates. This is true not only for the organizers who have to create sound systems, train with tripods, build props and compose info sheets, but also for those who just show up on the day of the protest in costume, with radios, drums, or fire-breathing apparatus, and ready to dance. An RTS action is like a potluck dinner. RTS secures the space and provides the music (and post-protest legal support), but what happens at the action depends upon what people bring with them and what they do once they are there.

This cultural ethic of DIY pulled RTS/NYC into being. The push, however, came from elsewhere. New York City's mayor, Rudolph Giuliani, a former federal prosecuting attorney, had run for office in 1993 and was re-elected in 1997 on a strong law-and-order message, with a "Quality of Life" campaign as the centerpiece of his policing policy. QOL campaigns are based on the "broken windows" thesis. Simply, it goes like this: if a window is broken and goes unfixed and unpunished, soon criminals will be breaking down the door, carting off the furniture and assaulting the inhabitants. This criminology theory translated into the daily NYPD practice of petty harassment for "crimes" that New Yorkers had long considered part of city life: drinking beer, lighting a joint, and playing a radio outside; not waiting until the light had changed to walk across a street and riding against traffic on a bicycle; or visiting sex shops and bars and dancing in small clubs with no cabaret license. In the past, police had used these violations selectively to harass poor black and Latino youth, homeless persons, gays, lesbians and other "undesirables," but now the NYPD's reach extended into middle-class, white life – the very population that spawned the young hipster troops of RTS.

While Giuliani was "improving" the quality of life, New York City was undergoing an economic renaissance. With the new money came entertainment and service corporations vying to get a piece of it. Times Square was "cleaned up", its sex shops and small businesses closed in order to make room for a renovation led by the Disney Corporation. In the East Village, small bookstores were forced out by the Barnes & Noble chain and cafés were replaced by Starbucks. The Do-It-Yourself spirit of small business was replaced with the corporate service mantra of We-Do-It-For-You. The megastores and strip mall culture of suburban America that the young bohemians of RTS had fled was following them to NYC.

"Mayor Giuliani's Quality of Life campaign hinges on his definition of 'quality of life.' Is this yours?" So began the single-page information sheet handed out at the first RTS action in New York. After a list of grievances against Giuliani and corporate America for "reshaping every neighborhood in their own image," RTS issued a proclamation: "If there is no place to freely assemble, there is no free assembly. If there is no place to freely express, there is no free expression."

This would be a theme repeated in nearly all of RTS/NYC's propaganda, articulating our core philosophy: if you do not act out your rights, then they mean nothing. It is only through participation and action that abstract rights become real. The street party thrown that day was meant as a symbolic action through which people would participate – even if only for a few hours – in actively reclaiming their rights by reclaiming the street. The action was a tableau of those things outlawed or priced out of the "new" New York. A carnival of freaks, culture for free. In the words of that first RTS info sheet: "We demand great feasts of public space" (RTS/NYC 1988).

While RTS openly positioned themselves against the policing and privatization of state and corporations, there was another – unspoken – opponent: the left itself. RTS's opposition to progressive movements had little or nothing to do with their politics. There were a number of excellent activist groups campaigning around QOL and public space in New York, and a number of members of RTS were also involved with these groups. Instead, the difference was one of style. With the notable exception of ACT UP and its spin-offs, the dominant progressive protest model in the US, throughout the 1980s and 1990s, was dull and deadly. It went something like this: leaders organize a "mass" demonstration. We march. We chant. Speakers are paraded onto the dais to tell us (in screeching voices through bad sound systems) what we already know. Sometimes we sit down and let the police arrest us. We hope the mainstream media puts us on the news for five seconds. Sometimes they do, often they don't. While these demonstrations were often held in the name of "people's power," they were profoundly disempowering. Structured within this model of protest was a philosophy of passive political activity: spectatorship. They organize; we come. They talk; we listen. And most of what was being said was negative and defeatist: "Hell No!" and "We're Against It!"

This model of protest holds little appeal to a generation who found their dissident voice, by rejecting spectator/consumer society and creating their own culture. Looking for models that resonated with DIY philosophy, RTS turned past the parade and rally model of the nineteenth century (Davis 1988) to the medieval carnival (RTS/London 2000; Bakhtin 1968; cf. Bey 1985).

During the carnival the world is temporarily turned upside down, the fool crowned king and the king made a fool. People glimpse what a different world might look like:

a world without priests or kings, or cops and corporations. "Carnival celebrates temporary liberation from the prevailing truth and established order; it marks the suspension of all hierarchical rank, privileges, norms and prohibitions," as RTS/London's website proclaims, borrowing freely from Mikhail Bakhtin, the famous scholar supporter of carnival. And, critically, the carnival is also a collaboratively constructed experience. "Carnival is not a spectacle seen by the people," RTS/London continues; "they live in it, and everyone participates because its very idea embraces all people."

In the carnival RTS found a model of protest in which the action itself was symbolic of its demands. RTS stages actions that perform a vision of the world we want to create. We demand collaboratively produced public space by going out and actually creating a collaboratively produced public space. To crib Marshall McLuhan: the medium is the message. As RTS/NYC's first flyer explained: "Reclaim the Streets is at once a unifying symbolic action, and a movement to reclaim public space." And on that damp day in October, RTS/NYC presented a message wrapped in a medium that spoke to a new generation of would-be activists in New York (McLuhan 1965; cf. Epstein 1991).

But something the boring old left – as well as state and corporations – did have that RTS did not was strategy. Grandiose claims of revolution and broad proclamations for public space aside, what did that action on Broadway actually accomplish? Were we creating a movement or bringing about change? Or was RTS merely engaging in "ether activism"? That is, was it putting an idea out there, hoping it catches, and then – magically – expecting change? (Kauffman 1998). Responding to this challenge, RTS/NYC decided to stage an action that had a tangible political effect. We decided to lend our support and protest style to an ongoing campaign, one which fitted with our concern for public space: the movement to save community gardens.

New York City's decline in the 1970s created thousands of empty lots, as landlords abandoned and torched their buildings and the city seized and demolished them. City residents responded by staking claims to blasted spaces, clearing them of garbage and rubble, and planting flowers and vegetables. Initially the city government blessed this practice and leased the land for a nominal cost to the gardeners. Amidst drab concrete, green spaces bloomed in New York City. In the 1990s all this changed. Pushed by a superheated real estate market and a mayor committed to privatization, the city revoked garden leases and began auctioning lots to developers. The East Village, once a poor neighborhood with many abandoned buildings, had a high concentration of gardens. Now, centrally located and imbued with bohemian allure, it was particularly attractive to luxury housing developers. In the spring of 1999 a large number of East Village gardens, as well as others around the city, were scheduled to be auctioned off. A loose coalition, including normally apolitical gardeners and radical urban environmentalists, formed to fight these auctions and stage protests ranging from permitted rallies to mass civil disobedience. Contacting this coalition (which wasn't difficult as a number of RTSers were also part of the garden movement), we offered our activist services. Working with members of the garden coalition we decided upon an action that would turn a street symbolically into a garden, timed to occur in the week between their rally and CD.

On April 11, 1999, RTS took over the main avenue of the East Village: Avenue A. With fire breathers, costumed dancers, a marching band, a seesaw made from police barricades, flower boxes, and two tripods on either side of the street, we turned a street into a garden party. During the action we distributed thousands of flyers explaining the garden struggle and giving simple "what you can do to save the gardens" action suggestions on the back. We also launched a fairly sophisticated press operation that netted appearances on the evening news as well as write-ups in a number of newspapers. A few weeks later, after mass arrests and amidst increasing publicity and public concern, the mayor backed down and cut a deal to sell many of the community gardens to a land trust bankrolled by a Hollywood star. It was a victory, limited perhaps, but a victory nonetheless. And it was a victory that RTS, by making gardens an issue for those protesting, and putting the issue on the news for one more evening, helped win. We felt great.

Unfortunately these warm and fuzzy feelings were not felt by all, particularly not by the New York Police Department, who responded to our future actions with increasing sophistication and brutality. Our relations with the NYPD had started off OK. Although they came with riot gear to our first action, they seemed more amused and bemused than threatened by us. They did arrest eleven people that day, but they also let us hold the street for a couple of hours and negotiate our sound system to safety. In the garden action they responded more aggressively, but again arrests were at a minimum (nine in total) and they allowed us to negotiate our way off the street after a couple of hours. Both our actions had caught them unprepared.

When they were prepared, it was because we wanted them to be. About a week after the initial October action we called the NYPD, tipping them off to an unspecified protest RTS was planning the following Sunday, again at The Cube in the East Village. On the appointed day and time about a half-dozen of us from RTS and another activist group, the Lower East Side Collective, met at The Cube. Wearing formal attire, we unfolded a table, assembled chairs, spread a tablecloth, and put out a tea service. As Vivaldi's *Four Seasons* wafted out of a tape deck, we sat down to high tea – surrounded by more than fifty uniformed cops, a cluster of high-ranking officers, a mobile command center, and a number of arrest vans. Predicting they would respond in this fashion, we printed up flyers asking the passersby why such a heavy police presence was necessary for such "civilized" behavior, thus calling the mayor's Quality of Life campaign into question. One cop even reinforced our message. When a curious onlooker asked why he was there in front of these people quietly drinking tea, he replied "to protect the public from this disturbance." Our point was made – courtesy of the NYPD. While most of the beat cops were amused, the white shirts were not, and RTS was on their shit list.

We staged a similar "prank" protest in the summer of 1999 when RTS organized groups of exactly twenty people to gather in Tompkins Square park for picnics, a croquet game, sunbathing, and so on. A twenty-first person then visited each group in turn, thereby making them "illegal" according to the draconian, and only recently enforced, Parks Department law that held that gatherings of over twenty people are illegal without a permit. With such bad publicity, which our protest contributed to, the Parks Police stopped enforcing the law soon after. We again invited the NYPD to this RTS "action," even going so far as to plan a bogus "massive demonstration" on an Internet listserv we knew they had infiltrated. The police initially showed up in force, with a half-dozen paddy wagons, but having learned their lesson last time, they retreated to the edge of the park and eventually left.

But these were not the only, or even the most important, factors in the NYPD's newfound interest in Reclaim the Streets. It's my hunch that their increasing concern had less to do with our antics, and more to do with those of our cousins across the Atlantic. In 1999 a number of groups had put out a call to protest the G8 meeting in Germany on June 18. RTS/London called for a Carnival Against Capital in the City of London as their contribution. Given RTS/London's track record in mobilizing thousands, even tens of thousands, of people for their protests, London police

were on high alert. Our connection with RTS/London
– or RTS anywhere else – was minimal. A former organizer with RTS/London was part of RTS/NYC, but
that was a coincidence of love and geography, not
coordinated international planning. In solidarity with
London and groups around the world, however, RTS/
NYC organized our own demonstration on June 18,
staged for the capitol of capital: Wall Street. It's my
guess that the NYPD saw – or were persuaded to
see by their overseas counterparts – our action as
proof of a global organization, ironically taking our
desire and intent to be part of larger movements
and campaigns far more seriously than we were
ourselves.

Dancers, actors, stilters, fire eaters, musicians, poets and preachers

Come and lend a hand, call the hotline for info.

RECLAIM THE STREETS NYC!
STREET PARTY PROTEST
JUNE 18TH
LIBERTY PLAZA 3:00 PM
HELP MAKE IT HAPPEN!!
(212)539.6746

Whatever the reason, on June 18 we got clob-
bered by the NYPD. We never took Wall Street, or
any street for that matter. Our – now huge – sound system was seized
after thirty seconds. We suffered thirty-seven arrests. And there was almost no
mention of the protest on the news. Part of this had to do with our own mistakes:
we were out of our home turf, our point people (the lead organizers) for the action
were engaged in an arrestable action (and were arrested) early on, and there was
minimal communication on the ground. Still, the biggest difference between this
protest and previous ones was that the police were ready for us, they knew what to
expect, and they were aggressive in responding. If you stepped onto the street that
day, you were under arrest.

It happened again five months later in Times Square. On November 26, RTS
threw a street party to celebrate Buy Nothing Day and demonstrate our solidarity
with the launch of the anti-WTO protests in Seattle. Although organizationally we
were much smarter, meeting in a place thirty blocks south of our destination and
taking a subway en masse, while keeping good communication throughout, the police
were even smarter. They showed up in force almost immediately. Special services
officers headed right for the tripods and shook the people out of them. The sound
system was seized. Forty-five people were arrested, some after being brutally tackled
to the ground. The party was squashed before it took off. (RTS also suffered – or,

Members of RTS, the Hungry March Band, countless garden folks and other neighborhood vagabonds all meet in a nearby community garden before the action.

you could argue, gained – from context confusion. In the heart of the Disneyfied Times Square, tourists mistook us for a film shoot or MTV video and cheered on their support.) It took a while, but the police had learned how to respond to RTS. They had help: two undercover police were identified trying to join RTS, and two short-term members of RTS were told they were under suspicion of being cops and left on their own accord.

RTS had built itself around a specific style of protest, the street party, and we were now discovering the weakness of fetishizing a certain protest style. The police had slowly, but surely and effectively, figured out how to respond and they had material resources and the law on their side. But we had creativity on ours. And so we rethought what it means to "reclaim the streets." This rethinking didn't happen in any sort of conscious planned strategy session, but organically in response to what had happened, new opportunities that arose, and new waves of leaders that took over as old ones stepped aside.

One direction in which RTS moved was pure cultural carnival. Some members of RTS organized a series of subway parties, in which revelers would meet at a certain place and hour and board a subway, taking over the entire train and transforming it into a moving party. Others of us worked with a local performance artist, Reverend Billy, in creating "permitless parades," illegal freak parades that would wind their way through lower Manhattan taking over the street where we could. Still another RTSer threw thousands of dollars into the air outside Macy's on the biggest shopping day of the year, each bill stamped with the question: "Satisfied?" There was no strategic goal in these actions, no coalition building leading to a larger movement. But through these actions, received notions of how things are, or how public spaces should be used, were gloriously and hilariously questioned and transformed.

Another direction for RTS was affinity groups. In the wake of Seattle and the success of the Direct Action Network in coordinating large numbers of semi-autonomous affinity groups, RTS/NYC went on the road to the International Monetary Fund/World Bank protests in Washington DC, the Republican National Convention in Philadelphia, and then back to DC for President Bush's Inauguration. To each of these demonstrations we brought our carnival style, dressing up and acting out the part of Loan Sharks, Billionaires for Bush (or Gore), and Students for an Undemocratic Society, respectively.

We also brought something new with us: irony. Instead of creating the symbolic embodiment of the world we wanted to create, we dressed the part of our opponents in order to parody them. Why this shift? Partly for strategic reasons. We engineered our image as a "culture jam," a way to break into mainstream media coverage while making it difficult for them to spin our radical critique into a reformist message. In order to cover us – which they did since we were appealing eye candy – the media also had to explain us. This meant making the connection between loan sharks and international funding agencies, billionaires and political parties, and youth fascists and a stolen election. Irony was also a way to continue our philosophy of participation when interacting with thousands of people (or millions of viewers) who were not part of our action. Irony only works in so far as people "get it," actively constructing a counter message and ideal in their own mind. In other words, we were creating a symbol of the world that we wanted to create, but one that only appeared if other people entered into our joke. And we also did it just to have fun. It was a refreshing act of personal and political catharsis to chant "No Justice? No Problem!" and "Wall Street! Our Street!" after years of mouthing earnest platitudes – not only for us, but for the other affinity groups we would meet in our duties as a "flying squad" blockading the streets.

At first glance these anti-capitalist globalization demonstrations seem a return to the dull and deadly "Mass March on Washington" protest model I described earlier. To be sure, people from all over the country descend upon one central location for a given demonstration on a given date. But there is also a critical difference. In this new style of mass action there are no marches or speakers. Instead the goal is to occupy public space and transform it through blockades, lock downs, or, in the case of RTS affinity groups, clowning and dancing (e.g. a fifty-person kick line blocking traffic, singing "Mac the Knife" while dressed as loan sharks in tuxedos). In other words, the new style of mass protest is very similar to the model of RTS. This is not the result of Reclaim the Streets' direct influence, but because both RTS and these demonstrations are created out of common experiences: positive familiarity with DIY ethics and practice, and shared distaste for spectator-style politics.

RTS/NYC still throws carnival-style reclamation protests. On May Day 2000, we reclaimed a fenced-off lot that the city had long promised as park land on the East River in Brooklyn. Working with More Gardens!, a local green space group, we cut the fence and erected a maypole, then cleaned up garbage and planted vegetables and flowers while the NYPD and television news crews looked on. In late November of 2000 we joined up with Critical Mass, organizing a bike ride for auto-free streets that ended in a street party fired up by our – temporarily – liberated sound system.

What's next? It's hard to know exactly. Reclaim the Streets in New York City has evolved and changed over the years we've been active, learning from our successes and – often painfully slowly – from our failures, responding to new opportunities and the closing of old ones, garnering new ideas from new people as they cycle through the organization, and spreading the ideas of RTS as people move on to other places and groups. Through all the permutations of RTS/NYC there has been one constant refrain: the form a protest takes needs to embody the politics of its participants. And if we are going to create a world worth living in, then that protest had better be fun.

Saving Esperanza Garden: the struggle over community gardens in New York City

KERSTIN MIKALBROWN

The Esperanza coqui

Walking down my street, I sometimes get the feeling that I don't belong. Between all the concrete paths and advertising billboards, genuine contact with other people often slips through the cracks. I eat in private – whether at home or at secluded tables in restaurants. I live with one roommate, whom I hardly see. And I when I go to work, I sit in a cubicle, by myself. Ironically, I am not alone in this. Being alone is par for the course in most large urban centers. In fact, it seems that cities are more and more designed for people to live very alienated lives. New York City is one of them. There are almost no public spaces in this city. Socializing is based around cafés, bars, restaurants, and shopping – private spaces where you need to pay a fee (whether a cup of coffee or a drink) to stay. They are commercial spaces designed to make a profit. And if you cannot afford endless $4 cappuccinos or $7 drinks, you find yourself with not a lot of places to go. Even the public parks – of which there are not many – are full of vendors, fences, and curfews. And I rarely have an encounter with someone else in the park.

That's why I was amazed to find myself sitting in front a campfire in a garden in the middle of Manhattan one night last winter, surrounded by strangers who were talking to me as though I were sitting in their own kitchen. The garden was called El Jardin de la Esperanza, Spanish for "The Garden of Hope." It was a community garden on the Lower East Side, a garden created and enjoyed by neighbors. It was destroyed by the city of New York.

Many of the gardens on the Lower East Side began in the 1970s. At that time the neighborhood was full of empty lots left by buildings burnt to the ground by landlords when the housing market crashed. These lots were full of trash and debris from the crumbled buildings, and the city made no effort to reuse them. The rubble-strewn lots threatened the safety of and demoralized the residents. The people in the community decided to do something about the situation. They went out and reclaimed the land that the city was wasting, clearing away the rubble to make room for something new and entirely their own. They cleaned up the trash, prepared the soil, and planted seeds. One by one, the old abandoned lots were covered in new greenery.

Esperanza was one of the most active community gardens developed in this period. It was planted in 1977 by Alicia Torres, her family, and the neighbors who lived next door to the empty lot at 221 East 7th Street. It took them an entire year to clear the trash and prepare the ground, but the result was well worth the effort. The birth of the gardens helped to transform the Lower East Side from a burnt-out ghetto into a vibrant, attractive community. This new beauty became a double-edged sword, though, because by the early 1980s the neighborhood began to attract real estate developers. New York City's government created the cross-subsidy plan, which allowed the gardens to be sold off for luxury developments so long as a small, flexible percentage of the housing was designated for low-income tenants.

Housing is a pressing concern in New York City. However, what is being built is primarily luxury rate housing, with rents out of reach of the people who actually live in the Lower East Side. And the city targeted lots where the gardens were growing for development, even though there are plenty of vacant lots available in the same neighborhoods, often on the same streets. Esperanza was one of these gardens.

Esperanza was first threatened in August of 1999, when the city offered to sell the garden to Donald Cappocia, a real estate developer who had donated more money than legally allowed to Mayor Giuliani's election campaign and whose company had already built luxury housing on top of the ruins of three other local community gardens.

The gardeners at Esperanza immediately began a campaign to save their 22-year-old piece of urban paradise. The fight against the city's development plans took many forms, from letter writing to direct action protests, but the heart of the struggle took shape with the construction of the giant coqui frog towering above the garden.

The thumb-sized coqui frog is native to Puerto Rico, and its history on that island makes it a perfect representation of the spirit of the garden. The coqui is so loyal to its community that it cannot survive outside of Puerto Rico, and it will do anything to protect the environment it lives in. In one story, the tiny creature defended an entire village from a monster.

Inside the coqui!

The coqui built at Esperanza was a larger-than-life representation, soaring fifteen foot above the ground and large enough for two people (or three or four children) to fit in comfortably. It took the gardeners and activists from the More Gardens! coalition three weeks just to build the foundation, and several more to cover the frame and complete the painting. Many of the local children who played in the garden helped with the construction, reminding the adults of all the fun and joy that the frog represented.

By early November 1999, the coqui was more than just a symbol of resistance. Faced with the threat of the city's bulldozers, activists and gardeners began sleeping in the frog every night. Every morning from 7 a.m. to 10 a.m., local residents and community activists gathered for a "stop the bulldozers party" with breakfast, coffee, and yoga sessions to keep up the spirits in the garden and support the dedicated souls sleeping outside through the freezing winter months.

The encampment protected the garden for much longer then the city would have liked, but the lot was sold and the developer demanded a return on his investment. On February 14, the blocks of 7th and 8th Streets between avenues B and C were covered in "No Parking"

Two years before he bulldozed Esperanza, Cappoccia bulldozed four community gardens. LESC borrowed from ACT UP's old know-your-scumbag flyer to make this comparison.

Viva el Jardin de la Esperanza!
Outside the garden with the coqui.

signs. The people keeping watch over the garden realized that the bulldozers would be coming the next day, and started calling the numbers on the emergency phone tree, letting people know that the garden needed urgent protection.

I was at a Valentine's Day party that night, where many of the guests were Esperanza supporters. One by one, or in small groups, people left the party to go to the garden. Some went home first to pick up sleeping bags or camera equipment, and I left with a neighbor to gather some wood from her apartment building to keep the campfire burning all night. The goal was to hold off the bulldozers long enough for the New York Supreme Court to issue a temporary stay against any further destruction of the gardens, but we knew that our chances were slim at best. As the night turned into dawn, more and more people came out to stand in the cold, support their community, and fight for their garden.

The bulldozers finally came at around eight in the morning. By then, hundreds of people were gathered inside and around the gates of Esperanza. The protesters shouted "Shame on you! Shame on you!" as the police arrested thirty-one people, several of whom were locked inside the coqui or chained to the fence, and pushed back the crowds to make room for the demolition crew. When the bulldozers tore the coqui off its steel perch and smashed the beautifully painted sculpture into the ground, several people in the crowd began to cry.

The temporary stay that would have protected Esperanza was issued at 11 a.m., three hours after the coqui was torn down and the garden was bulldozed. The front of the garden was covered with a tall plywood wall, as though people might forget what had once been behind it. But the next day "Viva Esperanza!" was painted across the wall in bold writing, and candles and flowers created a makeshift shrine.

"Walking home from jail, it all began to hit me," Ben Shepard, one of the thirty-one activists arrested said, "the photo of Brooke fighting off the cops, of the coqui, all the beauty of community courage, and of our loss. I'll say this much – never have I felt more joy and connection with New Yorkers from all walks of life … than standing in a blizzard, smiling by a bonfire, sharing stories at Esperanza.… After some eight years of HIV/AIDS work, I'm reminded of the simple point: loss lays fertile ground for community regeneration.… Let a thousand seeds bloom!"

These words are a direct call to action for all of us – a challenge to find new ways of bringing the spirit of community gardening to our own lives. When you walk down the street where you live tomorrow, try to see it with new eyes. Look for the cracks in the concrete where seeds could be squeezed in, and a community could start to grow. You don't have to plant a thousand at once, and you don't have to be a seasoned gardener or community activist to start. All you have to do is find a friend, or reach out to a stranger, and believe in your own power to make something beautiful for everyone to share.

At cross purposes: the Church Ladies for Choice

JAN COHEN-CRUZ

It is 7:30 a.m. on a Saturday morning, and the Church Ladies for Choice are getting dressed for a morning of street performances outside abortion clinics. Though usually the epitome of modesty, adorned in "sensible shoes, floral print polyester frocks, and earrings that pinch – that's what keeps us so angry!" – today they are in a daring mood. Phyllis Stein, "the Jewish Church Lady," shows off some pearls. "Are these too much?" he asks. "No," answers Sister Mary, aka Yasha Buncik. Stein is disappointed: "I'd hoped they were too much. I'll wear them anyway."

The Church Ladies are a pro-choice counterpart to right-to-lifers who "blockade women's health facilities that offer abortions, forcing the clients to run a gauntlet of harassment" (Buncik 1993). Like a radical chain of McDonald's, the first Ladies were established in Pittsburgh; a second group was founded in Washington DC. Impressed by their ability to entertain and defuse tension, two members of WHAM! (Women's Health and Mobilization) joined with two male ACT UPpers to inaugurate a New York contingent. The Church Ladies' goal is to get the pro-choice message out at the sites where the so-called pro-life message is most harmful. The strategy is to make themselves a news-attracting event: to "speak through, not to" the media (cited by Buncik 1993). This thinking reflects their roots in ACT UP, whose modus operandi was "to go to the furthest extreme in order to get the center to take notice" (Signorile 1993: 72).

ACT UP was founded in March 1987 in response to government passivity in the face of the AIDS crisis. It quickly became known for its brash direct actions to bring attention to, for example, the profiteering of pharmaceutical companies, insufficient governmental funds, homophobia, needle exchange, and issues of women with AIDS. At ACT UP, the Church Ladies' founding mothers experienced the power of theatrical street actions through a project called Action Tours. "Do you remember the Santa Claus who lost his job at Macy's in 1991 when they found out he was HIV-positive, and then it got a lot of publicity and he got his job back?" Buncik asks. "That's because twenty-eight of us dressed like Santas, converged on Macy's, chained ourselves to the cosmetics department and demanded that he be reinstated."

Membership in the New York Church Ladies is loose. Currently they number about eighteen, mostly gay men and a few straight women, all of whom dress as either ultra-feminine, church-going ladies or members of the cloth. Their character names are wordplays about sex, like Bessie Mae Mucho; religion, as Cardinal Sin; and pro-choice politics, as Harmonie Moore, who pleads, "How many more women must die of botched illegal abortions due to the fascist injustices of the American right and their psycho-Christian lapdogs?" They describe themselves as " 'gals' who lift spirits and provide comic relief at clinic defense and abortion-related demonstrations. The U.S.O. of clinic defenders; the cheerleaders for choice" (Church Ladies 1993a: 1).

The singing of "Hers – the word Hymns is just so sexist!" (Church Ladies 1993a: 7) – is at the heart of Church Ladies' performances. Sharon Flewitts explains the genesis of this choice:

> It was in New York, at the 1992 Democratic Convention. Randall Terry [founder of Operation Rescue, an anti-abortion group that blockades clinics under the banner of "rescuing unborn babies"] was surrounded by the media. We arrived, in our Church Lady garb, and redirected the media our way, a good thing in itself. But we didn't know what to do once we had their attention. That's why we developed the songs. (Flewitts 1993)

The songs are familiar melodies with rewritten pro-choice lyrics. For example, "This Womb is My Womb," sung to the tune of "This Land is Your Land," attests, "This womb is my womb/ It is not your womb/ And there is no womb/ For Wandell Tewwy." As the Ladies dress and make up this particular morning, some of them run through a new song that Bessie Mae Mucho has written to the tune of Mary Poppins' "Supercalifragilisticexpialidocious": "Christian-fasco-Nazi-nutso-psycho-right-wing-buuull-shit." The text renders the proper appearance of their personae suspect through its unladylike combination of "Christian fasco," colloquial "nutso," and unchurchlike "bull shit." The Ladies emphasize the gap between substance and form.

The use of drag also puts the normal into question, by underscoring the social construction of morality as embodied by church-going, conservatively dressed, sensibly shod, always smiling females. This might appear to be a self-defeating choice, given the group's feminist politics and drag's erstwhile hostile overtones. According to Carole-Anne Tyler, "Not so long ago camp languished, theorized as the shameful sign of an unreconstructed, self-hating, and even woman-hating, homosexual by gay, feminist, and lesbian feminist critics alike" (1991: 33). But in contrast to the glamour of most drag, the Ladies' careful exposure of a stubble of beard and fully hairy legs makes this a kind of Brechtian drag, whose seams are intended to show. Their obvious masquerade puts the "for realness" of their adversaries into question, too, by suggesting that any appearances can be put on or taken off. Still, aware that drag can be read as misogyny, the Ladies always include at least one biological woman dressed as a "Lady" or a nun (Buncik 1993). Women and men in drag together suggest that everyone is disguised to conform to social norms.

The Ladies also expose the ideological construction of words in the abortion controversy. Conscious of the power of language to shape public perception and aware that the religious right's term "pro-life" is emotionally stronger than "pro-choice," the Ladies have renamed their adversaries "antis," "lifers," and "the religiously challenged." The religious right also expresses its views through renaming, referring to the clients at clinics as "whores" and "dykes" (Phelan 1993: 131), an amazing conflation of women who choose abortion as either just into sex for the money or not attracted to men. Buncik refers to their local adversaries as "HOG-PI(E)s," the acronym for the New York City clinic attack group Helpers of God's Precious Infants. Members of HOGPI hold prayer meetings in front of clinics, hand out anti-abortion literature, and try to convince clients not to "murder their babies." Consequently, most clinics have clearly designated volunteer escorts waiting to whisk the women inside.

Today the Church Ladies plan to perform at four clinics, and I am to be their driver. I tend to be a strong advocate of street theatrics that direct attention to actual sites that deserve scrutiny. I think of such performances as acts of witness: acknowledging awareness of something even if there is no immediate means of stopping it. And I certainly perceive the religious right's performances outside of abortion clinics

as bullying women at a particularly vulnerable moment of their lives. But I begin this day dubious. The Church Ladies know that they will not change the antis' minds. Supporting the escorts is considerate, but why focus on a small group of people who already are pro-choice? I wonder about the clients. Having an abortion is no pleasure; nobody talks about "pro-abortion," only "pro-choice." How do they feel about these ostentatious people drawing more attention to the clinic? And why do gay men, who make up the Ladies' majority and are the adult population least directly affected by abortion rulings, get up early on Saturday mornings to do free street shows?

We arrive at the first clinic and, as carefully staged as conventional theatrics, the Ladies prepare their entrance a half block away. They unfurl a long banner that reads in bold large letters, "CHURCH LADIES FOR CHOICE." One Church Lady plays the bagpipes as they move ceremonially toward the clinic, holding the banner at their waists like a portable lower frame. The police direct them to one side of the clinic door, well apart from the antis. Once in place, the Ladies sing through their repertoire, with a little playful banter between songs, as the escorts cheer and the antis grimace. The Ladies are high-spirited and tuneful, sashaying along to the music and playing right to the audience, flirtatious toward the escorts and passersby, and with an undercurrent of one-upmanship toward the antis.

The songs are sung collectively, with occasional solos; some have choreography. "High Court Boogie," a song about the Supreme Court sung to the tune of "The Boogie-Woogie Bugle Boy from Company D," features three of the Ladies, while the rest do backup:

> Well George and Ronny put them on the bench to say
> Women in the kitchen they would have to stay
> When Casey came to town
> We-e-ell that's when they said
> Oh boy the shit will go down!
> They're on the High Court now
> They're after you and me
> They are Clarence, Tony, Billy, Dave and Sandra D.

The escorts flock around the Ladies, delighted with the energetic support. As they sing, the Ladies gather an additional audience of passersby, some delighted, some confused. They also give out pro-choice literature.

The right often frames its clinic appearances as religious revivals; according to Peggy Phelan, they "generate a feeling of terror, and thereby produce the feeling that one needs to be saved" (1993: 131). They do this through intense prayer and concentration, and through passionate efforts to convince women entering the clinics not to "murder their unborn children. "Sometimes the antis display two different posters of fetuses in what Faye Ginsburg has described as a pattern of dual representations: the one, an "innocent" fetus, photographed "in warm, amber tones, suffused with soft light … [and the other,] gruesome, harshly lit, clinical shots of mutilated and bloody fetal remains" (1989: 105). The Church Ladies juxtapose that energy with a totally contrasting display of irreverence and good humor, thus undermining the atmosphere that the religious right tries to create.

At one of the clinics we visit, an anti falls to her knees in prayer near the clinic door. She is holding a 3-inch-tall plastic model of a fetus that resembles a baby Jesus icon, sending clients a message that they are killing God. She rushes up to a woman entering the clinic, but the escorts get the woman in before the anti can say more than a few words. A police officer directs her to the side with the prayer group. A man waiting for his girlfriend who is inside getting an abortion says the right-to-lifers make them furious; an abortion is traumatic enough but the lifers only make them feel worse, not change their mind. They were both glad that people expressing the other side were at the clinic so that it did not appear "all bad" to get an abortion.

In front of another clinic, a male anti approaches me with a right-to-life magazine and shows me an article about a tortuous new method of abortion in which "they suck out a baby's brain." He speaks softly and with great concern. Were I not so ardently pro-choice, I can imagine wanting to dissociate myself from anyone who would do such a thing to a baby. But we are talking about fetuses, not babies. Again I am reminded, words are a weapon of this war. He refers to the Church Ladies as a "bunch of lesbians trying to mock what we're doing here." He not only misses the fact that most of the performers are men, complete with hairy arms, deep voices, and tall statures, but that they are a group of men and women. He also assumes that they are lesbians, as if that were the only reason one would be pro-choice.

Mimicry is another strategy here, the Church Ladies reflecting back their own version of the antis' gestures, songs, and clothing as through a funhouse mirror. Carole Anne Tyler links mimicry and camp, stating that in both realms "one 'does' ideology in order to undo it, producing knowledge about it" (1991: 53). When the lifers hold crosses up toward the Ladies, the Ladies hold up costume jewelry and make the sign of the cross back at them. When the HOGPIs sing "Amazing Grace," the Ladies join in, with their rewritten words:

Amazing grace, how sweet the sound
That saved a wretch like me
I once was lost, now I'm pro-choice
Was blind, but now I see.

The mimicry of tone with opposite words demonstrates that the same affect can be applied to any point of view.

Oddly enough, when the Church Ladies march up to the antis at this site, the police do not try to separate them and they are quickly surrounded by a crowd. Audience sympathy is clearly with the Ladies, causing the antis to pack up and leave. They would have only looked foolish if they stayed; a straight man automatically becomes part of the joke when partnered with a comic. The Church Ladies entertain for about forty minutes, then march out of the ad hoc performing space to vigorous applause.

Why do gay men, who make up the Ladies' majority and are the least likely to be directly affected by abortion rulings, get up early Saturday mornings to do clinic defense shows? I believe that they are cross-pollinating queer politics with traditionally feminist concerns. The term "queer," according to Michael Warner, "rejects a minoritizing logic of tolerance or simple political interest-representation in favor of a more thorough resistance to regimes of the normal" (1993: xxvi). The Church Ladies connect anti-choice and anti-gay actions, as articulated by a number of their songs. "Stand By Your Clinic" attests that "when they're done with the women, they're coming after us queers." "We're Off to Fight the Bigots" has one verse for women's healthcare and another in support of the Rainbow Curriculum. "Psycho Christians," to the tune of "Tiny Boxes," warns:

> Psycho Catholics, taunting homos
> That's the way they buy indulgences
> Psycho Catholics, taunting homos
> And they all look just the same
> There's a closet-case
> and a closet-case
> and a closet-case
> and a closet-case
> Psycho Catholics, taunting homos
> And they all hide just the same. (Church Ladies, 1993a)

They thus support the larger idea of sexual freedom, manifested as a woman's right to choose an abortion or anyone's right to choose his/her sexual partners.

Performing also functions as an anti-burnout strategy for activists. The male Ladies get a palpable pleasure from making-up, exchanging necklaces and earrings, and zipping each other's dresses. The biological women dressing in the moral authority of the nuns enjoy that unique pleasure. Yasha Buncik speaks with a compelling sense of moral outrage. She works as a copyeditor, correcting other people's mistakes for a living – but mistakes of form, not substance. As Sister Mary, she addresses people's ethical errors, and shows them the way.

The group's critique of the church may be seen as at cross-purposes because some religious people, who share their politics, are offended by songs like "God is a Lesbian" (sung to the tune of "God Save the Queen"). But others are attracted precisely to the connection between anti-choice, anti-gay attitudes and certain church politics. The Ladies fulfill their desire to take on the religious right by appearing with them on the only stage where such a duet would be possible, namely at the site of the controversy. And whereas in the late 1970s and 1980s, differences among people were stressed – for example, feminism became feminism*s* to acknowledge variances of race, class, ethnicity, sexual orientation, and concomitant political priorities – in the 1990s connections need to be forged among contingents with compatible goals. This the Church Ladies achieve by interpreting choice vis-à-vis the whole realm of sexuality. They thus please themselves, fight the good fight, and build coalitions, breaking the political hold that identity politics has had on leftist organizing over the past twenty years.

My day with the Church Ladies comes to a close. They thank me for being their driver, tell me to send my travel receipts to the Vatican, and disappear into the city.

The Adelante Street Theater Project: theatricalizing dissent in the streets of New York City

CARMELINA CARTEI

The press release from the Adelante Street Theater Project announced that George Bush and the Contras were to attack Nicaraguan civilians at Grand Central Station. On June 11, 1990, over thirty activists participated in a street theater action to inform the public that, contrary to the mainstream media's claims that the civil war had ended in Nicaragua, the US-funded Contras were still targeting the civilian population. In the action, the Grim Reaper walked down the grand staircase of the Grand Central terminal, followed by George Bush leading about twenty life-sized, skeletal Contra puppets against three women and a child identified as Nicaraguan civilians. Other activists distributed leaflets and provided security. Without police disruption, the Contras marched through the terminal, to 42nd Street and the New York Public Library. David L. Wilson, one of the participants, recalls the action brought "the war home" and a strategy to organize people against the US role in Central America.

By the fall of 1988, growing frustration with US foreign policies compelled Walter Ditman and a group of activists from the Nicaragua Solidarity Network of Greater New York to engage in an alternative form of political dissent from sending construction brigades to Nicaragua or demonstrating. Similar to the Rapid Transit Guerrilla Communications in Chicago or the City Street Theater in New York, Adelante came together in response to a political situation that required outrageous forms of political communication (*Culture and Agitation* 1972; Lesnick 1973; Weisman 1973). Adelante's intentions were to raise concern and consciousness among the public by presenting in public spaces "a living image of the truly hellish outcome of government policy which … spreads misery and death all over the world" (Ditman 1991). Adelante would be a people's guerrilla theater (Weisman 1973) which used theatre as a strategy to unleash the creativity of the solidarity community.

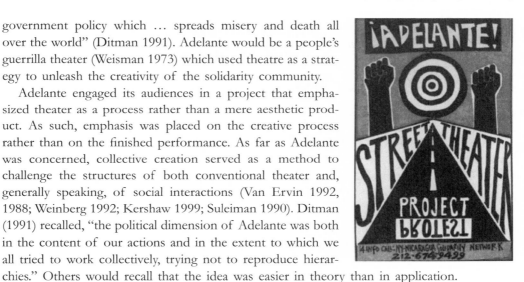

Adelante engaged its audiences in a project that emphasized theater as a process rather than a mere aesthetic product. As such, emphasis was placed on the creative process rather than on the finished performance. As far as Adelante was concerned, collective creation served as a method to challenge the structures of both conventional theater and, generally speaking, of social interactions (Van Ervin 1992, 1988; Weinberg 1992; Kershaw 1999; Suleiman 1990). Ditman (1991) recalled, "the political dimension of Adelante was both in the content of our actions and in the extent to which we all tried to work collectively, trying not to reproduce hierarchies." Others would recall that the idea was easier in theory than in application.

In its first action in 1988, Adelante staged a funeral procession, with a 6-foot cardboard coffin, pallbearers wearing long black cloaks, a drummer in a death mask and mourners, accompanied by activists who distributed leaflets about the Contras. The procession made its way into the streets of Manhattan, Brooklyn, the Bronx as well as spaces not sanctioned for guerrilla performances, such as Lincoln Center. Along the way, Adelante made the point that people actually dissented from US policy. In 1991, Adelante modified the procession, joining hundreds of members of ACT UP as they staged a demonstration inside Grand Central Station; at the same time Adelante performed along 42nd Street, calling attention to the US government's lethargy in the face of the escalating AIDS crisis.

Adelante was not an "imitative" theater, in so far as it did not engage in productions of conventional drama (McConachie and Friedman 1985). The skits or actions were created by the participants themselves, incorporating styles and content meant to reflect the needs of the group and, often, to energize the activist community itself. With the threat of war against Iraq, Adelante engaged over fifty participants in an action performed at the October 20, 1990 anti-war demonstration in New York City. The performance parodied a historical pageant with George Bush, armed with a golf club, leading the Vampire Pigs of Congress – in whiteface, bloody lips, pig's nose –

carrying two blood-stained oil barrels. In doing so, Adelante resignified a familiar image, using parody, irony, and masks "to unmask" Bush's duplicities (Hutcheon 1985). Other activists wore enormous cardboard US government checks made out to military contractors, while others wore cardboard pennies representing the "small change" meted out for domestic programs (Ditman 1991).

A scaled-down version of the action was performed in the subway on January 14, 1991. Working in teams, performers covered the major subway lines distributing over five thousand flyers challenging US manipulation of the crisis in the Persian Gulf and prioritizing the need for more constructive US foreign and domestic policies (Ditman 1991). This was Adelante's first action in the subway. While some were concerned about both police intervention and/or passengers' response, the police did not interfere, and riders generally agreed with the anti-war message. For Carol Skelsky this subway action was "a vibrant outreach to the community … people seemed excited … they grabbed the leaflets … and we had the opportunity to talk with people and answer their questions about the war."

One of the functions of political theater may be to dramatize issues that should enter the arena of public debate (Samuel et al. 1985). During the 1990s, Adelante created actions that advocated for a single-payer health-care system, protested Giuliani's war on the homeless, and re-envisioned the quincentennial festivities as a celebration of neocolonialism. In 1992, the group appropriated and then transmuted the familiar form of a game show to create a skit in which George Bush competes with Columbus for the conquest of the world in the "Master of the Universe Game". In this action Adelante relied heavily on humor and stylized acting. It mixed a serious political content with Bush and Columbus's buffoonery, evoking the work of the San Francisco Mime Troupe and their "festive-revolutionary" use of clowning antics as a cultural strategy to undermine the "aura" of the establishment (Orenstein 1998). In 1999–2000, Adelante's actions focused on the US war in Kosovo and sweatshops run by US companies abroad.

While it may be difficult to measure the social efficacy and the political impact of Adelante – that is, whether the group was directly responsible for specific policy changes in the manner that ACT UP's strategies forced changes (Solomon 1998: 43) – Adelante's unconventional performances provided the public with dissenting views and encouraged them to think critically about government policies. Today, long-time participant Jane Guskin wants to see Adelante move forward again, in full swing.

Irony, meme warfare, and the extreme costume ball

ANDREW BOYD

During the "Shutdown in Seattle" in November 1999, I watched a hundred sea turtles face down riot cops, a gang of Santas stumble through a cloud of tear gas, and a burly Teamster march shoulder to shoulder with a pair of Lesbian Avengers naked to the waist except for a strip of black electrical tape across each nipple. Several months later in Boston, a mutant freakshow with a cast of thousands – including hunchbacked rats, three-headed corn cobs, and strawberry fish – took to the streets against an international gathering of bio-tech industrialists. Protest has become an extreme costume ball.

To some it's just kids cutting up in the street. To others this brand of theatrical Do-It-Yourself (DIY) street politics represents a new kind of anti-corporate movement distinguished by creativity, self-organization, coalition building, and the will to take on global capitalism.

"The costume ball is the one formal convention in which the desire for individuality and extreme originality does not endanger collective performance but is actually a condition for it," the architect Rem Koolhaas once said, describing the urban chaos of New York City. He could just as easily have been describing the new sensibility of protest. "It works because we're all expressing a similar message in a different way," says Emily Schuch, twenty-two, who was in DC for the April 2000 anti-World Bank protest. The phalanx of corporate loan sharks, the Rube Goldbergian contraption that ate pieces of Earth and shat out coins, the contingents of indigenous peoples in striking native garb, combined artistically and politically to say: "More World! Less Bank!"

For Schuch, a recent graduate of the School of Visual Arts, the creative invitation offered by a carnival-like protest meshes well with her peers' do-whatever-you-feel-like attitude toward drugs, sex, and music, summed up in her mind by a recent bumper sticker – "My body is not a temple, it's an amusement park." This movement's costumed protest provides an exciting venue for self-discovery and artistic experimentation, where every giant puppet is a barricade and every outrageous act a challenge to the corporate-manufactured consumer sameness that passes for culture.

Its sources are many. In the 1980s and 1990s groups like ACT UP, Women's Action Coalition, and the Lesbian Avengers inspired a new style of high-concept shock politics that was both identity-affirming and visually arresting. In 1994 the Zapatistas burst from the Chiapas jungles and into the political imaginations of activists around the world. The "first post-modern revolutionary movement" set aside the dry manifesto and the sectarian vanguard for fable, poetry, theater and a democratic coalition of movements against global capitalism. The US labor movement, hit hard by globalization, began to innovate and seek out new allies. Among them was Earth First, which was experimenting with new technologies of radical direct action in the forests of northern California. The Critical Mass bicycle rides, dubbed "organized coincidences," provided a home-grown, working model of a celebratory, self-organizing protest. Even the Burning Man festival, while not explicitly political, helped spread an implicit politics of radical self-expression and radical self-organization. The Burning Man slogans "No spectators!" and "You are the entertainment!" were just as evident on the streets of Seattle as in the Nevada desert.

New ideas also migrated across the Atlantic. Reclaim the Streets began in London in the early 1990s, a loose collection of ravers, artists, and anti-car activists. RTS brought the underground rave dance scene out of the warehouses and clubs and into charged political spaces. An RTS action is part protest, part street party, part a gesture that reclaims the streets from the private exclusive use of the car and returns them to a collective use as a commons. Quickly, a tall three-pronged tripod structure is set up, blocking the street. Someone scampers to the top. A truck with a sound system arrives, and before the police can respond hundreds are dancing in the streets. It is both a negative act of resistance and a positive act of celebration, community-building, and self-expression. It is a mass civil disobedience in which ravers, per-

Andrew Boyd as sinister loan shark menacing police offers at the IMF protests in Washington DC, April 16.

formance artists, and fire jugglers set the tone. Exciting and easy to reproduce, these "festivals of resistance" quickly went global.

"We feel that art shouldn't be just an ornament, but rather an integral part of the movement," says David Solnit. "Everything is theatrical. Traditional protest – the march, the rally, the chants – is just bad theater." In the mid-1990s, Solnit helped launch the Art and Revolution collective, which was inspired by RTS and the diverse DIY alternative youth cultures of the hip-hop, punk, and rave music scenes. Pioneering a powerful fusion of direct action and Bread and Puppet-style street theater, Art and Revolution organized "Convergences" throughout the western US to train activists and artists in nonviolent tactics, prop and puppet making, and decentralized decision-making. "We put art and art-making at the center, not only of our actions, but of our organizing," says Solnit. Chapters formed. The model spread.

By the time of the WTO meeting in Seattle, RTS-style protest had taken hold of the activist imagination. The Direct Action Network (DAN), co-founded by David Solnit, had adapted the Convergence model to handle the democratic planning of a mass blockade. Activists divided a map of downtown Seattle into pie slices. Clusters of independent yet coordinated affinity groups took responsibility for each slice.

With this decision-making structure, thousands of people could organize themselves like so many rings in a many-ringed circus. We threw a costume ball that also successfully blockaded the WTO. On the street, each sideshow was part of the whole, every creative gesture was also an interruption of power.

"We were in Seattle for the world and for justice," says one Boston activist. "But we were also there for ourselves, to create a new culture." By bringing people together in a carnival-like format to challenge the major institutions of global capitalism, the movement found a shape that pushes beyond identity politics, yet creates a space for it. Like the Lesbian Avenger in Seattle who wrote "The WTO is bad for my body" in black Magic Marker on her mostly naked chest, participants can do their own thing in their own posse and still push a broader agenda. Traditional goal-oriented politics links up with the politics of being. People join the movement not only to take action but to feel alive and find out who they are.

Conquering irony

There was one sublime moment in Seattle when I realized that the wild yet focused energies in the streets could never be resolved into a folk song – we were now part of Hip-Hop Nation. The rhythms of the chants were rougher, more percussive. The energy was fierce and playful. The street resonated with an in-your-face confidence. The costumes – half Native American totems, half whimsical culture-jamming commentaries – made a joyous, friendly cacophony. The activists were comfortable with irony, but not bogged down by it. We were no longer mimicking the 1960s; nor were we distancing ourselves from its failures.

Something deep had shifted. This was not a new naivety. Somehow the movement had taken a Hegelian lurch forward – from thesis to antithesis to synthesis. In the 1960s the thesis was: "We can change the world." In the 1980s came the antithesis: "What good did it all do anyway." We knew everything was corrupt; we were bitter and defensive; we distrusted ourselves; we were too cool to care – or we played the self-righteous voice in the wilderness calling out, "Everyone else betrayed the ideals but me."

Maybe it takes the span of a generation to metabolize these kind of historical phases. Maybe the new generation of youthful activists are free to believe in themselves again because they are not invested in either the 1960s or the retreat from it.

Whatever the reason, on the streets of Seattle there was synthesis. Irony was no longer an expression of our lack of confidence; it was a playful tool we could wield and yet still be intensely passionate about our politics. We had somehow transcended and incorporated thesis and antithesis. Before Seattle, irony had the better of us; now we had the better of it. We were neither nostalgic nor snide. We had achieved a new attitude – sly and mischievous, yet full of hope for the future.

At the end of that long week in Seattle, as the last protest was winding down, I met a woman with whom I had the following conversation. I am not making this up. She was white, in her mid to late twenties, wearing conservative J.C. Penney slacks and blouse – no freak here – and was clearly moved. "This is my first protest," she said. "Well, I hope it won't be your last," I said. "We'll see what happens," she replied, "But I'm feeling very free."

What about the message?

But not everyone felt the way she did. Those watching on television might have thought it was just a chaotic party. The carnival protest, possibly by nature, often lacks a clear or unified message. If you aren't a participant or a direct observer, the true feeling may not come across – and the specific political message may also get lost. One of the great strengths of the new style of protest – its plural and expressive character – is also one of its greatest weaknesses.

In Seattle, and even more in the protests that followed the next year – in Boston, DC, Philadelphia, and Los Angeles – the mainstream media characterized the new movement as chaotic, superficial, self-indulgent, and faddish. As seen through the media our demands were a jumbled laundry list; we were against everything without knowing what we were for.

The corporate bias of mainstream media accounted for a portion of this negative picture, but we also opened ourselves up to it. Thousands of activists flooded into these mass protests without a shared analysis or allegiance to a common organization. Rarely did the ad hoc coalition hosting the protest have the authority to build a hard consensus around a tight message. Without positive agreement on long term vision or message, the highest expression of unity often defaulted to a potpourri of negative opposition to the target, whether that was the WTO, IMF, or Dubya.

Another problem was that many young activists distrust the corporate media to such a degree that they refuse to engage it at all. In their quest for authentic self-expression and resistance, they find no room to treat their protest also as an object for public consumption. Once you start to adjust your actions for the media, they believe, you're on a slippery slope of compromise and inauthenticity.

The vibrant culture of the new movement is a double-edged sword. As with all subcultures, it provides a home, a sense of identity and community, a shell to resist the dominant culture. Yet by that same very move, it can exclude and alienate, saying to others "You are not one of us." But cultural expression can also communicate values and vision to the outside world. "It's one thing to use creative expression to celebrate our own marginal subculture," says David Solnit. "It's another thing to use it as a bridge to other cultures. It's the best alliance-building tool I know."

The movement is smart enough to do both. We can celebrate our own culture of resistance *as well as* thoughtfully present ourselves to the public. Sometimes this balancing act can be quite simple. At a rally against the Free Trade Agreement of the Americas, Wesleyan students created placards which read, "The FTAA is bad for _____," letting participants write in their own reasons – the environment, labor, yo mama, and so on. Creative messaging like this can help bring out the unity and coherence of our resistance without suppressing its diversity. It can help provide a logic to the laundry list.

America looks at the new movement with a mixture of sympathy and alienation. If we want to broaden our appeal we need to cultivate the habit of seeing ourselves as others do. We need to cut our message in terms that link with the core values of the broad public – democracy, a basic sense of fairness, diversity and tolerance, and so on. We also need to understand what aspects of our style and sensibility are turn-ons – our humor, fun-loving free spirit, the sexy vibe on the street, our idealism, courage, commitment, compassion; and which are turn-offs – our negativity, freakishness, extreme behavior, burning American flags. We need to embody our visions and values in our actions and show how our target embodies the opposite. Forcing trade bureaucrats to hold their closed, secretive meetings "under a state of siege" is a direct challenge to their unpopular and undemocratic nature. Having an actual siege engine at the protest, like the catapult that hurled teddy bears into the old city of Quebec during the FTAA meetings, symbolically embodies this challenge for all to see.

We also need to design our message strategically and consciously so that it hits home with the public in spite of how it might get distorted by the media. In this

Billionaires for Bush (or Gore) at
the Republican Convention in
Philadelphia, August 2000.

respect, the "Billionaires for Bush (or Gore)" campaign is an instructive model. Conceived by United for a Fair Economy, the Billionaires campaign aimed to tap into the DIY energy, creativity, and daring of the new movement but maintain the tight message discipline and sustained focus of a campaign. As a consultant for UFE, and a member of RTS and DAN, I was at the center of the project.

In early May of 2000, I pulled together a team of talented volunteer designers, media producers, and veteran street theater activists – many of them associated with RTS in New York. With support from UFE, we began to put the pieces of the campaign in place. We created a stylish logo by splicing together a donkey and an elephant, and a "candidate" by digitally morphing photos of Bush and Gore into a single eerie image. Riffing off slogans like "Free the Forbes 400," "Corporations are people too," "We're paying for America's free elections so you don't have to," and "We don't care who you vote for, we've already bought them," we created bumper stickers, buttons, a series of posters, and a kick-ass website that eventually won more than a few awards (www.billionairesforbushorgore.com). The satire was compact, funny, and politically on target. The look was slick and the message was unified across a whole range of media. It was quite a package. And we launched it all with a "Million Billionaire March" at the Republican and Democratic national conventions.

We designed the campaign to be participatory: a simple concept that was easy to execute yet allowed for rich elaboration. Through the website, activists could download all the materials they needed to do actions in their own communities. By June, wildcat chapters were springing up. In Denver a Billionaires squad barged into the Green Party convention and tried to buy off Ralph Nader, much to the delight of delegates and the media.

By the time we arrived in Philadelphia for the Republican convention in late July, we were already a minor sensation. Advance articles and Internet buzz had put us on the map. Our website was getting 100,000 hits a day (20,000 unique page views). Everybody was asking for our buttons, stickers, and posters. Nearly a hundred Billionaires in full dress joined us in the streets, chanting, singing, burning money, smoking cigars. We also staged a "Vigil for Corporate Welfare" and auctioned off merchandising rights to the Liberty Bell (would it become the Taco Bell Liberty Bell or the Ma Bell Liberty Bell?). The media were all over us. An informal poll of photojournalists voted us "favorite protest." We were certainly one of the more focused and cohesive. The Democratic convention in Los Angeles was more of the same. My Billionaire character, Phil T. Rich, became a hit on the radio interview circuit and website traffic shot up to 200,000 hits per day. An editor at *The Nation* called us "the Sea Turtles of the convention protests."

As the campaign picked up, a hub–node structure arose. UFE became the organizational hub of an ad hoc network of Do-It-Yourself movement grouplets. In addition to the campaign framework, UFE was providing funding, infrastructure, research capacity, media contacts, and mainstream legitimacy. The grassroots injected energy, street smarts, and creative elaboration of the core ideas. In the weeks after the conventions, we'd get email every day from people across the country, raving about the project and eager to start local Billionaires chapters or informing us of actions they had already undertaken. Many had checked out the "Be a Billionaire" section of our website, chosen satirical names for themselves, and downloaded the slogans, posters, and sample press releases.

"The task of an organizer," says one movement veteran, "is to set up structures so people can participate." The Billionaires' hub played an essential role in shaping and steering the campaign. The hub designed the core ideas and launched the call to action. But what mechanisms helped us steer the campaign once things got rolling? One was the website. Another was the Million Billionaire March, which modeled the kinds of actions people could do in their home cities. Finally, it was the shtick and the materials themselves. Jokes were funny, content was thoroughly researched, graphic production values were high. People liked the package and were naturally drawn to stay on-message.

Meme warfare

The Billionaires campaign shows how hub and node can work together to invite open-ended DIY participation into creative actions and yet maintain artistic cohesion and a focused message. It demonstrates the potential of the Web for disseminating not just information, but ready-made organizing and message-making tools. It also shows how ingenious "meme warfare" can inject a message into corporate media in spite of editorial frames designed to filter it out.

Memes are "information viruses." The meme "Billionaires for Bush (or Gore)" was designed to have certain viral features – mobility, adaptability, self-protection, and so on – and was introduced into the media stream in a way that was calculated to maximize its propagation. In five words it encapsulated the two core ideas of the campaign: Big Money owns both candidates; both candidates are roughly the same. Its concision was an inoculation against distortion – even the most fragmented and decontextualized mention in the media tended to carry the name, and thus the message. The meme was easily attached to a range of "carriers" – logo, posters, fake radio ads, street actions, email, buzz, laughter, media story, and so on. Thus the meme "spread, reproduced, and mutated." None of this could have happened without tight message discipline across all the materials. Even when the wildcat DIY actions started to get scrappy, the core idea came through, and it was all of a piece.

Seattle showed that street protest can be a place where diverse subcultures can mix it up, where steelworkers and tree-huggers can learn how to party together, where young people can experiment with new ways of being and then pronounce, as much to themselves as the world, "*This* is what democracy looks like!" But the cacophony and free-for-all whimsy of the extreme costume ball can also undercut the seriousness of its political intentions, alienating or confusing people we want to reach. Perhaps the message discipline and media savvy of campaigns such as Billionaires can help to balance this out, without repressing creativity or the possibility for authentic self-expression.

Kneel before Bush! The origin of Students for an Undemocratic Society

JASON GROTE

> We have lost all sense of ritual and ceremony – whether it be connected with Christmas, birthdays, or funeral … we now find ourselves rejecting the very notion of a holy stage. It is not the fault of the holy that it has become a middle-class weapon to keep the children good. (Peter Brook)

Something strange happened on January 20, 2001. I don't mean George W. Bush, although that was weird too. There was a fleeting moment when I (and about fifty other people dressed like me) stood bellowing at a National Organization for Women rally. Behind them was a barricade, then Pennsylvania Avenue, then another barricade, then Republicans, and behind them the Capitol Building, its bland white concrete blending into the great gray sky above us all. And while I screamed "JOHN ASHCROFT DOESN'T DANCE!" in my fake British accent, boogieing jerkily like some amalgam of Charlie Chaplin and a member of Devo, the hard brick ground seemed to turn into the boards of a stage. The Capitol seemed like nothing more than pricey set dressing. Everyone, from the NOW protesters to the fur-clad Bushites to the forced-to-be-avuncular secret service agents, was transformed, simultaneously, into actors and audience. It wasn't as if DC had been suddenly transmogrified into a theater: it's always a theater. It had, temporarily at least, been transformed from a bad play into a good one. There was no question that the inaugural was intended to be tired melodrama: the authorities, having become competent if mediocre stage managers, were determined to prevent the rebels from upstaging them as they had done in Seattle and elsewhere. They knew the cameras thirsted for tear gas, race riots, hails of rotten vegetables thrown at the presidential limo. None of that was about to happen. The state knows as well as anyone the difference between the ceremonies that reinforce the status quo and the rituals that transform it.

The right wing and the corporate state are not, however, the only hack producers out there. The left has generated its share of turkeys. The stereotype is by now familiar: an unwashed white twentysomething in army surplus, screeching at passersby to take a copy of his newsletter. The cliché, always mean and frequently inaccurate, has become irrelevant. Activists have been growing increasingly mediasavvy, not to mention bored – one can only listen to so many speeches. As demonstrated by the Church Ladies for Choice, the Radical Cheerleaders, Reverend Billy – the list goes on – art has become an integral aspect of public protest. The affinity group with whom I work, Reclaim the Streets/NYC, is primarily known for blockading city streets, wheeling out a huge sound system, and holding dance parties.

Not that we were about to do that this time around. Besides the fact that our sound system would have ended up in a Pentagon basement until 2060 or something, none of us was ready to get shot or spend a month in jail. So, shivering in a poorly heated Lower East Side community center two weeks before the inauguration, we unanimously agreed on street theater. But what, exactly, were we protesting? None us was happy about black disenfranchisement or the Christian right, but we weren't exactly Gore supporters either. "I'm not going to protest about vote counting," said Jen, an anarchist. "The IAC is protesting the prison-industrial complex," said Simon, our DC point person. The International Action Center had applied for their permit months ago, having planned to protest no matter who won, and were in the news every day. "But the prison-industrial complex isn't funny," said Steve. This obvious truth was exacerbated by the inescapable fact that the room, unlike the prison system, was overwhelmingly white. "I say we have Jason come up with something. I'm no good with humor, but Jason's always funny." Steve has, I think, a gift for coercion by flattery. I didn't know whether to hug him or curse him. Either way, the heat was on. Like Mel Brooks said, dying is easy; comedy is hard. Suddenly, it hit me: "How about Students for an Undemocratic Society?"

It was decided. The SUDS hit that perfect note. Within a week, Amanda had designed a website, blithely celebrating horrific statistics about prisons, the military, and the impending Bush cabinet. The site was full of pictures of Bush looking moronic, a parody of SDS's Port Huron Statement, and the SUDS manifesto. The manifesto was an ecstatic recounting of American democracy's sorry state of affairs, framed with cheery taglines like "Whose Streets? Not Yours!", "Bombs Not Food!", and "You Say Sweatshop – We Say 'Swellfare'!"

Then came the costumes. Our plan was to cobble together various fascist tropes, from the classic Nazi to the tinplated dictator to the good old American fratboy. Armed with a few hundred dollars we had made at benefit parties, we wandered New York's fashion district, seeking black "W" baseball hats, mirrored aviator sunglasses, medals, and gold sashes. We got stuck on the medals: we agreed on miniature guns and plastic dollar bills, but disagreed on religious iconography. I had picked out crucifixes, but this was controversial. "We forget," Bill pointed out; "We live in New York. People in this country are really into God." We went with a subtler choice: little reflectors with saints on them.

Our shopping complete, we proceeded to Steve's to make signs. Steve had printed out giant, spooky pictures of Bush and Cheney underneath the word "OBEY," written in big black letters, and was gluing them to foam-core. The other side of the signs featured Oceania's aphorisms from *1984*: War is Peace, Freedom is Slavery, Ignorance is Strength. For our guerrilla theater skit, I created a character, Lieutenant General John Holy Cleansing Fire Smith, to be the SUDS' putative leader. I sounded like Ming the Merciless and I looked like a Contra.

On the big day we met in front of Union Station in Washington DC. As one may have guessed, there were quite a few people there who were looking for something interesting to gape at, and for a while at least we were it. As we practiced our act a bewildered crowd of Asian businessmen stood about 20 foot away from us, photographing us and shrugging to one another. An older white man in a cowboy hat

Inauguration protests. Grote as his alter ego, Lt. Gen. John Holy Cleansing Fire Smith, leading the crowd.

stood a few feet away from them, screaming at us what must have been verses from the Bible. "Who is the death and the life, the light and the darkness, our sex and our blood?" I shouted, in the British accent. "BUSH IS!", yelled the SUDS. "Kneel before Bush!" I shouted. I turned to the businessmen and the Jesus Cowboy. "We are the Students of an Undemocratic Society!" I said, by way of introduction. "And we don't have to take our clothes off to have a good time!" After a good twenty minutes of biblical verses the Jesus Cowboy left in disgust. "Government's not supposed to be fun," he spat contemptuously. It made a great chant, so we stole it. "Government's not supposed to be fun!" we yelled back. "Government's not supposed to be fun!"

We marched from Union Station to the Supreme Court, chanting "Brick by Brick! Wall By Wall! We're Gonna Smash, Imprison, and Oppress You All!" Two teenage Republican girls enthusiastically carried our Bush–OBEY signs for about four blocks until they caught on and threw them to the ground in disgust. We were going to the Court to meet the "Patriot March," a Republican rally sponsored by a political action committee from Virginia. They were a sight. It was like a Star Trek convention: all-male and full of weird obsessive behavior. This may have been the most satisfying part of our day. They would try to harass us with anti-Clinton chants, and we would pretend we were with them and start chanting the same thing. Eventually they got frustrated and left.

We did our act for passersby and the press. I screamed like a maniac as the SUDS knelt en masse. "Do you love George W. Bush with every fiber of your being?," I screamed. The people passing by seemed stuck between fear and laughter. "Would you die for him?" I demanded. "Say it!" "WE LOVE BUSH!" the SUDS chanted. "Yes," I affirmed. "We love Bush." Pause. "What about his retainer, Dick Cheney? Would you die for him?" "Yes! We love him!" the SUDS yelled. "Say it," I demanded. "Say you love Dick!" "WE LOVE DICK!" the SUDS chanted. "WE LOVE BUSH! WE LOVE DICK!" we chanted. We marched to the parade route.

At the parade route we experienced our first crisis of the day. Thankfully, it had nothing to do with non-lethal crowd control weapons. We had somehow lost everyone. The SUDS dwindled from almost fifty to fewer than twenty. Eventually we figured out that the back end of our parade had had to go to the bathroom and the back marshals neglected to tell anybody. One of us remained on the checkpoint line while we waited for our compatriots. I got some breakfast. By the time the missing SUDS caught up with us, our person was at the front of the line.

We tried to cut into where he was, but being fifty people in identical costumes, we weren't very inconspicuous. "Quick, let's do the act before they kill us," someone hissed. "Hey," said a large man who was standing near us. "You know what I think? I don't think you waited on line like the rest of us. I think you just cut in." This man was clearly not from New York. "We're fascists," I shrugged, then hid behind somebody.

We entered Pennsylvania Avenue by the Capitol building, where the National Organization for Women was holding an enormous rally. I imagine they needed a laugh that day. As we did our act for them, my voice grew hoarse and my head grew light. My pulse pounded in my ears as I realized that I was, in my tiny way, nudging the course of history. I once got to perform on a Broadway-size stage, but that experience didn't even compare. I stood in front of the throngs of laughing women piled five deep against the barricades on Pennsylvania Avenue, the bland beige Capitol blending into the gray sky beyond. For a moment the ground seemed to soften and everything seemed to become perfectly clear.

We proceeded west, chanting "What do we want? Fur coats! How do we want 'em? Full length!" A few blocks down we met up with some young people holding signs that said "Free Mumia" and "Ashcroft is a racist sexist pig." We started chanting at them, pretending to be enemies. They would yell real leftist chants, and we would yell our alternate-universe SUDS versions. "El Pueblo Unito Jamas Sera Vencido!" they yelled. "Learn English!" we yelled back.

By this time I was completely hoarse and had had enough of the parade route. Half of us decided to go to a hot spot a few blocks away, where a bizarre team-up between the Black Bloc and the Democrats was forming. The other half, including me, decided to go to Chinatown for lunch.

SUDS had not changed history, of course. Bush was sworn in, and continues to push that absurd Reaganite agenda of his. And aside from a good shot of his limo speeding up as thousands of people gave him the finger, the media coverage was predictably flaccid. But all of our efforts, even the bad old left theater, have their effect. Revolution is nothing if not cumulative, ripples in the vast pond of history that become waves and, in so doing, overwhelm the pond itself.

Video activists.

PART FOUR

Media and the new social movements

We have to find our own forms of gesture and communication. You can never depend on the mass media to reflect us or our needs or states of mind. (David Wojnarowicz)

All around us, it was just a typical Sunday afternoon in Greenwich Village. Thirty feet above, Louis was sitting atop a metal tripod that had stopped traffic on Broadway. Beneath him, police scratched their heads as members of Reclaim the Streets/New York danced to the sound system placed below the tripod. In a dangerous effort to dislodge Louis from his perch, one police officer began to shake the structure. "You are being filmed," Eve informed the officer as she pointed her video camera in his direction, demonstrating the utility of the video camera as an essential tool for activists (Harding 1998).

ACT UP's DIVA TV used mass media activism to build an audience through the crossover between spectator and participant. The point was simple: "When circumstances require that drastic measures be adopted, independent media activists assume a central role. This role is twofold: to assist other activists in clarifying and goals, and to represent those positions and goals to the world," posited DIVA TV's founder Greg Bordowitz in 1988. The media activist's role is to create armed propaganda. To do this, she must call into question established structures of the media while creating new ways to make and distribute it, all the while working toward participatory forms of representation that incorporate more and more people into the communication process. Over the years between ACT UP and the WTO, more and more activists would take this message to heart. The result was an independent media revolution. And video was just the beginning. From Los Angeles to Seattle, the new media – ranging from the Internet to guerrilla video feeds – has transformed the way we do activism.

Part 4 addresses the use of technology in creating resistance to censorship and political oppression. After all, radio and television communications between West and East Berlin helped bring down the Berlin Wall in 1989. Mass communication, including the Internet, have produced a cultural paradigm shift that influences not just organizing, but most everything in our culture. According to media critic and longtime ACT UP member Ann Northrop, "The Internet is the greatest tool we have, and they will do anything they can to take it away."

In her essay "The Vision Thing," Naomi Klein outlines the ways the new media, with their countless nodes and points of view, inform the new movements. She ponders the extent to which the new movements follow the shape of the highly decentralized Internet itself. The movement has no one ideology, just many points of view.

Ricardo Dominguez recalls the ways ACT UP's methods influenced Critical Art Ensemble's theory of electronic civil disobedience. In the same way that a crisis inspired the formation of ACT UP, Dominguez recalls how the crisis in Chiapas, Mexico, resulted in the Zapatista uprising in 1994. In the seven years since their uprising, the Zapatistas have come to represent two forces at once: first, rebels struggling against grinding poverty and degradation in the mountains of Chiapas; and, second, theorists of a new movement, another way to think about power, resistance, and globalization. Their theory – Zapatismo – not only turns classic guerrilla tactics inside-out, but much of left-wing politics on its head (Klein 2001b). Using the Internet as its most potent weapon, the Zapatistas sparked a movement that has spread around the globe at a speed unparalleled in human history. Ricardo Dominguez considers the links between his work with ACT UP and the Zapatistas and the use of a new method of direct action Internet politics called "hactivism." What emerges in Dominguez' narrative is one of the great case studies in the use of media as cultural resistance.

The ACT UP affinity group DIVA TV was founded in 1989. Founder Greg Bordowitz (2001) recalls: "It was an affinity group of ACT UP devoted to documenting ACT UP's efforts. We sometimes had as many as ten of us covering actions. This did two things: It ensured that activists were producing our own version of the events; taking ownership of our own history. Very important. And video cameras are also very useful deterrents against police violence." DIVA TV's anarchist model of the video activist video collective would go on to be a model for a generation of video activists, including the nascent IMC.

We would never have understood Seattle the way we did if it was not for the Independent Media Center (Indy Media Center). Ana Nogueira provides a brief history of Indymedia, a worldwide network of guerrilla news collectives designed and run by activists. It's the story of a generation of activists weaned on pop culture and their impulse to create an alternative media liberated from corporate information filters. The result has been a dramatic shift in information dissemination, as activists regained a grip on how the stories of movements are reported and understood. Alexandra Juhasz's "So Many Alternatives" looks at the Alternative AIDS Video Movement and its aim to create its own activist narrative line.

The mainstream media giveth and taketh away, commodifying movements and gestures. Sofía Quintero writes about how media and fashion appropriate and co-opt cultural markers, specifically the historic and political roots of hip-hop. Quintero frames questions of culture within the lens of media in considering "Black August," an international hip-hop festival that grounds hip-hop as music, medium, and movement of social change.

In this section's final essay, Bill Talen of the Church of Stop Shopping recalls some of the fun and headaches involved in putting together a made-for-TV demonstration, an invasion of a series of Starbucks throughout New York. What happens when we plan our actions for the cameras but lose focus on who and what we are targeting? Does the tail simply start wagging the dog? For better or worse, the media play an essential role in the way we experience social protest. Part 4 considers this question.

The vision thing: were the DC and Seattle protests unfocused, or are critics missing the point?

NAOMI KLEIN

"This conference is not like other conferences." That's what all the speakers at "Re-imagining Politics and Society" were told before we arrived at New York's Riverside Church. When we addressed the delegates (there were about a thousand, over three days in May), we were to try to solve a very specific problem: the lack of "unity of vision and strategy" guiding the movement against global corporatism.

This was a very serious problem, we were advised. The young activists who went to Seattle to shut down the World Trade Organization, and to Washington DC to protest the World Bank and the IMF, had been getting hammered in the press as tree-wearing, lamb-costumed, drum-beating bubble brains. Our mission, according to the conference organizers at the Foundation for Ethics and Meaning, was to whip that chaos on the streets into some kind of structured, media-friendly shape. This wasn't just another talk shop. We were going to "give birth to a unified movement for holistic social, economic and political change."

As I slipped in and out of lecture rooms, soaking up vision galore from Arianna Huffington, Michael Lerner, David Korten and Cornel West, I was struck by the futility of this entire well-meaning exercise. Even if we did manage to come up with a ten-point plan – brilliant in its clarity, elegant in its coherence, unified in its outlook – to whom, exactly, would we hand down these commandments? The anticorporate protest movement that came to world attention on the streets of Seattle in November 1999 is not united by a political party or a national network with a head office, annual elections, and subordinate cells and locals. It is shaped by the ideas of individual organizers and intellectuals, but doesn't defer to any of them as leaders. In this amorphous context, the ideas and plans being hatched at the Riverside Church weren't irrelevant exactly; they just weren't important in the way they clearly hoped to be. Rather than changing the world, they were destined to be swept up and tossed around in the tidal wave of information – Web diaries, NGO manifestos, academic papers, home-made videos, *cris de coeur* – that the global anticorporate network produces and consumes each and every day.

This is the flip side of the persistent criticism that the kids on the street lack clear leadership – they lack clear followers too. To those searching for replicas of the sixties, this absence makes the anticorporate movement appear infuriatingly impassive. Evidently, these people are so disorganized they can't even get it together to respond to perfectly well-organized efforts to organize them. These are MTV-weaned activists, you can practically hear the old guard saying: scattered, nonlinear, no focus.

It's easy to be persuaded by these critiques. If there is one thing on which the left and right agree, it is the value of a clear, well-structured ideological argument. But maybe it's not quite so simple. Maybe the protests in Seattle and Washington look unfocused because they were not demonstrations of one movement at all but rather convergences of many smaller ones, each with its sights trained on a specific multinational corporation (like Nike), a particular industry (like agribusiness), or a new trade initiative (like the Free Trade Area of the Americas). These smaller, targeted movements are clearly part of a common cause. They share a belief that the disparate problems with which they are wrestling all derive from global deregulation, an agenda that is concentrating power and wealth into fewer and fewer hands. Of course, there are disagreements – about the role of the nation-state, about whether capitalism is redeemable, about the speed with which change should occur. But within most of these miniature movements, there is an emerging consensus that building community-based decision-making power – whether through unions, neighborhoods, farms, villages, anarchist collectives, or aboriginal self-government – is essential to countering the might of multinational corporations.

Despite this common ground, these campaigns have not coalesced into a single movement. Rather, they are intricately and tightly linked to one another, much as "hotlinks" connect their websites on the Internet. This analogy is more than coincidental and is in fact key to understanding the changing nature of political organizing. Although many have observed that the recent mass protests would have been impossible without the Internet, what has been overlooked is how the communication technology that facilitates these campaigns is shaping the movement in its own image. Thanks to the Net, mobilizations are able to unfold with sparse bureaucracy and minimal hierarchy; forced consensus and labored manifestos are fading into the background, replaced instead by a culture of constant, loosely structured, and sometimes compulsive information-swapping. What emerged on the streets of Seattle and Washington was an activist model that mirrors the organic, decentralized, interlinked pathways of the Internet – the Internet come to life.

The Washington-based research center TeleGeography has taken it upon itself to map out the architecture of the Internet as if it were the solar system. Recently, TeleGeography pronounced that the Internet is not one giant web but a network of "hubs and spokes." The hubs are the centers of activity, the spokes the links to other centers, which are autonomous but interconnected. It seems like a perfect description of the protests in Seattle and Washington DC. These mass convergences were activist hubs, made up of hundreds, possibly thousands, of autonomous spokes. During the demonstrations, the spokes took the form of "affinity groups" of between five and twenty protesters, each of which elected a spokesperson to represent them at regular "spokescouncil" meetings. Although the affinity groups agreed to abide by a set of nonviolence principles, they also functioned as discrete units, with the power to make their own strategic decisions. At some rallies, activists carry actual cloth webs to symbolize their movement. When it's time for a meeting, they lay the web on the ground, call out "all spokes on the web" and the structure becomes a street-level boardroom.

In the four years before the Seattle and Washington protests, similar hub events had converged outside WTO, G7; and Asia Pacific Economic Cooperation summits in Auckland, Vancouver, Manila, Birmingham, London, Geneva, Kuala Lumpur and Cologne. Each of these mass protests was organized according to principles of coordinated decentralization. Rather than present a coherent front, small units of activists surrounded their target from all directions. And rather than build elaborate national or international bureaucracies, temporary structures were thrown up instead: empty buildings were turned into "convergence centers," and independent media producers assembled impromptu activist news centers. The ad hoc coalitions behind these demonstrations frequently named themselves after the date of the planned event: J18, N30, A16 and, for the IMF meeting in Prague on September 26, 2000, S26. When these events are over, they leave virtually no trace behind, save for an archived website.

Of course, all this talk of radical decentralization conceals a very real hierarchy based on who owns, understands, and controls the computer networks linking the activists to one another – this is what Jesse Hirsh, one of the founders of the anarchist computer network Tao Communications, calls "a geek adhocracy."

The hubs and spokes model is more than a tactic used at protests; the protests are themselves made up of "coalitions of coalitions," to borrow a phrase from Kevin Danaher of Global Exchange. Each anticorporate campaign is made up of many groups, mostly NGOs, labor unions, students, and anarchists. They use the Internet, as well as more traditional organizing tools, to do everything from cataloguing the latest transgressions of the World Bank, to bombarding Shell Oil with faxes and emails, to distributing ready-to-download anti-sweatshop leaflets for protests at Nike Town. The groups remain autonomous, but their international coordination is deft and, to their targets, frequently devastating.

The charge that the anticorporate movement lacks "vision" falls apart when looked at in the context of these campaigns. It's true that the mass protests in Seattle and DC were a hodgepodge of slogans and causes, that to a casual observer it was hard to decode the connections between Mumia's incarceration and the fate of the sea turtles. But in trying to find coherence in these large-scale shows of strength, the critics are confusing the outward demonstrations of the movement with the thing itself – missing the forest for the people dressed as trees. This movement is its spokes, and in the spokes there is no shortage of vision.

The student anti-sweatshop movement, for instance, has rapidly moved from simply criticizing companies and campus administrators to drafting alternate codes of conduct and building its own quasi-regulatory body, the Worker Rights Consortium. The movement against genetically engineered and modified foods has leapt from one policy victory to the next, first getting many GM foods removed from the shelves of British supermarkets, then getting labeling laws passed in Europe, then making enormous strides with the Montreal Protocol on Biosafety. Meanwhile, opponents of the World Bank's and IMF's export-led development models have produced bookshelves' worth of resources on community-based development models, debt relief, and self-government principles. Critics of the oil and mining industries are similarly overflowing with ideas for sustainable energy and responsible resource extraction – though they rarely get the chance to put their visions into practice.

The fact that these campaigns are so decentralized is not a source of incoherence and fragmentation. Rather, it is a reasonable, even ingenious, adaptation both to pre-existing fragmentation within progressive networks and to changes in the broader culture. It is a byproduct of the explosion of NGOs, which, since the Rio summit in 1992, have been gaining in power and prominence. There are so many NGOs involved in anticorporate campaigns that nothing but the hubs and spokes model could possibly accommodate all their different styles, tactics, and goals. Like the Internet itself, both the NGO and the affinity group networks are infinitely expandable systems. If somebody doesn't feel like they quite fit in to one of the thirty thousand or so NGOs or thousands of affinity groups out there, they can just start their own and link up. Once involved, no one has to give up their individuality to the larger structure; as with all things online, we are free to dip in and out, take what we want and delete what we don't. It is a surfer's approach to activism, reflecting the Internet's paradoxical culture of extreme narcissism coupled with an intense desire for external connection.

One of the great strengths of this model of laissez-faire organizing is that it has proven extraordinarily difficult to control, largely because it is so different from the organizing principles of the institutions and corporations it targets. It responds to corporate concentration with a maze of fragmentation, to globalization with its own kind of localization, to power consolidation with radical power dispersal.

Joshua Karliner of the Transnational Resource and Action Center calls this system "an unintentionally brilliant response to globalization." And because it was unintentional, we still lack even the vocabulary to describe it, which may be why a rather amusing metaphor industry has evolved to fill the gap. I'm throwing my lot in with hubs and spokes, but Maude Barlow of the Council of Canadians says, "We are up against a boulder. We can't remove it so we try to go underneath it, to go around it and over it." Britain's John Jordan, one of the founders of Reclaim the Streets, says transnationals "are like giant tankers, and we are like a school of fish. We can respond quickly; they can't." The US-based Free Burma Coalition talks of a network of "spiders," spinning a web strong enough to tie down the most powerful multinationals. A US military report about the Zapatista uprising in Chiapas even got in on the game. According to a study produced by RAND, the Zapatistas were waging a "war of the flea" that, thanks to the Internet and the global NGO network, turned into a "war of the swarm." The military challenge of a war of the swarm, the researchers noted, is that it has no "central leadership or command structure; it is multiheaded, impossible to decapitate."

Of course, this multiheaded system has its weaknesses too, and they were on full display on the streets of Washington during the anti-World Bank/IMF protests. At around noon on April 16, the day of the largest protest, a spokescouncil meeting was convened for the affinity groups that were in the midst of blocking all the street intersections surrounding the headquarters of the World Bank and the IMF. The intersections had been blocked since 6 a.m., but the meeting delegates, the protesters had just learned, had slipped inside the police barricades before 5 a.m. Given this new information, most of the spokespeople felt it was time to give up the inter-sections and join the official march at the Ellipse. The problem was that not every-one agreed: a handful of affinity groups wanted to see if they could block the delegates on their way out of their meetings.

The compromise the council came up with was telling. "OK, everybody listen up," Kevin Danaher shouted into a megaphone. "Each intersection has autonomy. If the intersection wants to stay locked down, that's cool. If it wants to come to the Ellipse, that's cool too. It's up to you." This was impeccably fair and democratic, but there was just one problem – it made absolutely no sense. Sealing off the access points had been a coordinated action. If some intersections now opened up and other, rebel-camp intersections stayed occupied, delegates on their way out of the meeting could just hang a right instead of a left, and they would be home free – which, of course, is precisely what happened.

As I watched clusters of protesters get up and wander off while others stayed seated, defiantly guarding, well, nothing, it struck me as an apt metaphor for the strengths and weaknesses of this nascent activist network. There is no question that the communication culture that reigns on the Net is better at speed and volume than at synthesis. It is capable of getting tens of thousands of people to meet on the same street corner, placards in hand, but is far less adept at helping those same people to agree on what they are really asking for before they get to the barricades – or after they leave.

For this reason, an odd sort of anxiety has begun to set in after each demonstration. Was that it? When's the next one? Will it be as good, as big? To keep up the momentum, a culture of serial protesting is rapidly taking hold. My inbox is cluttered with entreaties to come to what promises to be "the next Seattle." There was Windsor and Detroit on June 4 for a "shutdown" of the Organization of American States, and Calgary a week later for the World Petroleum Congress; the Republican convention will be in Philadelphia in July and the Democratic convention in LA in August; the World Economic Forum's Asia Pacific Economic Summit is on September 11 in Melbourne, followed shortly thereafter by anti-IMF demos on September 26 in Prague and then on to Quebec City for the Summit of the Americas in April 2001. Someone posted a message on the organizing email list for the Washington demos: "Wherever they go, we shall be there! After this, see you in Prague!" But is this really what we want – a movement of meeting-stalkers, following the trade bureaucrats as if they were the Grateful Dead?

The prospect is dangerous for several reasons. Far too much expectation is being placed on these protests. The organizers of the DC demo, for instance, announced they would literally "shut down" two $30 billion transnational institutions, at the same time as they attempted to convey sophisticated ideas about the fallacies of neoliberal economics to the stock-happy public. They simply couldn't do it; no single demo could, and it's only going to get harder. Seattle's direct-action tactics worked because they took the police by surprise. That won't happen again. Police have now subscribed to all the email lists. LA has put in a request for $4 million in new security gear and staffing costs to protect the city from the activist swarm.

In an attempt to build a stable political structure to advance the movement between protests, Danaher has begun to fund-raise for a "permanent convergence center" in Washington. The International Forum on Globalization, meanwhile, has been meeting since March in hopes of producing a 200-page policy paper by the end of the year. According to IFG director Jerry Mander, it won't be a manifesto but a set of principles and priorities, an early attempt, as he puts it, at "defining a new architecture" for the global economy. Like the conference organizers at the Riverside Church, however, these initiatives will face an uphill battle. Most activists agree that the time has come to sit down and start discussing a positive agenda – but at whose table, and who gets to decide?

These questions came to a head at the end of May when Czech president Vaclav Havel offered to "mediate" talks between World Bank president James Wolfensohn and the protesters planning to disrupt the Bank's September 26–28 meeting in Prague.

There was no consensus among protest organizers about participating in the negotiations at Prague Castle, and, more to the point, there was no process in place to make the decision: no mechanism to select acceptable members of an activist delegation (some suggested an Internet vote) and no agreed-upon set of goals by which to measure the benefits and pitfalls of taking part. If Havel had reached out to the groups specifically dealing with debt and structural adjustment, like Jubilee 2000 or 50 Years Is Enough, the proposal would have been dealt with in a straightforward manner. But because he approached the entire movement as if it were a single unit, he sent those organizing the demonstrations into weeks of internal strife that is still unresolved.

Part of the problem is structural. Among most anarchists, who are doing a great deal of the grassroots organizing (and who got online way before the more established left), direct democracy, transparency, and community self-determination are not lofty political goals; they are fundamental tenets governing their own organizations. Yet many of the key NGOs, though they may share the anarchists' ideas about democracy in theory, are themselves organized as traditional hierarchies. They are run by charismatic leaders and executive boards, while their members send them money and cheer from the sidelines.

So how do you extract coherence from a movement filled with anarchists, whose greatest tactical strength so far has been its similarity to a swarm of mosquitoes? Maybe, as with the Internet itself, you don't do it by imposing a preset structure but rather by skillfully surfing the structures that are already in place. Perhaps what is needed is not a single political party but better links among the affinity groups; perhaps rather than moving toward more centralization, what is needed is further radical decentralization.

When critics say that the protesters lack vision, what they are really saying is that they lack an overarching revolutionary philosophy – like Marxism, democratic socialism, deep ecology, or social anarchy – on which they all agree. That is absolutely true, and for this we should be extraordinarily thankful. At the moment, the anticorporate street activists are ringed by would-be leaders, anxious for the opportunity to enlist them as foot soldiers for their particular cause. At one end there is Michael Lerner and his conference at the Riverside Church, waiting to welcome all that inchoate energy in Seattle and Washington inside the framework of his "Politics of Meaning." At the other, there is John Zerzan in Eugene, Oregon, who isn't interested in Lerner's call for "healing" but sees the rioting and property destruction as the first step toward the collapse of industrialization and a return to "anarcho-primitivism" – a pre-agrarian hunter–gatherer utopia. In between there are dozens of other visionaries, from the disciples of Murray Bookchin and his theory of social ecology, to certain sectarian Marxists who are convinced the revolution starts tomorrow, to devotees of Kalle Lasn, editor of Adbusters, and his watered-down version of revolution through "culture-jamming." And then there is the unimaginative pragmatism coming from some union leaders, who, before Seattle, were ready to tack social clauses onto existing trade agreements and call it a day.

It is to this young movement's credit that it has as yet fended off all of these agendas and has rejected everyone's generously donated manifesto, holding out for an acceptably democratic, representative process to take its resistance to the next stage. Perhaps its true challenge is not finding a vision but rather resisting the urge to settle on one too quickly. If it succeeds in warding off the teams of visionaries-in-waiting, there will be some short-term public relations problems. Serial protesting will burn some people out. Street intersections will declare autonomy. And, yes, young activists will offer themselves up like lambs – dressed, frequently enough, in actual lamb costumes – to the *New York Times* op-ed page for ridicule.

But so what? Already, this decentralized, multi-headed swarm of a movement has succeeded in educating and radicalizing a generation of activists around the world. Before it signs on to anyone's ten-point plan, it deserves the chance to see if, out of its chaotic network of hubs and spokes, something new, something entirely its own, can emerge.

Mayan technologies and the theory of electronic civil disobedience

BENJAMIN SHEPARD AND STEPHEN DUNCOMBE
INTERVIEW RICARDO DOMINGUEZ

RD   I was born in Las Vegas, Nevada, May 2, 1959. Las Vegas was like living in three different worlds. One was the Happy Days world of the Mormons, where everyone was pure and nice and no one smoked, nobody drank, and nobody even had coffee. The other was the world of the Godfather, one of cool mobsters and occasional lawyers being blown up, and everything was legal: prostitution, gambling, everything else. And then the third was X-Files world: 98 percent of Nevada is owned by the government; some of the most secretive installations in the world are in Nevada. And right across the mountain, on the other side of Las Vegas, is the nuclear test site. So I grew up, every Saturday at twelve o'clock in the afternoon, hearing the sirens go off and we would get up, go run to the top of the Mint Hotel, and wait for the bombs to set off, and the entire earth would turn into these waves. In a certain sense my political consciousness came not so much from an exterior politicized context but more from a popular culture context. That is, at the same that these nuclear bombs were going off, I was watching Saturday afternoon matinées about people with nuclear radiation turning into giant bugs or growing third eyes. So I had an idea as a young boy that something was wrong, between the nuclear arms going off and what could happen to us, so Saturday afternoon monster flicks on TV were, in a certain sense, the genesis of my political evolution.

The other element of critique that emerged for me was that the only place that you could see Blaxploitation films was in North Las Vegas, where most of the black community was. Since neither the Mormons nor the Mafia were particularly fond of the black community and the only way I could go see any Blaxploitation movies was to make a trek into another zone, so I certainly began to comprehend that things were really divided into specific zones. And also Blaxploitation films – they were highly political; that is, they were attacking the white man, who was usually in power. For instance, I remember one of the important films for me was a film called *Three the Hard Way* with Jim Kelly, James Brown, and Fred Williamson, where they discover that there are Nazi fascists in Florida who are developing a virus that will kill only black people. So I certainly began to comprehend that there were spaces of division that were very real – a divide existed within my community based on race, and these Blaxploitation flicks spoke a certain truth about it. There were also science fiction films like *Soylent Green*, where they discover that governments will eat people, and *THX1138*, where the only value a human being has is the price of that individual and if you overrun that price then you are no longer of value. My political understanding of the world was both screenal and on the streets.

Then what occurred was that I was an explorer; I was very much a boy scout, a cub scout, an eagle scout. I met – because my mother by that time was a pathologist at Southern Memorial Hospital – what later became an atomic soldier. That's the name that I finally got for them. And these were men who during the late 1950s and early 1960s were asked to march to ground zero and, of course, were told that nothing could happen to them. They were asked to make foxholes five miles from ground zero and just cover their eyes. So as a young boy of maybe fourteen or fifteen, I certainly started seeing how the nuclear activists who were going out to the test site were participating in a kind of critique of this culture. And I certainly knew how all the Mormons, for all their purity, were accountants for the Mafia; that the Mafia were making all this money. So there was a sense of understanding.

And one of the things that occurred during this period was that I began to hear of the work of the Living Theatre. I began to see Bread and Puppet Theatre during the nuclear activist actions. So I began to comprehend that in film and in performance there was a way that one could critique this kind of condition – that one could actually do something – and I decided to become an actor; I decided to become a classical actor. So I spent most of my time from sixteen to about twenty just traveling doing Shakespeare around the country. All the while in the back of my head was floating the Judith Malina and Julian Beck treatise on the Living Theatre. This was 1975 to 1981. At the same time, I had been involved with the nuclear activist activities and getting information. Also you have to remember the Pentagon Papers had come out when I was twelve or so, so I knew governments were certainly capable of doing horrible things and not really being concerned about it.

So then, in 1981, I decided that perhaps what I really needed to do was some-how educate myself deeper in a critical theory, a discourse – of course I didn't have that language at the time. So I decided that I would go to school and get my MA in dramaturgy. And I ended up going to Tallahassee, Florida – the now famous Tallahassee, Florida, more famous that perhaps it deserves to be. And it was there that I started getting a deeper understanding of history and theory and so on. What I discovered was that in the academic bunker there wasn't a lot of interdisciplinary or transdisciplinary process. You were a dramaturg and you studied the classics of performance theory. You didn't go to sociology and read C. Wright Mills. You didn't go to philosophy and read Wittgenstein. It was just not done. And in a certain sense, I began to see the fault lines of the academy. And eventu-ally, I was asked kindly to leave the academy since I wasn't doing what I was supposed to do.

And what was lucky for me was that I said fine. I walked across the street and I got a job at Ruby Fruit books, a lesbian bookstore, the only lesbian bookstore in Tallahassee, Florida. And they were kind enough to make me their token male, if you will, and allowed me to order books; and it was through this that I started finding alternative presses. And some of the first Semiotext(e) books: Virilio, Baudrillard. I was reading a lot of the radical lesbian feminists that were coming out at that time. Certainly queer theory was beginning to emerge as the high edge of a new form of embodying theory… The theory would become not just a discourse but really playing itself out. And I thought that was very important.

At the same time, there was a small community. And at that time in the 1980s there was a lot of cocaine in Florida. There was so much that they would just give it to you. So you would end up going to a lot of cocaine parties. At these cocaine parties I started hearing people say, "Hey you should talk to so and so, cause they are talking in the same kind of yack that you are speaking," and you know, blah,

blah, blah. And eventually through one of these cocaine parties, I ran into some of the people who would later become Critical Art Ensemble. One of them was a filmmaker who hated film, a poet who hated poetry, a photographer who hated photography, the first person I ever met who actually worked with a computer who hated technology, a bookmaker who hated books; I was an actor who hated acting. And we all had a fetish for cocaine and we also had a fetish for theory. We developed this ritual where we would gather at Hope Kurtz's big glass table and she would put out lines and we would read Adorno – we would read all these great books and say "this is a great bit of critical theory," write that line down, and then do another line of cocaine. Basically we would take all the theory we could read that week… because that's all you had to do in Tallahassee.

But what happened was that we had a sense that something else could be created; that we could create a focus in this space, which we then defined as the cultural frontier. And that in the cultural frontier one could create a theoretical discourse, a practice which could be coequal to the nexus, to New York, Chicago, LA; which could be just as vital and specific. But, of course, it was very loose and not very lucid as yet. And unfortunately, like many of these things, what did bring it into focus, what did bring it into practice, was a crisis. And the crisis that hit us was AIDS.

A crisis

By 1986 and 1987, many of our good friends did indeed begin to get sick. And, of course, like many at first we didn't know exactly what to do or how to play it out. But we began to hear that there were very good groups, especially Gran Fury up in New York, who had begun to initiate directed aesthetic activist discourse and look. And we decided to do a show called 'cultural vaccines.' And we invited Donald Moffet from what would become ACT UP, but it was Gran Fury at the time and also Doug Ashford from Group Material, who also started doing early work, because those were two groups that we thought were doing very important work that we wanted to learn from. Gran Fury created Silence = Death, and the whole look of early ACT UP; they were designers, painters, artists. They had the show at the New Museum, I think around 1987. It was there, really, that ACT UP started unifying itself not only as a practice but as a look, as a design. Gran Fury created a kernel of what would become ACT UP, of course was Larry and so many others.

One of the things that developed from Critical Art Ensemble's "Cultural Vaccines" show was something that we didn't really expect. We rented a huge warehouse and on one side we invited the local community, all the way from kindergartners to the local skinhead to come put up their reading on AIDS; on the other side, we had Gran Fury and Group Material, which placed the audience in between the dialogue. What happened at the "Cultural Vaccines" show was that an ACT UP/Tallahassee emerged as a real collective that not only gathered and focused on spreading information to counter the hysteria but also looked at how HMOs worked with AIDS, and so on. We started working with ACT UP/Miami and ACT UP/Atlanta, doing coordinated actions with each other. Some of the first actions we did were what we called butt-ins. Because Tallahassee is the capital and of course the governor's mansion was there. Everybody was there. So we'd jump over the fence and pull down our pants. We'd have HIV or whatever comments we wanted. We'd slam our asses up against the window. But, of course, these butt-ins became media gestures. And we created T-shirts, which was one of the things that really established Critical Art Ensemble, in that it finally gained a name. I was an actor and a director, so I created the way actions would work.

BS   Theatre is a good training for activism.

RD   It's very good. It was a way that I could take all this kind of alternative, performative discourse – of the living theatre, of Teatro Campesino – and really bring it into focus. Like some of the T-shirts that we would do, like "AIDS: a kinder gentler genocide." We would have Hitler shaking Bush's hand. And we would create clothing for babies with the words "Healthcare not Warfare," and that sort of thing.

And one of the things that occurred out of these massive actions was that ACT UP really brought to the foreground one of the things that I think is really important and would later evolve in the 1990s with Zapatismo – that is, the politics of the question versus the politics of the answer. ACT UP was really calling for a single question to be answered: "Is there a cure?" It wasn't that we were saying that we were going to overthrow the state, that we were going to take over the

world, or that we had answers. But we were asking the single question that was
very difficult, one for the therapeutic state to answer, another for pharmaceuticals
to answer, and, of course, one for the regulatory bureaucracy to answer. Why
wasn't there a cure? What was going on? What was the hold-up? So this very basic
question started creating spaces – where now, of course, people living with AIDS
are on the boards of many pharmaceuticals, are now on the boards of the National
Health Institute, pushing drug trials forward. A lot of the community research
initiatives that were started in ACT UP/Miami and
ACT UP/San Francisco, a lot of those templates, are
now basic procedures that people are holistically
approaching living with AIDS – something that wasn't
being part of the AZT regime that was killing people.
So, it really brought into focus this kind of politics of
the question being pushed as active street leveraging.

   And one of the elements that began to occur during
these street actions is that we would do things like fax
jams. We would fax jam the National Institute of
Health. You know, what is AZT? How many people
has AZT cured? So to me it predates what electronic
civil disobedience could be. Electronic civil disobedience was doing these fax jams. Probably one of the
most important elements to the foreground was what
we called phone zapping. There was a large food
conglomerate in the south called Publix, which is found
everywhere all over the south. Probably around 1990 they decided that the best
way to deal with the AIDS hysteria was to stop selling condoms. How this worked
in their minds, we didn't know, but we certainly knew it was wrong. So what we
did – again, with this triumvirate of ACT UP/Atlanta, ACT UP/Tallahassee, and
ACT UP/Florida – was a phone tree of 24-hour action, 7 days a week, where
everybody (I was supposed to call 10:59, 11:59, 1:59) would say "look, I shop in
your store, I am happy to shop in your store, but I no longer want to shop in your
store if I can't buy my condoms in your store." And I really would. It wasn't a
kind of aggressive "we're going to take you down." It was look, we're shoppers, we
live in the community, blah blah blah. After two weeks of this they called us in,

and said yes we are going to start selling condoms in the stores. We said, "Great, now we want the condoms up front because we don't want to go all the way to the back." And you know there was a kind of simple leverage of a very simple tool, bringing this strong conglomerate into a more enlightened position as far as we were concerned.

And one of the things we also began to notice by 1990 was that, even though our actions were more highly organized, more specific, more directed, and much clearer in terms of all the information we had, they weren't getting the same kind of media attention that the early actions, say 1989 or 1988, were getting. And this was a turning point, at least for Critical Art Ensemble. We began to ask, what is it that we are doing wrong, what is it that we need to do, and can it be a simple thing? Is there something we can do?

Changing trajectories

And, of course, we took to heart the William Gibson metaphor of cyberspace being a mass hallucination. And that power had now shifted into cyberspace. You have to remember that came out in 1984. And for most of the 1980s nobody really had any access, except for maybe the science department and they weren't going to let you in to play with those machines. So we began to reread specifically *Neuromancer*. And in chapter 3 of *Neuromancer*, there is a section where Case, the hacker, and Molly Millions, the cyborg-women, need to break into this bunker of information but they can't. They need the help of a third group, which is mentioned, I think, only three times, the Panther Moderns. And what the Panther Moderns are is a highly self-conscious terrorist group that work in developing other types of mass hallucinations. So, if you imagine that cyberspace is already a master central hallucination, they were creating other hallucinations on top of that. And what happens is that these screenal hallucinations in effect blind power to what is actually occurring. And this allows Case and Molly Millions to enter the information bunker and get whatever it is that they were looking for. So, we began to think that perhaps what needs to happen is for Panther Moderns to emerge, an activist electronic community.

And one of the things that Critical Art Ensemble had always proposed was that plagiarism should be the predominant mode. Hypertext should be our mode of textual production. If you look at any of our books and if you want to spend any scholarship hours, you could look at every line and see where we stole it from — from Adorno or some other place. And all we would do was instead of saying "negative dialectic," we would say "electronic civil disobedience." And one of the things that we read at that time was "On Civil Disobedience." And all we did in the hypertext method was put 'electronic' in front of it. And that engendered in us the sense that this phrase "electronic civil disobedience" might be a very useful tool and focus for this kind of Panther Modern gathering and processing and putting it into practice. And we began to write and elucidate what later would be published in 1994 and 1995, *The Electronic Disturbance* and later on *Electronic Civil Disobedience and Other Unpopular Ideas*. We were lucky enough to do it through Autonomedia, who again had been very important to us in the 1980s by giving us access to this counter-discourse.

And one of the things you have to remember is that ACT UP and Gran Fury were, for me, the direct embodiment of queer theory. So we built what would become electronic civil disobedience on this kind of questioning, on this kind of processing. But, as in all things, by 1991 there was a sense of a divide in Critical Art Ensemble between theory and practice. I thought that there was a need for theory to hit the ground; in a certain sense to hit the street. It had to be put into practice or there wouldn't be anything else to really reflect on completely. It would just become another theoretical vein. But I didn't know how to do this, of course, not having had any training in code or computers. I had worked for a decade in a lesbian bookstore with books, which is a good training for some things but not very good training for what I was expecting to do.

So I began to hear that in New York City some artists had begun to build infrastructures. And these infrastructures were being built in terms of a certain level of access. And one of them was The Thing, which started in 1991. That was started by Wolfgang Staelhe, a painter and conceptual artist. Another was called Blast by Jordan Crandall. Both were among the first people who started investigating new space as an area of artistic development.

So, basically what I did was sell all the millions of books I had gathered during my ten years. I bought a little yellow Ford Fiesta for $200; it was guaranteed to get me to New York City before breaking down. I took the fifty books that I thought would be most important in developing the practice of electronic civil disobedience. It reminded me of H.G. Wells's *Time Machine*. The hero, at the end, before he goes back to the future, goes to his bookshelf and takes five books. So, I had taken my fifty books. And I drove as quickly as I could from Tallahassee, Florida. I went to where the BBS Thing.net was. I introduced myself to Wolfgang Staelhe. I was only there for maybe about twenty minutes. I came back out. They had broken into my car. They had taken all my clothes; they had taken all my books. So in a certain sense, I felt that New York was telling me how I needed to survive. And that is, I had to become a thief. Having been enamored of Genet, I felt that being a book thief was what I knew – that was the way I would live. And I started stealing very expensive Verso books and Lyotard's wallbook on Duchamp, price $350, and I would sell them at Mercer books. They were always very interested in theory since they were near NYU.

So in the mornings, I would study code at The Thing. The pedagogical method at The Thing is: there is a computer, there are books, good luck. Nobody was going to help me. It was all very do-it-yourself, which I think is a very strong tradition and is something I think all activists and artists should focus on. And it was there that I really began to understand how these networks were created. First thing: email. Just to train myself to think. And I would always introduce the concept of electronic civil disobedience. People would just shake their heads, "Well, that's interesting Ricardo. We don't know what that is."

Another crisis

In 1994, one minute after midnight, the Zapatistas emerged out of the jungle. They took over the state of Chiapas, calling for autonomy for the indigenous communities there. I had come stumbling home from the Tunnel. I think I was tripping on e or something. I couldn't sleep. I checked my email. I was living right by ABC No Rio, in basically a closet. One of the first things I got was the Declaration of the Lacandona. To me it really began the practice and formalizing of electronic civil disobedience. And the next day as I was stumbling out – I always went to the Odessa to get something to eat – I saw a little post-it note at ABC No Rio saying that if anybody had heard anything about the Zapatistas let's meet tonight. I think it was a Sunday night. And that night we met in the basement of

ABC No Rio. It was a cold, dank winter basement, full of big rats in those days. It wasn't nice like it is now. And basically the New York Committee for Democracy in Mexico was born. We instantly started doing civil disobedience, like hunger strikes, over at the Mexican Consulate, on 41st Street, I think.

We had predicted in Critical Art Ensemble's *Electronic Civil Disobedience* that: (1) hackers would never be politicized, and (2) activists would never be technologized, in terms of thinking of electronic culture as a useful form of leverage. One of the few areas open that didn't just disregard me was the net-art community. They seemed to be very open. They said, "Well, we don't know what it is but if you can do it, go ahead." So one of the things that occurred was that there were two blocks that I met during 1994 and a kind of open space. But I still didn't know enough code to even conceive of how that would work.

At the same time in 1994, Cecilia Rodriguez on *El Paso* had been chosen as the legal representative of the Zapatistas. So we kept trying to call her. We couldn't get hold of her because she herself wasn't prepared. She woke up one morning and found she was the legal representative. I think she didn't have a phone at the time because she was too poor. So it took her about a year even to establish some connection. At the end of that year, in December, we had the first gathering of Zapatistas in New York at Charas space to fundraise and Cecilia came.

I did a performance there called the run for the border, the Taco Bell War where I kindov emphasized what was then called cyber war or the net war by the military and the dot.coms. But it was still very difficult to elucidate. You have to remember this was 1994.

But you saw during 1994 a rising up of the ACT UP tradition of the politics of the question. What the Zapatistas soon learned out of net war was to begin to ask a question: "What does democracy mean for indigenous communities in Mexico? What is it? Is there a democracy for Mexico?" This began to break all sorts of barriers and questions, constitutional questions, NAFTA questions.

And we also started to see the gleaming of this kind of decentralized network, which would later be called the International Network of Struggle and Resistance or the Intergalactic Network of Struggle and Resistance. You started seeing the blooming of hundreds of Zapatista sites all over the world. Harry Cleaver at the University of Texas, Austin, had started, by 1995, the Zapatista listserv. So you started seeing a blooming around the Zapatismo, which hadn't occurred as strongly during the anti-NAFTA and the Peacenet movement in terms of this kind of practice or leveraging. And, unfortunately, again it was always through a series of crises that the electronic media started bringing themselves to the foreground. Probably the most important of these early gestures was the Chase Manhattan memo in early February 1996.

Remember that the Zapatistas had only had basically twelve days of fighting. In a certain sense the Internet radicalized them. Suddenly, they discovered they no longer had to be a modernist guerrilla movement that followed "death in arms." Instead they created an information guerrilla movement.

What occurred was that the Chase Manhattan memo was somehow leaked to the Zapatista community. It was an internal investment memo to be sent out only to the Chase Manhattan investment community. It stated that even though the Zapatistas had no direct influence on the value of the peso, it did create a certain psychological depression within the investor community. Therefore they called for the elimination of the Zapatista communities with extreme prejudice. A few days later, the first major offensive that had taken place since 1994, by Zedillo's Mexican military was initiated. You could see a direct connection between this memo and the offensive action.

Because we had this memo, we started doing posters of it. We did actions at Chase Manhattan. We sent the memo to the *New York Times*. We just spammed the entire world – and did street actions. I remember walking around with the memo with bloody handprints inside Chase Manhattan. And what occurred was that within three days the offensive stopped. I remember Comandante Ramona saying that an electronic force field had been created. And this electronic force field had not only created a protective device but had actually leveraged the possibility of bringing the worldwide community to Chiapas, which by 1996 forced the Mexican government to meet the Zapatistas face to face to create the San Andreas accords. If you look at the history of the Mexican guerrilla movements, it has been long term and very violent. So here the long-term violence hadn't happened. We had leveraged electronically a situation where power had actually to face this community.

SD   You had expanded the community from the jungle.

RD   Yeah, basically what the Zapatistas had shown was that you had the politics of the question, but that you can upload the singularity of the community and decentralize it. Chiapas globalized; it pushed itself around the world. It did end runs around the dominant media, the major media filters. We didn't need the *New York Times*. We didn't need these other spaces to allow the Zapatistas to speak to the world. And that they did it without electricity; they did it without computers, they did it without all the things that we have now. To become the dominant information force was truly amazing. If you look at the Rand Corporation book on social net war and the Zapatistas, they are still digging, digging to discover how they accomplished this and all the NGOs – all these things gathered together. It was bare bones. Somebody writes a note. They hand it somebody who rides a horse. The guy on the horse gives it somebody on a truck on a dirt road that takes it to San Cristóbal, who then probably goes to the church or someplace, then uploads it to *La Jornada*. I mean it's a long arduous process; nobody's uploading on their wireless Palm 7.

What occurred was that electronic leveraging began to occur. To me, these were direct signs of electronic civil disobedience. And I felt that something more could be accomplished in terms of direct action. Of course what happened was that the Mexican government never fulfilled any of the San Andreas accords whatsoever – the usual politics of the PRI government.

At the end of 1996, I was invited by MIT to do a performance, using early real video – very beta – and real audio. And this was called the Zapatista Port Action at MIT. And basically it lasted for four months into 1997. And what I did was communicate with all the Zapatista networks around the world, the Italian networks, Cecilia Rodriguez. And for two or three hours a week, I'd interview them and it would all be projected in a MIT laboratory onto huge screens. And this was the groundwork of what would become electronic civil disobedience and the creation of Electronic Disturbance Theatre. My software assistant and technology assistant at MIT was a woman named Carmin Karassic, who would later become a member of Electronic Disturbance. One of the people I interviewed, because I had read his MA on the drug war/information war in Mexico, was Stephan Wray. And what I had begun to do through The Thing was a pedagogical spamming of the networks that I was in contact with. I spoke to them about Zapatismo, about what was going on in Chiapas. I used these kinds of platforms to aggregate knowledge about the Zapatistas. Through this kind of networking I felt I was fulfilling the call that had been made through the Zapatista *encuentro* to create an intercontinental network of struggle and resistance.

SD   Can you explain what *encuentro* means?

RD   That was one of the vital and magnificent strategies that the Zapatistas used. *Encuentro* means encounter. What they started doing, as early as 1995, was inviting the world to come to Chiapas. And when there was a gathering, they would create tables. There was a table of music, a table of propaganda, a network table, and you could join any of these tables and you would share information that you brought to that table. And there was usually one Zapatista at the table who was silent and took in the information and then relayed it back to the command and the autonomous communities. And then there would be some response. Out of the network, there was a response: build the networks; start gathering.

The other thing the Zapatistas did was a very open gesture in which anyone or anything could participate in the Zapatismo in any manner they could. It could be a poem; it could be direct action on the street. There wasn't a specific Zapatista mode – you have to do this or you are not a Zapatista. So, again, it was quite an open gesture. And you use whatever tools you have at hand to create that gesture. Obviously the networks were what I had at hand. Unknown to me, out of the Zapatista Port Action show I had really created the ground for what would be the direct nonviolent use of the Internet, pushing it away from the paradigm of just communication and documentation. And again it happened because of a crisis. That's probably one of the most important things of all activism. It always comes from something horrible. You always say, "gosh, if we could only do better.…"

On December 22, 1997, the Acteal massacre occurred, in which forty-five women and children were killed by paramilitary troops trained and armed by the Mexican military using arms from the drug war; they went in and killed this Zapatista community. From what we understand, the police were only about 500 feet away. So a lot of rage and anger occurred in the Zapatista movement. I felt that something more needed to be done than send more emails and do more actions. I just wanted to shut them all down. Basically we were all so angry. So I started spamming everybody: "It's time for direct action, on the streets and online." And, of course, there were hundreds of thousands of actions, throughout the world.

After I sent out this email, I received an email from one of the groups I had interviewed in Italy called the Anonymous Digital Coalition. They said, Ricardo, why don't we do this: why don't we go to a specific URL of the Mexican government and by taking the refresh and reload button that exists on every public browser, just for an hour, in say Mexico City time, reload over and over and over. That is, in theory blocking the site, creating a disturbance. I thought: this is fantastico, let's go do it. I spammed everybody I knew. A few seconds later I received an email from Carmin Karassic, who had been my technical assistant and software engineer up at MIT. She said, "Ricardo, I have read some of your documents on electronic moments. What are the names of the Acteal dead? I would like to make an electronic monument." I thought that was a beautiful idea. A few beeps later, I got an email from Brett Stalbaum, a net artist and teacher from San José, California – the Cadre Institute – who said, "Ricardo, I think what I can do is a small java script which will take into account how many people participate and reload for us so we don't have to hurt our little finger reloading." I said, "Fantastico, lets do that." But, he said, "Ricardo, I'm not a good designer. I don't want to do the skin." And I said: "Brett, let me introduce you to Carmen." "Carmen, let me introduce you to Brett. Why don't you guys make an electronic monument to the Zapatistas that is active." And I let them go.

At that same time, Stephan Wray had been accepted into the doctoral program at NYU, in the media department under Neil Postman – who is not very media-friendly. He had come to visit me because he was also very angry. We had met early in December; he wanted to do his dissertation on electronic civil disobedience theory and practice and move it beyond what Critical Art Ensemble had done and wanted to know if I would help him and participate in this development. I said, sure. At that same time, I was developing a listserv for The Thing called Information Wars. So I said, "will you help me be, as it were, a co-moderator, and I'll help you," and he said sure. And, of course, this was without us knowing what was going to happen on December 22.

By the end of January, Stephan and I, Carmin and Brett, had begun to work together. The Zapatista FloodNet System emerged as a tool. And at that time we decided to become a theatre. I thought it was very important to continue the performative gesture. I didn't know how useful a tactic it would be. We decided that we would do a performance/action twice a month, throughout 1998. We would only do these actions in solidarity with the Zapatistas and we would only do them for a year. The main goal would be to spread information about the Zapatistas; the second to push the theory of electronic civil disobedience. We did our first action. Some 14,800 people participated around the world. Many people said President Zedillo's website responded, "I can't really fulfill your request," which to us was victory. The next day we were in the *New York Times*. And this started a new media level of discussion.

Hype and the information wars

On September 9, 1998, the morning of another performance, I received a phone call. I was getting a lot of journalists, so I thought it was a journalist. They said, "Is this Ricardo Dominguez?" I said, "Yes." "Of the Electronic Disturbance Theatre?" I said, "Yes." Then in very clear Mexican Spanish, they said, "We know who you are. We know where you are at. Do not go downstairs. We know where your family is. Do not do this performance. This is not a game. You understand." And they hung up. I said, "Wow, what a way to wake up." But I'm an addict. I need my cup of coffee. I'm gonna go downstairs and do all that sort of stuff. And, of course, I went downstairs. I told the cops. I told the festival. More spasm. And that's one of the things about information war: to outhype the hype, a very important strategy.

SD   What do you mean by that?

RD   To outhype the hype? To create a better look. If Prada is the look of whomever, then you create a better look, you create a better sense of style in a certain sense. That's what ACT UP did. It brought style into politics. All of a sudden the logo *was* "Silence = Death." Instead of being, "Oh my god, the police have called" (with doom in his voice): "Excellent, the police have called!" (spoken with optimism). "Let's let everybody know."

We counted victories if in the newspaper the first paragraph was about the Zapatistas. I would say about 81 percent of the time, in all the articles about the Electronic Disturbance Theatre, the very first paragraph or at least the second mentioned the Zapatistas and the conditions in Chiapas and what the Mexican government did.

SD   That's part of your action.

RD   Yes, because the main thing about the disturbance is not the shutting down of the space but about disseminating information. And what you want people to get is that information. It's not even so much the gesture. The performance isn't about your performance but about getting that information out there. Even in agitprop drama, you want to get this sort of information out there. And I think it worked extremely well. Because we used that level of hype and because the very system created the information.

And the other element that Electronic Disturbance Theatre hoped for was that by sending out the code, other cells, other groups, would begin to emerge, not necessarily following all the rules that we had set up. Certainly if you are an activist group in East Timor you can't be transparent, it would be suicidal, so certainly we understand the historical conditions. We certainly understand that every cell has to decide for itself its best tactics. This just happened to be our trajectory of what we thought was useful. And sure enough we began to see cells emerge, like the Electronic Hippies who started developing the major actions against the WTO, the slams against the WTO. We started connecting with other net activist groups like RTMark.

And because of the International Network of Struggle and Resistance the Zapatistas had started early on, you began to see in 1999 the networks not only coagulating but spilling out into the streets, which was, I think, of hyper importance. Again, electronic civil disobedience is only a tool. It's only one level. And if you can leverage the data bodies with the real bodies on the streets, you can have this kind of aggregated direct action like the WTO in Seattle, Washington, Melbourne. In fact, in Melbourne, there was a hactivist group, S11, that did a digital hijack of Nike.com and pointed it to the Reclaim the Streets/Melbourne action. And so as we saw in 1999, with the rise of e-commerce, you also saw the rise of international hactivism and its coordination of on-the-street actions. I think those kind of networks are so strong.

The rest is history… The Zapatista Revolution continues…

The birth and promise of the Indymedia revolution

ANA NOGUEIRA

> The problem is not only to know what is occurring in the world, but to understand it and derive lessons from it – just as if we were studying history – a history not of the past, but a history of what is happening at any given moment in whatever part of the world. This is the way we learn who we are, what it is we want, who we can be and what we can do or not do. (Subcomandante Marcos, 1997)

In 1835, Alexis de Toqueville wrote that "the power of the press is second only to that of the people." This ideal hasn't faired too well in the "Age of Corporatism," however. The recent AOL/Time Warner merger, the largest media merger deal in history, is the latest example of a media mentality that is based not on democratic ideals, but on profit. The corporate media are in the business of selling their audience to advertisers, and ensuring them that nothing aired or printed would hurt their public-relations campaigns. This forces us to update de Toquevilles's maxim: the power of the press is second only to the corporations that own them.

Today, most of the television stations we watch, the radio stations to which we listen, and the newspapers and magazines we read are owned by a core of five gigantic, multinational, cross-industry corporations, which exercise tight control of most everything we see and hear. At the last count, these were AOL/Time Warner/ CNN, Disney/ABC, General Electric/NBC, NewsCorp/Fox, and Viacom/CBS – all corporations that also own a host of other industries, and therefore have quite a lot at stake in the public-relations business (Shumway 2000).

This situation has earlier parallels in history. Revolutions facilitated by technological developments helped change the scene. Much has been said about how each technological innovation and media revolution has affected our lives, both positively and negatively. But perhaps Neil Postman (1991) expressed it best:

> Technological change is not additive; it is ecological. A new medium does not add something; it changes everything. In the year 1500, after the printing press was invented, you did not have old Europe plus the printing press. You had a different Europe. After television, America was not America plus television. Television gave a new coloration to every political campaign, to every home, to every school, to every church, to every industry, and so on.

Similarly, the introduction of the Internet has once again radically shifted the cultural and political paradigms of our age, transforming both corporate and civil society in one breath. The distinction is in the network. Jeremy Rifkin (2000) says that with the Internet comes a shift away from the twentieth-century age of capital and into the twenty-first century age of networks and access. No longer are corporations vying for first place in the race for more capital. Rather, "in the network economy, market transactions are giving way to strategic alliances, co-sourcing, and gain-sharing agreements."

But while governments and corporations struggle to control cyberspace and learn the game of networking, civil society is wasting no time using the same tools to organize and unite people's movements worldwide to fight this government sell-out and corporate takeover. "Advertisers and other opinion makers are now in a position where they are up against a generation of activists who were watching TV before they could walk," says Jamie Batsy, a Toronto-based network-security consultant and a member of the TAO Collective (www.tao.ca). "This generation wants their brains back and mass media is their home turf" (Wray 1998).

After half a century of being fed advertisement-driven, culturally homogeneous media, people are gluttonous for the ability to share stories and literally browse the world of people and places, organizations and institutions, facts and ideas, without a necessary corporate filter or bias. In this way, the Internet has radically empowered citizens to reclaim and redefine the public sphere, simultaneously providing access to uncensored and unfiltered information all over again.

What has surfaced is a diversity of culture that lies just beneath a "one-size fits all" corporate veil. That veil is woven by profit-driven media, which design notions of ourselves and present it to us as commodified reality. The Internet has radically empowered citizens to combat this presentation of a McWorld, to reclaim and re-define the public sphere, and access uncensored and unfiltered information the cor-porate elite would rather no one see. This tool is revolutionizing our understanding of culture, politics, and power just as the printing press, which played a great role in the demise of the religious elite and the birth of democracy, did in the sixteenth century. The peer-to-peer and network-to-network infrastructure of the Internet has created a method for interacting within a mediated world and publicly debating the important issues of our times, in turn spawning a new age of activism that allows people to keep up with the speed of globalization and to organize internationally to fight, or at least debate, its effects.

Ironically, the first person fully to understand this was David Ronfeldt, the most influential brain behind the right-wing military think-tank, the Rand Corporation. As early as 1993, in an article titled "Cyberwar is Coming," Ronfeldt and John Arquilla warned the military to prepare for the coming "netwar" with enemies that included activists who work on "human rights, peace, environmental, consumer, labor, immi-gration, racial and gender-based issues." They argue:

> First, the information revolution is favoring and strengthening network forms of organi-zation, while simultaneously making life difficult for old hierarchical forms. The rise of networks – especially "all-channel" networks, in which every node is connected to every other node – means that power is migrating to non-state actors, who are able to organize into sprawling multi-organizational networks more readily than traditional, hierarchical state actors can…. Second as the information revolution deepens, conflicts increasingly depend on information and communications matters. Conflicts will revolve less around the use of raw power than of "soft power" – that is, media oriented measures that aim to attract rather than coerce…. This may well turn out to be the next great frontier for ideological conflict, and netwar may be a prime characteristic. (Arquilla and Ronfeldt 1993)

"In breaking down barriers, sharing ideas with friends and peers, we are creating a new front in the cultural war to decommodify information and our lives," says Shane Korytko, a Vancouver Independent Media Center (IMC) volunteer. "I see this as an online front, working with journalism and activism at its core. Long-awaited by some, a beautiful surprise to others, the concept of a free and open exchange of ideas is now being built in earnest, thanks to a modestly conceived but paradigm-shattering open community called Indymedia."

Enter the Indymedia landscape

> We have a choice. We can have a cynical attitude in the face of media, and say that nothing can be done about the dollar power that creates itself in images, words, digital communication, and computer systems that invade not just with an invasion of power, but with a way of seeing the world, how they think the world should look. We can say, well, "that's the way it is" and do nothing. Or we can simply assume incredulity: we can say that any communication by the media monopolies is a total lie. We can ignore them and go about our lives. But there is a third option that is not conformity, nor skepticism, nor distrust: that is to construct a different way, to show the world what is really happening, to have a critical world-view and to become interested in the truth of what happens to the people who inhabit every corner of this world. (Subcomandante Marcos 1997)

Directly inspired by these Zapatista words, media activists, hackers, students, journalists, self-described "camcorder commandos" and "data dancers," "organic farmers of media," and "kamikaze, riot-chasing, direct-action journalists" are storming the world of journalism, taking full advantage of the do-it-yourself technology of the Internet, and just possibly taking the media industry through its next revolution. Challenging every part of the current media oligarchy, global networks are developing creative ways of disseminating information within society, sharing resources, educating and debating one another, and reversing the commodification of the intellectual commons. While they are at it, they are also offering an alternative model for how media institutions can and should be organized and structured. They have come together in a joint effort to democratize the media and have succeeded in creating the Independent Media Center, or Indymedia, a radical and democratic people's news network for the world.

"This is the essence of Zapatismo, and explains much of its appeal: a global call to revolution that tells you not to wait for the revolution, only to stand where you stand, to fight with your own weapon," says Naomi Klein (2001a). "It could be a video camera, words, ideas, 'hope' – all of these, Marcos has written, 'are also weapons.' It's a revolution in miniature that says, 'Yes, you can try this at home.'"

"Imperfect, insurgent, sleepless and beautiful, we directly experienced the success of the first IMC in Seattle and saw that the common dream of 'a world in which many worlds fit' is possible – step by step, piece by piece, space by space, pdf by pdf, word by word, over the net, on pirate broadcast, in the streets, streaming live, and most importantly: face to face," says Greg Ruggiero (2000), editor at Seven Stories Press.

From Seattle to Sydney, Chiapas to the Congo, the Indymedia phenomenon has indeed spread like wildfire, recklessly endangering the corporate media's monopoly on expression and intellectual property. After the success of the first IMC in Seattle, which received over 1.5 million hits in its first week, Indymedia has become the fastest growing, international, alternative media network in the world, mushrooming into dozens of physical and virtual sites that span six continents and work in a globally collaborative spirit which is a model to all. Born out of frustration with the way the mainstream media ignores or sensationalizes the almost daily anti-globalization protests occurring around the world, Indymedia has evolved into a hopeful vision that a new media landscape is on the horizon, one that gives voice to the millions of people who can only take to the streets to share knowledge about issues that affect them.

Arising out of the anti-globalization movement, Indymedia reflects many of the values, organizational methods, and contradictions of the larger movement. "In some way we are movement media," says Evan Henshaw Plath, a member of the Indymedia Tech Collective. "But given the nature of the movement, we don't advocate a particular ideological perspective. Rather, we have a terrain of ideologies which are both contradictory and complementary, but reflect the postmodern undercurrents of the anti-globalization struggle."

Like the Internet itself, power in the network is decentralized, allowing for immense freedom, creativity, and innovation on the part of each local center and each individual contributor, while each still remains connected to a network for the sharing of ideas, visions, analysis, research, stories, and even hardware.

Those working on the international network are still trying to put the pieces of the Indymedia puzzle together, while at the same time carefully avoiding the creation of yet another hierarchical and bureaucratic institution. Sheri Herndon (1999), a

Seattle IMC volunteer deeply involved in building the network, asks a most poignant question: "What is the relationship of the part to the whole, the node to the network, the cell to the organism? They are integrally related, yet remain unique; they are symbiotic, yet function to their own rhythms and needs; there is self-determination at all levels, local to global, yet there is always a link."

The most prominent link is the passionate desire to create a space where the people who are directly affected by social and economic policies can directly comment and share their news and views with the world. Indymedia has created that space, using innovative software that allows anyone with access to the Internet to instantaneously publish their texts, audio, and video files onto the cyber-network's newswires.

Self-publishing is as easy as cutting and pasting text documents and attaching an audio or video file to an email message. Additionally, once posted, viewers can "comment" on the article; the comments then appear directly below the original post, creating an open forum for important dialogue and debate. "The high level of participation and the high quality of content, despite a lack of editorial control, has shown the open publishing model to be enormously successful and useful to journalists and citizens," wrote Alex Kelly and Jason Gibson in *Arena* magazine. "The sheer enormity and breadth of information available has led to a greater level of engagement with … the issues, the readers, and the writers."

Conscious of the digital divide, many local IMCs work hard to create physical resource centers that welcome people into the media-making world by offering workshops in everything from how to get an email account, to newspaper layout, editing videos, or even performing system administration. In addition, several IMCs function as a unique space for collaboration on grassroots media projects, including regular newspapers or zines, documentaries and web radio stations, broadening the spectrum of participation and contribution.

Without much in the way of rules or style guides, Indymedia is a hub for the collection of eclectic and lush storytelling, a breeding ground for the exploration of new and creative journalistic styles, and an archive for history as it happens. "Open publishing" is redefining journalism by encouraging people to tell more than just the facts, but to tell their tale as they witnessed it. "People all over the world are dipping their storytelling toes in the water," says Matthew Arnison, also a member of the Indymedia Tech Collective and contributor to the creation of the rich-media-capable code, Active. "One of the big things with open publishing is this whole idea of getting away from a central bunch of editors or writers who know how to do journalism, know how to tell other people's stories, and are professional, and so on."

Operating on "copyleft" principles for both its content and its innovative software, the IMC has boundless potential for breaking the corporate media blockade. While forsaking the ownership of content would make most media outlets shudder, Indymedia strives to liberate media by claiming no ownership over them. The nonproprietary principle also applies to the very code on which IMC websites operate, contributing to the exponential growth of the network. "The free software ideology matches strongly our own in relation to breaking down monopolies and hierarchies of control of information and power," says Arnison. And it is helping to spread knowledge of the issues by allowing anyone to download content for free for redistribution (unless stated otherwise by the producer).

"We're not selling anything here – just offering a glimpse of something (some amazing moments of character and strength) that would otherwise be totally ignored by the mainstream or recontextualized as something very marginal," says Michael Eisenmenger, a videographer and member of Paper Tiger TV. "We do this work because we feel these are significant historical moments, that if not documented and allowed to be retold, will simply be treated as if they had never occurred, like much of the rest of our history." He continues,

> As a tactic, we view our work as potentially a key part of a larger struggle or mobilization. Neither a mouthpiece for someone's movement nor an arrogant self-appointed voice of a movement, but hopefully a means of amplifying voices within a critical context. All of our efforts have reached more people as a result. Will this ever result in radical change? Well – I hope we never lose sight [of the fact] that it's not the media creating social change, but the people themselves.

Indeed, Indymedia is fighting for a media "revolution to make revolution possible," and there are many obstacles that stand in the way before even that can happen. But the hurdles facing Indymedia are not so much that the international network has almost no money in its war chest, nor that dozens of people are going sleepless and unpaid to sustain the network. Rather, it is whether you, reading this right now, will grasp and take advantage of its purpose and stop conceiving of yourself as a mere media consumer, but think rather as an active media maker. As media activist Monsieur Jacobi (1999) says, "We don't change the world through newswires. But, Seattle and the Internet demonstrated that we can create media – in fact change its paradigm – directed not by profit, but by the passion to expose, educate, tell the truth, and change the world."

Indymedia is a potent next step in engaging in the battle of ideas that will win the future. "We are the next generation and we're building a media institution that is revolutionary," says Herndon. "We have a huge responsibility, by default. We've got huge hurdles ahead of us. We live in an oppressive, authoritarian, patriarchal system that likes discipline and punishment as the primary modus operandi for teaching us how to learn and grow. We are about something much different."

"Open publishing could make the tall tales of the Internet truly visible and accessible outside the mega-media monopolies," says Arnison. "And that's good news for 99.9 percent of the planet's population." And as the *Christian Science Monitor* notes, it is news that the major media moguls "ignore at their own peril."

"So many alternatives"
The alternative AIDS video movement

ALEXANDRA JUHASZ

In the years since AIDS was first identified with a name, thousands of programs about the crisis have been produced by videomakers who work outside of commercial television. Most critics, viewers, and producers refer to this large and diverse body of work as "the alternative AIDS media." The term distinguishes the unique conjuctions of finance, ideology, artisanship, profit, and style of independent video from the standardized, profit-oriented, seemingly authorless, and unbiased network television productions typically called "the mainstream media."

Of course, the binary terms "mainstream" and "alternative" obscure a great deal of cross-fertilization, mimicry, and hybridization: actually, both media use experimental as well as conventional forms; either format can espouse conservative ideology; "alternative" videos can have budgets larger than those of the "mainstream," and can make a lot more money.

Nonetheless, those of us who make and use AIDS media have held on to this sometimes obscuring terminology because while connoting processes of production, it has equally served to signify production ideology. The terms express our understanding that the "mainstream" media have consistently represented dominant (bigoted, distanced, judgmental) ideology about AIDS for the "general public," while the "alternative" media represent a critique, re-evaluation, or resistance to these "bad" images for a smaller, more committed audience. This simplistic understanding of the media has functioned to describe what has proven to be a relatively straightforward history of AIDS media. It has also contributed to a movement-wide awareness of the power of representation, giving words to a recognition of the negative consequences of mis- and under-representation by dominant institutions as well as the immense significance of resistant, critical, or alternative representations.

This terminology, however, does not allow us to see how the "alternative" AIDS media are themselves composed of individual tapes which are conceived, funded, produced, and distributed in an infinite variety of ways. The case studies which follow are examples of "alternative" projects based within the New York AIDS video community. They range in budget from $2,000 to $1.3 million, and in form from art tape to traditional documentary; they are shot on camcorders, Betacam, and 16 mm film by producers who are self-identified as amateurs and professionals; and they range in distribution strategy from screenings at high schools to airings on PBS.

But their similarities are also telling. Several agencies and names involved in these projects appear in more than one case study, which indicates a commitment broader than one distinct project, and also points to the interrelation between alternative producers who are highly aware of each other's work. Yet, while interaction within the alternative community provides inspiration, all eight of these projects explicitly position themselves in some relationship, however diverse, to the form, reach, or agenda of the "mainstream media." Equally crucial, each one of them would never have been made without the highest level of passion and tenacity by their respective producer or collective. Such projects are based primarily upon the urgency of politics and, according to Sean Cubbitt, the notion of struggle: struggle to find funding and equipment, struggle to learn skills, to organize distribution, and to invent the best forms for new content; struggle for specific real-world goals because the work is primarily and consistently motivated by a shared commitment to altering the course of the crisis.

Testing the Limits

Originally a group of six artists and AIDS activists who knew each other from the Whitney Independent Studio Program and/or ACT UP, the Testing the Limits Collective (TTL) has produced five videos since their formation in 1987: *Testing the Limits Pilot* (1987); *Testing the Limits Safer Sex Video* (1987); *Egg Lipids* (1987); *Testing the Limits: NYC* (1987); and *Voices from the Front* (1992). Part of the collective's struggle has been to strike a balance between the desires to reach a mass audience, and to remain true to their art-school training, and to their commitment to the movement which they document and in which they also participate. Currently in production on four hour-long documentaries about the gay and lesbian liberation movement, the collective's transition away from AIDS-specific video marks a significant change in its work, as does this project's million-dollar-plus budget.

In 1986, David Meieran and Gregg Bordowitz conceived of a video project which would represent the resurgence of lesbian/gay/AIDS militancy in New York City. Bill Olander's Homo Video show at the New Museum served as an inspiration, bringing together for the first time a developing movement of art and activist video centered upon the politics of AIDS, homophobia, and gay identity. In the meantime, ACT UP was forming. It was a heady, exuberant, dynamic time; anything and every-thing was happening in the just-forming AIDS activist community, and it all needed to be documented. "ACT UP drove us, galvanized us, gave us a focus. There was a direct alignment between the group's history and our own. We were caught up in it – documenting daily … constantly."

In early 1987, Sandra Elgear, Robyn Hutt, and Hilary Joy Kipnis joined Meieran and Bordowitz in the production of the first documentary video about the fledgling AIDS activist movement. Their intention was to produce the first mass-release AIDS documentary for Middle America, so they set their sights on PBS.

The organizing principle for the pilot they were producing to help raise funds for their thirty-minute PBS-style documentary was "document everything." The group taped countless demonstrations, ACT UP meetings, public roundtables, and inter-views with AIDS activists. This documenting occurred however it could, which most typically meant "down and dirty footage" shot by whomever had a camera. This is what Meieran calls "alternative media": media production motivated by a commit-ment to a social issue where production occurs because it has to, by unpaid staff who are themselves insiders to what they document.

Testing the Limits immediately began "to distribute itself" to AIDS service organi-zations, as well as within the art and activist scene. Although the tape used a hybrid of conventional if roughly produced forms (talking-head interviews with AIDS ac-tivists interspersed with sexy footage of AIDS demonstrations which is, in best MTV manner, rapidly cut to music), its content, the early history of ACT UP/New York, was even less conventional. *Testing the Limits* never had its PBS airing: the style was too rough, the politics were too explicit. Thus, the group make its first steps towards professionalization, which, among other things, resulted in ideologically bound splits within the collective.

The group's next project, *Voices from the Front*, took two and a half intense years to complete and began where *Testing the Limits* ended – the 1988 March on Washington for gay and lesbian rights. The great diversity of issues, organizations, and activist strategies covered in this 90-minute tape demonstrate how the AIDS activist movement and agenda had expanded and diversified since 1988. Transferred to film, *Voices from the Front* went on to play at art and independent theaters across the country and, with even greater success, on the international film market. In October 1992, it aired on HBO for a $15,000 fee. Nevertheless, the tape ran up a $40,000 deficit, and never aired on PBS, perhaps because of the group's continued reliance on "guerrilla coverage footage." But Hutt and Elgear think there is another reason: "We were too close to the material. Our friends, our lives, were in that tape. If we didn't have that type of intimacy, it wouldn't have been made. We wouldn't have gotten those interviews."

The year 1992 also brought about an escalation in anti-gay violence, and lesbian and gay militancy. TTL began documenting the birth of Queer Nation, and the response of gays and lesbians to anti-gay initiatives across the country. Now consisting of Elgear, Hutt, and Meieran, the group continued their attempt to professionalize, working on the transition from "alternative" to "independent" media production: work that, they explain, requires funding before production; work that is job- rather than issue-driven; work that is organized, structured, and neat in its form and production strategies; work that answers first to its funders; work that is paid; work that is viewed by millions. After receiving a $1.3 million grant from ITVS in 1993, TTL is currently producing *Rights and Reactions*, a four-part series of hour-long documentaries about the history of the gay liberation movement. In this case, their political commitments will be marked by the process and professionalism that only money can buy.

DIVA TV (first incarnation)

In 1989, DIVA TV (Damned Interfering Video Activist Television) was formed as an affinity group of ACT UP, "organized to be there, document, provide protection and countersurveillance, and participate." Catherine Saalfield, who co-founded DIVA

TV along with Ray Navarro, Jean Carlomusto, Gregg Bordowitz, Bob Beck, Coasta Papas, Ellen Spiro, George Plaggianos, and Rob Kurilla, points out that DIVA "targeted ACT UP members as its primary audience and made videos by, about, and, most importantly, for the movement." The group produced three tapes in its first phase: *Target City Hall*, which chronicles ACT UP's March 28, 1989 demo against Ed Koch's administration; *Pride*, about the twentieth anniversary of NY's gay and lesbian pride movement; and *Like a Prayer*, five seven-minute perspectives on the ACT UP/ WHAM demo "Stop the Church" at St Patrick's Cathedral on December 10, 1989.

Testing the Limits and DIVA TV often shared footage, covered the same actions, and were committed to AIDS activism, as was also true of GMHC. But the AIDS video scene itself was diversifying and expanding along with the AIDS crisis. As their production histories reflect, by 1989 none of these groups necessarily shared ideological assumptions about AIDS video.

While Testing the Limits and DIVA TV had a close affinity in membership, content, and political commitment, the groups also differed significantly. With PBS as its goal, Testing the Limits always attempted to professionalize. DIVA, on the other hand, was remaining staunchly antiprofessional. As Saalfield explains, "Watching Testing the Limits evolve into an institutionalized organization reinforced DIVA's commitment to working as a collective. We remain fluid, make decisions with whomever comes to a meeting, and resist assigning a treasurer by dedicating any income to buying tape stock." According to Saalfield, DIVA's commitment to "the quick and dirty approach" of alternative production led to a "limited audience, inconsistent participation by collective members, and more process than product." But at the same time there remained "the essential goal of inclusivity, with open lines of communication among collective members for expressing opinions and offering analyses. Here protest is the process, communication is our form of resistance, and everyone has a say."

Tom Kalin

The film and video artist Tom Kalin has made at least eight videotapes and films about AIDS since 1985, although he believes that all of his work (including, for instance, his feature film *Swoon*) is impacted by the crisis. His AIDS work has been financed, produced, and distributed in a variety of ways – from personally funded, individually produced montage-based experimental "art tapes" to collectively produced, glossy television. Kalin believes that he combines two models of the artist-as-producer: the "heroic artist," who gives form to the issues and feelings of his own personal/political landscape, and the "collaborative activist," whose work reflects a collective interpretation of experience and ideology.

Kalin's first AIDS tape, *Like Little Soldiers* (made while completing his MFA at the Institute for the Arts in Chicago), marks his initial response to AIDS – a personal and profound fear untempered by any interest in organizing or politicizing with others. The tape intercuts the brutal image of a pair of hands washing and picking off the white and then brown paint which color them, with the image of a burning shirt. In 1987, Kalin together with Stathis Lagoudikis produced *News from Home*, which renders the anxiety of disclosure of sero-status within a relationship and the society at large.

Kalin's search for and move towards a community represents a second stage in his AIDS work. His 1988 production, *they are lost to vision altogether*, reflects his move to New York and exposure to the activist politics of ACT UP. The tape strings together found and stolen footage from television, movies, reshot television, and Kalin's own images of sexuality, history, and activism, into a rapid and disorienting montage juxtaposing mass media hysteria with individual fixation, desire, and fear.

Until 1991 Kalin also produced work with the ACT UP artists' affinity group, Gran Fury. In 1990 the group produced *Kissing Doesn't Kill*, which consists of four thirty-second public service announcements for racial and sexual diversity in the face of AIDS; all emphasize the group's belief that, although culture is made in a lot of places, the mainstream media set the global and national agenda about AIDS. Therefore, to reach people and to reach for change, it is necessary to speak to people where they listen and in a language they understand. Kalin insists that "the ideal distribution" for even alternative AIDS video is television, "plop in the middle of the market place. You need to work to engage in the politics of Michael Jackson, Madonna, and Benneton. There is no outside the market place in relation to art production – the best you can do is to tease its margins."

Kalin makes tapes for ghosts – the people he's lost to AIDS, the faces he's seen on city streets or at AIDS demonstrations. "I don't have anything more to say about AIDS than the proverbial Latina mother of two infected babies who is also sick herself. But I do have cultural access, entitlement, privilege." Kalin used his privilege like an artist, like an AIDS activist. He represents what he knows and how he lives in a mass-mediated society which is unaware that it is dripping with infection, and unaware of Kalin's grief and anger unless he represents it.

James Wentzy/DIVA TV 2/AIDS Community Television

AIDS Community Television, a half-hour public access show devoted to programming "for greater advocacy, coalition building and greater public awareness of AIDS activism," first went on the air on January 1, 1993. There are twelve airing times monthly in all five boroughs of New York, and many of the shows have been aired by ACT UP affiliates across the country. Since its second inception, the new DIVA TV (James Wentzy) has produced over twenty shows, including *AIDS Community Television: Introduction to AIDS Video Activism* (January 5, 1993), *Target Bush: Last Night in Office* (January 9, 1993), and *Tim Bailey Political Funeral Washington* (July 6, 1993). That's one show a week, without break, for over twelve months and counting: 101 shows as of December 5, 1994. Wentzy's raw, angry, and thorough coverage consists entirely of long and unedited shots – as if you are there – usually intercut with interviews of activist participants who contextualize or critique the event covered.

DIVA TV, the media affinity group of ACT UP, was defunct for a variety of personal, structural, and historical reasons when James Wentzy, who had joined ACT UP in 1990, reenergized it with the goal of commencing a weekly activist cable show. With his Hi8 camera, and no experience editing or producing video, Wentzy produced *Day of Desperation*, which documented the first ACT UP action he attended. A slow accumulation of grants (approximately $17,000 since 1992) has allowed DIVA to purchase a ¾-inch off-line editing system, currently housed in Wentzy's living room.

Wentzy claims he has documented 95 percent of ACT UP's demonstrations since his reconstitution of DIVA. "The weekly show is my life. If you want to know how I'm doing, tune into the Manhattan Public Access Tuesdays at 11:00 p.m. or Fridays at 9:00 am." Wentzy's new goal is a national media network devoted to reflecting the "struggles, needs and state of mind" of people affected by AIDS. He believe his television coverage of the AIDS crisis has an activist perspective. "It's the only weekly series in the world devoted to covering AIDS activism, and it's political. All activists see the crisis as a political problem." On the other hand, he sees that "the nature of the broadcast media is that it is fleeting, with so little for perspective or evaluation."

It is telling that the first action Wentzy documented was the last action covered by Testing the Limits. Wentzy is in effect a third-wave AIDS video activist in a movement that has had only a six-year history, re-creating a wheel only four years after the first video collective devoted to covering AIDS activism was formed (Testing the Limits), and two years after a group was formed as an arm of ACT UP (the origional DIVA TV).

Meanwhile, other individuals and organizations have been using both high- and low-end video to educate diverse communities of color, artists, PWAs, caregivers of PWAs, the "home viewer" of broadcast television) about safer sex, the interpersonal, physical and emotional consequences of HIV infection and the politics of the representatioin of AIDS.

Having concentrated here upon the production histories of a diverse group of alternative projects (and having made many such alternative tapes myself), one conclusion about this work rises above the expected remarks upon the similarities of commitment, struggle, and ideology which set apart the alternative AIDS media. In the second decade of the AIDS crisis, and nearing ten years and tens of hundreds of alternative AIDS video projects, what I see is a crisis of multiple perspectives, diverse dimensions, countless communities, and limitless personalities and a response, in video, which attempts to take this web into account. There are "so many alternatives" because a complex and mutating social crisis needs as many responses as there are forms in which to respond.

As is evidenced in the projects above, mediamakers come to AIDS with camcorders and 16 mm cameras, with their sights on national television and individual video monitors, and with political inclinations which range from the left to the center to the apolitical. And it is precisely this feature of the alternative AIDS media, as opposed to the bounded and closed nature of so much mainstream television, which I celebrate and applaud: a form as rich, open, and malleable as are the individuals and communities who have been scarred and scared into action against AIDS and the cultural and political indifference it has continued to breed.

Black August continues: an exemplary blend of hip-hop and political history for social justice

SOFÍA QUINTERO

[T]here is a seed of revolution within the essence of all forms of hip hop culture that transcends ideological constraints. Our mission, therefore, is to bring these various political and cultural elements together and naturally evolve into a unique hip hop consciousness… The Black August Collective actively opposes the criminalization of youth and youth culture, the advancing global prison industry, the continued existence of political prisoners in the United States, and the persistence of white supremacist propaganda. This opposition is reflected through the effective merging of hip hop culture and political information. (Black August Collective 2000)

The significance

Calls for the hip-hop community to wield its power for the sake of justice are as old as the subculture itself. Numerous and varied efforts to answer this call exist in the United States, thriving in the shadow of the entertainment industry's commercialized products and the consumerism, misogyny, violence and other oppressive ideas they promote. Examples include but are hardly limited to:

- Independent production of socially conscious music such as *No More Prisons*, a compilation album by Raptivism Records whose proceeds benefit the Prison Moratorium Project, a youth-led organization dedicated to the creation of a more humane criminal justice system.
- The establishment of grant-making institutions like the Active Element Foundation,

"investing in the political leadership of the hip-hop generation to save our ass in the 21st Century" (www.nomoreprisons.net/ae.html).

- Grassroots publications like *Blu* which eschew the Puff Daddy interviews and fashion spreads for the writings of Mumia Abu Jamal and profiles of Zapatista women.

The unsung organizations utilizing hip-hop as a tool for building community and promoting social change are too numerous to list. One, however, deserves attention, not only because of its growing success but also because of its historical foundation, international scope, and collaborative model. In the spring of 1998, the Malcolm X Grassroots Movement and *Stress* magazine came together to answer the call. Charged by their elders, they formed the Black August Collective and organized a hip-hop concert in New York City to raise awareness of the continued existence of political prisoners, the explosion of the prison industrial complex, and the international growth of hip-hop. Known simply among its supporters as Black August, the now annual event is inspiring proof that indeed hip-hop can return to its roots in resistance.

The context

Ask the average hip-hop "head" who might conceive of organizing a concert to introduce the concept and history of resistance to the hip-hop community, she might cite the usual suspects – Chuck D; KRS-One; maybe a handful of more commercial rappers who, while not as overtly and consistently political, have been known to drop a socially conscious lyric or lend their celebrity to progressive causes.

Yet such activism has become the exception rather than the rule. Having its cultural roots in African practices such as Brazilian *capoeira* to Egyptian hieroglyphics, hip-hop evolved among African-American and Latino youth of the South Bronx during the late 1970s, a period of extreme political disenfranchisement and economic devastation (Rose 1994). Relying on little more than the youths' own bodies to express themselves creatively and find meaning amid squalor, hip-hop exhibited revolutionary elements at its birth. This rebellious undercurrent may not have always been evident to its practitioners, but it is no less deniable than that of the lyrics of current emcees.

But the rise of hip-hop as capitalist enterprise coincides with its decline as revolutionary force. In 1999, one out of ten albums sold were recorded by rap artists to the tune of $1.4 billion (Goldstein 1999). Estimated as a $5 billion market in 1996, hip-hop fashion sales continue to explode (Hunter 1996). FUBU – the nation's largest urban apparel company, with its $115 baseball jackets and $67 baggy jeans – made $300 million in 1999, up from $3 million only three years earlier (Goldstein 1999; Schoolman 2000). Increasingly, hip-hop clothing lines like PHAT Farm and Sean John are cited as factors in the financial descent of fashion giants like Tommy Hilfiger and Donna Karan, mainstream designers for the affluent once popular among hip-hop celebrities and their fans. While graffiti is still punishable by law (and beating by the police) in the streets or railyard, on the SoHo gallery circuit it finds wealthy patronage. A culture that once only thrived underground now commands significant attention from the likes of the *New York Times*, the *Wall Street Journal* and *Nightline*. With the exception of a few individuals, however, this commercial success has meant little to the social, political and economic advancement of the communities who create hip-hop or those who consume it.

The origin

So while the true architects of the Black August concert are indeed activists who have been challenging oppression for years, one won't find them on the cover of *VIBE* magazine or see them on BET. "The annual benefit concert was the brainchild of two freedom fighters living in exile right now," explains Malcolm X Grassroots Movements (MXGM) member Lumumba Akinwole-Bandele. These exiles – Assata Shakur and Nehanda Abiodun – both reside in Cuba and they are both women.

Former Black Panther and Black Liberation Army leader during the 1970s, Assata Shakur is perhaps the most famous victim of racial profiling by New Jersey state troopers. As she explains in a 1997 letter to Pope John Paul:

> I was captured in New Jersey in 1973, after being shot with both arms held up in the air, and then shot again from the back. I was left on the ground to die and when I did not, I was taken to a local hospital where I was threatened, beaten and tortured. In 1977 I was convicted in a trial that can only be described as a legal lynching. In 1979 I was able to escape with the aid of some of my fellow comrades. I saw this as a necessary step, not only because I was innocent of the charges against me, but because I knew that in the racist legal system in the United States I would receive no justice. I was also afraid that I would be murdered in prison. I later arrived in Cuba where I am currently living in exile as a political refugee. (www.afrocubaweb.com/assata.htm#new interview)

In 1982, organizer and healer Nehanda Abiodun went underground when she and several others were indicted for a Brinks truck expropriation. She writes:

> After the liberation of Assata Shakur on November 2, 1979, our clinic [the Black Acupuncture Association of North America] was labeled a terrorist hangout, and following the October 21, 1981 Nyack Brinks expropriation attempt, we were an excuse for the FBI to intensify their war on progressive people. On April 26, 1982, a number of us were either arrested or sought by the FBI for violating the federal RICO laws. I was one of the people they were looking for, and it was this day… that I went underground. (Abiodun 2000)

A member of the Malcolm X Grassroots Movement, Sister Abiodun was also a Black Panther; she is currently one of the organizers of Cuba's hip-hop festival held annually in Havana (Billboard 2000).

Amidst other kinds of solidarity work, MXGM had been travelling to Cuba for some time to participate in the annual hip-hop festival there and build relationships with its organizers. Independently, Sisters Abiodun and Shakur raised, both with members of MXGM and with *Stress* magazine, the idea of using hip-hop culture (rap music in particular) to celebrate freedom fighters.

"*Stress* was a publication with two strong qualities," explains Akinwole-Bandele. "One, it definitely had a heavy street and authentic element to it. Two, it was open to politicizing that element." On returning to the United States, the representatives of MXGM and *Stress* met to answer the call of their elders. It was then that the newly formed collective conceived of holding the concert in August both to evoke the history of Black resistance and to raise awareness of the contemporary struggles of political prisoners. The funds generated would go to support the development of a hip-hop studio in Cuba as well as to send US artists to participate in the nation's annual hip-hop festival.

The legacy

"Our Nation is primarily a racial, cultural, and social fusion of various ethnic groups and Nations – the Yoruba, Akan, Fante, Hausa, Fulani Ibo and several other," reads the MXGM explanation of the term "New Afrikan" (www.mxgm.com/newafrikans. html). "Since being brought to north america, New Afrikans have been called Niggers, Colored, Negroes, Black Americans, and African American. We believe these terms are misnomers and serve to confuse a unique New Afrikan Nation. By stating 'We are New Afrikans,' *we* inform the world *we* no longer want the ruling class of the american empire to determine *our* political, economic, and socio-cultural affairs."

During the 1970s, New Afrikans incarcerated in California prisons established August as the month of discipline and reflection in recognition of the many acts of resistance that have taken place during the month throughout Black history. Consider that in the month of August:

- In 1791, over one hundred thousand enslaved people in Haiti revolted against their French colonizers to ultimately establish the first independent Black nation in the Western hemisphere;
- Led by Nat Turner, approximately seventy-five enslaved Africans in Virginia rebelled in 1831.
- The escape network known as the Underground Railroad launched in 1850, enlisting the support of three thousand abolitionists and leading tens of thousands of enslaved people to fourteen free states.
- Marcus Moziah Garvey (himself born in August 1887) addressed a crowd of twenty-five thousand at the first convention of the Universal Negro Improvement Association at Madison Square Garden in New York City in 1920.
- Black people marched on Washington for civil rights in 1963 and rebelled in Watts two years later.

Even the event that demanded these acts of resistance occurred in August 1619: the arrival of the first enslaved Africans in the Americas.

The assassinations by agents of the state of George Jackson, Jonathan Jackson, and Khatari Gaulden, in particular, inspired imprisoned New Afrikans to found Black August in 1979. George Jackson entered prison at the age of eighteen and became radicalized after discovering various Marxists thinkers and their works. In his renowned autobiographical work *Soledad Brother*, Jackson recounts how he and other imprisoned revolutionaries' attempts to politicize fellow inmates made them targets of vicious repression.

On August 7, 1970, Jackson's brother Jonathan attempted to free three of his comrades. He entered the Marin County Courthouse during the trial of James McClain, accused of assaulting a guard after the brutal murder of another inmate. But before he, McClain, and two others could flee, the San Quentin police arrived and opened fire on their van. Jonathan was only seveteen years old. After several failed attempts, the state finally killed George Jackson on August 21, 1971, gunning him down in San Quentin under suspicious circumstances during a prison revolt. Khatari Gaulden continued organizing inmates. Soon after Gaulden was killed in the prison infirmary.

In commemoration of these and other resistors throughout Black history, the observant inmates wore black armbands, studied revolutionary literature, boycotted the prison canteen, abstained from drugs and alcohol, and shunned television and radio. Today New Afrikans also fast throughout August, between the hours of 6 a.m. and 8 p.m in remembrance of the hardship of their ancestors. Whenever possible, they break bread at sundown with other comrades, and eventually break the fast on the 31st with the People's Feast (Nyasha 2000; Black August Collective 2000).

The event

Many recognize the need to educate politically and mobilize hip-hop artists, but few attempt and fewer succeed (Caramanica 1999). The collective remains selective about the artists it allows to grace its bill. Perhaps the most commercial artist ever to participate in the benefit concert was Fat Joe, a Latino rapper more known for the braggadocio typical of mainstream artists. While raising the consciousness of such artists was not on the collective's initial agenda, it opened itself to the challenge. "He expressed an intent to become politicized and learn more," says Akinwole-Bandele, "and we're always willing to struggle with people."

But the Fat Joes at Black August are rare. Rather, the program usually consists of performers, like dead prez, already engaged in conscious struggle, not merely through their art but also through their acts on the streets. Unlike most socially conscious rappers who become politically active after launching their artistic careers or limit their activism to their creative output, this activist duo earned their organizer stripes as members of National People's Democratic Uhuru Movement. dead prez not openly embrace socialist economics and armed resistance in their songs, they – like many other Black August artists, such as Common and Mos Def – rhyme about themes so threatening that radio keeps them off its playlist: respect for one's elders; sex with emotional meaning; and regard for one's health, community and environment.

At every level, the Black August benefit is an educational experience as much as it is a good time. Instead of self-aggrandizing videos of the artists, slide shows celebrating the freedom fighters are shown. Concerts are prime opportunities for marketing hip-hop products for profit, but political petitions and leaflets promoting causes for justice are more likely to circulate amidst this crowd. Merchandising does occur at the event, but the faces emblazoned on the T-shirts sold belong not to the headliners but to Fred Hampton and Malcolm X. And despite the persisting notion that conscious rap does not sell, each year the collective has the unpleasant task of turning people away at the door.

The challenges

Given hip-hop's rebellious nature, however, implementing such an event is not without its challenges. Industry exploitation of and media emphasis on the more negative aspects of the subculture make it very difficult for hip-hop acts of any kind to find venues despite their commercial viability. Nevertheless, in 2000 Black August earned the distinction of losing a secured venue when its management learned dead prez were on the bill, objecting to their song "Police State" (Lee 2000).

Furthermore, because the concert supports and benefits the self-determination of socialist Cuba, government authorities consistently attempt to disrupt it. "We've experienced typical anti-Cuban harassment from Customs and the State Department," says Akinwole-Bandele. "They send harassing letters to the artists and other people who travel down for the concert."

Nevertheless, all the challenges the Collective faces in organizing the event are anticipated. "We don't get major support from any of the major labels. We don't expect to get that," Akinwole-Bandele says. "We never ask them for it." Most of the Collective's support comes from Internet sites like platform.net, minor labels such as Loud Records, and other small enterprises.

There may be another challenge on the horizon due to the event's growing success: replication. Such a possibility could be blessing depending on who does it and towards what end. The Reverend Al Sharpton recently expressed his desire to organize hip-hop exchanges with Cuba, generating media attention over his mere expression of intent never enjoyed by the collective. His interest invites legitimate suspicion not only because of his questionable political motives and alleged history with the FBI, but because what he proposes as some kind of personal innovation has been occurring successfully for years to his knowledge.[1]

Furthermore, unlike Sharpton whose visits create demands on the limited resources of the Cuban people, not only does the Black August Collective finance its own travel and bring resources to its hosts; it does so at great risk. In other words, in the spirit of true solidarity, members travel to the island *in open defiance of the US blockade against Cuba.*

In a subculture that revels in its homophobia, the Black August collective also breaks ground with its celebration of Kuwasi Balagoon – New Afrikan anarchist, member of the Black Liberation Army, defendent in the Black Panther 21 case, and openly bisexual man. Author of such provocative works as *The Myth of the White Proletariat* and *The Continuing Appeal of Anti-Imperialism,* Balagoon died in jail of AIDS-related pneumonia in 1986 (and some would contend murdered by medical neglect.) "Kuwasi Balagoon was an analytical, articulate, conscious, fearless freedom fighter," says Akinwole-Bandele. "We make sure to include this brother in all we do because to exclude his name from our history would do our community an extreme disservice" (See also Balagoon 1971, 2000).

The lessons

When asked how the strategies used by the Collective differ from those of their predecessors in the movement, Akinwole-Bandele insists they are the same. "There has always been this side of hip-hop. It's just our intent to continue that legacy." If anything, the experience of organizing this celebration of hip-hop and freedom fighters reinforces the necessity of self-determination. "Unless we're able to develop our own venues and performance spaces, we'll continue to be in a position of disempowerment, " he explains. "We'll continue to have to shuck and jive and work our way around whatever politics to try to get something to happen. Self-determination is very real and not just the second day of Kwaanza." His point is particularly resonant because Black August is a form of cultural activism. When culture becomes commodity, it becomes too easy to forget that it is a natural vehicle for self-determination. Subtle and overt attempts to repress events such as Black August – from media oversight to police boycott – prove that culture is indeed political.

By embracing that truth and placing itself on the historical continuum of Black struggle, the Black August concert bears significance not enjoyed by similar hip-hop benefits. Even now, with its tremendous commercial success, hip-hop remains the voice of disenfranchised youth, a voice that rages doggedly against police, prisons, and other trustees of the status quo. Indeed, in the hands of capital, hip-hop rails against agents of repression while simultaneously glorifying the self-destructive actions that court them, although they need no invitation.

Thus, the profundity of the Black August benefit comes not so much in its defiant stance against police terror and prison expansion, for such rhetoric has become commonplace. Rather, the genius lies in showcasing hip-hop that does *not* normalize excessive substance abuse, dominate television and radio, reference popular (as opposed to revolutionary) culture, promote consumerism (especially name-brand clothing), glorify misogyny or homophobia – presenting the event as part of the legacy of freedom fighters who have meaningfully challenged the status quo by avoiding the same.

The future

In 2001, Black August blazes a new trail to Johannesburg, South Africa, to coincide with the United Nations conference. "It'll give us an opportunity to have our own platform to talk about racism and xenophobia in America and not have handpicked representatives from so-called NGOs talking about it," Akinwole-Bandele says. The locale may have moved but the overall objective remains unchanged, for Black August will continue to celebrate Black resistance in America as well as the existence of hip-hop beyond its borders – with artists that have the courage to write rhymes like this:

Yo, little Khadijah pops is locked,
she wanna pop the lock
But prison ain't nothin but a private stock
And she be dreamin' 'bout his date of release, she hate the police
But loved by her grandma who hugs and kisses her
Her father's a political prisoner, free Fred
Son of a Panther that the government shot dead
Back in twelve-four-nineteen-sixty-nine

4 o'clock in the mornin', it's terrible but it's fine
Cuz Fred Hampton Jr., looks just like him
Walks just like him, talks just like him
And it might be frightenin, the feds and the snitches
See him organize the gang brothers and sisters
So he had to be framed yo,
you know how the game go
18 years because the 5–0 said so
They said he set a fire to a A-rab store
But he ignited the minds of the young black and poor
It will do both at the same time. (dead prez 2000)

Wednesday, July 12:
invasions of three NYC Starbucks

BILL TALEN, AKA REVEREND BILLY

Preachin' at The Cube

About thirty people participated in two actions at Astor Place, in downtown Manhattan, and then later that evening another eight or nine of us interrupted the sippers at Park Slope on 7th Avenue. There were three basic improvisatory themes, where two people indulged in "Spat Theater," shouting their comic — but absolutely about Starbucks — positions. Nearby shills would then join sides, up the decibels, and break down the barriers that exist between a conversation and the larger shop. We also planned to employ our "Cellphone Opera" — a time-honored approach from the Disney interventions. I recently had the honor to hear, just before an interview on KCR, the classic "The Revolution Will Not Be Televised" by Gil Scott Heron. Well this action was. A television crew had interviewed me shaving, talking on the phone, ranting and pacing… for three hours on Wednesday morning. I was recovering from a flu of the day before, and felt woozy anyway, but seven people with all their gear in the smallish apartment added a nice craziness to it all. Gradually I could feel the television crew beginning to agree with the points I was making in the interview and, you know, that happens so much. I constantly go through this strange conversion. People think I'm a small-time comedian at first, and then, after I've raved about "We're all turning into extras from dawn of the dead" and "We're drowning in The Sea of Identical Details" and "New York is turning into a Vertical Mall," before you know it everyone's head is bobbing yes… yes…

I wonder, in retrospect, if I got in over my head with the media people. If they make a nice show from it, well, then it would reach many more people with the anti-consumerist message then we've had here-tofore. But, for instance, I saw the camera guy taping my Obie, there near the wall. Suddenly I'm wondering if I want that appearing that way on TV. The fact is I don't have enough experience to know if that's inappropriate or not. Later, during the action, one of my friends declined to go into the Starbucks with us because of the rushed way that they asked her to sign a release for the taping. I agreed that the action was the point, not the TV show, although in the ideal world you could have the local and radiate out from it, too.

Going to the action then with the TV crew in tow, I visited Post-Al and Jones Diner, two owner-run bizzes on Lafayette. I shouted at the workers up on the Absolut sign on Bond, which is a luxury apartment in the famous bottle shape. "We can't pay the rent in this neighborhood anymore but so much dough has shifted to advertising that we have luxury pads sprouting from the billboards. What is this ad's message? Get drunk because you've lived here for years and can't afford it now?"

We stopped to buy some red adhesive dots to put on the Mermaid sign, to give her nipples (the red nipples were still up there on the Astor Place mermaid yesterday, Saturday the 15th), but Starbucks might read this and peel them off. They erased the nipples and navel three years ago as an executive decision designed, one suspects, to expand into more conservative markets. So every action we put the nipples back on, but we always have women do it. After gathering at the huge black cube that spins on its point in the middle of Astor Place, we retired into the shadows under the scaffolding on the front of the K-Mart (used to be the National Theater). I handed out the scripts you see on the "Invasion Kit" page and rehearsed folks as the TV cameras rolled. Dietmar from Germany was also there doing his doc, and Iris was taking the pix. Could've used sound recordings too… could've wired everyone and gotten great stuff for the site, and for radio, but – next time. Anybody out there expert at doing these things, contact us. It inspires others to break into contested spaces with retail-distorting dramas if they sense the charged fun of it. And just-if people understand how we do it. It's like the Marx Brothers but we go in with a unifying theme.

The Starbucks 30 went off, led by our best acting coaches, and I paced in my collar and now "alarmingly cantilevered" hair. On my signal I walked in and, yes, it did remind me of early Disney invasions, the scariness of it. For the last fifty feet before the door I sort of put the psycho-blinders on, then stopped, then started preaching before I went in. I decided on the spot to preach my way in.

The media cover the event!

So I hit the place at high volume, and people tell me that was the dramatic point of the whole thing, the first few seconds. The TV folks told me to announce "I'm Reverend Billy. Welcome to the Church of Stop Shopping." I must admit to the pleasurable sensation of causing latte-sippers to just not register the volume of my little hand-held amplifier. A part of me observed a large number of people stopped in mid-facial maneuver, almost like a photograph.

I don't remember what I preached, but it started at break-neck pace and at a high volume, and looking back, I contrast this with the Park Slope performance later in the day, where I starting by personally whispering to everyone at every table. When you start out like Moses parting the sea, you can't sustain it. I remember at one point leaning over the counter and shouting at the workers that the church would find them better jobs. I'm considering apologizing to them for saying that, because I was temping and restaurant-working very recently in my life and, well, it felt wrong to insult their jobs. A very big Starbucks worker came out to insist that I leave and we did a dance together; he was smiling. I did leave, having preached about sweatshop beans and the destruction of Astor Place by chain stores – pretty basic information – and out. The congregation left with me, after distributing sheets of information about the bean lords.

We walked to Cooper Union, where I preached from a kind of natural stage, a landing, overlooking an outdoor table area that was packed. This is right at the mouth of St Mark's Place, and I felt that more people heard a more detailed sermon. With a more natural audience sitting there, I was able to observe closely the sides of people's heads, or the backs of their heads, in some cases. I was prepared for this, as a longtime sidewalk preacher. In a perhaps related development, I have come to fetishize the feminine nape. I've become a nape man, and on a hot summer day, there's nothing like the whisps of hair that loll like feathery mirages above a nape that is shimmering with delicate sweat. There are times when a sprig of nape hairs will be stuck in the sweat, stuck there on the nape flesh, fastened in the sweat. I preached for some time on that landing with this meditation on the warm nape continuing in an ongoing rhapsody.

Later that evening I said goodbye to the TV people and we took the F to 7th Avenue and walked down to 1st Street for our virgin voyage in this new Morebucks location. It is already famous, because, like the Starbucks on 47th and 9th Avenue in Hell's Kitchen, this one violates a string of owner-run businesses that are essential to the community's identity. Now rents will triple. Also, this particular store had a loud air conditioner that kept people up all night – but now replaced with a more quiet model, I'm told. Once again I cast people in roles and rehearse their "spats." They went in and I waited. It was a wonderful night in Brooklyn. People walking slowly in the neighborhood, a slow confidence about everyone. On my signal I entered and this time, after my blasts in Manhattan, I decided to counsel these children. Built like a duplex, the café invites a kind of theater. While the workers ran to the phone (their directions are to call the police if I refuse to leave; the company memo is also posted on the site) I whispered the good news to the sippers, gradually escalating the preacherly passion. I remember the height of the whole thing was an appraisal of the graphics, the art on the walls, textured and statementless, but referencing certain famous artists whose identities you inevitably end up guessing: Morris Lewis? Jean-Michel Basquiat? The action-folks called this among their favorite, partly because it was so quiet in there that their conversations were radiating out at lower volumes. We discussed ways to improve, to create more articulate interventions, at a dinner of buttered catfish and Dixie lager in a place called Sweet Mama's, right next to the Starbucks, and a place that we had offered as an alternative, should the latte vente drinkers have their coffee ruined by our efforts.

STOP THE
RACIST
IMPRISONMENT
BINGE

PART FIVE

Race, poverty, and world making

The 1990s began with the LA riots over the acquittal of four police officers who brutalized Rodney King; the decade ended with mass civil disobedience over the use of forty-one bullets against unarmed African immigrant Amadou Diallo, racial profiling, and new revelations of widespread discrimination by the LAPD (Purdam 2000). In between, consciousness about institutional racism grew, leading to new approaches to the problem of race in America. The result was a burgeoning activism aimed at addressing racial injustice and the imperative to rebuild communities outside the parameters of racial disparity (Marable 2000; Wilson 1999). The essays in part 5 consider this new politics.

As the continued persistence of police brutality and racial profiling demonstrates, urban disadvantage in the US today is still concentrated among racial minorities, especially African Americans, Latinos, and new immigrants. Beneath the surface, hierarchies of race – from "whiteness" to "blackness" – reveal historical legacies that continue to produce social and economic inequality as combinations of culture, ideology, economy, public policy, and institutional practices interact to reproduce a hierarchy of color. "Whiteness" is privileged, while "blackness" is marginalized in today's apartheid (Massey and Denton 1993; Thompson 1998). Occasionally, combinations of these forces bubble to the surface, manifesting themselves in urban unrest. Roger Keil begins the final part of this volume with an essay that assesses the causes and consequences of the riots that erupted in Los Angeles in 1992. Thirty years after the passage of the Civil Rights Act, the fires in South Central Los Angeles offered a rare glimpse of a deeply embedded anger, once again putting racial politics on the US political agenda. This critical event, one of the largest riots in US history, set off reverberations from coast to coast. Part 5 considers a series of new responses to the age-old dilemma of race in America.

Keil's contention is that Seattle was the consequence rather than the beginning of an urban-based movement which has challenged globalization locally for the past two decades. Poverty-reduction advocates have always waged the war on poverty on local battlefronts. Throughout the last decade, AIDS activism moved to the center of these struggles. As activism moved from ACT UP to the WTO, one of ACT UP's most vital chapters became ACT UP/Philadelphia, over half of whom are people of color. The group's strength was adapting ACT UP's mission to an AIDS epidemic which was becoming increasingly intertwined within the mosaic of poverty in America. Just consider, by the late 1990s AIDS cases in prisons were five times more than the rate in the US population. In response, ACT UP/Philadelphia linked AIDS activism with mobilizations to free Philadelphia-based political prisoner Mumia Abu-Jamal, and in the summer of 2000 they organized the mass protests to end the death penalty at the Republican National Convention. In so doing, the group placed struggles against the prison industrial complex at the center of the global justice movements.

Yet, ACT UP/Philadelphia was just one of many AIDS activist groups which have successfully pushed AIDS activism beyond treatment issues toward questions of social justice and poverty reduction. New York's Housing Works, which was born out of ACT UP, has spent over a decade attacking the twin epidemics of homelessness and HIV/AIDS, utilizing a harm-reduction approach to break the link between drug addiction and criminal justice. Keith Cyler, Housing Works' co-executive director, reports on his organization's birth from ACT UP's Majority Action Committee and the history of the battle for housing for people with HIV and AIDS. Alan Greig and Sara Kershnar outline how the harm-reduction movement has taken on the inequalities of a US drug policy which has placed nearly a generation of young men of color behind bars.

As AIDS activism found its way into the anti-poverty struggle, the movement was forced to recon with its shifts and contradictions. In the battle to reduce poverty in the 1990s, there were numerous setbacks – from "empowerment zones" to "welfare reform." With the de facto triumph of the market, new movements emerged that

utilized the tools of both governments and markets to fight poverty by creating jobs, assets, and housing (Center for Community Change 2000). At the same time, poverty-reduction initiatives like Low Income Housing Tax Credits and the Community Reinvestment Act (CRA) bore fruit. The community economic development movement took these tools and ran with them. With full implementation of the CRA, redlining was slowed. As a result, historically low-income communities from the South Bronx to South Chicago were able to emerge from social isolation. Community groups established credit unions, developed strategies to renovate housing, and provided aid to small business development, all as part of the burgeoning community economic development movement, reported on in part 5.

All the while, AIDS activists argued, "Housing is an AIDS Issue, Housing Equals Health." In linking housing and healthcare, AIDS housing activists successfully built a movement and model around housing formerly homeless people with AIDS and other co-occurring disorders, including substance abuse. And they did it by using tax credits and market-based solutions to create more housing.

Reports by Randy Stoecker, Margaret Groarke, and Jordan Moss outline how old-school community organizing serves as an integral component within the community economic development movement. While many activists would rather not work within a system they do not believe in, the link between the community economic development movement and the new community organizing is producing significant rewards and stronger communities.

Roger Keil concludes his essay by suggesting, "As destructive as the four days in April and May of 1992 were to the social fabric and built environment of Los Angeles, they also created the basis for new forms of cooperation of various forms of protest politics, neighborhood activism, social movements (old and new) as well as reformist politicians." The riots inspired call for fresh thinking about what low-income communities need to thrive. For many, the answer was community organizing. Not long after, the Black Radical Congress (BRC) was born. A founding member, Bill Fletcher, discusses relations between old and new generations of radical black activists as the group engaged in a broad reassessment of the shifting terrain of racial politics in America. While many shied away from market-based approaches to community problems, others were less reticent. Fletcher analyses these strains of black radicalism – including black nationalism, the Civil Rights Movement, and the critical role of labor – in building viable solutions to the dilemma of social and economic inequality faced by African Americans.

Part 5 includes an examination of the Living Wage Campaigns, an integral component of a new agenda for racial and economic justice, springing up across the country. Stephanie Luce details how new coalitions between labor unions and community groups have advanced the circumstances of working people by winning wage increases for workers. She analyzes the impacts of living-wage laws on the employment patterns and economic development in the cities where they have been enacted. In the spring of 2001, the Harvard Living Wage campaign galvanized the nation, bringing together the diverse campus in ways few can recall. Such are the world-making possibilities of the campaigns for racial and economic justice addressed in the final part of *From ACT UP to the WTO*.

March of young New Yorkers marked forty-one days since the acquittal of four police officers for shooting Amadou Diallo forty-one times, April 4, 2000.

From Los Angeles to Seattle: world city politics and the new global resistance

At the beginning of the new century, the world is characterized by a political divide and a type of social conflict which runs like a fault line through both the globe in its entirety and through every nation, region, and city of the world. With the first decade of a willfully stated New World Order over, as we look back on the period since the fall of the Berlin Wall and the collapse of the Soviet system, a new breed of activism and politics has entered the world stage. And in contrast to earlier such events, which tended to spread from one place outward – think of the Paris Commune, for example – the current round of global anti-capitalist activism and anti-globalization politics comes from many points at once. While symbolically enlarged in cases such as the anti-WTO protests of Seattle in late 1999, these conflicts are really ubiquitous, decentralized, and unpredictable.

Much has been written in recent months and years about the reasons for the emergence of new coalitions of steelworkers and turtles, about the meaning of Seattle as an inspiration for the movement against globalization worldwide, and about the genealogy of the new protest politics (see the range of contributions to this volume for an excellent review). In my contribution to this debate here, I am suggesting a specific interpretation which is anchored in my research on insurgent politics in large cities: so-called "global cities" or "world cities." It is my contention that some of the activism we see presently around the world is, in fact, the extension of protest politics which have existed in some form or other in large globalizing cities for some time. Based mostly on the experience of Los Angeles, I will argue that "Seattle" was, at least to some extent, the consequence rather than the beginning of an urban-based movement which has challenged globalization through local action for the past two decades (for Los Angeles, see Keil 1998).

Riot politics

In the afternoon of April 29, 1992, in Simi Valley, in the north of Los Angeles, a jury consisting entirely of whites, with the exception of one Asian man, acquitted four white policemen who on the night of March 3, 1991, had beaten African American Rodney King so brutally he almost died. The beating had been caught on tape by an amateur videographer and would soon be broadcast to millions of people around the world. On the afternoon of the verdict, Los Angeles erupted into the gravest civil unrest the city saw in the twentieth century.

On May 4, after almost all of the 623 documented fires had been extinguished (initial press reports had spoken of 5,000 fires), 60 people had been killed (perhaps "only" 45 of them in immediate connection to the violence in the street), 10 by security forces; another 2,383 people were counted as injured. The estimated damage was one billion dollars. In Koreatown alone, more than three hundred stores had been set on fire or looted. Twenty thousand jobs had disappeared, five thousand of which were considered long-term losses. Eight hundred and fifty families had been made homeless as a consequence of the rioting. Between April 20 and May 5, 12,545 arrests were reported; 51 percent of those arrested were Latino, 36 percent were African American. The police forces of the city and the county were joined by the National Guard and by the Marines in their effort to control the imposed curfew. It was estimated that 40–50,000 persons participated actively and 200,000 passively in the uprising. Many thousands helped in the rebuilding efforts right after the event and more than 30,000 people joined in a peace march through Koreatown.

Among the general explanations often given for the uprising were the restructuring of the US economy, institutionalized racism, Reaganite urban policies, austerity policies on all government levels. We can add a few local peculiarities to this catalogue of contextual causalities. Los Angeles has been at once the most vivid expression of the crisis of American Fordism, and also the experimental field of new urban and regional modes of regulation. An essential feature of these new developments has been the globalization of the city, which has led Los Angeles astray from the trajectory of American urbanism. A new urban world has emerged. Conversely one can argue that globalization has prompted a redefinition of the very concept of the "American city." Still, most publications on the riots have operated with images of American cities etched into our collective mind during the post-World War II era. These are comfortable images because they suggest a simple understanding of the events: the ghettoization of African Americans, the suburbanization of the white middle class, racism and police brutality are the terms we carry in our tool bag from the previous round of urban uprisings in the 1960s. But these notions may ultimately fog our view on the reality of contemporary Los Angeles. Literal black and white thinking is not sufficient for the interpretation of what happened in 1992.

Almost a generation passed between the uprising of Watts 1965 and the rebellion of April 1992. In these twenty-seven years, Los Angeles changed its face. A majority white city with small black and Latino minorities became an international melting pot, a world city with a non-white majority. Whereas black impoverishment and cultural and racist exclusion continue in Los Angeles, the situation has also changed dramatically: Watts and similar riots in the 1960s, like those in Detroit or Newark, were a reaction by African-American inner-city residents against the repressive power of white America; in contrast, the rebellion of 1992 was the first full-scale explosion of a multinational metropolis, in which the black–white antagonism was only one – albeit essential – moment.

Instead, the Los Angeles events of 1992 foreshadowed a decade of globalization and internal diversification of protest politics and resistance in many large cities around the world. Although the event that immediately triggered the uprising was the verdict of a white jury acquitting white policemen who had brutalized a black man, the uprising was mostly seen as a multicultural affair. A multi-ethnic coalition of disenfranchised and poor people had blown off some steam by attacking the symbols and institutions of their oppression in the new Los Angeles. And they had done so in an area not as spatially restricted as Watts but in places as far apart as Pacoima in the north, Pomona in the east and San Pedro in the south of the urban region. Any attempt to streamline our understanding of "the riots" into a singular explanation (such as the two nations thesis of the Kerner Commission twenty-five years earlier) could not succeed in the face of a tremendously diverse reality (and its diverging readings). Analytical unidimensionality appeals mostly to those in power.

Instead, the inherent fragmentation of counterhegemonic discourses and explanations can be turned into an asset in the face of a rigid and inflexible power structure which looks for simple explanations (and solutions) in a period of complexity by introducing a newly invigorated discourse of solidarity to the fragmentation. The explanations will remain multiple and contradictory. My own interpretation of the event was at the time that in Los Angeles the model of "global city" development implemented by the city's ruling politicians and businesspeople had exploded. But, while unintentional as an event, the riots also provided an insight into and strengthened an emerging movement of at times radical, community-based, neighborhood-scale, grassroots activism, which was to become the beacon of renewed progressive urban politics throughout the decade that followed.

Press reports on the 1992 riots depicted a situation of destruction of both the built environment and the civility of Los Angeles. In the popular media, the impression of an epidemic social pathology was nurtured. The repeated representation of Los Angeles as the protoplasm of urban pathology and violence in this context served – perhaps not without intention – to eclipse the humanistic aspects of civil society in Los Angeles. There was little discussion, at the time, about how it was possible that a society as diverse as the one of Los Angeles had been able to sustain itself in the pressure cooker of globalization and restructuring without erupting into full-scale social violence before 1992. Yet, over the past two decades in Los Angeles, there was also a countervailing force which created much interethnic solidarity and interracial unity usually unnoticed by the common depiction of the 1992 events. Still, in all common depictions, Angeleno/as as social activists, everyday antiracists, class-conscious trade unionists, or defenders of their living environments were completely disregarded. Yet, these were the people who were instrumental in maintaining the latent antihegemonic civility and quotidian humanity of the urban region.

Social movements, community groups, neighborhood associations, labor unions have contributed to politicize and civilize the terrain in Los Angeles. Particularly the convergence of territorial and workplace-related movement segments in Los Angeles during the 1980s and 1990s, the struggle of a labor and community coalition against the closing of the General Motors plant in Van Nuys, the community-oriented strategy of labor organizers in the garment industry during the late 1980s in downtown Los Angeles, the movement for community economic development tied to the struggle against the destruction of housing in South Los Angeles, and the environmental justice activism of the 1990s can be cited as movements against the grain of restructuring, racism, oppression, and injustice – the very causes of the 1992 rebellion.

Los Angeles has become one of the major sites for the nascent environmental justice movement in the United States. One of the major organizations to focus on the relationship of social class, race, gender to environmental and human health has been the Labor/Community Watchdog, founded by the Labor/Community Strategy Center. This group has been very successful in contextualizing issues of political emancipation and economic justice in environmental discourses. More recently, this organization has become instrumental in the emergence of a Bus Riders Union in Los Angeles which represents the interests of low-income customers of the Metropolitan Transportation Agency. While this struggle reconnects the Center with its civil rights tradition, it also maintains the environmental aspects of public transportation as its mandate in fighting for the rights of the poor. Meanwhile, the environmental justice movement has had additional organizing successes. One important case in point has been the Communities for a Better Environment/La Causa, who have rallied around an agenda of social liberation and environmentalism. In a prominent case, CBE together with local communities and politicians fought the pollution caused by a commercial construction waste facility in a poor residential neighborhood in Huntington Park in the southeast of Los Angeles. Like the L/CSC, other community groups have participated to redefine their political space innovatively. In almost all such cases, there is an aspect of territoriality and political control over space involved. A slew of initiatives to renaturalize and resocialize the LA River and to make it an axis for community development along its banks as well as a research and action project of the Department of Urban Planning at the University of California, the Los Angeles Manufacturing Action Project (LAMAP) in the 1990s, which sought to organize workers along the industrial Alameda corridor in Los Angeles' industrial core, are cases in point.

These (and other) cases of applied insurgent civility have usually been left out of the analysis of social relationships in Los Angeles, particularly out of common interpretations of the 1992 uprising. I have argued here that what happened in those few days in April and May 1992 has to be seen in conjunction with the activities of many antiracist, labor, community, church, and environmental groups to create an alternative Los Angeles. The riots of 1992 did not make these politics irrelevant but highlighted their importance in the face of the breakdown of the official plans for the formation of the "world city."

World city politics

To a large degree, progressive politics in LA has been characterized by a careful dance around the confines of a post-Cold War anti-communist climate and an explosive racialized environment. Radical activists have operated in communities which are often more conservative than the activists are themselves. When middle-class radicals took power in combination with tenant and gay rights movements in Santa Monica and West Hollywood, these were exceptions. In these relatively small urban enclaves in the Los Angeles metropolitan area, a specific brand of local progressive politics did not just claim local control over "the urban"; it also aspired to hold a proactive mediating position between the global and the local. It became a negotiator of globalization. Individualized power brokerage around single policy issues prevails in Los Angeles. A large number of innovative community initiatives are tied into the campaigns of Democratic politicians at all levels, but their main activity is grassroots mobilization around bread-and-butter issues. Coalition building is part and parcel of any progressive strategy. While in Los Angeles any reference to social class had been almost inaudible in official political parlance, progressive coalitions have tended to place it at center stage. In the late 1970s, middle-class activists rushed to East-end communities to lend strategic support to anti-plant-closure struggles from inside and outside the factories. In the 1980s, community support for the struggle to keep the General Motors plant in Van Nuys open was considered crucial to the success of the threatened boycott strategy used by the workers. At the end of the 1990s, with the success of the newly invigorated labour movement in Southern California, such as the mass organizing of home-care workers, the Justice for Janitors campaign, and successful strike in 2000, the continuing presence of various living-wage campaigns – including the Los Angeles Alliance for a New Economy (LAANE) – things started to look much different. The Los Angeles progressive tradition of "labor/community" coalitions achieved some hard-won victories in the public realm. Organizing drives of garment workers and janitors in the 1980s and 1990s were built on a program of social unionism which afforded a central role to mostly immigrant inner-city communities. When labor organizers in the 1990s set out to mobilize hundreds of thousands of LA County manufacturing workers (mostly Latinos), they explicitly built part of their strategy on "community assets" and existing political infrastructures in immigrant communities. The rhetoric of labor/community coalitions in Los Angeles usually implies the notion of a cooperation of local working-class activists and residents from communities of color. Los Angeles' progressive social activists have mostly restricted their coalition-building efforts to the mobilization of partial territories and political spaces. The agents in these spaces are not members of any middle segments of urban society but rather are peripheralized by economic exploitation and racism. In Los Angeles, progressive politics has been the attempt by displaced industrial workers, impoverished and marginalized citizens (and noncitizens) and radical activists to fight the wave of Republicanism and globalization that threatens to wipe them from the landscape of their city.

The politics of resistance to restructuring in Los Angeles has often been the object of ridicule. In contrast, I would argue that the transition from American Fordist to globalized post-Fordist Los Angeles has been characterized by lively, at times violent, struggles of social classes and collectives. In the face of economic and political power of the protagonists of restructuring on the side of global capital and the local state, the social and political organizations in the described spectrum have suffered many defeats. Yet new coalitions of workplace, community, identity, and environmental movements in Los Angeles have forced more than negligible concessions. The practical intervention of newly assembled movement fragments in Los Angeles represents the latent civility of a multicultural society which has organized itself from the grassroots up and which has attempted – often successfully – to counteract the destructive tendencies of the "project world city."

The forced ethnicity of the world city has brought people from all over the globe into immediate urban proximity. In contrast to earlier periods of immigration, however, the classical integration mechanisms of the American melting pot have all but ceased to function properly as a release valve. As part of this dramatic socioeconomic and demographic restructuring, new modes of regulation have come into existence, in which immigrants and natives, the Korean middle class and the African-American working class, Chinese bankers and Central American refugees are directly forced into sociospatial relationships with one another. These new proximities are the seams of the regulation of the world city as the typical locality of the globalized world economy. The 1992 uprising represented not the failure of a concept of multiculturality per se, but the failure of multiculturalism understood as hierarchization of ethnic groups under the hegemony of the world city economy. The riots of April 29, 1992 were the death knell for the world class city as proposed by the ruling elites of the urban region. Perhaps they represent the birth of an international city with a human face. In order for this to occur, however, it will be necessary to strengthen the popular or insurgent civil society of the poor, the marginalized, and the oppressed.

Lessons from Los Angeles

The Los Angeles uprising of 1992 was unintended, spontaneous, and unorganized. But the faultlines it disclosed were structural. So were the political forces that aligned themselves after the event. As destructive as the four days in April and May of 1992 were to the social fabric and built environment of Los Angeles, they also created the basis for new forms of cooperation of various forms of protest politics, neighborhood activism, social movements (old and new), as well as reformist politicians. And to take this one step further, I would argue that the specific conditions of world city formation – the internationalization of the regional economy; the diversity of the population; the increased world market integration; social polarization; immigration and settlement issues; questions of ethnicity and "race" – were the basis in other cities for similar developments. To some degree, then, the endogenous conditions of world city formation, the urban contradictions in large metropolitan centers, were the fertile breeding ground for a new type of social action, which the world saw in full view in Seattle in late 1999. In Toronto, for example, emergent forms of multi-cultural, multi-class activism characterized much of the 1990s. A large popular movement against neoliberal policies in the province of Ontario and in the city brought 200,000 people to the streets of Toronto in 1996. In June 2000, more than one thousand antipoverty demonstrators showed up on the steps of the provincial legislature and demanded to be heard by the assembly. When access was denied, a riot started which was largely incited by the police. In both the large and the small demonstrations in Toronto, the kind of increasingly anti-capitalist coalition we saw in Seattle – labor, environment, anti-poverty, gender, gay and lesbian, anti-racist – was present and active. Seattle, in the light of this argument, was not really a beginning. It was, rather, the product of many decentralized, diverse, and innovative local urban mobilizations that occurred like a brushfire during the 1990s and has set the tone of global urban organizing in the new millennium. The kind of radical, multicultural, diverse politics discussed here in sketchy terms will need our attention as researchers, strategists, and activists.

Can Black radicalism speak the voice of Black workers?

BILL FLETCHER, JR.

From 19 to 21 June 1998, some two thousand activists and scholars came together in Chicago as part of an initiative called the Black Radical Congress (BRC). Constructed by 150 Black activists from around the United States over a period of more than two years, the conference generated a response which took everyone by surprise. The BRC was sparked by an effort to rebuild Black radicalism in the United States, particularly in the face of the neoconservative political and economic programs emerging in America. There were many striking features of the conference and of the project as a whole. One was the significant turnout of Black workers and trade unionists. In addition, there were caucus meetings of Black labor activists interested in helping to shape the Congress, as well as build ties among themselves. The BRC and the activism it has generated are among the most promising recent developments in Black radicalism.

Still, two aspects of the founding BRC conference illustrate the challenge of refusing Black radicalism and the Black working-class experience. The first regards the Black working-class/trade union segment of the BRC. The activity of this segment was not qualitatively different from the role of the Black labor segment of the National Black United Front (NBUF), formed in 1980. The labor committee of the NBUF set out to build a network of labor activists within the NBUF itself – particularly from the perspective of working-class Blacks (epitomized by the slogan "Black workers take the lead") – but that perspective did not end up dominating or leading the NBUF.

Though much has changed during the past two decades, there were some tendencies towards a similar approach in the BRC labor section. At the conference, concerns were expressed that efforts be made to shape the BRC in ways that were pro-working class, and discussions were held about independent Black worker initiatives. The lingering question was what specifically had to be new and different about the BRC in order to make it a powerful and effective voice of the Black working class.

A second aspect is reflected in an incident that shortly followed the BRC conference. I later had a discussion with a young trade unionist in another city who had attended the Chicago conference and who expressed a great deal of support for the BRC, radiating enthusiasm. The trade unionist mentioned discussions with other activists who had also been at the conference and who were attempting to decide upon appropriate follow-up activities, including building a special day to support Black business. They saw no inconsistency between the platform of the BRC (which is anti-capitalist and pro-worker) and the notion of building, as a first major campaign of the BRC in that particular locale, an initiative around supporting Black business. While I suggested other activities, the fact of the matter was that Black radicalism was seen in very different terms by this trade unionist, despite the person's job and focus of activity.

The paradigm of Black radicalism

Black radicalism has always been a multi-tendencied phenomenon, going back to the days of slavery. Within this tradition, there have been faith-based activists (Christian, Muslim, Jewish), radical democrats, socialists, communists, revolutionary nationalists, and feminists. None of these traditions has ever been able to claim, credibly, the sole legacy of Black radicalism. At the same time, Black radicalism has principally been about the interconnection between "the masses – struggle – defiance – transformation." It is a tradition that has advanced "independence," broadly defined, in a manner reminiscent of the South African/Azanian slogan "We are our own liberators." That is, Black radicalism has identified the source of Black liberation as in the power of the Black masses, even when or where Black radicals believed it necessary for strategic alliances with other sectors or ethnic groups, or have advocated territorial independence within the current borders of the United States.

It should not be surprising that, in the 1980s, as the larger left, socialist, and national liberation movements faced strategic crises, Black radicalism also declined.

In the 1980s and early 1990s, as racist oppression intensified, and the Black left was noticeably absent as a force from the field of battle, Black radicalism came to be seen as anyone or any organization which expressed defiance in the face of white supremacy and promoted some version of independence, irrespective of whether such independence was derived from left-wing or right-wing ideological sources. "Independence" came to mean not a reliance on the Black masses to struggle for Black liberation but, rather, some degree of autonomy from white people and, to varying degrees, from the "system."

This set the stage for sociopolitical trends such as the Nation of Islam to emerge and be perceived as radical. Standing up in the face of white supremacy and insisting on the humanity of people of African descent came to be seen as a radical act, despite the fact that the Nation of Islam draws most of its social philosophy and practice from sources on the ideological right rather than the ideological left. Similarly, national liberation struggles in the former colonial world – some of the most militant and radical advocates of national liberation – can, at the same time, advance a pro-capitalist agenda. Thus, while it was somewhat unsettling, it should not be surprising that younger activists, in connecting with Black radicalism, could come to the conclusion that an assertion of independence through the promotion of Black business was entirely consistent.

Class and Black radicalism

Black radicalism, like other manifestations of a progressive, populist approach to politics, has a multi-class character. In broad strokes, it embraces the struggle of the "have-nots" against the "haves," the poor against the rich, the disenfranchised against those in power. Different tendencies have coexisted within Black radicalism, particularly as manifested in African American Brotherhood at the beginning of the twentieth century, in the Communist Party, and in the growing militant Muslim movement.

Militancy evolved into radicalism under the leadership of individuals such as Malcolm X and organizations such as the Revolutionary Action Movement (RAM). With respect to Malcolm X, post-Nation of Islam and post-1963, his radicalism was characteristically populist. Although class issues could easily be inferred from his speeches and remarks, the reality is that his approach, so well captured in his metaphors of the "house Negro" and the "field Negro," focused on the individual's relationship to the struggle against national/racial oppression (i.e. whether one was willing to take up that struggle militantly or whether one was a capitulationist). While Malcolm had an evolving interest in socialism, class was not a major preoccupation for him; nor did he offer an explicit class interpretation of the African-American struggle against white supremacist national oppression.

In part because of this articulation of the struggle, many of those radicals who saw themselves following in the tradition of Malcolm (a) were silent on the class question; (b) were openly opposed the utilization of such a framework in the African-American situation; or (c) came to embrace it as, at least, a factor for consideration. Many of the latter radicals subsequently adopted a class viewpoint as central both to understanding the oppression of African Americans and for the future of the African-American movement.

By the 1970s and 1980s, the voice of Black freedom, while sung by Black workers, was all too often written by the Black petty bourgeoisie – a petty bourgeoisie which had changed and grown as a direct result of the struggles of the civil rights and Black Power movements. Greater numbers of Black college graduates, together with the entry of African Americans into corporate America in professional positions, formed part of the social base for this change. This sector was also represented by emerging political elites (primarily at the municipal level), which advanced pro-business agendas.

The response by many Black radicals to the fracturing of the African-American movement was frequently formulaic and dogmatic: an assertion that the Black working class must lead the African-American movement. But such an approach failed on all counts, never rooting such projects in the Black working class itself and, more often than not, chasing away badly needed allies.

At the same time, for those who shied away from or actively opposed dogmatism and abstract rhetoric, practice involved the type of activity carried out within the NBUF (i.e. claiming a place at the table and working to build the visibility of labor activists). While this generally constituted a better practice, a Black working-class project was not fundamentally advanced. This shortcoming is what the BRC sought to remedy.

Writing the words

A Black radical working-class project needs two principal elements. It has to interpret Black freedom via the demands of the Black working class and it has to have the

Black working class as central to its construction. The collapse of the civil rights consensus in the 1970s coincided with the offensive of US capital against the working class. Although the demands of the movement, which were primarily political and legal, had been largely accomplished, the question of economic justice remained unanswered. This question had plagued Martin Luther King Jr. before his assassination, and it was an issue which sections of the African-American movement would raise again, but around which there was no general agreement. As living standards for average US workers declined after 1973, for Black workers this decline has been matched by a growing gap between themselves and white workers.

By and large, established civil rights organizations paid only formal attention to this polarization. Resolutions were passed in conventions and by executive boards, but little was done in terms of organizing, mobilizing, or other relevant assistance. For many non-left-wing nationalists, the declining living situation of the Black worker was not necessarily a focus for organizing either, except in so far as it was connected to various "self-help" programs. For the left, this could have been a source of greater mobilization and organizing, but the weakened state of the Black left specifically, and Black radicalism generally, limited both the possibilities and effectiveness of such efforts. Black radicals faced an additional dilemma: the way in which the issues were framed. Some important work was carried out by Black radicals against police brutality, for example, or over electoral issues, but little was done in organizing the unemployed (or semi-employed).

Thus, for a project such as the Black Radical Congress, it is not enough for economic justice to be an add-on to its programmatic thrust. Economic justice (nationally and internationally) has to be at the core of its work. Three examples of such work illustrate this point: living-wage campaigns, organizing former welfare recipients, and support for trade-union organizing efforts.

Living-wage campaigns were initiated in the early 1990s by several unions and community-based organizations as a means of attacking declining wages and addressing the privatization of public services (See essay by Stephanie Luce below). Essentially, living wage campaigns attempt to set a municipal, county, or state wage level – for publicly administered funds and contracts to privatized service providers – so that it more closely approximates what is necessary for a family to survive. During the Reagan/Bush years, the minimum wage was not adjusted to inflation and declined in real terms. With the steady rise in privatization, the incentive existed for public agencies to utilize substandard contractors to carry out work previously done by public-sector workers.

The living wage initiative has two advantages. It provides a line of defense for the public-sector workforce (a high proportion of which are Black workers). It also addresses marginal workforces which are employed by contractors – who include immigrants and African Americans – who often remain at or below the poverty line, the "working poor."

Organizing former welfare recipients. In the late 1960s, the National Welfare Rights Organization (NWRO) led welfare-rights organizing, which was a direct outgrowth of the civil rights movement, and carried on the proud history of direct action and civil disobedience. It represented the possibilities contained in Dr King's "Poor People's Campaign," initiated shortly before his death. When welfare was repealed in 1996, the situation for unemployed and semi-employed welfare recipients changed dramatically. Its replacement with a time-limited program, which combines a work requirement, has created a situation of near-indentured servitude for millions of former welfare recipients. A stratum has been created immediately beneath the existing workforce who will do much the same work, but for substantially less pay.

Welfare repeal created a new terrain of struggle. The battle now has been turned into a struggle for economic justice, for jobs, and to rebuild a social safety net. It is a battle that has the potential to unite "workfare" participants with existing work-forces. Organizing in support of workfare workers offers an opportunity to tackle the larger question of poverty and its growth over the last twenty years.

Trade-union organizing has been an important part of the Black experience in the United States. While Black workers have had an admittedly contradictory relationship to organized labor, it is also the case that Black workers, and the African-American movement as a whole, have tended to support those trade-union efforts which seek to include the disenfranchised and dispossessed, and have played an important role in influencing such efforts. After years of inertia and decline, new efforts at union revitalization came to a head in 1995 with the victory of John Sweeney to lead the AFL–CIO. This new leadership has committed itself to a significant increase in resources for organizing and outreach to build coalitions with nonlabor groupings.

While important victories have been achieved, what remains lacking is a broader sense of a worker's movement and a general fight for economic justice. A trade-union movement will not be fully revitalized, nor will a labor movement be reborn, without the active input of progressive social movements such as the African-American movement.

These three examples – living wage, organizing workfare workers, and support for trade-union organizing – are identified because they represent key sites of struggle where the Black working class is currently engaged. In some cases, these struggles take the offensive – for example, living-wage campaigns – and in other cases they may be defensive – for example, some of the organizing among workfare workers. But in every case, there is motion going on at the base. What is lacking is a coherent set of national politics that ties this work together into a transformative sociopolitical movement against capitalism. The BRC was born out of an effort by Black radicals to address this need. The BRC sees these sites of struggle as opportunities for Black radicalism to base itself in the real experiences of the Black working class.

Moreover, basing Black radicalism in these struggles also offers the opportunity to rearticulate more profoundly the essence of Black freedom. Black freedom involves a combination of the fight for political power with the fight for economic justice. Thus, Black freedom is defined less by a legal victory on affirmative action (which is nevertheless important) or the expansion of Black entrepreneurs than on the success of the Black working class in getting organized and changing power relations, first locally and then nationally. Yet building Black radicalism as the voice of Black workers is not solely a matter of choosing these sites of struggle. Integrally linked to this must be the mobilization of Black workers to participate in the construction of this project.

The issue facing Black radicalism is whether the Black worker is an actor on his or her own behalf, or whether things are being done for and about the Black worker by others. In practice, the add-on programmatic approach, such as in the NBUF, involved more doing *for* the Black worker than the Black worker doing for him- or herself. Workers are already involved in the Black radicalism project generally and in the Black Radical Congress in particular. The BRC has stressed that workers already involved in the Black radicalism project must be central to choosing sites of struggle and developing overall strategy. This means that worker-radicals are involved in looking at the big picture in launching local campaigns.

The BRC has also focused on popular education and leadership development through study/discussion groups, which form the basis of organizing campaigns. There is a long history of study groups and book clubs in the African-American movement generally and within the radical movement in particular. The BRC is building upon that tradition. Their approach draws upon popular education methodologies such as those of Brazilian theorist Paulo Freire. The existing knowledge of the participants has to be drawn upon and strengthened with analysis and the introduction of new knowledge, in order to create a higher level of unity and practice.

One of the most important things about the BRC – particularly in the context of other radical Black and labor organizations – is its stand against homophobia and heterosexism from its founding. The BRC has made a point of reaching out to LGBT activists to say that there is a home in the BRC. As AIDS has increasingly affected Blacks, the BRC has made itself more open to these issues. One option discussed was to focus on AIDS and pharmaceutical genocide in Africa. And discussion within the BRC continues to include how to address these issues more effectively in its national campaigns.

As I have argued, this involves far more than an additional point on a long program. It involves the identification and strengthening of existing leaders within the Black working class, the engagement in a dialogue towards a more advanced theory for the strategic direction of the African-American movement, and the prioritization of critical sites of struggle which are relevant to the Black working class. This is what the BRC is doing. If we are successful in this, Black radicalism will not only be reborn as a national current within the African-American movement; it will have transformed itself to address the needs of building a transformative social movement for the twenty-first century.

Note

For the Black Radical Congress, see their website: www.blackradicalcongress.org

The fight for living wages

STEPHANIE LUCE

By the end of the 1990s, as the United States was experiencing the longest period of economic growth in its history, the proportion of people earning poverty-level wages had grown to almost 30 percent of all workers. Although the federal minimum wage had been raised to $5.15 in 1996, its real value was still 20 percent below its value in 1979, far below the level needed to provide a full-time worker the income necessary to support him/herself and a family (Brocht 2000). Despite experiments in "trickle-down economics," "Clintonomics," and high-tech stock "option-omics," many workers were still living in or on the edge of poverty.

Perhaps this was inevitable. With the growing integration of the world economy, employers had gained power over workers with an increased ability to move their companies overseas – or at least to threaten to do so. Standard rhetoric about globalization stated that cities, let alone individual citizens, could not make any claims against business interests lest that provide them further incentive to leave, taking all jobs, money, and resources with them.

But this past decade also saw the emergence of the living-wage movement: a national effort to raise the wages of some of the poorest-paid workers in the country. This movement, which began in the early 1990s, was a way for workers and activists to fight back at the local level, demanding from their governments that any firm doing business with the city be required to pay a wage high enough to bring a worker with a family up to the poverty level.

This article tells the story of a living-wage campaign in one city: Tucson, Arizona. This is the story of how clergy members, union members, students, environmentalists, and community organizers came together in one city to fight for living wages on a local level while thinking on a global scale.

The Tucson campaign

Tucson was not the first city to pass a living-wage ordinance. In fact, the movement began in 1994 when several pastors in the city of Baltimore realized that a number of the people coming into their food pantries were people who held jobs but didn't earn enough to buy adequate food for their families. The pastors worked with a local organization affiliated with the Industrial Areas Foundation (IAF) and with a local of the American Federation of State, County and Municipal Employees (AFSCME) to pressure the city to adopt a living-wage ordinance, which required firms holding city contracts to pay their employees a wage high enough to meet the federal poverty line. Since the victory in Baltimore, the idea spread around the country. By the time Tucson began its campaign in 1998, a couple of dozen cities and counties had passed ordinances.

Organizers in Tucson had tried a few times to pass legislation mandating higher wages. Another IAF-affiliated Tucson area organization, called the Pima County Interfaith Council (PCIC), had attempted to put forward a living-wage ordinance but failed. And the Southern Arizona Labor Council had introduced a ballot initiative to raise the city minimum wage to $7 per hour in 1996, but the state legislature stepped in to pass a measure banning city minimum wage laws.

Around the time that the minimum wage measure was defeated, the national AFL–CIO began promoting a new educational curriculum called Common Sense Economics. The president of the Labor Council, Ian Robertson, began to go into the community to look for people who were like-minded on economic justice issues. Through this effort, the Labor Council outreached to about seventeen religious leaders, including leaders of the Interfaith Council. The two groups came together via a new local coalition, the Southern Arizona Alliance for Economic Justice (SAAEJ). While the PCIC continued to play the major coordinating role behind the campaign, SAAEJ worked to mobilize around the campaign and to make it into a community project. Robertson states that the living-wage campaign "had two missions: to educate people on economic issues, and to build a group that could be mobilized around these issues."

The groundwork was laid for a new living-wage campaign, one that built on the strength of both organizations. The campaign began with fifty to eighty activists, about half from labor and half from the Interfaith Council. Based on a PCIC tactic, the campaign was officially launched with a Living Wage Walk through neighborhoods in Tucson, where church and labor activists paired up to canvas neighborhoods. According to Communications Workers of America (CWA) Local 7026 organizer Rolando Figueroa, the group chose neighborhoods that were close to schools and churches, and over one thousand volunteers went door to door, talking to residents about their work, concerns about their schools and neighborhood, and their opinions on the living-wage campaign.

In addition to the walk, the campaign organized one-on-one meetings with lawmakers. They held roughly one hundred meetings with city council members, the mayor, the chair of the City Procurement Office; and they attended council hearings and Fiscal Subcommittee meetings. Through the Living Wage Walk, the coalition was able to identify low-wage workers willing to tell their story firsthand at council meetings.

The Living Wage coalition also sponsored two large group study sessions, one in a church and one at the Carpenters Hall. To run the study sessions, the campaign worked with the group Scholars, Artists, and Writers for Social Justice (SAWSJ) to connect with two professors, a sociologist and an economist. The professors helped run the meetings to brief people on the issues. The first hearing had 450 people, and the second had 650.

Throughout the campaign, SAAEJ continued to build itself as a coalition, and eventually brought in over fifty organizations. Ian Robertson describes it:

> like a shopping mall, anchored by two big groups – the Interfaith Council (itself a coalition of fifty-seven religious groups) and the Labor Council; and then lots of small ones: Students Against Sweatshops, Jobs with Justice, SAWSJ, Labor Party, Earth First, Southwest Biodiversity Center, Stop the School of the Americas, American Friends Service Committee, Primavera Foundation, homeless organizations, Community Food Bank, the labor liaison at United Way.

The campaign had opposition from the start from elements of the business community and the Chamber of Commerce. For example, city contract holder Lynn Kastella was a vocal opponent, stating that the ordinance would cost the city lots of money, and would add an administrative burden. Furthermore, Kastella argued, "It's extremely unconstitutional to dictate to any private company what in the world they pay their people" (*Arizona Republic* 2000).

However, the opposition to the campaign was never as organized as the support. Unlike the previous efforts, this time the campaign came out of a broad community-wide coalition. Most of the city council members supported the effort fairly early on, once they realized which forces were behind the campaign. With thousands of residents demonstrating their interest in the issue, it was clear that public support was now behind this idea.

The education and organizing went on for about two years, until the campaign felt it had built up enough momentum to push for passage. On September 13, 1999, with over five hundred people in attendance at the hearing, the city council voted 5:2 to pass the ordinance.

The ordinance

The living-wage ordinance requires any firm with a city service contract to pay their employees, whether full- or part-time, $8 per hour with health benefits, or $9 without health. The wage is indexed to increase every year with the Consumer Price Index. The ordinance also requires that 60 percent of the employees hired by contractors on city projects be city residents.

The original estimates produced by the city suggested that the ordinance would affect workers at forty-one companies. According to City Procurement Director Wayne Casper, these firms provide services ranging from general cleaning and repair to commercial property management and specialized maintenance (Devine 2000). However, estimates also suggested that only about five hundred workers would actually receive mandated wage increases through the ordinance. Clearly, a wage increase of a few dollars per hour for five hundred workers would not make a large dent in poverty in Tucson. Pima County had a poverty rate of 20 percent in 1997, and almost 100,000 workers were earning poverty-level wages. So was the campaign a success? What did the coalition win for all its hard work?

Outcomes of the campaign

Tucson's case is typical for many cities with living-wage campaigns. Although some cities like San Francisco and Los Angeles have living-wage ordinances covering thousands of workers, most cover much smaller numbers. Yet it would be a mistake to judge the impact of the campaign only by its ability to win wage increases for all low-wage workers. The Tucson campaign, like campaigns in many other cities, achieved victory in numerous other ways.

Real gains for workers and employers

Some critics discount the impact of the ordinances because they do not cover large numbers of workers. However, for those workers who are covered, the wage increase can make a significant difference. For example, Debra Oliver, one person affected by the ordinance in Tucson, had worked as a security guard and supervisor on a city contract for six years. The living-wage ordinance raised her wages from $6.25 to $8.25 per hour. With the raise, said Oliver, "I'm actually able to put money in a savings account. If my vehicle breaks down, now I have a little money set aside. One of these days, I can think about taking a vacation" (*Arizona Republic* 2000).

Aside from workers, some employers find benefits to the ordinances. Oliver's boss, George Corti, said that with the higher wage his company has experienced a large drop in staff turnover. Now, he has a pool of workers eager to work, and he doesn't have to pay overtime.

Building coalitions and organizations

Perhaps one of the greatest successes of the campaign was its ability to build new coalitions. Although some of the groups had worked together before, many had not. In fact, some of the groups involved had historically been on opposite sides. Ian Robertson, a member of the United Steelworkers of America, commented on the way in which the living-wage campaign helped build new alliances: "Come on, I work in a mine, and now I'm sitting down with people from Earth First!" Paula Arnquist, staff member of SAAEJ, agrees. "The relationships built, between faith communities, labor, and even student groups, is the main thing that Tucson got out of this campaign."

The campaign also helped build up the Workers Rights Board, in conjunction with a Jobs with Justice chapter. The Workers Rights Board is made up of a diverse cross-section of leaders from the community who use "education, moral persuasion, personal contact, community outreach, and public pressure to encourage employers to abandon practices such as discrimination, poor safety practices, and interfering with workers' efforts to exercise their democratic rights to organize." (*CWA Local 7026*, 2000). The purpose of the Board is to provide a collective, community voice for unorganized and vulnerable workers, and to set a community standard for workplace justice.

In their first public activity, not long after the living-wage ordinance was passed, the Workers Rights Board took on the issue of environmental racism and workers' rights. The Board held a hearing on Brush Wellman, one of the largest manufacturers of beryllium in the world. The company was not only fighting the workers trying to organize with the Machinists Union in several states; it has also been exposing workers and the community to toxic pollutants for over fifty years.

Organizing and empowering workers

Beyond the work done through the Workers Rights Board, at least one union has already been able to convert momentum from the living-wage campaign into organizing success. About a year after the ordinance was passed, the media began pointing out that despite city living-wage ordinances, city employees themselves were not necessarily guaranteed a living wage. In fact, according to the city's own human resources department report, almost 20 percent of city workers received less than $9 per hour and received no benefits. CWA organizer Rolando Figueroa, who had been active in the living-wage campaign, began talking to city employees about their low wages.

An organizing campaign developed, and in August 2000 the workers had a 94 percent "yes" vote to join the union. Fifteen hundred city employees are members of the Tucson Association of City Employees (TACE/CWA). CWA is now working with SAAEJ to build support for a large-scale community-based organizing drive to organize up to sixteen thousand teleservice workers in the area. SAAEJ has also been providing support for the effort to unionize graduate student teaching assistants at the University of Arizona.

Some union leaders around the country argue that the living-wage movement is a bad idea for unions. They say that if workers win wage increases through legislation they will have no incentive to join unions. But Figueroa disagrees. He argues that fighting in a living-wage campaign can help workers develop the confidence in themselves, to see that they can make a difference. Many workers are reluctant to join unions because they are afraid to make the commitment, or think the effort is futile. But joining together to fight for and win a living-wage ordinance opens their eyes to the power of collective action, and the potential power of working with other workers in a union.

Expanding the movement

Living-wage activists have a number of projects on their plate. Robertson declared after the living-wage campaign, "The momentum is there, the ball is rolling, we don't want to let it stop." The group has gone on to a range of activities to push themselves into new directions. They continue to fight on local living-wage and prevailing wage issues, but have also tied their local work into global organizing. SAAEJ works with the American Friends Service Committee to promote economic literacy workshops that focus on international and border solidarity. They helped organize a delegation of workers and activists from Kentucky to visit the new facilities of a company that has recently moved from Providence, Kentucky, to a *maquiladora* (low-wage assembly or manufacturing plant) in Nogales, Mexico. The steel company Moen eliminated 144 jobs in Kentucky and now operates with about five hundred workers in Mexico, who receive $3.50 a day. Delegates from SAAEJ were able to see the new plant, talk to workers and organizers there, and learn about life on the border.

SAAEJ continues to organize around global issues. On September 26, 2000, the group helped organize a rally in solidarity with protests against free-trade meetings that day in Prague. A much larger rally was organized on April 20, 2001, in solidarity with the anti-Free Trade Area of the Americas activities in Quebec City. But, according to Arnquist, the group's main work on globalization issues is not so much the public rallies, but the day-to-day organizing they are engaged in, trying to build relationships between worker organizations in the US and Mexico. "The real work is what takes place when we take a labor organizer from the US to spend a day in Mexico with a Mexican labor organizer," Arnquist says. "We are trying to frame the globalization here with voices from both sides of the border, through a real coalition."

What is interesting about the Tucson campaign is that activists were able to connect local and global issues in a new way. In a number of cities, activists have recently worked to link their local work to new protests around trade agreement struggles. But in Tucson, globalization work had been going on for some time. "It hasn't been hard to talk about global issues in Tucson," Arnquist says. "Everyone here wants to talk about the poor conditions the *maquila* workers face in Mexico. But it was hard to get people to see that workers right here in Tucson were also living in poverty." What the living-wage campaign did was to educate Tucson residents about conditions in their own community. Arnquist feels that this step is crucial in building a real movement around globalization: "Before, people here just felt pity for people in other countries. That kind of thinking will keep the movement from growing. People need to see how globalization affects us in our own communities as well." Through living-wage outreach and education, Tucson residents saw how their economy was part of the global community.

Future challenges

These stories suggest that the Tucson campaign was a success, even if the original ordinance covered few workers. But the campaign has not been all easy. In fact, organizers in this movement have faced serious problems. The first challenge is the opposition to the ordinances from employers and legislators. As mentioned earlier, initial efforts to pass living-wage ordinances were not successful. And when the ordinance did pass in 1999, the state legislature began working to overturn the law. The bill was voted down, but there is clear and ongoing opposition to the ordinance from employer groups and some legislators. Given the significant opposition to the measures, their implementation remains a challenge. Activists must remain vigilant. Coalitions have adopted a variety of strategies to improve enforcement, ranging from targeting certain employers for media campaigns and issuing "report cards" for the city implementation efforts to winning formal representation on living-wage task forces to oversee the law's administration.

Clearly, the movement has momentum and has not been slowed by the forces ranged against it. But to keep going it needs to convert temporary coalitions into lasting, democratic organizations, and local victories into national political power. For now, the strength of the living-wage movement is that it truly is a grassroots movement. The campaigns look different in every city, as do the coalitions forming to run them. There is no national leadership or any one organization in charge. This allows for creativity and flexibility, and a chance for each campaign to develop its own character. Yet there is not one clear vision of another type of society. The unifying demand of the movement is a simple one: higher wages for low-wage workers.

Unfortunately, the living-wage movement has not yet translated into building political power in most cases. This is because, for the most part, the campaigns are not run by or tied to political parties or local political coalitions. The New Party had been active in early campaigns, but this is no longer the case. Now, the best that campaigns can do is to use the issue as a qualification for endorsement by the Labor Council. This may help move Democrats to the left, but without building any mechanism of accountability the strategy can only go so far. In fact, the Montgomery County ordinance lost when two of the candidates endorsed by Progressive Montgomery (a New Party affiliate), who had promised to support the effort, decided to vote against it. Living-wage supporters have vowed revenge on the council members who betrayed their campaign, but so far they haven't ousted them or gotten the living-wage ordinance passed. In the future, living-wage activists will need to find ways to build themselves as a political power in order to ensure that their movement has real teeth, and that their gains are translated into further victories.

In the meantime, the movement's strength is the impact it is having on ideological debates about wages and poverty, and about the ability of cities to pass effective policy in a global economy. While the challenges are large, the Tucson campaign shows how a dedicated group of activists, thinking broadly and working together, can make an impact.

Sources

Brocht 2000 and Communication Workers of America 2000.

Building a healing community from ACT UP to housing works

BENJAMIN SHEPARD INTERVIEWS KEITH CYLER

Keith Cyler began our interview on AIDS activism and community building by explaining:

> For many of our clients the first step toward becoming whole is to forgive themselves for all the scary and insane things that happened to them, and they may have done to others. It requires the staff to develop a real sense of compassion, as the clients often become abusive, self-destructive and angry toward them because that's how they relate to a world that has been hostile and abusive to them. And finally these people must develop the courage to face these behaviors and to begin to heal from these events and move forward with their lives in spite of having a life-threatening illness that will kill them sooner or later.

It wasn't an unusual argument from the co-executive director of an organization whose mission is to reach the most vulnerable and underserved among those affected by the AIDS epidemic in New York City – homeless persons of color whose positive HIV diagnoses are complicated by a history of chronic mental illness and/or chemical dependence. In the ten years since its founding, Housing Works has had to balance between the competing pressures of both a social service and a social movement organization. Through programs such as their Second Life Job Training Program, Social Ventures Development Program, and primary care clinics, Housing Works utilizes the tools of community economic development to open up spaces for an often invisible population. Their literature states:

> The Social Ventures Development Program includes several entrepreneurial ventures which were created to meet two critical challenges facing most AIDS service and anti-poverty organizations: the need to generate unrestricted income for our social service programs and the need to create employment opportunities for clients who wish to enter or re-enter the workforce. (www.housingworks.org/about.htm)

Despite its development role, the agency was founded within the trajectory of activism. Cyler and I talked about the creation of different kinds of spaces for a population the dominant culture would just as soon ignore.

BS   When did HIV/AIDS first cross the path of your life?

KC   1984, and 1983, when I was in Boston and with a very good friend that I had met. I had developed an incredible network of young black gay professionals, who were my core group of friends. It was an awesome support group of people who were gifted and lovely. In 1983, the first of our group died from some rare blood disease – it was AIDS, only the world didn't know it. As the epidemic began to show its true nature, we became increasingly uncomfortable. And at some point around then, we began to count the years of unprotected sex and drug use against the years of monastic-life behavior, knowing all the time that any one of us could be the next. And one by one they died. Of that circle, I happen to be, I believe, one of the last ones still alive, and I'm infected and scared.

At that point I was having sex wherever. It was really schizophrenic; there was the fear of contagion, but the unforgiving presence of hormones and the need to have sex. I don't regret it. I actually wish that I had had more sex than I had back then but I was a prude. I was a nerd. I cried a lot back then because of how lonely I was. It was a very alienated world, which didn't necessarily know how to deal with a strong, black, intelligent, jock male who is also a faggot who loves men and loves kinky sex…

BS   A little of that James Baldwin feeling?

KC   Absolutely, James speaks to that kind of pain and isolation, and where do you go to find safe harbors. And so as the epidemic began to rage, literally, we would count years. It was very painful coming up as a sexual person within the

AIDS epidemic… which is another story that I really wanna write and talk about…

BS   Now, what about your first arrest?

KC   My first arrest was actually kind of amazing. It was at the Waldorf, probably 1988 or 1989. And it was an affinity group – whoever was president was coming there, right. And we thought we were so cool and so smart because we had rented a room [*laughs*] under somebody else's credit card, not tied to ACT UP at all. You know, we all filtered in one by one and made our way up to the room. And we were doing a banner drop. And we thought we were going to handcuff ourselves on that big expensive clock in the middle of the lobby. We were going to leaflet and we had all the multi things going on that we were going to do while a banner was being dropped out of the roof. There was a demonstration on the outside and those of us going in were so cool. We were [*whispers*] and we had a password, all of that, all of that… just total covert.

So we finally all get into the room and we have it timed, bom, bom, bom, bom … very James Bond, right? I go to the fucking door of the hotel room that we are renting under this name and the fucking secret service had reversed the god damn key hole. They were fucking watching us… [*laughs*] You know? So we do the whole thing. We're handcuffed behind the great big clock in the middle of the lobby. And the banner drop happens while the demonstration is going on – all this craziness. And we're arrested and we're handcuffed. And my partner Charles was there to walk me through it.

We spend a couple of hours in jail. They spring us. We're done. And then it was, for a while, an arrest here, an arrest there. Where are we getting arrested next? This action, that action. And the only arrest I missed that I wish I'd gone to, I was supposed to be part of the group, the Power Tools, that went down to South Carolina to drill themselves into Burroughs Welcome. I was supposed to go but I chickened out at the last minute.

BS   How come you chickened out?

KC   Because I'm a black man and going down to the South and having them put fucking handcuffs on me was more than I wanted to experience. I'm from the South.

Majority Action/ACT UP

BS   So when did you first go to an ACT UP meeting?

KC   In 1987, the love of my life died from AIDS. And he died within four days of the official diagnosis. And I didn't know what to do, and I just freaked. And I thought I was going to die and I didn't know where to go, and I didn't know what to do, and I wanted my man back. Somehow I found out the Community Health Project was at the Gay and Lesbian Center. And they had this program for the worried well, which back then gave information about drug use on your system and counseling; it was a very holistic center. I went there and my appointment happened to be on a Monday evening. And when I walked down after my appointment, quite shell-shocked, I saw this table full of paper and all of these people in black leather, this guy in drag with big earrings shouting at everyone and all these dykes. At that point in time, I was very much into wearing black leather. And they started talking about AIDS. Larry Kramer was up talking. And I saw all this literature and information so I walked in and I stood in the back of the room and I crossed my arms. There were all these faggots, people running around, and so I wanted to hear the information. So I listened and I took all of the information off the table.

And the next week I came back. And what I would do was… I would stand in the back of the room. And I wouldn't talk to anybody and I was mumbling, "get the fuck out here" about all these white people. And I did that a couple of times. And this guy, Dan Williams, who was also black, was also standing in the back of the room. He started standing behind me. He could hear me. And I'd nod and he'd nod. And I'd listen to this craziness that was going on but I wanted the information so I had to come. The real deal was us dishing on everyone there.

Then one day he said, "Hi, my name is Dan" and we started to talk and Dan decided I needed to come to the Majority Action Committee of ACT UP. It was called the Majority Action Committee because the majority of people dying of AIDS were people of color. Majority Action focused on Black and Latino issues in the epidemic. And I started to go there. And then they needed somebody to be a representative to Treatment and Data, which was the treatment committee of ACT UP, where everything was happening with drug development and treatment issues.

Slowly, one day at the large meeting, I raised my hand and all of a sudden people realized that I had something to say. And then the next thing I know, we were doing the next Wall Street action. So I go and I'd never been to a demonstration in my life. And the television cameras picked up on me being there. They walked up to me. They stuck the microphone in front of my face and said, "What is this all about?" So I responded and the next thing I know, I'm it. And I'm going to this committee and that committee. I'm goin' here, I'm goin' there.

And that was a period in my life when I wore nothing but black. And all of a sudden I knew all this stuff about AIDS and HIV. And I was very much into the leather scene. And I was a drug dealer, and people in the gay bar scene, the leather scene, began to realize that I knew something about AIDS and HIV. And they began to ask me questions. So I was at after-hours dealing with safer sex issues and helping people deal with losing this one and that one... And AIDS became a focal point in my life. And I had dropped out of social work school [at Columbia] at that point. I was swept away.

Housing is an AIDS issue

BS   What about this Housing Committee? When did housing become an AIDS issue? When did housing and AIDS become linked? It's not part of everybody's consciousness.

KC   Let me tell you what was happening. There was a gridlock in the hospital system. Charlie King, Ginny Shubert, Eric Sawyer started recognizing the issue in 1988, 1987. For me working in the hospital... I couldn't get people out of the hospital because they didn't have a place to live. We'd get 'em well from whatever brought them in; they wouldn't have a place to live. They'd stay in the hospitals and they'd pick up another thing and then they'd die. Remember, 1988, 1990, 1991, 1992 – New York City literally had hospital gridlock and that was when they were keeping people out on hospital gurneys in the hallways. That was when people were not being fed, bathed, or touched. It was horrendous. You can't imagine what it was like to be black, gay, a drug user, transgender, and dying from AIDS.

So housing all of a sudden became this issue. ACT UP recognized it and formed this Housing Committee. I got involved in the Housing Committee when

they came to the Majority Action Committee to do a presentation, asking us to help them get money from the floor to go to the First National African American Conference on AIDS. It was going to be in Washington [DC]. There was this guy there, Charles King, I sort of ripped into Charles King. We started working together.

The strategy was to push, push, push. It wasn't different than the general ACT UP strategy about inclusion. But it was always to get those populations also included. It was easy for the world to deal with gay white men. People of color were so far off the Richter scale, and it was also to hold people-of-color organizations accountable.

A lot of this stuff for me became very emotional but I have not focused on it because I plan to do this work for a long time and I have learned. This is the problem that happened with ACT UP. You cannot last forever on anger. You cannot last forever on the negative side of emotions. And you really have to learn how to love. And you have to go to much more positive spaces ultimately if you are going to do this for a long time.

And part of what happened with ACT UP was its evolution had to do not only with this intense creative thing and very brilliant people who created and populated and ran organizations. They were so competitive and so angry and bitter at the outside world and they needed to be because we were literally fighting for our lives. But inside we needed to learn how to love. We needed to learn how to care for each other. We needed to learn that I wasn't necessarily your enemy.

BS   There was also the recognition that doing AIDS work meant doing race, class, and gender work.

KC   That came for people of color. We were trying to do that and they were doing "Drugs into Bodies." So there was always this contention. When ACT UP worked well and there was a real consensus process and you could talk about stuff and you could talk it through, you could work together. And that was when it worked well. The fights that happened out of that led to people splintering. You cannot build a community in hate, you cannot build a community on anger. You cannot build a community on death and dying. The overwhelming thing about the AIDS epidemic is they died.

Housing Works, shelter kills

KC   Housing Works, how did we get there from ACT UP? I was a social worker working in the hospital system. Charles was at the Coalition for the Homeless doing legal entitlements, getting arrested as often as he could with the Housing Group. Eric Sawyer was with the Housing Group in ACT UP. His big dream was he wanted to build shit. He wanted to be a real estate developer. He had a white boy grandiose dream that he's actually living out. That was cool.

And there was this women who was Charles's supervisor, Ginny Shubert, who wanted to do this impact litigation 'cause she was a lawyer. She was originally from Alabama; she was doing death penalty work in Florida. She likes attacking the system. And there was the three of us – me, Eric, and Charles – and it was literally out of frustration. AIDS service organizations kept telling us that they couldn't take our clients, and all of the agencies had these stupid rules that said you had to be clean and sober. You had to be this, you had to be that.

But there was this old social work principle that you have to take people where they are. If you believe that then you have to take them taking their drugs with their homelessness. And if you think about the fact that back then having an AIDS diagnosis meant that you were going to die in six to nine months, can you give me one reason why I would not want to get high? For me as a social worker, it just made sense to say, "Okay, get high. But how do we manage your life so you can live a little longer?"

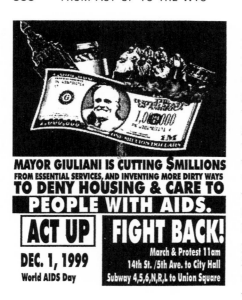

And sometimes it wasn't about just living longer but what is the work you have to do to help them die well. So it takes you into the family dynamics and the very reasons why you were getting high. So when you do that kind of work with people, you understand that they are going to get high. Getting high is a very sane reaction to a very insane world. And sometimes the world that we live in is completely fucked up and you need to change it. This is where I think most social workers and most schools of social work fail. Social work school should be training people to be social-change people. And instead they train people to fix people so that they fit in with these insane systems. And that's just wrong and counter to what I thought they were teaching in social work school, but I was one of those people who they kept wanting to throw out of social work school.

Housing Works started when after demonstrating, fighting, and working in the AIDS community, the people that I cared the most about were the people least likely to get served. And so we decided we had to do it ourselves. All of a sudden, we got this arrogant streak. Fuck it – nobody else can do this. We're gonna do it. So we started writing about it and talking about it. And we started a process that involved actually twenty to thirty people. And we talked about what kind of bylaws and organization it would be that was a shared responsibility and would empower clients. And then we recruited a whole lot of people who were in this group, AIDA – it was AIDS Into Direct Action. And it was made up of homeless and formerly homeless people, many people of color who did direct action around these issues. We included them in all of the discussions because it was important to design something that they had insight into. It was important for their voices to be heard throughout. We got a lot of them on the board so that if push came to shove, they could stop it. And we wanted to be different than AIDS Inc. And then we became this radical housing provider/service agency/advocacy thing.

All of them were interrelated and the people who you were trying to get services to needed you to be in all of those arenas. And Ginny, Charles, and myself had our own areas of expertise. So as not to re-create the kind of traditional social service model, we all were going to be co-executive directors. And we were going to run this thing together and there was going to be a consensus process. And our bosses were going to be our clients, and it was going to be this new model or at least a way to prevent all the kinds of crap that prevent the other social service agencies [from succeeding].

And this is where it all becomes blurred because you are doing the activist stuff over here and you're doing the social service stuff over here. But the social service work we do is actually at the extreme of social service work because nobody knew how to treat an active drug user. No one knew how to deal with an active person who was dying from AIDS and HIV, and they didn't want to confront that. They didn't fit within their nice, neat little models. And here we were saying, "Fine, everybody that you can't work with in your program, I want. I want to work with them and I'll find ways to move them." And a lot of that just had to do with... first of all you had to listen.

You had to listen to the people. And when they told you that they were hungry, then you needed to fuckin' feed 'em. And when they needed this and this and this, if you met them and did this, this, and this, then, you know what, they would try a little bit to do what you needed them to do, which meant that they might need for you to go with them to the doctor's office. You had to sit there and you had to explain why the doctor needed to take their bloodwork and you had to explain what this meant and you had to talk to them because the doctors and the nurses didn't have time. And the doctors and nurses were looking at them and seeing them simply as problems. They were people. They were wonderful people and they had lots of stories. They had lots of life and they had lots of wisdom. And they had a lot to give back but nobody ever valued them. Nobody ever loved them. And so you became this great positive cathartic thing to them that gave them this opportunity to reclaim their lives.

WE DIE -

[PEOPLE OF COLOR, WHETHER WE ARE AFRO AMERI-
CAN, NATIVE AMERICAN. HISPANIC LATINO, OR
ASIAN, WOMEN, MEN, IV DRUG USERS, PARTNERS OF
IV DRUG USERS. LESBIANS, GAYS, STRAIGHTS, THE
HOMELESS, PRISONERS AND CHILDREN AFFECTED BY
THE AIDS CRISIS]

[16,834* OF OUR LIVES LOST ACCORDING TO THE CEN-
TERS FOR DISEASE CONTROL. THIS IS 42% OF ALL OF
THE DEATHS. WHILE...]

THEY

[RONALD J. REAGAN • GE____ CHAEL DUKAKIS
• NATIONA____ Dr. Fauci ___ LYN • FOOD AND DRUG
ADMIN. ___ NIAID / IGRESS • THE CON-
GRESSIONAL ___ HISPANIC CAUCUS • OUR
NATIONAL M____ OUR NATIONAL MINORITY LEADERS]

DO

[absolutely]

NOTHING!

MAJORITY ACTION COMMITTEE OF ACT UP
ADDRESSING ISSUES OF ALL COMMUNITIES AFFECTED BY AIDS
P.O. Box 7832 F.D.R. Station, New York, N.Y. 10150

*as of July 1988

Harm reduction in the USA:
a movement toward social justice

ALAN GREIG AND SARA KERSHNAR

Roxbury is the poorest neighborhood in Boston. Over half of its population, primarily African American and Latino, live below the poverty line. People living in Roxbury suffer more ill health and are more likely to die from heart disease and cancer than people who live in other, wealthier parts of Boston. They are also more likely to die of AIDS – twice as likely. If you look at women and men separately, the women of Roxbury are over three times as likely to die of AIDS as women living elsewhere in Boston (Boston Public Health Commission 1998).

This local situation is repeated in poor, urban communities across the nation. The highest rate of new cases of HIV infection in the United States is now among young women of color. Official reports will tell you that the greatest risk factor for these young women is sex with a male injection-drug user. But this is to miss the larger picture. Drug policy, in the form of the War on Drugs, has denied people access to life-saving, clean injection equipment. Incarcerating nearly a whole generation of young men of color from the inner city, the bulk for nonviolent drug offenses, has damaged their life prospects for good. Not only do their chances of getting HIV increase in prison, through sharing dirty needles and having unprotected sex (both common realities inside), but their options for making a better life for themselves on the "outside" are reduced.

More fundamentally, US social and economic policies over the last thirty years have worsened poverty and social disintegration in the inner cities, depriving their communities (mainly people of color) of the resources and opportunities to deal with the problems that drugs can bring. Widening income inequalities, the flight of jobs and investment, rollbacks in affirmative action, coupled with welfare "deform" and lack of access to basic health care and drug treatment have laid the groundwork for a drug-related HIV epidemic in communities like Roxbury all over the United States.

These realities birthed and continue to confront the harm-reduction movement in the United States. Born of syringe exchange and HIV/AIDS activism in the late 1980s, the movement continues to grow as a coalition of syringe exchange workers, AIDS activists, health and social service providers, drug policy reformers, researchers, women's rights advocates, local and state politicians, and progressives on health care and criminal justice reform (some of whom are current or ex-drug users). Telling the story of the US harm-reduction movement is to document a unique coalescing of a diverse group of individuals, institutions, and interests around an analysis of and resistance to the regressive and repressive public policy of the last thirty years.

Outlaw public health

"The first syringe exchange programs in New York City were set up by 'grass roots activists'" (Henman et al. 1998). Harm reduction as a self-identified practice in the United States began on the street, in the mid to late 1980s, as HIV prevention. Its first "programs" were outreach bleach and teach, peer education, and syringe exchange on street corners, in violation of a range of prescription and paraphernalia laws designed to deprive drug users of clean injection equipment and to punish those who tried to provide them with it.

Faced with official denial and hostility, and recognizing the explosion of an HIV epidemic in poor urban communities related to the shared injection equipment, activists took their clean syringes and sharps containers onto the streets, as direct-action public health and civil disobedience. They were inspired and influenced by the politics and strategies of both ACT UP and the civil rights movement. ACT UP members, front-line workers in AIDS service organizations, civil rights activists, and frustrated drugs workers came together to get the syringes and the message out to everyone who wanted them. Their goal was saving lives through prevention of HIV transmission, and they explicitly rejected the "abstinence" orthodoxy of the time –

that drug users could only be helped by getting off drugs. They described their work as "harm reduction" – in other words, working to reduce the harms related to drug use (in this case HIV/AIDS) without necessarily reducing the consumption of drugs.

Harm reduction as an "outlaw practice" was in stark contrast to the experience in other countries. As a self-conscious approach and philosophy, it first emerged in the Netherlands in the early 1980s as a pragmatic partnership between drug users and city officials, who started a needle exchange in order to tackle the growing problem of hepatitis B among users. In the late 1980s, Reagan's ideological soulmate, Margaret Thatcher, founded and funded a network of syringe-exchange and broader harm-reduction programs as a part of the United Kingdom's National Health Service. This development was echoed in other parts of Western Europe, Canada, and Australia. The distribution of clean injection equipment to drug users in those countries was, and continues to be, supported and frequently sponsored by the state. In such countries, the consensus remains that AIDS constitutes a greater immediate threat to the public health than drug misuse.

The civil war

No such consensus was possible in the Reagan and Bush era and remains problematic to this day in the United States. By 1996, this lack of consensus had cost the United States 146,359 cases of drug-related HIV (Centers for Disease Control 1996), in contrast to the United Kingdom, which, with one-sixth of the US population, had just over six hundred cases (Stimson 1995). The contrast in these statistics is largely a direct consequence of the civil war that has raged in the United States over the last thirty years. Its more common title, the "War on Drugs," runs the risk of misdefining both its intent and focus, and of course its consequences. War was declared in 1972 when Richard Nixon announced the federalization of supply reduction and prosecution of drug offenses previously under state auspices. While a portion of the budget went into the introduction of methadone maintenance in the United States, a bulk of resources went into military and police interventions in both drug sales and drug use.

Its intent was clear from the start. "People are poor and violent not because of grand social pressures ... but because they are bad individuals deserving only of discipline and punishment" Nixon declared when he switched the federal budget away from social programming. Drugs, the icon of the 1960s, and the "bad individuals" who used them were now defined as the problem. The drugs war became a "political spectacle that depicted social problems grounded on economic transformations as individual moral or behavioral problems that could be remedied by simply embracing family values, modifying bad habits, policing mean streets, and incarcerating the fiendish 'enemies within'" (Reeves and Campbell 1994).

The most feared "enemies within" were communities of color; those whose involvement in civil rights protest and potential for social revolution offered the most serious threat to the American political class since the radicalism of the early 1930s. "The history of drugs and drug policy in the United States has always been racialized" (Moore 1995) and the racism of the drugs war is striking. Though five times as many whites are estimated to use drugs as African Americans, the latter are five times more likely to be incarcerated for drug use than their white counterparts. While black men make up about 13 percent of drug users, they constitute 62.7 percent of all drug offenders imprisoned. Similarly, despite equal rates of drug use amongst pregnant women, and a greater absolute number of white women using drugs during pregnancy, African-American and Latina women account for 80 percent of those prosecuted for delivering drug-exposed babies (Coffin 1997). The front lines of this new American civil war have been and remain the inner city and its main casualties, poor people of color.

Communities of interest?

In addition to damage from harmful social, economic, and drug policies, such communities have also been devastated most by the harms caused by drug use and the drug economy. For many people in those communities, understandably, AIDS has not been the priority. Addiction and dependency, drug-related violence and criminality, and the resulting impacts on the social and economic life of the most affected communities have been experienced as more serious problems. When drugs, drug "addicts," and drug "pushers" are identified as the source of these problems, the War on Drugs has seemed to many to be the right response. Far from being seen as a life-saving measure, syringe exchange and harm reduction more generally were for many years resisted and denounced by the leaders and representatives of communities of color as enabling the very behavior that was killing their people and deeply damaging their communities.

In order to work with and within the most affected communities, there was a need to take harm reduction beyond HIV prevention and toward an analysis of and response to the multiple harms related to drug use, drug sales, and drug policy. The formation of the Harm Reduction Working Group in October 1993 was a momentous step in meeting that need. The Working Group was a unique grassroots think tank, bringing together previously isolated syringe-exchange and drug-policy activists, and AIDS and drugs-service providers, across color, gender, sexuality, and class, to articulate a vision for an emergent harm-reduction movement.

This vision acknowledged the very real harms associated with drug use but insisted on the innate rights and capacities of individuals and communities to deal with those harms. It castigated current drug policy and drugs service provision for denying people their rights and capacities, and argued that not only had the War on Drugs failed to reduce the supply and the demand for drugs, but that it had increased the harms associated with drugs (notably the spread of HIV and other infectious diseases). Crucially, the Working Group, informed by its developing alliances with drug-policy reform movements, recognized that the War on Drugs was a key component of a resurgent neoliberal public policy that rejected the structural explanations and social programming of the 1960s. Pathologizing drug users as the cause of social problems distorted the real picture that showed that social and economic policies in the 1980s had created the conditions for an explosion of drug-related harm in the inner city. As has been noted,

> In the midst of decreasing educational and economic opportunity within the legal labor market, the allure of the illegal drug economy as a source of income became more powerful during the early 1980s.... Residents of neighborhoods fraught with economic impoverishment, social disintegration, and boredom were, and continue to be, susceptible to use of psychoactive drugs for relief and stimulation. Not surprisingly higher prevalence of drug traffic and drug use occurs in such neighborhoods. Among the people living there are economically poorer women of color and the families that they support. Young men living in these communities also have been and remain at extremely high risk of violent death, unemployment, and arrest. (Zierler and Krieger 1997)

The first strategic outcome of the Working Group was the formation of the Harm Reduction Coalition (HRC), tasked with stimulating, supporting, and expanding harm-reduction efforts across the United States. From the beginning, HRC's work was guided by the progressive political vision of the Working Group. Thus, in its mission statement, HRC "locates itself as part of a broader movement for progressive change that challenges social, cultural and economic structures – including current drug policy – that foster and sustain disadvantage, discrimination, and denial of civil liberties and human rights."

In from the outside

HRC has played a key role in moving harm reduction toward a vision of social justice. Through the training activities of its Harm Reduction Training Institute (a joint project with The Lindesmith Center, a national drug-policy think-tank) as well as its quarterly newsletter, *Harm Reduction Communication*, and allied educational materials, HRC has argued the case for reducing drug-related harm through progressive public policy and programming. Its biennial national conferences (three to date) have brought together an extraordinarily diverse group of individuals, institutions, and interests around a common agenda of radical social change. This has included criminal justice reform (for example, ending mandatory minimums for drugs offenses and shifting to noncustodial sentencing), universal health care, AIDS policy (such as access to treatment and housing issues), and women's and reproductive rights (for example, in prosecutions of drug-using pregnant women, challenging the status of the unborn child as a "victim" of their mother's drug use), as well as civil liberties (reversing the "creep" of occupational drug testing and search and seizure), drug user organizing, and voter registration.

The practices, strategies, and philosophy of harm reduction have evolved from the experiences and efforts of people working across these issues and fields, including those currently or formerly using drugs or affected by drug-related harm. These activists have helped to move harm reduction "in from the outside," from its origins as an outlaw public health practice. Health and social service providers, law enforcement and criminal justice staff, drug policy reformers and treatment providers, policy think-tanks, and political leaders now routinely discuss drug users and drug-related harm in the context of harm reduction. This was unthinkable a few years ago.

But there are tensions within such a move. Some of these have been felt most acutely at the program level. "In acquiring official status, syringe exchange programs (SEPs) have shed their spontaneous and autonomous, even sometimes overtly anarchist character, and come to resemble other 'street-oriented' nonprofit organizations" (Henman et al. 1998). But where syringe exchange has left its outlaw origins and has been accepted by public health bureaucracies, SEPs have also come under greater official regulation and scrutiny. Far from seeing harm reduction in political terms, many such bureaucracies still regard SEPs as a technical public-health intervention directed at Them (drug users) for the sake of Us (the public). The attitude appears to remain that there is "something distasteful about helping addicts to their fixes; but in public health terms, this may be an acceptable trade-off to slow the spread of AIDS" (*The Economist* 1996).

This "Them vs. Us" mentality is one of the clearest legacies of the War on Drugs. One of the functions of the war propaganda has been to identify drugs and drug users as the cause, rather than a symptom, of problems in society. "Drug users are extremely vulnerable to scapegoating, and such scapegoating can divide workers and neighborhoods in ways that weaken opposition to socioeconomic changes and policies" (Friedman 1998). This issue has confronted harm-reduction efforts to organize at community level. It has been hard to translate the model of gay community organizing, which was built on a clear consensus about the main problem (AIDS) and the main cause (homophobia). "Unlike the gay community, which 'came out' and responded to AIDS with its own autonomous organizations, drug injectors were — and still are — attempting to find a political voice in the context of drug prohibition, which generates a climate of alienation and pervasive suspicion among users, and between users and the wider society" (Henman et al., 1998).

Building a movement

This climate makes it hard to build a harm-reduction movement with and within affected communities most impacted by drug-related harm. It makes it hard for drug users to articulate a legitimate community voice, when they are blamed for the problems faced by the community. And it makes it hard for people in low-income, urban communities to come together across lines of difference (drug use, HIV status, gender, sexuality, and color) to name and confront the common causes of their oppression.

The harm-reduction movement's emphasis on linking individual responsibility with institutional accountability makes this possible, however. Its political analysis recognizes that the 425 percent increase of HIV amongst African-American women in the

United States between 1987 and 1995 (CDC 1996) cannot be understood simply as the result of sex with a male injection-drug user, separate from the contexts of gender inequities, racism, and economic disempowerment that shape such behavior. At the same time, the day-to-day practice of harm reduction acknowledges the need to work with women and men to address issues of power, responsibility, and vulnerability as they play out in their lives.

Practical examples of bringing together these individual and institutional perspectives toward a vision of social justice are emerging in disenfranchised communities of color. One such example comes from Roxbury, where a group of Latino men, all self-identified current and ex-drug users, have formed Fuerza Latina. The group was started in response to the racist stereotyping of the drugs war that identifies poor, urban men of color as deadbeat dads, abusers of women, vectors of HIV, and social derelicts. In understanding the role of drug use in coping with their social reality and as a self-fulfillment of such stereotyping, Fuerza realizes that the struggle to establish meaningful alternatives can only be won if men can "recover" and re-define their relationships and roles within their community, and become agents of social change. They meet to share their struggles with the drug use as it has and, at times, continues to cause harm in their lives and for their families and the communities in which they live. But they also come together to understand and mobilize against these struggles and harms in the broader context of social and economic problems of their community and the failure of public policy to address them. Rather than divide communities into "the guilty" and "the innocent," Fuerza Latina, like other harm-reduction agencies around the country, has become a site for beginning to develop leadership from within some of the most marginalized members of an already marginalized community.

Harm reduction's emphasis on mobilizing leadership and movement for change from within affected communities is supported by its efforts to reach out to and ally with other movements for social change. In its work defending the rights of pregnant (predominately poor, African-American) drug-using women, the National Advocates for Pregnant Women urges that "we [the harm reduction movement] need to not only strengthen ties with feminist, civil rights, gay rights and civil liberties groups, we need to understand that fundamentally their issues are our issues." Intersecting with such issues in poor, urban communities of color are basic issues of political marginalization and economic impoverishment. A more explicit class analysis offers the potential for locating the harm-reduction movement's efforts to reduce drug-related harm within "common struggles against repression, marginalization, impoverishment, cutbacks, unsafe working conditions – and FOR health and solidarity" (Friedman 2001). Nor should such a class analysis be confined within national borders, as an expanded harm-reduction movement of social justice needs to join with international human rights and anti-imperialist efforts, such as the WTO protests, that have been activated against the global impact of US economic and social policies, including the War on Drugs. Integrating these international, national, and local dimensions of social justice pushes harm reduction beyond its origins as outlaw public-health practice, but holds the promise that it can continue to become a much needed site for a coalition-based progressive movement for change.

Notes

The authors would like to thank Heidi Behforouz, Allan Clear, and Denise Paone for their contributions to this chapter.

For more information on harm reduction, please access the following resources: Harm Reduction Coalition – www.harmreduction.org; The Lindesmith Center – www.lindesmith.org; National Advocates for Pregnant Women – www.napw.net

The Northwest Bronx Community and Clergy Coalition

MARGARET GROARKE AND JORDAN MOSS

In June 1995, the House Banking Committee passed a bill to exempt 88 percent of the nation's lenders from the Community Reinvestment Act (CRA). The law, which required banks to lend in the communities where they do business, had brought more than $60 billion in private investment into disadvantaged communities since 1977.

The Northwest Bronx Community and Clergy Coalition (NWBCCC), one of the community organizations that had fought for passage of the CRA in 1977, was concerned. After making numerous phone calls to get a meeting with their senator, Banking Committee chairman Al D'Amato, Coalition members decided it was time to up the ante. They rented a bus, and headed for Park Avenue, armed with a large greeting card, banners, and flyers explaining their mission. The card was addressed to Senator D'Amato, and the NWBCCC members aimed to bring it to the swanky, doorman-protected Park Avenue building where D'Amato's girlfriend lived. The next day, an irate D'Amato called NWBCCC president Dalma DeLaRosa. He complained about the Coalition's tactics, but he also agreed to meet with the group. That fall, CRA was preserved, with support from D'Amato.

The Coalition's campaign to save CRA, like all its campaigns, involved the mobilization of its grassroots membership, confrontational tactics, and preparedness to negotiate. The modus operandi of the Northwest Bronx Coalition sounds much like the direct action tactics of ACT UP, but the Coalition has been using that strategy successfully since 1974.

What has happened to the many community groups like the Coalition that were born in the 1970s? Some have disappeared. Studies of grassroots organizations, and social movements in general, show us that most groups are transitory. Many of the survivors are now more engaged in housing management, development, and social services than organizing – if indeed they continue to do organizing at all. The Northwest Bronx Community and Clergy Coalition has survived, thrived, and adapted itself to the changing times while continuing to focus on its central mission: community empowerment. This essay will explore what characteristics made the Northwest Bronx Coalition adaptable to new circumstances.

Community organizing

> We are concerned with how to create mass organizations to seize power and give it to the people; to realize the democratic dream of equality, justice, peace, cooperation, equal and full opportunities for education, full and useful employment, health and the creation of those circumstances in which man can have the chance to live by values that give meaning to life. (Alinsky 1971)

The term "community organizing" is often loosely used to refer to almost any kind of community improvement effort – organizing a tenant association, picketing an irresponsible neighborhood merchant, planning a block party or neighborhood clean-up. For our purposes, a more specific definition is necessary: community organizing is bringing people together to identify issues of common concern, identify the parties responsible, and demand from those parties appropriate action – in Saul Alinsky's words, "creat[ing] mass organizations to seize power and give it to the people." (Alinsky 1971). The parties from whom action is demanded, who are usually referred to as "targets," may be private entities (landlords, corporations, businesses located in the neighborhood), public agencies (on the city, state or federal level), or elected officials.

Community organizing tactics range from the conventional to the radical, often escalating as necessary to achieve the group's goal. A tenant association may first, for example, write to the landlord requesting that a problem be addressed. If he does not respond, they might take him to court, or make a surprise visit to his office – or home – to demand a meeting.

Origins of NWBCCC

The Northwest Bronx Community and Clergy Coalition was founded in 1974, to combat the wave of arson and abandonment that was moving through the South Bronx. A Jesuit priest from Fordham University and his students, organizers recently arrived from the Midwest, local Catholic and Episcopal pastors, and pre-existing organizations and concerned residents came together to form the Coalition. They formed eight neighborhood associations, covering a large northwest section of the Bronx, from the Cross Bronx Expressway north to Van Cortlandt Park and the City line, including all the neighborhoods west of the Bronx River.

The NWBCCC today operates as a coalition of ten neighborhood associations, each representing a different geographic area within the coalition's turf. The NWBCCC's board consists of representatives elected from each neighborhood association, some clergy representatives, and neighborhood residents appointed at-large. The central organization does the lion's share of the fundraising, and commits to pay the salary of at least one organizer to work in each neighborhood. Most of the organization's funds come from grants or government contracts, although an annual dinner dance and donations from members supplement the budget. Neighborhood associations also raise money to support their organizing. Each neighborhood association determines for itself the issues on which it wants to organize. Staff organizers in each neighborhood spend a lot of time building tenant associations. A few neighborhoods also employ organizers who focus on mobilizing teen leaders.

Coalition-wide committees, consisting of interested members from several neighborhood associations, are formed around issues that several neighborhoods are working on, to address jointly a common agenda. Such committees serve as a forum for neighborhood associations to share information and strategies; it also allows them to bring common issues to a higher level. On policing issues, for example, neighborhood associations might meet with the captain of their precinct, but there are three or four Coalition neighborhoods in each precinct. The Coalition's Safe Streets committee can easily meet with the Bronx Borough Commander, and has met with several successive police commissioners. This is particularly effective when the target is a high-level official; it is easier for the NWBCCC, with a membership of 2,000, to win a meeting with a US senator than it is for three or four smaller neighborhood associations, each with 100–500 members, to do so.

The NWBCCC is driven by grassroots leadership development. Organizers play a critical role in getting neighborhood folks involved on issues of concern to them, and provide them with the information and support they need to do their work, but the organization's members are the decision-makers, sitting on the boards of the local affiliates and on the board of the larger organization.

Because the goal of the Coalition is to enable community residents to realize their own power, its members speak for themselves. At meetings, it is only the group's leaders – never the organizing staff – that present demands to targets. When the press comes calling, organizing staff may offer background, but it is only community members of the group that speak for the record.

Staying true to the organizing mission

The late 1960s and early 1970s were a growth time for community organizing in New York. The conditions of rental housing were an area of primary concern; by 1974 there were 83 neighborhood tenant organizations, 67 of which were founded after 1969 (Lawson 1986). Their primary focus was on basic housing conditions, such as heat and hot water, which were major problems in many buildings.

In Bronx neighborhoods, housing problems were the result of complex forces. Banks and insurance companies were "redlining" neighborhoods, refusing to re-finance mortgages or renew insurance policies in neighborhoods they had determined were no longer viable. Financially strapped landlords cut back on services, abandoned buildings, or hired arsonists to torch their properties so they could collect the in-surance money. Tenants and organizers tried to pressure, cajole, and threaten land-lords to fulfill their responsibilities to their buildings – sometimes successfully – but for buildings abandoned by the landlord, or taken by the city, alternative management was needed. And if neighborhood dreams to rehabilitate vacant buildings were realized, who would run them?

Many community organizations solved this problem by taking on the management of apartment buildings, or the redevelopment of vacant buildings. In this way, a trusted neighborhood organization would become the landlord. Among community organizations, the NWBCCC is unusual in that it chose, back in the 1970s, not to do housing management or development. At that time, tenant organizing was far and away the most important thing the organization did, and many of the buildings it organized were in need of better management. Unlike many kindred organizations, however, the Coalition chose to encourage the creation of completely independent nonprofit housing companies which would oversee rehabilitation work and manage residential buildings. Other community organizations in the Bronx took on the management tasks themselves, and expected that the fees from building management would support continued organizing. However, as many of these organizations grew, their organizing was constrained by the interests of the management arm of their organizations. The Coalition didn't face this problem; while it remained on a cordial basis with the housing companies, there were no ties between the groups. As a result, the housing companies have redeveloped more than three thousand once-vacant units as affordable housing, and have provided management for two thousand additional apartments. Meanwhile, the Coalition has continued to engage in confrontational organizing, without concern for the interests of the housing companies.

Local needn't be small

Most NWBCCC leaders don't start out wanting to change the world. They just want heat in their apartment, or the drug dealer off their corner, or a cleaner park. But for many, winning those things leads them to pursue greater justice for themselves and their neighbors, and often that leads to wider policy changes beyond the Bronx. Organizers and leaders encourage this progression: local victories are celebrated and used as inspiration for bigger battles; issues that aren't resolved on a local level are analyzed to determine where the important decisions are really made.

The development of the group's education organizing is a good example of this. The Coalition had dabbled in education organizing before when crises arose at one school or another, but it didn't form an education committee until the early 1990s. Bronx School District 10, where most coalition neighborhoods lie, is the second most overcrowded school district in the city. Virtually every school has, in the place of their play yards, portable classrooms or mini-schools. Against this backdrop was the hope offered by two new schools, PS 20 in Norwood and PS 15 in University Heights. After two years of delays, the coalition began organizing around the issue. Parents whose kindergartners were being bused a mile or more away, or whose kids went to school in shifts (7–12 and 12–5) due to crowding, formed a natural constituency for this campaign.

The School Construction Authority, a quasi-public agency that was set up by the state to build schools faster and better than the Board of Education was able to, was not used to public scrutiny. But they got it in spades from parents involved in the new organizing campaign, who grilled and graded SCA officials (giant score cards are a standard prop at Coalition meetings and serve the practical purpose of keeping track of what officials have agreed to) and occasionally paid unannounced visits to SCA headquarters.

In the end, the school was completed three years later than it should have been, but it is clear that the scrutiny and pressure prevented further delays. And in September 1999, six new schools were finished in District 10 with relatively few problems. The success drew the coalition deeper into education organizing specifically around school construction issues, and it joined with other organizations citywide to push the city and federal governments to give all city kids "room to learn." Currently, it is pushing federal legislation that would create $25 billion in tax-free bonds for school construction, of which New York City would expect to get $1.2 billion.

The effects of the Coalition's brand of organizing can be seen not only in the revival of the northwest Bronx's bricks-and-mortar landscape, but also in uncountable personal transformations over the group's quarter-century history. Dalma De La Rosa, a self-described "shy Puerto Rican housewife," became one of the Coalition's most outspoken and effective leaders after going toe-to-toe in the 1980s with city housing bureaucrats when her landlord stopped providing heat and the boiler froze. She later served as president of the Coalition's board. A decade later parent Ronn Jordan stepped into public life when he found out his kindergartner was being bused a mile away from his local school due to overcrowding. Now he knows as much about federal school construction legislation as Congressman Charlie Rangel. De La Rosa and Jordan and scores of others are conversant on the city, state and federal policies on issues of concern to them. Meetings and negotiations with mayors, senators, police commissioners, and cabinet secretaries are common fare for residents who had little if any prior experience in public speaking or public policy.

Organizing in racially diverse communities

In an era of identity politics, the coalition – with African Americans, Latinos, Asians, and whites – has largely avoided the internal racial tensions that have bedeviled other organizations. Although white residents probably harbored suspicions of the newer

African-American and Latino arrivals, neighbors were able to unite across ethnic and racial lines for a common purpose. The strategy could best be summed up in the phrase, "When the heat's off, we're all cold."

Anne Devenney, an Irish-American grandmother, had much to do with weaving that belief into the group's DNA. John Reilly, a former organizer who runs one of the spinoff housing companies, remembers the day Devenney, who lived in Norwood, at the north end of the Coalition's turf, visited the southeastern neighborhood of Crotona. The city had cleared four square blocks of apartment buildings for Fordham Hospital. After the plan was abandoned during the fiscal crisis, the city added insult to injury by using the vacant lots as a temporary dumping ground for street cleaning trucks. Devenney insisted on traveling to Crotona to support Dominican Republic native Astin Jacobo, another Coalition leader, and his neighbors for a meeting at a local church.

"I think at the time there was still some concern whether all these neighborhoods were going to work together, that they were going to see their common interest," Reilly said, adding that Jacobo told him it changed his view of what the coalition could accomplish. The two would collaborate on many issues, and they tagged themselves Salt 'n Pepper. This philosophy has served the organization well, as the communities it covers have become more and more diverse.

Attracting a more diverse staff has also been a goal, and one that has not always been so easy to accomplish. To help in training the next generation of community organizers, and to recruit good people from diverse backgrounds who would stay with the organization, the Coalition worked together with ACORN and Mothers on the Move to create Training Institute for Careers in Organizing (TICO). Potential organizers spend three months in TICO, attending trainings and working with an experienced organizer. After three months, most TICO participants are offered jobs in one of the three organizations, or assisted in finding other employment.

Keeping up the fight

At a critical 1995 meeting with bank representatives, Coalition leaders demanded to meet with the institutions' CEOs. When a Citibank staffer told the Coalition that that would be impossible because Citibank is a global organization, a campaign was born: "The Bronx is on the Globe." Once again buses were boarded, this time to CEO

John Reed's house in Princeton, NJ. He wasn't home but the hit, complete with papier mâché globes, got local press coverage and it led to a meeting with a top Citibank executive in charge of branches worldwide. From that session, Citibank agreed to put an automated branch on Burnside Avenue. A new Chase branch – the first new branch in the area in twenty-five years – also resulted from the Banking Committee's work during that time (Ritter, 2000).

Globalization can be disempowering as the locus of power shifts farther away from people's everyday lives, and can seem more and more difficult to influence. When power shifts from the local banker to a John Reed, getting action on community concerns would appear to be an uphill battle. But as the Citibank example shows, global institutions are hardly impervious to community organizing that takes aim at corporate power. The task is undoubtedly harder, so joining together with like-minded groups, as the Coalition does with National People's Action, a Chicago-based umbrella group of grassroots organizations, is now more crucial than ever. And staying true to the organizing mission, without the distraction of running programs or managing housing, is also key, and may be the most important lesson the Northwest Bronx Community and Clergy Coalition has to offer.

Community development and community organizing: Apples and oranges? Chicken and egg?

RANDY STOECKER

Much of this volume is focused on the flashier, sassier, funkier side of community activism. Those who brought infamy to the period between ACT UP and the Battle of Seattle did so because of their willingness to get arrested and beaten for disrupting business as usual, and on occasion breaking things. But during the 1990s there was an equally powerful community-based activism that amassed probably more power, but less change. The *community development* movement in the United States, mostly based in community development corporations, or CDCs, is now well entrenched in the community landscape. For every group opposing global capital through disruption and blockades, there is a group attempting to counteract global capital through micro-enterprise development, community housing development, and other forms of community-based basic needs development. But as the presence and activity of CDCs in poor neighborhoods has grown, so has the debate surrounding them. Recently, community development analysts and practitioners have been trying to combine community development with the more politicized community organizing model.

This essay begins by defining and describing these two approaches. Next, it explores the extent to which they are complementary or contradictory – apples and oranges. Finally, it reviews ways of combining them, exploring their chicken-and-egg relationships. Community development, in this essay, is defined as nonprofit organizations – CDCs – doing physical development of impoverished communities. CDCs are supposed to be "community-based," having some connection with the residents who live there. They are also expected to do "comprehensive development" – creating jobs, housing, safety, and other changes (though most emphasize housing). Finally, they are supposed to accomplish all this within the existing political economic system (Stoecker 1997).

Critics of the CDC model, however, point out how CDCs often fail at projects that left their host neighborhoods in as bad or worse shape than when they started, fold under funding shortages that allow elites both to prevent real redevelopment and to blame CDCs for failure, or disrupt neighborhood empowerment by purporting to speak on behalf of a community that they barely know (and that barely knows them) (Stoecker 1994, 1997). These critics have led a call to bring back community organizing.

Community organizing works in local settings to empower individuals, build relationships and organizations, and create action for social change (Beckwith and Lopez 1997; Bobo, Kendall, and Max 1991; Kahn 1991; Alinsky 1969, 1971). Community organizers have historically focused on building localized social movements in places as small as a single neighborhood. Consequently, the bulk of community organizing occurs "backstage" (Goffman 1959), building relationships and networks in the quasi-private setting of the neighborhood community (Stall and Stoecker 1998) that can create a larger social movement.

Community organizing has a much longer history than community development, including the early-twentieth-century settlement house movement and other women-centered efforts (Stall and Stoecker 1998), the civil rights movement (Morris 1984), and others. The most well-known influence was Saul Alinsky (1969, 1971) who, in the 1930s, created a community organizing model in Chicago's Back of the Yards neighborhood that was rowdy, bawdy, and confrontational (Finks 1984). The civil rights movement is the other crucial source of community organizing; though its influence on community organizing practice has been as profound as Alinsky's, it has been historically neglected. The accepted founding event of the movement, the Montgomery Bus Boycott, was coordinated through local African-American networks and organizations and created a model that would be used in locality-based actions throughout the south (Morris 1984). Out of these efforts grew the Welfare Rights Movement (Piven and Cloward 1979) and eventually the famous Association of Community Organizations for Reform Now (ACORN) (Delgado 1986; Russell 2000).

Today, community organizing is experiencing a resurgence, with an explosion of small efforts and the growth of better-publicized efforts by the Industrial Areas

Foundation (IAF) (Tresser 1999), by ACORN (1999) and the New Party (1997) in their living wage efforts, and by many other groups and networks (COMM-ORG 2001), including the rapidly expanding National Organizers Alliance (2001), which supports and connects independent and network organizers across North America. The definition of community is also expanding well beyond place-based neighborhood groups. As this collection shows, community organizing practices are now used also to build and shape new identity formations and communities. And community organizing practices are also evident in the movement against global capitalism. One of the things that made the Battle of Seattle so important was its integration of community organizing practices. As Starhawk's essay in part 1 of this volume illustrates, solidarity tactics, affinity groups, and other community-building practices provided the glue that bound activists together to feed and shelter and even protect each other.

Apples and oranges?

Can these two models – one that works within the system and the other that tries to change it – be combined? Or are they the proverbial apples and oranges? Steve Callahan et al. (1999) argue for combining *project-based community development*, which delivers social, economic, and housing services to poor communities, and *power-based community development,* which employs polarizing and militant tactics to develop the power of low-income people and hold officials accountable.

The challenge is that these models are rooted in fundamentally different theories of how society works, which sociologists refer to as functionalist and conflict models. The functionalist model argues that society tends toward natural equilibrium and its division of labor develops through an almost natural matching of individual talents and societal needs. For functionalists, healthy societies maintain some basic degree of equilibrium and place all of their members into the roles for which they are fit. The implication (though few today admit it) is that the poor and the oppressed are supposed to be poor and oppressed. Of course, those who don't belong there (i.e. those who are willing to work hard) are provided with new roles. This theory also assumes that people have common interests even when they have different positions in society. Healthy, persistent societies are in a constant state of gradual equilibrium-seeking improvement. Thus, a group organizing to force change is actually unhealthy, as it can throw off equilibrium; cooperation to produce gradual change is a better alternative (Eitzen and Baca Zinn 2000). In this model, poor people need only opportunity, not power, and cooperation between the "haves" and the "have-nots" is the best means to provide opportunity. But because the model does not recognize structural barriers to equality, it can only provide opportunities determined by existing power holders.

Conflict theory sees no natural tendency toward anything but conflict over scarce resources. In this model society develops through struggle between groups. To the extent that stability is achieved, it's not because society finds equilibrium but because one group dominates the other groups. Conflict theory sees society as divided, particularly between corporations and workers, men and women, and whites and people of color. The instability inherent in such divided societies prevents elites from achieving absolute domination and provides opportunities for those on the bottom to create change through organizing for collective action and conflict.

The CDC model, rooted in the functionalist tenets of common interest and cooperation, can only work if functionalist theory is correct. In other words, there can be no barriers to poor communities rebuilding themselves. The problem is that, while individuals can lift themselves up and attain greatness, not all poor people can lift themselves up simultaneously because there are not enough better spaces available in society – not enough good jobs, not enough good housing. This problem is multiplied when the focus is trying to lift up poor communities, which can only occur if the people in those communities are simultaneously lifted up. If there's no space for all those individuals in the economy, there's no chance for that community. The simultaneous improvement of poor people everywhere requires a drastic redistribution of wealth, violating the fundamental tenets of functionalist theory, which argues that trying to create an artificial equality would actually upset equilibrium.

So what happens in the community development model is that people's need for a transformed economy providing a wealth of good jobs becomes replaced with training programs for people to compete within an extremely limited good-job pool. People's need for affordable housing that is controlled by its occupants becomes replaced by a trade-off between expensive home ownership and affordable rental housing. People's need for high-quality health care, daycare, and other services becomes translated into sporadic, overcrowded, and inefficient low-quality stopgap programs. Not only can a model emphasizing cooperation and denying class conflict not work to end poverty and oppression; it's not even supposed to work.

The community organizing model is much better suited for attacking the structural barriers that prevent poor communities from lifting themselves up. In a capitalist society, equal competitors make deals because each either has something to offer or something to take away. But when CDCs attempt to make deals with these power holders, they have nothing with which to bargain. They are in the powerless position of begging for lower loan rates, reduced construction costs, more open hiring practices, and so on. CDCs have little to offer as inducement for power holders to say yes, and little to withhold if they say no. The community organizing model, however, substitutes the lack of money resources with people resources. The bargaining chip poor communities have is their cooperation. If they can collectively withhold their cooperation or, even more powerfully, can disrupt the activities of power holders, they have something to bargain with (Piven and Cloward 1979).

The community organizing model, and its conflict theory underpinnings, also has limits. When community organizations wrest concessions from corporations or government they often discover that those wins are only as good as the community's ability to implement them. When the Cedar–Riverside neighborhood beat back a government–developer coalition out to displace the neighborhood with massive highrises, they were faced with the prospect of their existing housing being condemned unless they found resources to fix it up (Stoecker 1994). When the Dudley Street Neighborhood Initiative won city approval of their neighborhood redevelopment plan, they had to find funding and eventually even do the development themselves (Medoff and Sklar 1994). ACORN had to create a community development arm when it began winning housing through squatting and other tactics (Russell 2000; ACORN 1997). Because of the incompatibilities of the theories on which they are based, many community organizing groups make the transition to development gagging and retching. Some of them destroy themselves in the process (Stoecker 1995a).

Community organizing is necessary to get the power. Community development is necessary to keep it. So what do we do?

Chicken and egg?

Regardless of how hard it is to combine community organizing and community development, we must figure out how. This is the chicken-and-egg problem. Which is more important? Which is more powerful? Which comes first? Can you move from development to organizing and actually build power? Can you move from organizing to development without disrupting organizing? There are two basic strategies. One is to combine organizing and development in a single organization. The other is to separate them into allied organizations.

Organizing *in* development

The initial efforts to combine organizing and development came as effective organizing groups were forced into doing their own development. Because of the shift in funding during the 1980s from development to organizing, staff and directors of organizing groups found themselves forced into becoming developers. But many really wanted to be organizers and kept looking for ways to bring organizing back (Rubin 2000). Given the funding constraints, however, traditional organizing that threatened funders' power was not to be and it is no mistake that community building, consensus organizing, and women-centered organizing are in the spotlight today. The avoidance of confrontation, the lack of focus on structural change, and the absence of conflict in these models makes them well suited to CDCs.

Community building is defined as "projects which seek to build new relationships among members in a community and develop change out of the connections these relationships provide for solving member-defined problems" (Hess 1999). Linked to Kretzmann and McKnight's (1993) asset-based community development model, and to communitarianism, the emphasis in community building is creating and restoring relationships between community residents. The focus is internal, finding and building the community's own "assets" or "social capital" rather than confronting or negotiating with external power and resource holders (Smock 1997).

Consensus organizing includes relationship building but also focuses on moving people from welfare to work, improving school achievement, promoting inner-city reinvestment, and developing housing and businesses, among other things. This model specifically opposes the "Us versus Them" model of community organizing (Eichler 1998). The purpose of consensus organizing, consistent with functionalist theory, is to build cooperative relationships between community leaders and business and government, to improve poor communities (Consensus Organizing Institute 2000).

The women-centered organizing model emphasizes relationship building that is not rooted in self-interest but in an understanding of mutual responsibility. And while it does see a structural division in society that holds women back, it also emphasizes that power is infinitely expandable rather than zero-sum, thus reducing the need for conflict. Like the community building model, women-centered organizing emphasizes small group development and has more of an internal problem-solving focus. The goal is as much the development of individuals as it is the development of communities (Stall and Stoecker 1998).

Some CDCs are now able to break free of these limited community organizing models through new funding sources. The largest and most well-known effort to help CDCs do community organizing is the $1.5 million Ricanne Hadrian Initiative for Community Organizing (RHICO), sponsored through the Massachusetts Association of CDCs and the Neighborhood Development Support Collaborative. The program supports and trains CDCs throughout Massachusetts to do community organizing (Winkelman 1998a 1998b).

A similar project to promote community organizing through CDCs was the Toledo Community Organizing Training and Technical Assistance Program sponsored through the Toledo Community Foundation. Over a two-year period, ACORN provided training and technical assistance to three CDCs, though one dropped out due to a lack of fit. The Organized Neighbors Yielding Excellence (ONYX) CDC adopted a combined organizing and development group model, where leadership and authority over the organizing effort remained vested in the CDC board of directors, though they gave tacit approval to developing an informal community-organizing leadership structure. Conversely, the Lagrange Development Corporation established a relatively autonomous community organizing group, adopting a written code of principles to prevent the CDC from interfering in the organizing effort even while it paid the organizer's salary. The Lagrange Village Council, the relatively autonomous community organizing group, practices a more traditional Alinsky-style community organizing model, using actions and pressure tactics to close problem businesses in the community, improve trash collection, and manage a long-drawn-out campaign against a predatory property speculator. ONYX has practiced a much more subdued approach consistent with the community development model, and with fewer subsequent victories.

What are the outcomes of this combined model? CDCs in the RHICO initiative have seen more community involvement in CDC decision-making, less funder-driven project development, and more effective CDC advocacy efforts (Winkelman 1998). This also appears to be the case with the Lagrange Development Corporation and

Lagrange Village Council in Toledo, which has got a number of problem businesses to shape up or leave, can turn out dozens of people for a demonstration, and has hundreds attend its annual meetings.

There are also important problems. The first is the potential restriction on militancy. One of the RHICO CDCs lost government funding when it moved to organizing. However, this CDC continued down the organizing path, weathering the cut and actually freeing itself from restrictive funding (Winkelman 1998a). Other groups are less able to make such bold moves. In Toledo, ONYX's organizing effort has been hindered by the fear of funding loss, and the organization has been threatened with government-funding reductions.

A second, related, problem is the internal conflict that the combination can produce. The East Toledo Community Organization (ETCO), an Alinsky-style community organization in Toledo, Ohio, turned to development to support its staff during the 1980s when funding shifted from organizing to development. ETCO began conducting home energy audits, providing advice on how to reduce energy costs. They took on city contracts to board up vacant houses. They got a grant to start a jobs bank. And the organization imploded as infighting between organizing proponents and development proponents broke into open warfare (Stoecker 1995a, 1995b). The Dudley Street Neighborhood Initiative in Boston began by reclaiming a city park from drug dealers, closing area garbage-transfer sites, curbing illegal dumping. They also developed a plan to build new housing in their community, fighting off a government redevelopment plan that would have wiped them off the map. They won government and foundation support for their plan, and found a developer who would do the project. But they had problems finding a reliable development partner and ended up doing the development themselves. The time-consuming technical and financially risky aspects of managing housing construction badly distracted the organization (Medoff and Sklar 1994).

Organizing *and* development

In this model, organizing and development are separated into different organizations. In a 1997 article I argued that the ideal-type model was a small locality-based community organizing group partnering with a high-capacity multi-local CDC. The reason was that CDCs, to be successful, needed technically skilled (and thus expensive) staff and enough capitalization to do development in higher-risk situations. Larger CDCs would be more likely to have those qualities. But because those characteristics would also increase the separation of the CDC from the community, small neighborhood-based community organizing groups were necessary to maintain community control of development. I have had great difficulty finding examples of this model.

The Cedar–Riverside neighborhood redevelopment movement is the source of my model, as they consciously kept their organizing and development activities separate, gaining a combination of political power and redevelopment resources that I have not seen matched since. They were very concerned (and it was from them that my own thinking developed) about the compromised politics of CDCs that might prevent them from truly following the neighborhood's direction and abiding by their demands. At one point the neighborhood's community organizing group brought in a private developer to build housing when its own CDC was behaving too insensitively (Stoecker 1994).

In contrast to my model of a highly capitalized CDC partnering with local community organizing groups, more common are cases of large community organizing networks partnering with small development and service organizations. The Toledo Community Organizing Training and Technical Assistance Program discussed above has expanded to a partnership between the two local participating CDCs and an independent ACORN organizing effort now in the city. The Sacramento Valley Organizing Community (SVOC), an organization of nearly thirty predominantly Latino Catholic and African-American Protestant churches across a three-county area in Northern California, is part of the Industrial Areas Foundation community organizing network founded by Saul Alinsky. In one instance SVOC brought 1,800 members to a meeting with area health system officials, successfully demanding two hundred jobs. To implement the win, SVOC partnered with the Private Industry Council (PIC), the county welfare department, and a community college to do job training and preparation (Callahan et al. 1999). The famous Communities Organized for Public Service (COPS) in San Antonio practiced a similar model, and ended up directing a large proportion of San Antonio's federal Community Development Block Grant budget over a number of years to COPS-defined projects. But COPS refused to do any of the development themselves to preserve their organizing focus (Cortes 1995; Warren 1995).

Perhaps the most famous case is the Northwest Bronx Community and Clergy Coalition. The NWBCCC, with a 25-year history, organizes with ten neighborhoods and approximately twenty local religious communities in the Northwest Bronx area of New York City and has spawned a number of CDCs. Because NWBCCC is an affiliate of groups, different subcoalitions can work on issues they have in common. They consciously put organizing first, understanding the technical constraints placed on development. Consequently, they came up with the idea of "Neighborhood Improvement Plans ... as opposed to fitting into existing programs[;] leaders were asked to think about what they wanted to see in the area and then we would try to figure out how to get there" (Buckley n.d.). Two of the CDCs formed through NWBCCC – Fordham Bedford Housing Corporation and Mount Hope Housing Company – are highly capitalized, multi-local CDCs with hundreds of employees and thousands of housing units. The NWBCCC's housing committee, or neighborhood groups, determine projects and then negotiate with one of the CDCs about how to implement them (Dailey 2000).

The problem with this multi-organizational model is not its theoretical desirability but its practicality. In many poor communities, even with the resurgence of community organizing, we are more likely to find a neighborhood CDC than an organizing group. Corvallis Neighborhood Housing Services, in Corvallis, Oregon, is looking for community organizing groups to partner with so they can "direct development to organized neighborhoods instead of building a project and then organizing around it." But the neighborhoods in Corvallis, with rare exception, are not organized (Smith 2000). It makes no sense to tell CDC staff with a knowledgeable commitment to community organizing that they shouldn't do it just because they don't fit the ideal model.

There are also risks in separating organizing and development into independent organizations. When separate organizations forget their complementarity, they can compete rather than cooperate. In a single neighborhood, the infighting that can occur within a CDC trying to do both organizing and development can also occur between a neighborhood-based CDC and a neighborhood-based organizing group.

So how do we decide whether to implement the organizing *in* development or the organizing *and* development model? Based on lessons from RHICO and the Toledo Community Organizing Training and Technical Assistance Program, here are some guidelines.

First, it is important to assess what exists in the neighborhood already. If there is an organizing group and a CDC, it is probably counterproductive for the CDC also to do organizing. Instead, it should find ways to partner with the organizing group. If there is a CDC but no organizing group in the neighborhood, it is important to assess the CDC's readiness and capacity to do community organizing. How knowledgeable is the executive director about organizing in general and different organizing models? Is there anyone else highly skilled in organizing on staff? Is there an organizer in place and, if so, what do they know about organizing in general and which organizing model do they prefer? Who is or would be responsible for supervising the organizer? How are leaders (board members) identified/recruited? Are leaders elected or appointed (elected is better for organizing)? What do leaders know about organizing in general and different organizing models? How do organization leaders and director respond to a series of organizing versus development dilemmas (such as doing an action against a bank that also gives loans to the CDC projects)? What procedures are in place for replacing staff and leadership without losing internal organizing culture? Does the CDC have a broad mission statement that could easily include community organizing? In general, the more skill, knowledge, and support for community organizing, the more successfully a CDC will be able to develop its organizing capacity.

Second, it is important to assess what exists beyond the neighborhood. If the neighborhood has neither a CDC nor an organizing group, are there high-capacity CDCs or multi-local organizing networks working in the area? If there are both, what are their histories of working cooperatively across the organizing–development divide? If there is a neighborhood CDC, but it is not structured to support organizing, what is its history of working cooperatively with other organizations? Also, what is its level of power? Numerous neighborhoods have small CDCs which do little or nothing, and would be better replaced with a combination of community organizing and high-capacity community development.

It is clear there is no single correct way to combine organizing and development. It is also clear that the two models, contradictory as they are, are inseparable. So we must continue the search for ways of combining them where organizing will not be compromised and development will not be limited.

Note

Many thanks to Lee Winkelman for comments on an earlier draft. This essay is part of a larger project studying the relationship between community organizing and community development, supported by a grant from the University of Toledo Urban Affairs Center.

Joy, justice, and resistance to the new global apartheid

BENJAMIN SHEPARD

It could be said that over the twelve years between ACT UP's first Wall Street demo in 1987 and the protests against the World Trade Organization in 1999, activism has freed itself. The theme of a revitalized activist project runs throughout the essays within *From ACT UP to the WTO*. Parts 1 and 2 report on the links between ACT UP's early years and its expansion into battles against colonialism, unjust trade laws, worker rights and debt reduction at the center of the global justice movement. In many respects, ACT UP has taken the lead in the struggles against the new global apartheid. While its early slogan, "People with AIDS under Attack, What do We Do ACT UP Fight Back!!!" remains, new slogans – "Donate the Dollars, Drop the Debt, Treat the People, Save the Lives, NOW!" – speak to the globalization of AIDS activism in solidarity with countless movements. Instead of a single-issue politics, we have been forced to reconcile ourselves to the links between our movements, identities, and politics. Instead of looking at life as an either/or game in which economic issues overwhelm identity groups, we are learning that it is impossible to separate struggles for economic justice from racial equity or sex and gender liberation (see Krupat and McCreery 2001). The result is a liberated activist project able to honor countless strategies of engagement. As a result, countless players have been freed to act.

Over the last few years, we have encountered a shift in the way we do activism. By 1999, Andrew Boyd could write:

Somehow the movement had taken a Hegelian lurch forward – from thesis to antithesis to synthesis. In the 1960s the thesis was: "We can change the world." In the 1980s came the antithesis: "What good did it all do anyway?" We knew everything was corrupt; we were bitter and defensive; we distrusted ourselves; we were too cool to care – or we played the self-righteous voice in the wilderness calling out, "Everyone else betrayed the ideals but me." (Boyd, part 3 above)

With Seattle, we had reached a bold synthesis in which history became something to build upon instead of longing for. With the lessons of the 1960s and ACT UP under its belt, a new generation found faith in its communities and re-engaged. Reverend Billy, of the Church of Stop Shopping's contention, "It feels good to have something to believe in," speaks to this optimism.

Building the recognition that small groups are always the ones that change the world, a generation of young activists stopped looking for someone else to take the lead. In her essay in part 3 above, "How We Really Shut Down the WTO," Starhawk points out that there is no way activists would have voluntarily ingested teargas or engaged in weeks of jail solidarity if they were being led by a charismatic leader. "People were empowered to make their own decisions, and the centralized structures were for coordination, not control. As a result, we had great flexibility and resilience, and many people were inspired to acts of courage they could never have been ordered to do."

But something else was at hand. Whether it was the feeling of doing the right thing or being part of a vast democratic civil society, joy re-entered the fold, allowing us to embrace a new level of justice in our activism. Along the road, our movements were linking without erasing our differences. Not that any of this is a simple process. The essays within *From ACT UP to the WTO* outline the complexities of the project. As Randy Stoecker says in the final essay, inherent tensions between activism and development are an inevitable by-product of the effort to rebuild after tearing down the barricades.

That is not to say that everyone is fully on board within this project. For example, a vast gap has emerged between queers who see their movement as a broad-based human rights movement, inherently involved in struggles for sex and gender liberation, and racial and economic justice, and those who see gay rights as a single issue. The idea of today's queer activism is not just to make the world better for lesbians and gays, but for everyone. In order to do this, many are studying the lessons of generations of activism. A friend from queer activist circles sent a winter solstice card to a number of activists. On it were trade unionist Victor Debs's famous words:

> While there is a lower class, I am in it,
> While there is a criminal element, I am of it,
> and while there is a soul in prison I am not free.

It's this spirit that runs throughout the new social movements. The Zapatistas consistently link their cause with the struggles of all marginalized people around the world. Building on Debs, Subcomandante Marcos (1994) proclaims: "Marcos is gay in San Francisco, black in South Africa, Asian in Europe, a Chicano in San Isidro, an anarchist in Spain, a Palestinian in Israel, a Mayan Indian in the streets of San Cristobal…a woman alone in the Metro at ten [p.m.] … an underground editor, an unemployed worker … a nonconformist student, a dissident against neoliberalism … and of course a Zapatista in the mountains of southeastern Mexico." Instead of looking at competing oppressions, we have developed a healthy respect for their links. In his interview, Bob Kohler recalled Lois Hart's slogan from Gay Liberation: "Oppression is like a large tree with many branches. Each branch being a part of the whole. They cannot be separated; they draw from each other." In the end, the new activism has taught us – to borrow from Emerson – that in every person there is something; in this we can all be pupils.

   To the extent that activists called for us to globalize liberation, we were forced to recognize that there are countless things we need to be doing if we really believe this. You do not need to be an activist to learn that your college T-shirt is made in a sweatshop or understand that the park bench you sit on is made of wood from a rainforest. By recognizing the significance of our choices as consumers and voters, we are forced to acknowledge that there is a great deal that each person can do. There is a sphere of influence we can all control – even if that means just buying clothing with a union brand. Somewhere along the road, a generation stopped letting what they could not do keep them from doing what they could.

The urgency of AIDS activism demanded such action. "History will recall, you were the one who did nothing at all!" activists chanted at Reagan and Bush. But the chant also extended to all of us. Eric Sawyer, one of ACT UP's co-founders, writes:

> History will recall how we responded in the face of the AIDS pandemic, and will judge us if we fail to act. It is time to stand up as human beings concerned about our brothers and sisters in the developing world to demand that the human right to health care be provided to everyone in the world, no matter how much money they have, what country they live in, what religion they practice, what color they are, who they love, what drugs they take, or how they make the money they need to feed themselves and their children. Just as a virus recognizes no national borders, our solidarity must encompass all who are affected by the AIDS epidemic.... We must never forget that access to health care is a human right. And we must not rest until every man, women, and child has access to safe shelter, sufficient food, clean water, and good health care. (Sawyer, part 1 above)

To back up their words, the remainders of ACT UP's final standing chapters shaped history by helping us recognize they could actually make a difference in the fight for AIDS drugs abroad. In order to accomplish this goal, ACT UP brought together organizations concerned with issues ranging from economic fairness, to gender equity, to the human right to health care. In June 2001, Jubilee USA, AIDS activists, and labor leaders marched on New York demanding: "STOP GLOBAL AIDS NOW!" Within days of the demo, the US dropped its lawsuit against Brazil for making their own generic AIDS drugs. "We're seeing the dawn of a powerful move-ment," explained Kim Nichols, of the African Services Committee, which worked with ACT UP to organize the demo. "International AIDS activist groups, like ACT UP, people of faith, like Jubilee US and American Jewish World Service, and people who are simply moved by the AIDS crisis are coming together – and out into the streets. We are beyond showing dramatic photos of AIDS victims and entering an era of mobilizing resources. That means dollars, drugs, and debt cancellation. When enough people come together," Ms Nichols concluded, "change can happen" (see Ascribe July 2).

Success began with an understanding that our lives were intricately, almost chemically, woven with people all over the world. "Increase reduce... and I am you and you are me..." What was emerging was a Whitmaneque faith in democratic vistas which allowed us to see the poetry in our interconnections. Such are the world-making narratives of the new unrest.

Borrowing from Marx, Marshall Berman (1982) suggests that just as capitalism is rapidly rearranging the elements of our world, so that "all that is solid melts into air," so too are activists developing new strategies and tactics to reclaim the world as our own. While Seattle was the culmination of thousands of protests, pranks, and street parties, its our responsibility to continue the high jinks, instead of fetishizing its memory. There will never be another Seattle, just as there will not be another Woodstock. So long as we keep proposing alternative, more sustainable models of community building, our new movements will thrive – one prank at a time.

The root goal of these movements is to democratize the public sphere and project of globalization at large. While much of the movement is about building something external, our movements are additionally about building a new series of civil societies. In this, everyone can play a role. Before you close this book, please take a second to consider the Syracuse Cultural Worker list of ways each of us can help build community. So much begins by just introducing yourself to a neighbor.

HOW TO BUILD COMMUNITY

TURN OFF YOUR TV LEAVE YOUR HOUSE
KNOW YOUR NEIGHBORS
LOOK UP WHEN
YOU ARE WALKING
GREET PEOPLE
SIT ON YOUR STOOP
PLANT FLOWERS
USE YOUR LIBRARY
PLAY TOGETHER
BUY FROM
LOCAL MERCHANTS
SHARE WHAT YOU
HAVE HELP A
LOST DOG TAKE
CHILDREN TO THE
PARK GARDEN
TOGETHER SUPPORT
NEIGHBORHOOD
SCHOOLS
FIX IT EVEN IF YOU
DIDN'T BREAK IT
HAVE POTLUCKS
HONOR ELDERS PICK
UP LITTER READ
STORIES ALOUD
DANCE IN THE STREET
TALK TO THE MAIL CARRIER
LISTEN TO THE BIRDS

PUT UP A SWING HELP CARRY
SOMETHING HEAVY BARTER
FOR YOUR GOODS
START A TRADITION
ASK A QUESTION
HIRE NEIGHBORHOOD
YOUNG PEOPLE FOR
ODD JOBS
ORGANIZE A
BLOCK PARTY
BAKE EXTRA AND
SHARE
ASK FOR HELP
WHEN YOU NEED
IT OPEN YOUR
SHADES SING
TOGETHER
SHARE YOUR SKILLS
TAKE BACK THE
NIGHT TURN UP
THE MUSIC
TURN DOWN THE
MUSIC LISTEN BEFORE
YOU REACT TO ANGER
MEDIATE A CONFLICT
SEEK TO UNDERSTAND
LEARN FROM NEW AND
UNCOMFORTABLE ANGLES

KNOW THAT NO ONE IS SILENT THOUGH MANY ARE NOT HEARD
WORK TO CHANGE THIS

Bibliography

Abiodun, Nehanda (2000) Underground. *Blu* 2, no. 9.

Acme Collective (1999) N30 Black Bloc communique, 4 December. http://flag.blackened.net/~global/1299bbcommuniqe.htm

Active Element Foundation. www.nomoreprison.net/ae.html.

Adkins, Warren D. (1997) New York's free love advocates blast new puritanism; Republican Mayor Giuliani charged with anti-sex agenda; Gay authors calling for marriage and monogamy critiqued. *Badpuppy Gay Today*, 25 June.

AFL–CIO (American Federation of Labor and Congress of Industrial Organizations) (2001) Article XXI Decision, 13 January.

AfroCubaWeb. www.afrocubaweb.com/assata.htm#new interview.

Agnew, Michael (2001) Theatre of the oppressed: Interview with Augusto Boal. *New Art Examiner* 28, no. 5 (February).

Alinsky, Saul (1969) *Reveille for Radicals*. New York: Vintage.

——— (1971) *Rules for Radicals*. New York: Vintage.

Amar, Akhil Reed (2000) A state's right; A government's wrong. *Washington Post*, 19 March.

American Psychiatric Association (APA) (2000) *Diagnostic and Statistical Manual of Mental Disorders*. 4th edn, text rev. Washington, DC: APA.

Applebaum, Richard and Peter Dreier (1999) The campus anti-sweatshop movement. *The American Prospect* (September–October).

Arizona Republic (2000) Pay, benefits top issues to contract workers; "Living wage" movement grows, 1 August.

Arquilla, John, and David Ronfeldt (1993) Cyberwar is coming! Philadelphia, PA: Taylor & Francis. www.well.com:70/0/Military/cyberwar

Arno, Peter, and Karyn Feiden (1992) *Against the Odds*. New York: HarperCollins.

Arronchic, Warren (1997) Mainstream media keeps provocative gays distant; Why do anti-sex neoconservatives get prime time access to public pulpits? Right wing group is strongly opposed in academic circles. *Badpuppy Gay Today*, 9 July.

Art and Revolution (2001) Introduction. www.artandrevolution.org

Ascribe (2001) Global AIDS movement gathers momentum as disparate groups come together; Funds grow from millions to billions. (3 July) Boston.com

Aspen Institute Roundtable on Comprehensive Community Initiatives (1997) *Voices from the Field: Learning from the Early Work of Comprehensive Community Initiatives*. Washington DC: Aspen Institute.

——— (1995) *New Aproaches to Evaluating Community Initiatives*. Washington DC: Aspen Institute. www.aspenroundtable.org

Association of Community Organizations for Reform Now (ACORN) (1997) Capital and communities: A report to the Annie E. Casey Foundation on ACORN's work to revitalize low and moderate income communities. www.acorn.org/ACORNarchives/studies/c-and-c/capital-and-communities.html

Bacon, David (2000) Immigrant workers ask labor "Which side are you on?" *Working USA: The Journal of Labor and Society* 3, no. 5 (January–February): 7–18.

Bacon-Blood, Littice (2000) Tulane protest finally pays off; Sweatshop vote in favor of WRC. *Times Picayune*, 21 October.

Badpuppy Gay Today (1997) Entrapment: Are outdoor cruisers sex-offenders? Outdoor cruise spots nationwide find increased police entrapments arrests up in New York, San Diego, Atlanta, Salt Lake City. Compiled by *Badpuppy Gay Today*, 27 August.

Bakhtin, Mikhail (1968) *Rabelais and His World*. Cambridge, MA: MIT Press.

Balagoon, Kuwasi (1971) *Look for Me in the Whirlwind: The Collective Biography of the New York 21*, New York: Random House.

——— (2000) *A Soldier's Story: Writings by a Revolutionary New Afrikan Anarchist*, Montreal: Solidarity.

Barber, Benjamin R. (1995) *Jihad vs. McWorld*. New York: Times Books.

Bartlett, Donald L., and James B. Steele (1992) *America: What Went Wrong?* Kansas City: Andrews and McMeel.

Beck, Allen J. and Harrison, Paige M. (2001) Prisoners in 2000. US Department of Justice, August. www.ojp.usdoj.gov/bjs/pub/pdf/p00.pdf

Beck, Juliette (2000) Interview by Ed "Redwood" Ring, 6 December. www.ecoworld.com/Articles/global exchange.cfm

Beckwith, Dave, with Cristina Lopez (1997) Community organizing: People power from the grassroots. COMM-ORG Working Papers Series, http://comm-org.utoledo.edu/papers.htm

Benderson, Bruce (1997) *Toward the New Degeneracy*. New York: Edgewise.

Bennet, James (1981) *Oral History and Delinquency*. Chicago: University of Chicago Press.

Berlant, Laura, and Michael Warner (1999) Sex in public. In Simon During, ed., *The Cultural Studies Reader*, 2d edn. New York: Routledge.

Berman, Marshall (1982) *All That Is Solid Melts into Air: The Experience of Modernity*. New York: Simon & Schuster.

Bérubé, Allan (1996) The history of the gay bathhouses. In Dangerous Bedfellows, ed., *Policing Public Sex: Queer Politics and the Future of AIDS Activism*. Boston: South End Press.

———— (1997) A century of sex panics. In *SexPanic!* New York: Sheep Meets Sheep Collective.

Bey, Hakim (1985) *T.A.Z.* Brooklyn: Autonomedia.

Billboard (2000) Black August hard at work in N.Y., Havana, 29 August. www.billboard.com

Black August Collective (2000) Statement of purpose. *Blu* 2, no. 9.

BFC (Black Feminist Caucus of the Black Radical Congress) (2000) Statement of support of the World March of Women, 4 October. http://blackradicalcongress.com/organizing/pressrelease/release100400.html

Boal, Augusto (1979) *Theatre of the Oppressed*, trans. Charles A. and Maria-Odilia Leal McBride. New York: Theatre Communications Group.

———— (1992) *Games for Actors and Non-actors*, trans. Adrian Jackson. London and New York: Routledge.

Bobo, K., J. Kendall, and S. Max (1991) *Organizing for Social Change: A Manual for Activists in the 1990s*. Washington, DC: Seven Locks Press.

Bolin, A. (1987) Transsexualism and the limits of traditional analysis. *American Behavioral Scientist* 31, no. 1 (September): 41–65.

Bordowitz, Greg (1988) Picture a Coalition. In Douglas Crimp, ed., *AIDS: Cultural Analysis/Cultural Activism*. Boston: MIT Press.

———— (2001) Fast trip, long view: Talking to Gregg Bordowitz. *Artery: The AIDS-Arts Forum*. www.artistswithaids.org/artery/artist2.html

Boston Public Health Commission (1998) *Health of Boston Report*. Boston, MA.

Brecher, Jeremy, Tim Costello, and Brendan Smith (2000) *Globalization from Below*. Boston: South End Press.

Brocht, Chauna (2000) The forgotten workforce: More than one in 10 federal contract workers earn less than a living wage. Washington, DC: Economic Policy Institute.

Bronski, Michael (1998) *The Pleasure Principle: Sex, Backlash, and the Struggle for Gay Freedom*. New York: St. Martin's Press.

Brown, G. (1995) Cross-dressing men often lead double lives. *Menninger Letter* (April): 4–5.

Buckley, James (2000) Interview by Joseph Muriana. Oral history project, transcript no. 131 (25 July).

Buckley, Jim. n.d. Statement. www.nwbccc.org/History/Stories/Buckley.html

Bull, Chris (1999) Still angry after all of these years. *Advocate*, 17 August.

Buncik, Yasha (1993) Interview with Jan Cohen-Cruz. June 10.

Burke, P (1996) *Gender Shock: Exploding the Myths of Male and Female*. New York: Anchor Books.

Burr, Tom (1998) Sleazy city, 42nd Street structures, and some qualities of life. *OCTOBER* 85 (Summer).

Burtless, Gary, ed. (1990) *A Future of Lousy Jobs*. Washington, DC: Brookings Institution.

Butler, Judith (1990) *Gender Trouble: Feminism and the Subversion of Identity*. New York: Routledge, Chapman, & Hall.

Butterfield, Fox (1997) Study links violence rate to cohesion of community. *New York Times*, 17 August.

Callahan, Steve, Neil Mayer, Kris Palmer, and Larry Ferlazzo (1999) Rowing the boat with two oars. Paper presented on *COMM-ORG: The On-Line Conference on Community Organizing and*

Development. http://comm-org.utoledo.edu/papers.htm

Caramanica, Jon (1999) It's Nation time. Again. *Village Voice*, 1–7 September.

Carlson, Virginia, and Nikolas Theodore (1995) *Are There Enough Jobs? Welfare Reform and Labor Market Reality.* The Job Gap Project. The Woods Fund of Chicago.

Cauvin, Henri E. (2001) Access to AIDS drugs at issue in South African trial this week. *New York Times*, 5 March.

CDC (Centers for Disease Control) (1996) *HIV/AIDS Surveillance Report* 12, no. 1. Atlanta: CDC.

Center for Community Change (2000) Transforming lives and communities: Community organizing for YOU!, November. www.communitychange.org

——— (2000) *HIV/AIDS Surveillance Report* 12, 12, no. 1. Atlanta: CDC.

Christopherson, Susan (1994) The fortress city: Privatized spaces, consumer citizenship. In Ash Amin, ed., *Post-Fordism: A Reader.* Cambridge, MA: Blackwell.

Church Ladies for Choice (1993a) *Starter Kit.* New York.

——— (1993b) *In Your Face With Amazing Grace.* Video. New York: Land of Fire Productions.

City Record (1999) Parks and recreation: Amendment to Chapter 1 of Title 56 of the Official Compilation of the Rules of the City of New York. 16 August.

Cockburn, Alexander, Jeffrey St. Clair, and Allan Sekula (2000) *Five Days that Shook the World.* New York: Verso.

Coffin, Phillip (1997) *Cocaine and Pregnancy.* New York: The Lindesmith Center.

Cohler, Bertram (1982) Personal narrative and the life course. In P. Bates and O'Brim, eds, *Life Span Development and Human Behavior.* New York: Academic Press.

COMM-ORG: The On-Line Conference on Community Organizing and Development (2001) CO groups and networks. http://comm-org.utoledo.edu/orgs.htm

CWA (Communication Workers of America) Local 7026 (2000) Home page. www.cwa7026.com

Consensus Organizing Institute (2000) www.consensusorganizing.com

Cortes, Ernesto (1995) Remarks as panelist, special session on "The legacy of Saul Alinsky". American Sociological Association annual meeting.

Cowen, Scott S. (2000) Thanks to democracy; Sit-in ended well. *Times-Picayune*, 13 April.

Crain, Caleb (1997) Pleasure principles: Queer theorists and gay journalists wrestle over the politics of sex. *Lingua Franca* (October): 27–37.

Crass, Chris (2000) Beyond the whiteness – global capitalism and white supremacy: Thoughts on movement building and anti-racist organizing. www.tao.ca/~colours/crass4.html

Crimp, Douglas (1988) How to have promiscuity in an epidemic. In Douglas Crimp, ed., *AIDS: Cultural Analysis/Cultural Activism.* Boston: MIT Press.

——— (1997) Liberation backlash. In *SexPanic!* New York: Sheep Meets Sheep Collective.

Crimp, Douglas, Ann Pelligrini, Eva Pendleton, and Michael Warner (1997) This is a SexPanic!. In *SexPanic!* New York: Sheep Meets Sheep Collective.

Culture and Agitation: Theatre Documents (1972) London: Action Books.

Dailey, Mary (2000) Message posted on COMM-ORG: The On-Line Conference on Community Organizing and Development. http://coserver.sa.utoledo.edu/pipermail/colist/2000-December/001212.html

Danaher, Kevin, ed. (1996) *Corporations Are Gonna Get Your Mama*. Monroe, ME: Common Courage Press.

Danaher, Kevin, and Roger Burbach, eds (2000) *Globalize This!* Monroe, ME: Common Courage Press.

Dangerous Bedfellows (1996) *Policing Public Sex*. Boston: South End Press.

Davis, Mark (1997) *Gangland: Cultural Elites and the New Generationalism*. St Leonards, NSW: Allen & Unwin.

Davis, Susan (1988) *Parades and Power*. Berkeley: University of California Press.

dead prez (2000) Behind enemy lines. *Let's Get Free*. Loud Records.

Delany, Samuel R. (1999) *Times Square Red, Times Square Blue*. New York: New York University Press.

Delgado, Gary (1986) *Organizing the Movement*. Philadelphia: Temple University Press.

Desert, Jean-Ulrich (1997) Queers space. In Gordon Brent Ingram, Ann-Marie Bouthillette, and Yolanda Retter, eds, *Queers in Space: Communities, Public Spaces, Sites of Resistance*. Seattle: Bay Press.

De Toqueville, Alexis (1994) *Democracy in America*. New York: Knopf.

Devine, Dave (2000) Payday dismay: The city doesn't abide by its own living wage ordinance. *Tucson Weekly*, 14 September.

Ditman, Walter (1991) Adelante hits the street. *New York Nicanews* 3, no. 2 (April): 4–5.

Do or Die (1997) *Do or Die* 6 (Summer). Reprinted as The evolution of Reclaim the Streets at www.gn.apc.org/rts/evol.htm.

Dowbiggin, I. (1997) *Keeping America Sane: Psychiatry and Eugenics in the United States and Canada, 1880–1940*. Ithaca, New York: Sage House.

Duberman, Martin (1999) *Left Out: The Politics of Exclusion: Essays, 1964–1999*. New York: Basic Books.

Dunlap, David W. (2000) In city canyons, slivers of public space erode. *New York Times*, 28 September.

The Economist (1996) 18 May.

———— (2000) Anti-capitalist protests: Angry and effective, 23 September.

Eichler, Michael (1998) Organizing's past, present, and future. *Shelterforce Online*. www.nhi.org/online/issues/101/eichler.html

Eigo, Jim (1998) What's the use of being queer if you can't be different? (December). www.cruisingforxsex.com

———— (2000) The asshole is a revolution. *Playguy* (December).

Eitzen, Stanley, and Maxine Baca Zinn (2000) *In Conflict and Order: Understanding Society*, 9th edn. Boston: Allyn & Bacon.

Ekins, Paul (1992) *A New World Order*. London: Routledge.

Elbaz, Gilbert (1993) The sociology of AIDS activism: The case of ACT UP, 1987–1992. Unpublished dissertation. New York: ACT UP archive.

Elliott, Michael (1999) The New Radicals. *Newsweek*, 13 December.

Epstein, Barbara (1991) *Political Protest and Cultural Revolution*. Berkeley: University of California Press.

Epstein, Steven (1996) *Impure Science*. Berkeley: University of California Press.

Fair, Gary Allen (1995) Public narration and group culture. In Hank Johnson and Bert Klandermans, eds, *Social Movements and Culture*. Minneapolis: University of Minnesota Press.

Fajardo, Brenda, Socrates Topacio et al. (1989) *BITAW: Basic Integrated Theater Arts Workshop*. Quezon City: Philippine Educational Theater Association (PETA).

Fineberg, David (1994) *Queer and Loathing*. New York: Viking.

Finks, P. David (1984) *The Radical Vision of Saul Alinsky*. New York: Paulist Press.

Fishkin, Joey (1999) Our generation finally sits in. *Yale Daily News*, 10 February.

Flewitts, Sharon (1993) Interview with the author, 29 May.

Flynn, Kevin (1999) 8 arrested near City Hall in protest on police shooting. *New York Times*, 23 February.

Folbre, Nancy, James Heintz, and the Center for Popular Economics with the National Priorities Project and United for a Fair Economy (2000) *The Ultimate Field Guide to the U.S. Economy*. New York: The New Press.

Foucault, Michel (1980) Introduction to *Herculine Barbin: Being the Memoir of a 19th Century French Hermaphrodite*, trans Michel Foucault. New York: Random House.

Freeman, Jo (1999) A model for analyzing the strategic options of social movement organizations. In Jo Freeman and Victoria Johnson, eds, *Waves of Protest: Social Movements since the Sixties*. Lanham, MD: Rowan & Littlefield.

Freeman, Richard B (1999) *The New Inequality: Creating Solutions for Poor America*. Boston: Beacon Press.

Freire, Paulo (1973) *Pedagogy of the Oppressed*, trans. Myra Bergman Ramos. New York: Seabury Press.

Friedman, Samuel (1998) The political economy of drug-user scapegoating – and the philosophy and politics of resistance. *Drugs: Education, Prevention, and Policy* 5, no. 1.

——— (2001) New times, new dangers, new possibilities. In *Harm Reduction Communication* 11 (Spring).

Galbraith, John Kenneth (1996) *The Good Society: The Humane Agenda*. New York: Mariner Books/ Houghton Mifflin.

Gamson, Joshua (1991) Silence, death, and the invisible enemy: AIDS activism and social movement "newness." In Michael Burowoy et al., eds, *Ethnography Unbound*. Berkeley: University of California Press.

Gaywave (1997) Sex-lib activists confront "SexPanic!" *Gaywave*, 2 December.

Gereffi, Gary (1994) The organization of buyer-driven global commodity chains: How U.S. retailers shape overseas production networks. In Gary Gereffi and Miguel Korzeniewicz, eds, *Commodity Chains and Global Capitalism*. Westport, CT: Greenwood Press.

Ginsburg, Faye (1989) *Contested Lives: The Abortion Debate in an American Community*. Berkeley: University of California Press.

Goffman, E. (1959) *The Presentation of Self in Everyday Life*. Garden City, NY: Anchor.

Goldstein, Laura (1999) Urban wear goes suburban. *Fortune* 138, no. 12.

Goldstein, Richard (1997) The crackdown on cruising: Just when you thought it was safe to be gay; Police harassment is on the rise. *Village Voice*, 1 July.

Greenhouse, Steven (2000a) A Vallone bill bars purchases in sweatshops. *New York Times*, 8 February.

———— (2000b) Despite defeat on China trade bill; Labor on rise; New efforts alter dinosaur image. *New York Times*, 30 May.

———— (2000c) With some victories in hand, battered labor flexes muscle. *New York Times*, 9 September.

Gross, Dave (2001) Encyclopedia of culture jamming. What its all about, anyway. www.syntac.net/hoax/commerce.php

Hathaway, Will, and David S. Meyer (1997) Competition and cooperation in movement coalitions: Lobbying for peace in the 1980s. In David S. Meyer and Thomas R. Rochon, eds, *Coalitions and political movements*. Boulder, CO: Lynne Reinner.

Hayduk. Ron (2002) The anti-globalization movement. In John Berg, ed., *Teamsters, Turtles, and Others: Left Movements in the 20th Century*. New York: Rowan & Littlefield.

Hayes, Roger (2000) Interview by Jordan Moss, 6 November.

Healy, Michelle (2000) Sweatshop protests gain momentum on campuses. *USA Today*, 17 February.

Henman, Anthony, Denise Paone, Don Des Jarlais, Lee Kochems, and Samuel Friedman (1998) From ideology to logistics: The organizational aspects of syringe exchange in a period of institutional consolidation. *Substance Use & Misuse* 33, no. 5: 1213–30.

Herndon, Sheri (1999) http://lists.indymedia.org

Hess, Doug (1999) Community organizing, building, and developing: Their relationship to comprehensive community initiatives. Paper presented on *COMM-ORG: The On-Line Conference on Community Organizing and Development*. http://comm-org.utoledo.edu/papers.htm

Hirschfeld, M. (1910) *Die Transvestiten*. Leipzig: Max Spohr; English translation by M. Lombardi-Nash, *Transvestites*. New York: Prometheus Books, 1991.

Horowitz, Craig (1998) Whose Village? *New York Magazine*, 9 November.

Humphries, Laud (1999) Tearoom trade: Interpersonal sex in public spaces. In William Leap, ed., *Public Sex/Gay Space*. New York: Columbia University Press.

Hunter, Karen (1996) Fubu fitted for success: Taking urban gear to top through Macy's. *New York Daily News*, 11 November.

Hutcheon, Linda (1985) *A Theory of Parody: The Teachings of Twentieth-century Art Forms*. Urbana and Chicago: University of Illinois Press.

International Collective Media Gathering (1996) Toronto, Canada, 27 October.

Jacobi, Monsieur (1999) http://lists.indymedia.org

Jenkens, Philip (1998) *Moral Panic: Changing Concepts of the Child Molester in Modern America*. New Haven, CT: Yale University Press.

Jobs with Justice (2000) Fighting for social justice: Highlights from around the nation. *National workers rights resource directory, 2000*. http://www.jwj.org/OrgTools/ResDir00–5.htm

Jonnes, Jill (1986) *We're Still Here: The Rise, Fall, and Resurrection of the South Bronx*. New York: Atlantic Monthly Press.

Jordan, John (1998) The art of necessity: The subversive imagination of anti-road protest and Reclaim the Streets. In George McKay, ed., *DIY Culture: Party and Protest in Nineties Britain*.

London: Verso.

Kahn, S (1991) *Organizing: A Guide for Grassroots Leaders*. Silver Springs, MD: NASW Press.

Kamansky, Mark (1992) Introduction to *Remembered Lives: The Work of Ritual, Storytelling, and Growing Older*. Ann Arbor: University of Michigan Press.

Kaplan, Marla B., and Gregory S. Krauss (2000) Apparel companies put factory locations within mouse click. *Harvard Crimson*, 21 January.

Katznelson, Ira (1994) *City Trenches*. Chicago: University of Chicago Press.

Kauffman, L.A (1998) Unpublished manuscript on post-sixties protest.

———— (2000) Whose movement? *Free Radical* 6.

———— (2001) Militants and moderates. *Free Radical* 15 (January).

Keil, Roger (1998) *Los Angeles: Globalization, Urbanization, and Social Struggles*. Chichester: John Wiley & Sons.

Kelly, Alex, and Jason Gibson (2000) Being the media. *Arena* 49. http://home.vicnet.net.au/~arena/archives/Mag Archive/issue 49/against the current3 49.htm

Kershaw, Baz (1999) *The Radical in Performance*. London and New York: Routledge.

King, Martin Luther (1986) *Strength to Love*. Minneapolis: Fortress Press.

Klein, Naomi (2001a) Not dreaming of revolution, but a dreaming revolution. [London] *Guardian*, 3 March. www.guardian.co.uk/weekend/story/0,3605,445513,00.html

———— (2001b) The fate of the end of the end of history. *The Nation*, 19 March.

Kohut, Heinz (1959–78) Introspection, empathy, and psychoanalysis. In *The Search for the Self: The Selected Writings of Heinz Kohut, 1950–1978*, edited by P. Ornstein. New York: International Universities Press.

Kramer, Larry (1994) *Reports from the Holocaust: The Making of an AIDS Activist*. New York: St. Martin's Press.

Kretzmann, John P., and John L. McKnight (1993) *Building Communities from the Inside Out*. Evanston, IL: Center for Urban Affairs and Policy Research Neighborhood Innovations Network, Northwestern University.

Krupa, Gregg (1999) The battle cry against sweatshops resounds across college campuses; Activists score in campaign targeting athletic retailers. *Boston Globe*, 18 April.

Krupat, Kitty and Patric McCreery (2001) Introduction to K. Krupat and P. McCreery, eds, *Out at Work: Building a Gay Labor Alliance*. Minneapolis, MN: University of Minnesota Press.

Lamborn, Peter, and Bill Weinborg (1999) *Avant Gardening: Ecological Struggle in the City and the World*. Brooklyn: NY Autonomedia.

Lawson, Ronald, ed. (1986) *The Tenant Movement in New York City, 1904–1984*. New Brunswick, NJ: Rutgers University Press.

Lee, Chisun (2000) Taking the rap. *Village Voice*, 6–12 September.

LeRoy, Greg, Fiona Hsu, and Sara Hinkley (2000) *The Policy Shift to Good Jobs: Cities, States, and Counties Attaching Job Quality Standards to Development Subsidies*. Washington, DC: Good Jobs First.

Lesnick, Henry (1973) *Guerrilla Street Theater*. New York: Avon Books.

Levin, Richard (2000) Private correspondence to Eli C. Messinger, MD.

LGNY (1998) LGNY Review '97. 19 January: 16–17.

Lin, Jennifer (1999) Students create groups to fight sweatshops. *Houston Chronicle*, 5 December.

Lucas, Daniel (1999) Interview, 31 December.

Luce, Stephanie (1999) The role of secondary associations in local policy implementation: An assessment of living wage ordinances. Ph.D. dissertation, University of Wisconsin.

McAdam, Doug (1982) *Political Process and the Development of Black Insurgency, 1930–1970*. Chicago: University of Chicago Press.

McAdam, Doug, Sidney Tarrow, and Charles Tilly (2001) *Dynamics of Contention*. Cambridge: Cambridge University Press.

McConachie, Bruce, and Daniel Friedman (1985) *Theatre for Working Class Audiences, 1830–1980*. Westport, CT: Greenwood Press.

McFarland, Melissa (1999) Cal Poly cat walk sends labor message. [California Polytechnic State University, San Luis Obispo] *Mustang Daily*, 16 November.

McKay, George (1998) DIY culture: Notes towards an intro. In George McKay, ed., *DIY Culture: Party and Protest in Nineties Britain*. London: Verso.

McLuhan, Marshall (1965) *Understanding Media*. New York: McGraw-Hill.

McNight, John (1987) Regenerating community. *Social Policy*, Winter: 54–8.

Mair, M. (1988) Psychology and storytelling. *International Journal of Personal Construct Psychology* 1: 125–38.

Malcolm X Grassroots Movement (MXGM). www.mxgm.com/newafrikans.html

Maller, Peter (1999) Students set up mock sweatshop in protest: They promote awareness of working conditions for those making UW goods. *Milwaukee Journal Sentinel*, 11 November.

Mander, Jerry, and Edward Goldsmith (1996) *The Case against the Global Economy: And for a Turn to the Local*. San Francisco: Sierra Club Books.

Marable, Manning (2000) *How Capitalism Underdeveloped Black America: Problems in Race, Political Economy, and Society*. Cambridge, MA: South End Press.

Marcos, Subcomandante Insurgente (1994) Zapatista Communique (May).

——— (1997) Statement to the Freeing the Media Gathering, New York City, 31 January–1 February.

Martinez, Elizabeth (2000) Where was the color in Seattle? *Color Lines* (Spring).

Massey, Douglas and Nancy Denton (1993) *American Apartheid: Segregation and the Making of the Underclass*. Cambridge, MA: Harvard University Press.

Mayor, M. (1974) Fears and fantasies of the anti-suffragists. *Connecticut Review* 7, no. 2 (April): 64–74.

Medoff, Peter, and Holly Sklar (1994) *Streets of Hope: The Fall and Rise of an Urban Neighborhood*. Boston: South End Press.

Melendez, Michele M. (1998) Oberlin considers stand on sweatshops. [Cleveland] *Plain Dealer*, 19 May.

Melucci, Alberto (1985) The symbolic challenge of contemporary movements. *Social Research* 52.

Meyer, David S., and Thomas R. Rochon (1997) Toward a coalitional theory of social and political movements. In David S. Meyer and Thomas R. Rochon, eds, *Coalitions and Political Movements: The Lessons of the Nuclear Freeze*. Boulder, CO: Lynne Rienner.

Miller, D.W. (1999) Sweatshop protest ends at U. of Michigan. *Chronicle of Higher Education,* 2 April.

Milstein, Cindy (2000) Reclaim the cities: From protest to popular power. www.infoshop.org/rants/cindy reclaim.html

Mollenkopf, John and Ken Emerson (2001) *Rethinking the Urban Agenda: Reinvigorating the Liberal Tradition in New York City and Urban America.* New York: Century Foundation Press.

Mission Statement (1997) *SexPanic!* New York: Sheep Meets Sheep Collective.

Moore, Harmonie (1993) Interview with Jan Cohen-Cruz. May 29.

Moore, Lisa (1995) In harm's way. *Crossroads.*

Moore, Robert (1990) Ritual process, initiation, and contemporary religion. In Stein, Murry and Moore, eds,. *Jung's Challenge to Contemporary Religion.* Wilmette, IL: Chiron Publications.

Morris, Aldon (1984) *The Origins of the Civil Rights Movement: Black Communities Organizing for Change.* New York: Free Press.

Moss, Jordan (2000) Fighting fires with fire. *City Limits* (April).

Nader, Ralph (1999) Socialism for the rich. *New York Times,* 14 May.

National Organizers Alliance (2001) www.noacentral.org

Neff, Lisa (1997) Police "sex" stings on the increase. *Windy City Times,* 28 August.

Ness, Immanuel, and Nick Unger (2000) Union approaches to immigrant organizing: A review of New York City Locals. UCLEA Labor Education Conference, April, in Milwaukee, Wisconsin.

New Party (1997) Living wage and campaign finance reform initiatives. www.newparty.org/reforms.html

Nichols, Jack (1997) Journalist's "call to arms" exposes gay conservatives; advises: End sodomy laws and think beyond "having what 'they' have" David Scorr Evens: Marriage and baby carriages; Spare Us!" *Badpuppy Gay Today,* 12 September.

——— (1999) Beheading: A gristly murder in Virginia. *Gay Today,* 9 March. http://gaytoday.badpuppy.com/garchive/events/030999ev.htm

Nicklin, Julie L. (1998) Developing codes of conduct for manufacturers of college apparel. *Chronicle of Higher Education,* 13 November.

No More Prisons. www.nomoreprison.net.

Nussbaum, Bruce (1990) *Good Intentions.* New York: Atlantic Monthly Press.

Nyasha, Kiilu (2000) Black August: A celebration of hip hop and our freedom fighters. Unpublished essay.

Orenstein, Claudia (1998) *Festive Revolutions: The Politics of Popular Theater and the San Francisco Mime Troupe.* Jackson: University Press of Mississippi.

Osterman, Paul (2000) Report on the impact of the Valley Interfaith living wage campaign. Unpublished report.

Palms, Katherine (1999) Sweatshop workers tell of making Yale apparel. *Yale Daily News,* 20 October.

Pendleton, Eva (1997) Love for sale: Queering heterosexuality. In Jill Naggle, ed., *Whores and Other Feminists.* New York: Routledge.

Phelan, Peggy (1993) *Unmarked.* London and New York: Routledge.

Piven, Frances Fox, and Richard A. Cloward (1979) *Poor People's Movements: Why they Succeed, How they Fail.* New York: Vintage.

———— (2000) Power repertoires and globalization. *Politics and Society* 28: 413–30.

Plummer, Ken (1995) *Telling Sexual Stories: Power, Change, and Social Worlds.* Routledge: London.

Pollin, Robert, and Stephanie Luce (1998) *The Living Wage: Building a Fair Economy.* New York: New Press.

Postman, Neil (1991) Six things worth knowing about technology. *Cause/Effect* (Fall): 48. www.agricola.umn.edu/Library/Postman.htm

Purdam, Todd S. (2000) Justice department warns Los Angeles police; May act to gain oversight if city doesn't stem abuse by officers. *New York Times*, 9 May.

Reeves, J., and R. Campbell (1994) *Cracked Coverage.* London: Duke.

Reissman, Catherine Kohler (1993) *Narrative Analysis.* Qualitative Research Methods Series, no. 30. London: Sage Publications.

Reitzes, Donald C., and Dietrich C. Reitzes (1987) *The Alinsky Legacy: Alive and Kicking.* Greenwich, CT: JAI Press.

Rifkin, Jeremy (2000) *The Age of Access: The New Culture of Hyper-capitalism Where All of Life is a Paid-for Experience.* New York: Tarcher/Putnam.

Ritter, Jennifer (2000) Interview by Jordan Moss, 8 May.

Rofes, Eric (1997) The emerging sex panic targeting gay men. Speech given at the National Gay and Lesbian Task Force's Creating Change Conference in San Diego, 16 November.

———— (1998) *Dry Bones Breathe: Gay Men Creating Post-AIDS Identities and Subcultures.* Birmingham, NY: Harrington Park Press.

Rose, Tricia (1994) *Black Noise: Rap Music and Black Culture in Contemporary America.* Middletown, CT: Wesleyan University Press.

Rotello, Gabriel (1997) *Sexual Ecology.* New York: Dutton.

RTS/London (2000) Reclaim the Streets website: www.gn.apc.org/rts/

———— (2001) Propaganda. www.gn.apc.org/rts/prop10.htm

RTS/New York City (1998) Reclaim the Streets New York City action flyer.

Rubin, Gayle (1984) Thinking sex: Notes for a radical theory of the politics of sexuality. In Carole S. Vance, ed., *Pleasure and Danger: Exploring Female Sexuality.* Boston: Routledge.

Rubin, Herb (2000) *Renewing Hope within Neighborhoods of Despair: The Community-based Development Model.* Albany: State University of New York Press.

Ruggiero, Greg (2000) http://lists.indymedia.org.

Russell, Dan (2000) Roots of a social justice movement, 1970–75. http://www.acorn.org/history-content.html

Russo, Vito (1988) Why we fight. Speech delivered during a demonstration, October 10, in front of the Department of Health and Human Services building in Washington, DC. www.actupny.org/documents/whfight.html

Samuel, Raphael, Ewan MacColl, and Stuart Cosgrove (1985) *Theatres of the Left, 1880–1935: Workers' Theatre Movements in Britain and America.* London: Routledge.

Sandalow, Marc (1990) New push in US for divestment. *San Francisco Chronicle*, 29 June.

Sanger, David E. (1997) The last liberal (almost) leaves town; Labor Secretary Reich offers "a last word" on U.S. social policy. *New York Times*, 9 January.

Sanjek (1998) *The Future of Us All 1998*. Ithaca: Cornell University Press.

Sassen, Saskia (2000) *The Global City: New York, London, Tokyo*. Updated edn. Princeton, NJ: Princeton University Press.

Schattschneider, E.E. (1975) *The Semisovereign People: A Realist's View of Democracy in America* [1961]. Hinsdale: The Dryden Press.

Schmitt, Eric (2001) New census shows Hispanics are even with Blacks. *New York Times*, 8 March.

Schoolman, Judith (2000) Low profits hit high fashion bigs. *New York Daily News*, 7 February.

Schulman, Sara (1993) *My American History*. New York: Routledge.

Sedgwick, Eve (1990) *Epistemology of the Closet*. Berkeley: University of California Press.

Selznick, Philip (1992) *The Moral Commonwealth: Social Theory and the Promise of Community*. Berkeley: University of California Press.

Sex Panic! (1997) Mission statement. In *SexPanic!* New York: Sheep Meets Sheep Collective.

Shepard, Benjamin (1997) *White Nights and Ascending Shadows: An Oral History of the San Francisco AIDS Epidemic*. London: Cassell Press.

———— (2001) Queer and gay assimilationists: The suits vs. the sluts. *Monthly Review* (May).

———— (2002) Notes on ACT UP! In John Berg, ed., *Teamsters, Turtles, and Others: Left Movements in the 20th Century*. New York: Rowan & Littlefield.

Shindler, Paul (1997) Is it a gay thing or a Giuliani thing? *LGNY*, 3 August.

Shumway, Chris (2000) News media, corporate power, and democracy. http://members.tripod.com/chris.shumway/id19.htm

Signorile, Michelangelo (1993) *Queer in America*. New York: Random House.

Silverman, Robert K. (1999) Harvard anti-sweatshop group models in protest fashion show. Harvard *Crimson*, 29 October.

———— (2000) Students stage sweatshop protests at colleges nationwide. *Harvard Crimson*, 3 March.

Smith, Jackie (2000) Globalizing resistance: The Battle of Seattle and the future of social movements. *Mobilization* 6: 1–2.

Smith, Jackie, Charles Chatfield, and Ron Pagnucco, eds (1997) *Transnational Social Movements in Global Politics*. Syracuse, NY: Syracuse University Press.

Smith, Ken (2000) Message posted on *COMM-ORG: The On-Line Conference on Community Organizing and Development*. http://comm-org.utoledo.edu/pipermail/colist/2000–December/001213.html

Smock, Kristina (1997) Comprehensive community initiatives: A new generation of urban revitalization strategies. Paper presented on *COMM-ORG: The On-Line Conference on Community Organizing and Development*. http://comm-org.utoledo.edu/papers.htm.

Solomon, Alisa (1998) AIDS crusaders ACT UP a storm. In Jan Cohen Cruz, ed., *Radical Street Performance: An International Anthology*. London and New York: Routledge.

Soule, Sarah A. (1997) The student divestment movement in the United States and tactical diffusion: The shantytown protest. *Social Forces* 75: 855–82.

Spitzer, R., ed. (1994) *DSM-IV Casebook: A Learning Companion to the Diagnostic and Statistical*

Manual of Mental Disorders, 4th edn. Washington DC: American Psychiatric Press.

Stagg, Bethan (1998) Reclaim the Streets goes global. *Car Busters*.

Stall, S., and Stoecker, R. (1998) Community organizing or organizing community? Gender and the crafts of empowerment. *Gender and Society* 12: 729–56.

Stimson, Gerry (1995) Personal conversation.

Stoecker, Randy (1994) *Defending Community: The Struggle for Alternative Redevelopment in Cedar–Riverside*. Philadelphia: Temple University Press.

———— (1995a) Community, movement, organization: The problem of identity convergence in collective action. *The Sociological Quarterly* 36: 111–30.

———— (1995b) Community organizing and community development in Cedar–Riverside and East Toledo: A comparative study. *Journal of Community Practice* 2: 1–23.

———— (1997) The community development corporation model of urban redevelopment: A critique and an alternative. *Journal of Urban Affairs* 19: 1–23.

Suleiman, Susan Rubin (1990) *Subversive Intent: Gender, Politics, and the Avant-garde*. Cambridge, MA: Harvard University Press.

Tarrow, Sidney (1999) Beyond globalization: Why internationalization is unlikely to make agents freer but under what conditions it might. Paper presented at the Workshop on Contentious Politics at Columbia University.

Tyler, Carole-Anne (1991) Boys will be girls: the politics of gay drag. In Diana Fuss, ed., *Inside/Out*. London: Routledge.

Teal, Donn (1971) *The Gay Militants: How Gay Liberation Began in America, 1969–1971*. New York: St. Martin's Press.

Tedlock, B. (1991) From participant observation to observation of participation: The emergence of narrative ethnography. *Journal of Anthropological Research* 47: 69–94.

Thompson, J. Phillip (1998) "Universalism and Deconstruction: Why Race Still Matters in Poverty and Economic Development." *Politics and Society* 26. no. 2.

Thomson, Tom (2001) The gay rights movement goes to the mall: Envisioning an anarchist alternative to queer political co-optation. *Onward Anarchist Newspaper* (Spring).

Tilly, Charles (1978) *From Mobilization to Revolution*. New York: Random House.

———— (1995) *Popular Contention in Great Britain, 1758–1834*. Cambridge, MA: Harvard University Press.

Tönnies, Ferdinand (1957) *Community and Society*. New York: Harper.

Toronto Star (2000) U of T protesters end sit-in. *Toronto Star*, 25 March.

Trebay, Guy (1999) Mayor taunts city and a coalition forms; Disobedience training. *Village Voice*, 30 March.

Treichler, Paula (1988) AIDS, homophobia, and biomedical discourse. In Douglas Crimp, ed., *AIDS: Cultural Analysis/Cultural Activism*. Boston: MIT Press.

Tresser, Thomas (1999) The work of the industrial areas foundation – Building strong citizens organizations for power – action – justice. http://my.voyager.net/ttresser/iaf1.htm

Vaid, Urvashi (2000) Bridging the political gap. *The Advocate*, 5 December.

Van der Werf, Martin (1999) "Sweatshop" protests raise ethical and practical issues. *Chronicle of Higher Education*, 5 March.

———— (2000) Sweatshop issue escalates with sit-ins and policy shifts. *Chronicle of Higher Education*, 10 March.

Van Erven, Eugene (1988) *Radical People's Theatre*. Bloomington: Indiana University Press.

———— (1992) *The Playful Revolution: Theatre and Liberation in Asia*. Bloomington and Indianapolis: Indiana University Press.

Warner, Michael (1993) Introduction to Michael Warner, ed., *Fear of a Queer Planet: Queer Politics and Social Theory*. Minneapolis: University of Minnesota Press.

Warren, Mark Russell (1995) Social capital and community empowerment: Religion and political organization in the Texas Industrial Areas Foundation. Ph.D. dissertation, Harvard University.

Watney, Simon (1987) *Policing Desire: Pornography, AIDS, and the Media*. Minneapolis: University of Minnesota Press.

Weeks, Jeffrey (1985) *Sexuality and its Discontents: Meanings, Myths, and Modern Sexualities*. New York: Routledge.

Wehling, Jason (1995) Netwars and activists power on the Internet. http://spunk.etext.org/texts/comms/sp001518/Netwars.html

Weinberg, Mark S. (1992) *Challenging the Hierarchy: Collective Theatre in the United States*. Westport, CT: Greenwood Press.

Weisman, John (1973) *Guerrilla Theater: Scenarios for Revolution*. Garden City, NY: Anchor Books.

Wessel, Paul (2000) Message posted on *COMM-ORG: The On-Line Conference on Community Organizing and Development*. http:/comm-org.utoledo.edu/pipermail/colist/2000-December/001212.html

Wilson, K., and B. Hammond (1996) Myth, stereotype, and cross-gender identity in the DSM-IV. Association for Women in Psychology, 21st Annual Feminist Psychology Conference, Portland OR.

Wilson, Kathy (2001) Transgender madness. Unpublished paper.

Wilson, William Julius (1996) *When Work Disappears: The World of the New Urban Poor*. New York: Knopf.

Wilson, William Julius (1999) *The Bridge Over the Racial Divide*. Berkeley: University of California Press.

Winkelman, Lee (1998a) Organizing: An investment that pays. *NeighborWorks Journal* 16, no. 2 (Winter). www.nw.org/resources/pub/nwjournal/1998/vol16no2/

———— (1998b) Organizing renaissance: Twin Cities CDC leads exploration of organizing by Massachusetts CDCs. *Shelterforce Online*. (September/October). www.nhi.org/online/issues/sf101.html

Wise, T., and J. Meyer (1980) The border area between transvestism and gender dysphoria: Transvestic applicants for sex reassignment. *Archives of Sexual Behavior* 9: 327–42.

Wray, Stephan (1998) E-guerrilla in the mist. *Ottawa Citizen*, 26 October. www.ottawacitizen.com/hightech/981026/1964496.html

Zierler, S., and N. Krieger (1997) Reframing women's risk: Social inequalities and HIV infection. *Annual Review of Public Health* 18: 401–36.

Zinn, Howard (2000) A flash of the possible. *The Progressive* (January).

Contributors

Andrew Boyd is an organizer, propaganda artist, and writer. Andrew (aka Phil T. Rich) is currently a creative action consultant with United for a Fair Economy and one of the driving forces behind Billionaires for Bush (or Gore) and the Million Billionaire March. He was the founder, and until recently director, of the arts and action program at UFE, which uses guerrilla theater, media stunts and creative direct action to fight growing economic inequality. He has conducted workshops around the US on activist art and artful activism. Boyd is also the author of *The Activist Cookbook: Creative Actions for a Fair Economy*, a how-to guide for artist-organizers. His most recent book, *Life's Little Deconstruction Book: Self-Help for the Post-Hip* was published by W.W. Norton and Penguin UK in 2000. His next book, "The Agony of Being Connected to Everything in the Universe – A Book of Daily Afflictions" is a dark, twisted, existential manifesto posing as a parody of new age inspiration books. He is thirty-eight, lives in New York, has no kids, no wife, no same-sex partner, and minimal health insurance. Phil T. Rich is the Co-Chair of Billionaires for Bush (or Gore). (Strangely, Mr. Boyd and Mr. Rich have never been seen together.)

Carmelina Cartei is an activist with the Nicaragua Solidarity Network on Latin America and labor issues; an educator at Hunter College; a Ph.D. candidate in the Theater Program at the CUNY Graduate School and University Center; and a member of the Theater of the Oppressed Laboratory in NYC and of the Adelante Street Theater Project in NYC.

Jan Cohen-Cruz is an associate professor of Drama at NYU. She co-edited *Playing Boal: Theatre, Therapy, Activism* and edited *Radical Street Performance: An International Anthology*, where an expanded version of her essay in this volume first appeared.

Ricardo Dominguez is a co-founder of The Electronic Disturbance Theater (EDT), a group that developed Virtual-Sit In technologies in 1998 in solidarity with the Zapatista communities in Chiapas, Mexico. He is senior editor of The Thing (bbs.thing.net); a former member of Critical Art Ensemble (1987 to 1994 – developers of the theory of Electronic Civil Disobedience in the late 1980s); and currently a Fake_Fakeshop Worker (www.fakeshop.com), a hybrid performance group, presented at the Whitney Biennial 2000. Ricardo has collaborated on a number of international net_art projects: with Francesca da Rimini on Dollspace (www.thing.net/~dollyoko), the Aphanisis Project with Diane Ludin (www.thing.net/~diane). He also presented EDT's SWARM action at Ars Electronica's InfoWar Festival in 1998 (Linz, Austria). His first digital Zapatismo project was in 1996–97, a three-month RealVideo/Audio network project: *The Zapatista/Port Action* (MIT). His essays have appeared at Ctheory (www.ctheory.org); an article appears in *Corpus Delecti: Performance Art of the Americas*, edited by Coco Fusco (Routledge, New York 2000). He edited EDT's *Hacktivism: Network_Art_Activism* (Autonomedia Press 2001). EDT: www.thing.net/~rdom/ecd/ecd.html. Home: www.thing.net/~rdom. The Thing: bbs.thing.net.

Stephen Duncombe has been with Reclaim the Streets/New York City since its first meeting, beginning as a loyal skeptic and becoming a passionate advocate and committed organizer. He is also the author of *Notes from Underground: Zines and the Politics of Alternative Culture* (Verso 1997). He teaches media and politics at New York University's Gallatin School, and has edited a collection of writings entitled *Cultural Resistance* (Verso 2002).

Jim Eigo is a writer and editor living in New York City. An early AIDS activist, he co-founded ACT UP's Treatment and Data Committee and wrote the first draft of the federal policy that expanded access to experimental AIDS drugs. He later worked for AIDS prevention and sexual freedom with the grassroots groups the AIDS Prevention Action League (APAL) and SexPanic! His short fiction has appeared in numerous anthologies, little magazines and art tabloids. His theater and dance writing has appeared in such publications as *Theatrical Gamut* and *Dance Ink*. As a model he has appeared on gallery walls, in city murals, and on the pages of *Honcho* and *Visionaire*. His (homo)erotic fiction has been published in several anthologies and literary magazines (most recently, *Best American Gay Fiction 3*, *Quickies 2* and *The Harrington Press Gay Male Fiction Quarterly*). He is managing editor of *Playguy* and *Inches* magazines.

Bill Fletcher is the national organizer for the Black Radical Congress (BRC) and one of the three co-chairs of the BRC. He is a long-time trade-union activist and writer. Bfletcher4@compuserve.com.

Alan Greig is an independent consultant, working at the intersections of HIV prevention, harm reduction, and gender equality. For the past ten years, Alan has worked with nongovernmental and community-based organizations in countries of the economic North and South to locate HIV prevention and harm-reduction programs within a broader agenda of social justice. As a white, straight, northern European middle-class male, Alan is engaged with the tensions between privilege and justice, between identity and community, and between the margin and the center. He draws inspiration from the writings of Gilles Deleuze, Gayatri Spivak, and Adam Phillips, and from the struggle against all those who seek "to again take the world from us."

Margaret Groarke is an assistant professor of government and director of the Peace Studies Program at Manhattan College in the Bronx, New York. She received her Ph.D. from the City University of New York. She has been involved in the Northwest Bronx Community and Clergy Coalition since 1985.

Jason Grote is a playwright and activist. His plays include *Pipe Bomb Sonata: The 1988 Tompkins Square Police Riot* and *Teachings*, a monologue written for NOW's *My Choice My Voice* project. He is the literary manager of the Hoboken, NJ Waterfront Ensemble and a founding member of Toolbox Productions. As an activist, Jason has worked with numerous groups in New York City, including the Lower East Side Collective, The Committee to Save CHARAS/El Bohio, and Reclaim the Streets/NYC. He has developed guerrilla theater with Bill Talen and studied Theater of the Oppressed techniques with Claire Picher. He lives in Brooklyn.

Liz Highleyman is a writer and health educator who has been involved in radical activism for over fifteen years. She has been active in the anarchist movement, the women's health and pro-choice movements, bisexual and sex worker organizing, and AIDS activism. She is co-editor of the anthology *Bisexual Politics: Theories, Queries, and Visions* (Haworth Press 1995). Her work has appeared in a number of anthologies: *Bi Any Other Name* (Alyson 1990), *The Second Coming* (Alyson 1996), *Whores and Other Feminists* (Routledge 1997), *Encyclopedia of AIDS* (Fitzroy Dearborn 1998) and in several progressive and queer publications (*Sojourner, Anything That Moves, Anarchy: A Journal of Desire Armed, San Francisco Bay Guardian, Gay Community News, Bay Area Reporter, The Fifth Estate*). She has worked as a street medic at the Seattle WTO, Washington DC IMF/World Bank, and Los Angeles "D2K" actions.

Alexandra Juhasz is a theorist, maker, and teacher of alternative media. She is an associate professor of Media Studies at Pitzer College, and is the producer of activist videos on subjects ranging from women and prison, to feminist film, and AIDS. She is the author of *Women of Vision: Histories in Feminist Film and Video* (University of Minnesota Press) and *AIDS TV: Identity, Community and Alternative Video* (Duke University Press 1995).

Esther Kaplan is an editor with *POZ*, a national AIDS magazine, and is a member of the board of directors of Jews for Racial and Economic Justice, which she directed from 1995 to 1997. She was trained in civil disobedience by ACT UP, an organization she was active in for seven years. In 2000, she worked with American and South African women to organize South Africa's first Women and AIDS conference; in New York City, her recent activism has focused on the public schools, including a successful campaign to defeat a for-profit takeover of five city schools and an ongoing attempt to rescind an agreement that put the New York Police Department in charge of school security. She lives in Brooklyn.

L.A. Kauffman is, among other things, perhaps the first person in US history to be arrested for allegedly committing a crime by fax machine. (The Manhattan District Attorney declined to prosecute.) Her involvement in radical organizing and journalism spans two decades. She was part of an on-the-ground tactical squad for the IMF/World Bank protests in Washington DC, in April 2000. She was also a key organizer of the two-year direct-action campaign that saved 114 New York City community gardens from development in 1999. Kauffman's journalistic work has ranged from undercover infiltration of the religious right to international investigative reporting. Her writings on activism and radical politics have appeared in *Spin*, *The Nation*, *Village Voice*, *The Progressive*, *Salon.com*, *SF Weekly*, and elsewhere. Kauffman is at work on *Direct Action: The Roots of the New Unrest*, a history of American radical activism from the early 1970s to the present, and writes an online column on the current movement, *Free Radical: Chronicle of the New Unrest* (www.free-radical.org).

Roger Keil teaches Urban and Environmental Politics at the Faculty of Environmental Studies at York University. He has published widely on matters of urban governance and local politics. His most recent book is *Los Angeles: Globalization, Urbanization and Social Struggles* (Wiley 1998). He has been involved in urban activism in Frankfurt, Los Angeles, and Toronto and is a founding member of the International Network for Urban Research and Action (INURA).

Sara Kershnar was a co-founder of the Harm Reduction Coalition, started in 1993 to mobilize a national movement to reduce drug-related harm and an alternative, public health alternative to the damaging and racist War on Drugs. After over ten years of activism in the fields of harm reduction, HIV/AIDS, and women's and sexual health and rights, she returned to the Harvard School of Public Health for a Master's degree. Sara currently works with Generation Five, an activist organization committed to ending child sexual abuse over the next five generations through the development and support of local leadership throughout the US and in collaboration with international efforts against sexual exploitation. Her heroes, mentors, and inspirations include Los Mariposas, Simon Kershnar, Mark Gerse, Lynn Paltrow, Professor Richard Levins, Dr Nancy Krieger, Me'shell NdegeOcello, many great writers, and the 1959 Cuban revolution. Her work is dedicated to her father, Harvey Elliot Kershnar, a compassionate and ethical man who died of HIV in 1992.

Naomi Klein, born in Montreal in 1970, is an award-winning journalist and author of the best-selling book *No Logo: Taking Aim at the Brand Bullies*. The New York Times called *No Logo* a "movement bible," and the *Guardian* newspaper shortlisted it for their first book award. Her articles have appeared in numerous publications including *The Nation*, *New Statesman*, *Newsweek International*, *New York Times*, *Village Voice*, *Ms.*, *The Baffler*, and *Saturday Night*. She writes a weekly column in the *Globe and Mail*, Canada's national newspaper. For the past five years, Klein has traveled throughout North America, Asia, and Europe, tracking the rise of anti-corporate activism. She is a frequent media commentator and has guest-lectured at Harvard, Yale, and New York universities. Naomi Klein lives in Toronto.

Bob Kohler, long-time queer activist, has been a member of CORE, The Gay Liberation Front, ACT UP, SexPanic!, and Fed Up Queers. He is currently working with homeless youth and is a volunteer with the NYC AIDS Housing Network.

Joel Lefkowitz teaches classes on protest movements, political activism, and other political science topics at the State University of New York at New Paltz. He is the author, with Christine Kelly, of "Radical and Pragmatic: United Students Against Sweatshops" in *Teamsters, Turtles, and Others: Left Movements in the 20th Century*, edited by John Berg.

Stephanie Luce is an assistant professor at the Labor Center, and a research associate at the Political Economy Research Institute, both at the University of Massachusetts at Amherst. She received her Ph.D. in Sociology in 1999 from the University of Wisconsin at Madison. Luce has done extensive research on the political and economic impact of the living-wage movement, and is the co-author with Robert Pollin of *The Living Wage: Building a Fair Economy* (New Press 1998).

Bronwyn Mauldin is a member of the Jubilee Northwest steering committee. In organizing the human chain, she was responsible for mainstream and alternative media communications. She is a longtime Ustawi volunteer and activist against IMF and World Bank structural adjustment policies.

Kerstin Mikalbrown is an overextended college student living in New York City. In addition to her studies, she is an active member of the activist group Reclaim the Streets, a getcrafty intern, and a copywriter.

Kelly Moore lives in two worlds that she constantly tries to bridge. As a sociology professor at Barnard College, she writes and teaches about activism, organizations, and the sociology of science. She is the author of *Disrupting Science* (Princeton University Press 2003). As an activist, she works on making public space truly public, and eliminating cars from the planet and replacing them with bicycles.

Tracy Morgan has an M.Phil in history, a CSW, and is pursuing certification as a psycho-analyst while maintaining a private practice in New York City.

Jordan Moss has been editor of the *Norwood News*, a Bronx community newspaper, since 1994. He has covered the Northwest Bronx Community and Clergy Coalition's activities for that paper and for *New York Newsday* and *City Limits* magazine.

Immanuel Ness is assistant professor of Political Science at Brooklyn College, City University of New York. His research focuses on labor, politics, union organizing, and immigrants. His books include *Trade Unions and the Betrayal of the Unemployed*. He is editor of the *Encyclopedia of Third Parties in America*. Ness is also the author of numerous articles and reviews on labor and politics in *Labor Studies Journal, Working USA, Social Policy, The Nation*, and is a contributing author to *Organizing to Win*. He is co-editor of *Central Labor Councils* and *The Revival of American Unionism* (M.E. Sharpe 2001) and is currently working on a book on immigrant organizing and union jurisdiction in New York City. Ness is also conducting a research project on privatization's impact on workers of color. He is editor of *WorkingUSA: Journal of Labor and Society*.

Ana Nogueira is a volunteer with the New York City IMC, so madly in love with Indymedia that she just quit her job to go gallivanting around Latin America visiting start-up IMCs there. She is investing all her time and energy into helping Indymedia develop into a participatory, international network in the hope that the tools of open communication are shared with all who envision a better world. Ana has been published in a diverse range of publications, including the *Washington Peace Letter*, the *New Internationalist, Punk Planet*, as well as several IMC newspapers.

Sofía Quintero is a writer, activist, and performer whose work has appeared in *Ms., Blu* and 360hiphop.com. She serves on the board of several organizations committed to social justice, including the Brecht Forum and the Organizing Support Center in New York City, the Advocacy Institute in Washington DC, and We Interrupt this Message in San Francisco. Sofia also sits on the advisory board of Doula, the only scholarly publication devoted to hip-hop culture.

Eric Rofes is a professor of education at Humboldt State University in Arcata, California, and a long-time community organizer. He is the author of *Dry Bones Breathe: Gay Men Creating Post AIDS Identities and Cultures* (Harrington Park Press, 1998).

Eric Sawyer is the co-founder of ACT UP/NY, Housing Works, and the HealthGAP coalition.

Sarah Schulman is the author of seven novels, two nonfiction books, and fifteen plays. For twenty years, she was involved in a number of emblematic feminist and gay organizations including CARASA (Committee for Abortion Rights and Against Sterilization Abuse), the Reproductive Rights National Network, ACT UP, the Lesbian Avengers, the Irish Lesbian and Gay Organization, the New York Lesbian and Gay Experimental Film

Festival, and others. She has been a pioneer of lesbian representation in US, European and Japanese book publishing and in the American theater.

Starhawk is a long-time activist and the author of *The Spiral Dance*, *The Fifth Sacred Thing*, and other books that link an earth-based spirituality to action to change the world. www.starhawk.org/index.html.

Randy Stoecker is Professor of Sociology, and Research Associate in Urban Affairs, at the University of Toledo. He is moderator and editor of COMM-ORG: The On-line Conference on Community Organizing and Development (comm-org.utoledo.edu) and the author of numerous works on community development, community organizing, and community computing. He also works in collaboration with community organizations and community–university partnerships doing participatory action research and empowerment evaluation.

Bill Talen is the founder of the Church of Stop Shopping.

Lesley J. Wood is a doctoral candidate in sociology at Columbia University and part of New York City's Direct Action Network. Stumbling back and forth across the academic–activist divide, she studies contentious politics and migration, and organizes around issues of police brutality, anti-racism, and immigrant rights.

Susan Wright is the policy director for the National Coalition for Sexual Freedom.

The photographers

Diane Greene Lent is a photographer and activist. She combines her political experience with her talent in photography to document the political movements now emerging in the twenty-first century. Lent has been an activist for three decades, working in the women's movement, Central America solidarity movement and most recently in the movement against the Criminal Injustice System. Lent worked for with the Committee in Solidarity with the People of El Salvador for thirteen years in the 1980s and 1990s. Lent studied photography at New York's International Center of Photography. She has had photos published in many publications including the *Progressive*, the *Village Voice*, *New York Magazine*, the *Amsterdam News*, and *Time Out New York*. Lent currently works as a photographer and web designer. She works with Praxis Consulting Cooperative, a worker-owned cooperative providing computer services for nonprofit organizations and small businesses.

Caroline McNamara Shepard has been attending demonstrations since she learned to walk. Her photos have appeared in the *New York Times*, *LA Times*, *Keyboard Magazine*, *People Magazine*, *Guitar World*, the London *Independent*, *Entertainment Weekly*, *New York*

Magazine, Details, and others. She first developed her love of photography at Sarah Lawrence College and is currently fulfilling her dream of attending art school at the graduate photography department, School of Visual Arts. She lives in New York City with her adorable husband and their two cats.

The editors

Benjamin Shepard is a social worker moonlighting as a social historian. By day he combines his work as a deputy director of a South Bronx harm-reduction agency/needle exchange with his doctoral studies in social welfare at Hunter/CUNY; by night he is involved in campaigns to save New York's public spaces. Shepard is author of *White Nights and Ascending Shadows: An Oral History of the San Francisco AIDS Epidemic* (Cassell 1997). His work has appeared in *Monthly Review, WorkingUSA: A Journal of Labor, Minnesota Review, Antioch Review*, and three book collections, Hayduk and Mattsson's *Democracy's Moment: Reforming the American Political System in the Twenty-first Century* (Rowan & Littlefield 2002), John Berg's *Teamsters, Turtles, and Others: Left Movements in the 20th Century* (Rowan & Littlefield 2002) and David Colbert's *Eyewitness to the American West: 500 Years of Firsthand History* (Penguin 1999). He can be reached at benshepard@mindspring.com.

Ronald Hayduk teaches political science at the Borough of Manhattan Community College of the City University of New York (CUNY). Hayduk has written about political participation, social movements, immigration, race, and regional planning, including as co-editor and contributing author of *Democracy's Moment: Reforming the American Political System in the Twenty-first Century* (Rowan & Littlefield 2002). Hayduk has also contributed essays in the several books and journals, including: "From Anti-Globalization to Global Justice: A 21st Century Movement," for *Teamsters, Turtles, and Others: Left Movements in the 20th Century* , edited by John Berg, (Rowan and Littlefield 2002); co-authored an article in *In Defense of the Alien*, edited by Lydio Tomasi, (Center for Migration Studies 2000); "Immigration, Race and Community Building," (www.aspenroundtable.org, 2000); and in *Mobilization: The International Journal of Research and Theory about Social Movements, Protest, and Collective Behavior* (1998), and in public affairs magazines. Hayduk is currently finishing a book, *Gatekeepers to the Franchise: Election Administration and Voter Participation* and an article "Spatial Dimensions to Racial Disparities and the Promise of Democratic Regionalism," in *Structural Racism and Community Building* (forthcoming).

Formerly a social worker, Hayduk has worked in the Anti-Apartheid and Latin American Solidarity Movements. He worked in New York government as the director of the NYC Voter Assistance Commission, and consults to several policy organizations, including The Aspen Institute Roundtable on Race and Community Revitalization (www.aspenroundtable.org); Demos (www.demos-usa.org); and The Century Foundation (www.tcf.org).

Acknowledgements

In the fall of 1998, shortly after the Matthew Shepard political funeral, Steven Gendin invited me (Ben) to his offices at Poz. Over the next two hours, the veteran activist opened up files of over a decade of activist work he had completed with ACT UP, AIDS Prevention Action League, and SexPanic! It was one of those quiet, generous gestures from an activist who made a career of such moments. Some three years later, Stonewall legend Sylvia Rivera permitted me to interview her, reviewing her career over the thirty-two years since the Stonewall Riots. Neither of them is around to see their contributions to this anthology. The world is simply a transformed place because of their activism.

We cannot thank Jennifer Shepard, Liz Highleyman, and L.A. Kauffman enough for their invaluable editorial assistance. Without them, the prose would have been unreadable. In addition, countless individuals and institutions contributed photos, flyers, and illustrations. Dianne Greene Lent and Caroline Shepard provided the bulk of the work for the photos. But there are so many who deserve thanks – especially Sylvia's old GAA nemesis Rich Wandel and the New York City Lesbian and Gay Community Services Center Staff, who took the time to open up their ACT UP archives for us. Countless others, including Jennifer Berkshire, Peter Huffacker, Heather Hadden, Vicki Larson, Bert Cohler, Katherine Wilson, Aresh, and Bill TimesUP! Aspen Institute Roundtable on Race and Community Revitalization, and the Brecht Forum, contributed to this volume in untold ways. In addition, we would like to acknowledge Crimp and Rolson for inspiring us with their seminal work

AIDSDEMOGRAPHICS (Bay Press 1990). If our text is half as dynamic, we will be pleased. AIDSDEMOGRAPHICS allowed us to think about what it means to participate in the nexus of theory and activism. To organizations – from LESC, to SexPanic!, to ACT UP, to Direct Action Network, and all the other happy warriors out there fighting for joy and justice, as you remind us to forgo cynicism: you are the ones who make telling this story such a pleasure. Essentially, these stories are about countless activists who, in their own small ways, are doing the only thing any generation has the responsibility to do – plug the cracks in the dam.

We certainly cannot express our full gratitude to the folks at Verso – especially Niels Hooper and Colin Robinson for their support. And finally, to our parents and significant others – Caroline Shepard and Susanna Jones – for helping us with the printer crashes, downloading jpegs, and handling 2001 kvetches and excuses: no need for the bla, bla, blas; you know you guys are the greatest.

Credits

We wish to thank the following people and institutions for granting us permission to reprint their materials:

Naomi Klein , "The Vision Thing: Were The DC And Seattle Protests Unfocused, Or Are Critics Missing The Point?" was originally published in the *Nation* on July 10, 2000. Copyright © 2000 Information Access Company. All rights reserved. Copyright © 2000 The Nation Company L.P.

Kerstin Mikalbrown, "Saving Esperanza Garden: The Struggle over Community Gardens in New York City", was originally published on Get Crafty website, www.getcrafty.com.

Leslie Feinberg, "Jail House Rocks: 'Matthew Shepard lives!'", was originally published by Copyright Workers World Service: For more information: Workers World, 55 West 17th St, New York, NY 10011; via email: ww@workers.org. Copyright © 1998 workers.org.

An earlier version of Bill Fletcher Jr's "Can Black Radicalism Speak the Voice of Black Workers?" appeared in *Race and Class*, vol. 40, no. 4, April–June 1999.

An earlier version of Jan Cohen-Cruz's "At Cross Purposes: The Church Ladies for Choice" appeared in *Radical Street Performance*, Routledge, New York 1998.

"How to Build Community" was originally published by, and is still available from, The Syracuse Cultural Workers, PO Box 6367, Syracuse NY 13217. (315) 475–1277. www.syrculturalworkers.org.

Alexandra Juhasz, "So Many Alternatives", the Alternative AIDS Video Movement, was first published in *Cineaste*, vol. 20, no. 4, 1994; vol. 21, nos 1–2, 1995.

Illustrations

Page: 8 photograph by Caroline McNamara Shepard; 10 photograph by Diane Greene Lent; 15 flyer by Vincent Gagliostro, 2001; 24 Car Free NY flyer by Caroline McNamara Shepard; 58 photograph by Diane Greene Lent; 59 poster by Emily Schuch; 62–3 flyer by L.A. Kauffman and Immanuel Ness; 77 photograph by Diane Greene Lent; 79 photograph by Diane Greene Lent; 82 photograph by Melissa A. Wall; 83 photograph by Liz Highleyman; 93 poster by Sharonann Lynch, 2001; 95 poster by Sharonann Lynch, 2001; 97 photograph by Diane Greene Lent; 105 flyer by David Pasquarelli; 110 photograph by Liz Highleyman; 111 photograph by Liz Highleyman; 123 photograph by Diane Greene Lent; 127 photograph by Diane Davies; 129 photograph by Diane Davies; 137 photograph by Diane Greene Lent; 143 photograph by Liz Highleyman; 196 photograph by Diane Greene Lent; 211 photograph by Diane Greene Lent; 231 flyer by L.A. Kauffman; 237 photograph by Diane Greene Lent; 251 photograph by Diane Greene Lent; 247 photograph by Caroline McNamara Shepard; 257 photograph by Caroline McNamara Shepard; 264 photograph by Diane Greene Lent; 325 photograph by Diane Greene Lent; 360 poster by Dan Williams; 390 poster by Vincent Gagliostro, 2001; 394 poster by Syracuse Cultural Workers © 1998.

Index